WE SHALL OVERCOME

We Shall Overcome

A History of
Civil Rights and the Law

ALEXANDER TSESIS

Yale University Press   New Haven & London

Set in Caslon by Keystone Typesetting, Inc. Printed in the United States of America.

Library of Congress Cataloging-in-Publication Data
Tsesis, Alexander.
We shall overcome : a history of civil rights and the law / Alexander Tsesis.
p. cm.
Includes bibliographical references and index.
ISBN 978-0-300-11837-7 (cloth : alk. paper)
1. Civil rights—United States—History. I. Title.
JC599.U5T74 2008
323.0973—dc22   2007035453

A catalogue record for this book is available from the British Library.

The paper in this book meets the guidelines for permanence and durability of the Committee on
Production Guidelines for Book Longevity of the Council on Library Resources.

10 9 8 7 6 5 4 3 2 1

For my lovely children

There is no Negro problem. There is no Southern problem. There is no Northern problem. There is only an American problem. . . . It is all of us who must overcome the crippling legacy of bigotry and injustice. And we shall overcome.

—President Lyndon Johnson, special message to Congress,
"The American Promise"

I have a dream that one day this nation will rise up and live out the true meaning of its creed: "We hold these truths to be self-evident: that all men are created equal."

—Dr. Martin Luther King, Jr.

Contents

Acknowledgments

As with any book, this one would have been impossible but for the help and guidance of innumerable people. Some of them stand out most prominently. Richard Delgado has continued to be an exceptional mentor and a great friend. He is a rare individual. A person who strives for intellectual rigor while demonstrating his compassionate humanity in each communication. His suggestions on the proposal and critique of the entire manuscript were invaluable. Eric Foner's comments on the proposal likewise helped me establish an outline and topical concentration. I often relied on him for guidance.

James McPherson, Cass Sunstein, John Braithwaite, Geoffrey Stone, Rogers Smith, and J. Alex Schwartz helped me in the preliminary stages of the project. Marcia McCormick critiqued an early synopsis and engaged me in vibrant discussions. And it seemed like I could always count on the encyclopedic knowledge of Alfred Brophy, who read the entire manuscript. Andrew Taslitz and J. Gordon Hylton seemed to enlighten me on virtually any historical question I posed to them.

The editors at Yale University Press have been wonderful from start to finish. Christopher Rogers and Laura Davulis provided fresh perspectives into the substance of the book and the publishing process. Jonathan Brent, Larisa Heimert, and Keith Condon were enormously helpful in their generous support for the project. Dan Heaton meticulously advised me in matters of style and caught several of my analytical oversights.

Bernard Bailyn and Mary Dudziak directed me to resources I might have otherwise missed. I relied on the support of many libraries. I found most of the books I needed at the Northwestern University Library. I have been using that library since my first major writing project in eighth grade and have always found it a delightful place to spend my days. Russell Maylone and

Sigrid P. Perry were always generous in my frequent trips to the Special Collection. I am indebted to Rosemarie Fogarty and Jennifer A. Norman at the U.S. Census Bureau and to Mariam Touba at the New-York Historical Society.

Although it is impossible to mention everyone whose ideas contributed to this book, some are particularly memorable. I was fortunate to tap into Winthrop Jordan's knowledge of how white indentured servitude ended and black slavery expanded during the 1760s and 1770s. Marylynn Salmon elaborated on women's lives during the colonial period. Melanie S. Gustafson was incisive on the women's suffrage movement. George Rutherglen clarified the distinctions among various Reconstruction-era statutes. I gained a more accurate comprehension of blacks in the New Deal period through e-mail exchanges with Harvard Sitkoff and Roger Biles. Discussions with Mark Tushnet and Reva Segal on American democracy were enlightening about the evolving conception of American citizenry. James Lindgren was as generous as ever with his time in breaking down the difference between formal equality and equality of results. Scott A. Moss made me better informed about reproductive rights issues. During his convalescence from a difficult surgery, Howard M. Sachar nevertheless had the strength to provide me with advice about parts of the book dealing with Jews in the United States. Amy Dru Stanley and Risa Goluboff gave me valuable advice on the book's subtitle. Spencer Waller gave helpful ideas on the cover.

I have done my best to incorporate all their wise counsel. Any remaining deficiencies are mine alone.

Following Jack Rakove's and Jim McPherson's advice, I found that without research assistants I could conduct more exhaustive research and better understand what I found. After the manuscript was complete, however, Robert Gratzl, Charles Stone, Maria Ryan, and Kimberly Lekman diligently checked my sources and citations. Over the years, I have been lucky to have two helpful administrative assistants, Gloria Sanders and Debra Moore, who saved me enormous time with their typing. Debbie even read the entire manuscript and provided me with her impressions.

My wife, Alexandra Roginsky Tsesis, is an inexhaustible wellspring of inspiration. Her achievements as a surgeon and mother make me aware of the heights to which I can aspire. At every stage of this book, the faces of our children, Ruth and Ariel, have been in my mind's eye.

We Shall Overcome

Introduction

The convergence of liberty and equality has been integral to the evolution of American identity. The aspiration to found a country committed to these two ethical standards came to fruition at a time when racial slavery and gender inequality were widely accepted. The young nation meandered through a series of controversies that no compromise between slave and free states resolved. Eventually, sectional disagreements became so acrimonious that brother fought brother in the Civil War.

After the Union victory over the Confederacy, state ratification of the Reconstruction Amendments altered the dynamic between federal and state governments in matters of civil rights. Yet even with the end of slavery, the prejudices born of centuries stood in the way of realizing the ideals of a free and equal citizenry. Soon after Reconstruction, the path of liberal equality became rocky, and the next major bend in the road appeared when the New Deal government instituted a variety of programs designed to improve general welfare. Despite the New Deal's many social achievements, African Americans were even then unable to secure their coequal entitlement of nationally recognized rights. Great Society programs of the 1960s were intended to end lingering injustices; some of the most significant progress came with the Civil Rights Act of 1964, which prohibited practices like segregation and employment discrimination. Thereafter, the nation continued its introspective quest for rehabilitation. It was only in the 1970s that the Supreme Court recognized that gender discrimination is suspect, and it took until 2003 for the Court to realize that gays and lesbians, like any other Americans, have an intimate right to privacy.

The winding path of social justice in the United States left the scars of slaves and the corpses of civil rights activists in its wake. What is remarkable about the United States is that, through fits and starts, the ideal of an independent and coequal citizenry has led to overall improvements, although not always in a linear path. The cultural demand for equal treatment has brought into sharp relief partial achievements and outright exploitations. When viewed over an extended period of time, as in this book, the steady expansion of liberties is inspiring. But the story is also melancholy, for instances of state and private prejudices appear throughout it. The achievements of America's quest to live up to its ideals can be measured, at least in part, by the improved quality of life and increased opportunities for groups that had historically been excluded from the bounty of democracy.

This is a book about the birth pains of civil rights. The venture begins with the American Revolution and continues through contemporary struggles. The work's premise is that the United States Constitution, through a variety of provisions such as the Equal Protection Clause, obligates the federal government to protect individual liberties in a way that is beneficial to general welfare. This perspective stands apart from those of legal theorists like Herbert Wechsler or John Hart Ely, for whom the Constitution is a procedural device. Their constitutional methodologies are process based, requiring only consistent application of law to meet standards of fairness.[1] I argue, to the contrary, that the Constitution, as it applies to civil rights, guarantees substantive protections of fundamental and basic interests.[2] No procedural consistency in legal application can justify infringement against life, liberty, and property. Government's *raison d'être* is the development of liberal equality for the overall good, not the following of neutral principles, as Wechsler would have it, nor the preservation of democratic neutrality, as Ely thought. When principles and democratic processes are neutral, they lack any judicially recognized fulcrum to check the behavior of dominant majorities.

The federal government's role has not always been expansive enough to protect individuals against group discrimination. In the early days of the Republic, the Bill of Rights protected only against federal encroachment. Reconstruction, however, changed the federalist structure, making the national government supreme in protecting the rights of identifiable groups. After the New Deal, following the lead of Justice Hugo Black, the Supreme Court found that the post–Civil War constitutional change made most of the Bill of Rights applicable to the states. The civil rights era and later the Warren and Burger Courts took this premise a step further, finding that the Constitution protects even unenumerated rights, such as privacy, racial intermarriage, and parental autonomy.

These and other rights are not absolute. Even "liberty" has at various times been abused as a clarion call for the right to own slaves or expand territorially at the expense of Native American tribes. Coming to terms with the licentious excesses that have been perpetrated under the banner of "liberty" has led the country to understand that individual freedom is not absolute and must sometimes be curbed for the common good.

The American Constitution's use of generalities, about equality, the general welfare, and due process, has helped each generation evaluate its treatment of underprivileged groups under the microscope of history and the hindsight of contemporary sensibilities. Constitutional interpretation has expanded to include groups of freeborn people, like blacks and women, to participate in the workings of civics and the enjoyment of public goods, even though their involvement would have been anathema to many Americans of the revolutionary period. The Constitution has proven to be flexible enough to adapt to an increasingly empathic understanding of civil rights. By themselves, however, humanitarian concerns have little value to the average person seeking legal redress against arbitrary treatment at school, court, or work. The equality of personal liberties, which while mentioned in the Declaration of Independence made its first appearance in the Constitution only in 1868, constrains the abuse of power. It provides a criterion for governmental action against intrusion into fundamental human dignities.

While both equality and liberty have often been mere abstractions used as catchwords for political gain, real progress has come when these principles inspired action for the sake of fairness and national improvement. The most effective changes have arrived through the efforts of coalitions capable of winning popular and political support. Law is an essential component of progressive change, which is best achieved through coordinated efforts of the legislative, executive, and judicial branches. But the reality is that coalitions can act destructively or constructively. Law can be the culminating accomplishment of special-interest groups that gain at the expense of other members of the polity.

Neither do insignificant reforms provide anything other than hollow hopes or, at best, short-lived victories. Authors in the "interest convergence" school of thought, Derrick Bell and Mary Dudziak foremost among them, perceive the history of civil rights as a series of expedients, driven by the exploitive convergence of white interests with those of blacks. According to their view, even the landmark rejection of school segregation in *Brown v. Board of Education* was nothing more than a false victory for the benefit of the white establishment. Whites, according to this view, help blacks only when to do so benefits white interests.[3]

My perspective differs from theirs. The improvement of civil rights in the United States has been made possible by individuals and organizations committed to ending injustices, sometimes at great personal, professional, and political risk. For this reason, I am optimistic about America's constitutional vision of equal justice, along the lines of Gunnar Myrdal's guiding American Creed.[4] This view also differs from Rogers M. Smith's. While Smith is correct that "successful American political actors have not been pure liberals, democratic republicans, or ascriptive Americanists, but have instead combined politically potent elements of all three views," I believe that he is mistaken that "American liberal democracy is not the 'core' meaning" of United States national purpose. Although he is undoubtedly right that American civic development exhibited many contrary strains, progress came in pursuit of a goal rather than by force of political whim.[5]

Civil rights advancements come from a genuine commitment to liberal equality, which is promised by the Declaration of Independence and the Preamble of the Constitution. While the reality is that at every point in its history America has failed to live up to its ideals, universal freedom has always been the underlying core of lasting civil rights advancements. The arbitrary restriction of liberty has worked against American betterment. Eric Foner, a leading historian of American freedom, has pointed out a limit of this ideal: "If the universalistic American Creed has been a persistent feature of our history, so too have been efforts to delimit freedom along one or another axis of social existence."[6]

The ability of governing majorities to exploit minorities was well known even in James Madison's time. A student of the struggle for equality must analyze events in which civil rights flourished and declined, especially where successes and failures were long term. Neither is it sufficient to examine the revolutionary generation's original perception of rights. It matters relatively little whether the abolitionists were right that the Constitution's framers believed that slaves had the same natural rights as they because it is likely that a large proportion of them did not think so. Nor is it important whether the Seneca Falls Convention (1848) on women's suffrage could legitimately claim the Declaration of Independence for its inspiration since eighteenth-century politicos had an unmistakable strain of chauvinism. What is key is how the constitutional machine, running of itself, to reword Michael Kammen's terminology, was adept at shedding prejudices and why it so often failed to do so.[7] In a representative government, political decisions are linked to people's choices, and when special interests run amok in the legislative process, the judiciary has the power to step in. The truth of the matter is that popular consensus has at various times been on the side of oppressive measures, as with the passage of the Fugitive Slave Act of 1850. The judiciary has often left minorities unprotected, with *Dred Scott* or *Plessy v. Ferguson* being the most glaring examples of this pattern. If national citizenship implies the possession of individual entitlements, not mere aspirations but federal civil rights statutes must protect them. Vigorous law enforcement and adjudication can punish and deter group harms and safeguard universal rights on which the country is founded. Without the Civil Rights Act of 1964 and *Brown v. Board of Education* it is unlikely that the country could have made substantial advances in the treatment of women and minorities.

Slavery, lynching, Indian removal, Japanese internment, employment discrimination, and restrictive economic laws are among our failures to live up to the universal freedoms on which the nation is founded. The many racial, gender, ethnic, and nationalistic discriminations perpetrated pursuant to both laws and cultural norms have been miscarriages of justice, not indications of American values. They were not central to the U.S. mission but an abrogation of it. I take liberal equality to be not a national myth but a driving force of social and civil improvement. Without the ideal of liberal equality to strive for, the United States could not have advanced from the clutches of slavery, provided women with the right to vote, and punished segregation in public places. Placing this book within the context of some schools of constitutional thought is merely an attempt to identify its niche. In it, for the most part, I avoid scholarly debates in favor of exploring key developments of U.S. civil rights.

The book's main focus is on the treatment of disempowered groups in the United States. Most of the illustrations are drawn from African American history. Treatment of other groups, such as women and Asian Americans, also is a theme, but the book is not meant to provide an exhaustive investigation of the innumerable facets of the topic.

The United States has always been a land that racial, cultural, national, and religious minorities have shared. The early American colonists were locked in class and religious conflicts to assert their rights as British citizens. They fought for "life, liberty, and the pursuit of happiness," but the Revolution brought a more abundant bounty to some than others.

The book begins with the severing of the colonists' monarchical ties to

Britain, which seemed to herald the advent of universal rights. In the first two chapters I discuss the intellectual framework of the new republic, primarily manifest in the Declaration of Independence and the Preamble. I examine the extent to which the framers lived up to some of the ideals that they left as their legacy to future generations. Their willingness to protect the institution of slavery, even while their writings indicated an awareness of its incompatibility with national purpose, indicates the extent to which self-interest undermined their goals. In the third chapter I look carefully at how slavery came to be essential to southerners. The abolitionist movement also receives careful scrutiny because from humble beginnings it was able to influence a generation of politicians who came to power in the 1860s. The fourth chapter covers the period of compromise, when slave power cajoled the nation into a series of agreements, beginning with the Missouri Compromise in 1820 and ending with the Kansas-Nebraska Act of 1854. These compromises only made the South more ambitious to protect its peculiar institution of slavery. The sectional differences that intensified over the decades were resolved through civil war that began in 1861.

The fifth chapter begins with the cataclysmic changes in the federal protections of rights that emerged in the aftermath of Civil War. I examine the monumental changes radical politicians were able to make to the Constitution. They strove, with limited success, to bring literacy to newly freed slaves and grant them voting privileges. The end of the reconstruction project is described in chapter six. There I seek to explain how the United States Supreme Court used its power as the interpreter of the Constitution to undermine the new commitment to liberty and equality. In chapter seven I discuss political changes in the late nineteenth and early twentieth centuries. I cover the systematic southern disenfranchisement of blacks as well as the woefully slow progress of women's suffrage.

Much of this period, as I describe in chapter eight, was dominated by a notion of liberty that ignored the equal interests of citizens. That sense of self-absorption bred exclusionary policies in the treatment of minority groups and immigrants. In this poisonous atmosphere, the Ku Klux Klan was reborn. The emphasis on personal success also came through in economic laissez-faire, which gave credence to business claims of liberty that worked to the detriment of laborers.

The New Dealers, whose work I discuss in chapter nine, took a different track in trying to resolve the old problem of unequal distribution of rights. With Franklin Delano Roosevelt in the presidency, reformers were able to use the Commerce Clause to improve the prospects of the underprivileged. While the most glitzy initiatives came from the White House, this chapter also concerns the Supreme Court's new prominence in scrutinizing discriminatory practices and advancing participatory democracy. The success of the New Deal in creating legally recognized rights also came about because of the increasing effectiveness of civil rights and labor organizations.

The slowdown in civil rights in the period immediately following World War II is the focus of the tenth chapter. The levees to long-awaited progress broke in the 1960s, most auspiciously during Lyndon Johnson's presidency. In chapter eleven I cover the contributions of all three branches of government to the improvement of people's lives and the equalization of opportunities. The achievements of that era, exemplified by the Civil Rights Act of 1964 and the Voting Rights Act of 1965, have profoundly moved the United States in the direction of liberal equality. In the twelfth chapter I investigate the Warren Court's deep civil rights legacy, from the realms of desegregation, voting rights, and family privacy to criminal procedure.

I reflect in the final chapter on some of the most recent advances of individual rights. Here, too, I selected several topics out of an unceasingly creative effort to make real the American dream across classes, genders, and races. Accordingly, I discuss some recent feminist, affirmative action, children's rights, and gay rights issues.

Issues of liberty and fairness have confronted Americans from the earliest stages of their history. Ever since the nation's founding there have been incompatibilities between national ideals and practices. The core aim of protecting individual rights for the general welfare of equal citizens has remained firm, but injustices and exclusionary tactics have often been the norms of politics, law, and custom.

Addressing the continued abuse of power and privilege requires a realistic look at the past. Changes to existing institutions emerge within the context of developing traditions. How a society reacts to its strengths and shortcomings subsequently influences persons who are yet unborn. History, then, is an investigative tool that can help focus debate about present policymaking. For anyone seeking meaningful improvement in the lives of ordinary citizens, a critical look at the past can establish baselines for measuring achievements and establishing goals.

CHAPTER ONE

Liberty through Revolution

The founding generation of Americans thought of liberty in objective terms as an abstract principle requiring the state to protect natural rights. The revolutionary outlook on government differed from the twenty-first century's relativistic perspective. Eighteenth-century writers believed that human reason could discover the characteristics of liberty and happiness. Like John Locke before them, revolutionary leaders believed that reason made people naturally free and capable of establishing political entities for the common good. Civil law, in the words of Samuel Adams, had to follow the "law of natural reason and equity." Civil rights could be discovered from an examination of human nature, as Alexander Hamilton forcefully explained. They "are not to be rummaged for, among old parchments."[1] Given their declared affinity for equal natural rights, the framers' discriminatory practices were glaring.

Natural Rights

Revolutionary literature abounds with rationalistic arguments deducing rights from natural law. These rights were considered to be innate. In contemporary terms, we might think of them as biologically intrinsic to the human organism. In eighteenth-century terms, the rights were God-given and inborn: the rights people "possess at their births are equal, and of the same kind." Since these rights were divinely granted, they could not be "repealed or restrained by human laws" and were antecedent "to all earthly government." Inalienable rights were thought to be so intrinsic to human nature—the rights to life and liberty fit into this category—that no person could dispose of them.[2]

Given the absolute nature of inalienable rights shared by all members of a civil society, cooperation for mutual improvement was possible only when the governed were willing to place some limits on their conduct. A future justice of the Massachusetts Supreme Court, Theophilus Parsons, succinctly explained that "each individual parts with the power of controuling his natural alienable rights, only when the good of the whole requires it; he therefore has remaining, after entering into political society, all his unalienable natural rights, and a part also of his alienable natural rights, provided the good of the whole does not require the sacrifice of them."[3] The legitimacy of civil government was predicated on individuals' consent to give up coequal rights to self-defense and self-indulgence.

Nothing justified infringing on another's equal right to natural freedom, but a person could willingly submit to the authority of a government designed to benefit the entire community. In more specific terms, Spartanus wrote that persons enter into social compacts for "mutual defence, and for the equitable and peaceable enjoyment of their lives and properties." Accordingly, the people's representatives were to enact laws that placed constraints on individuals for the good of entire polity.[4]

From their opposition to the Stamp Act of 1765, Americans regarded their political struggle with Britain in moral terms. They reckoned that British policy was not merely impolitic but unjust. They relied on principles of human nature and governmental responsibility to convince others, in America and Britain, of the justness of their cause.

"Liberty" was the central principle of the Revolution. The Sons of Liberty rallied colonists against taxation without representation, Liberty Polls were assembly places, Patrick Henry exhorted his fellow colonists with the statement "Give me liberty or give me death," and the great orator Thomas Paine declared America to be "the place where the principle of universal freedom could take root."[5] One pamphlet after another argued that liberty was part of human nature. Freedom was more than an individual trait; it was a right that everyone shared "equally with other men." Silas Downer, the corresponding secretary for the Sons of Liberty in Providence, Rhode Island, gave voice to the commonly accepted view that the source of liberty is God. Despotism was so common, wrote Arthur Young, that "nine-tenths of the species" were "miserable slaves of . . . tyrants." Their notions of human nature catalyzed rebellion against British rule, but they also condemned the colonial practice of slavery.[6]

Even slaveholders of that age aligned themselves with natural-rights philosophy, but they preferred personal gain to acting on the logical implication of that theory. Their attitudes were not indicative of the colonies as a whole. Abolitionists of the nineteenth century would come to understand the political philosophy of the Revolution to mean that protections of slavery, especially the Fugitive Slave and the Slave Importation Clauses of the Constitution, were unconscionable anomalies in a nation professing universal rights. Constitutional protections for slave owners' commercial interests undercut American justifications for independence. If the founding generation left the rights of blacks and women on the threshing floor of statecraft, they nevertheless established national principles that later generations relied on to end injustices tolerated at the time of independence.

Embracing the Common Good

Governmental pursuit of the common good was prescribed as the antidote against despotism. Developing institutions designed to meet public needs was just as much a purpose of government as was securing individual liberties. Colonial writers often merged the two. Members of the community shared an equal interest in consenting to laws that would treat them justly. Members of the polity "love those with whom they live on terms of equality, and under a sense of common interests," as Thomas Shippen put it. "It engages them in the exercise of their best talents and happiest dispositions." Paine regarded general welfare to be measurable in terms of the cumulative good of individuals composing the body politic. A Virginia clergyman echoed these sentiments, analogizing public good to "a common bank, in which every individual has his respective share." Personal Liberty, John Dickinson wrote in his *Farmer's Letter*, was intrinsic to living happily.[7]

In its advocacy of the Constitution, the widely read *Federalist* often spoke of government's obligation to secure the "public good" for the "great body of the people." When state interests conflicted with the people's happiness, "let the former be sacrificed to the latter." All three branches of government were responsible for the "preservation of liberty" and justice. According to James Madison, one of the *Federalist* authors, securing the public good was intrinsically associated with private rights. Religious pamphlets, too, agreed that "legislators have a right to make, and require subjection to any set of laws that have a tendency to promote the good of the community." While the gospels did not endorse any particular type of government, they only favored a polity with "the common good of mankind for its end and aim."[8]

Persons were willing to subordinate their ambitions and interests to those of the community, expecting that "equal justice be done" for them and others. Individuals who consented to be members of political bodies expected to be treated fairly. On rare occasions, even natural liberty could be "abridged or restrained, so far only as is necessary for the great end of society," explained Samuel Adams.[9]

A representative republic's ultimate goal was to provide laws conducive to happiness. By establishing a central authority, the people could augment the number of opportunities available to them for living contentedly. Adams expressed an oft-stated theme in his *Thoughts on Government* that "happiness of society is the end of government." Along these lines, Dickinson thought the "right to be happy" was attainable only in a free society. Where a government did not promote the welfare and happiness of the people, it was their right to "amend, and alter, or annul, their Constitution, and frame a new one." Years before the Revolution, James Otis, Jr., eloquently described the government's duty "to provide for the security, the quiet, and happy enjoyment of life, liberty, and property. There is no one act which a government can have a *right* to make, that does not tend to the advancement of the security, tranquility and prosperity of the people."[10]

To protect these interests, the Virginia Declaration of Rights provided that the "majority of the community" may "reform, alter or abolish" a maladministered government "in such manner as shall be judged most conducive to the public weal." James Wilson of Pennsylvania advocated that the "majority of people wherever found ought in all questions to govern the minority." This perspective regarded majorities to be facilitators of the people's good.[11]

Not everyone shared this optimism. During a speech delivered to the Constitutional Convention, Madison warned that majorities could prey on minorities and thereby endanger the general welfare. Yet even Madison, along with virtually all the other delegates to the Philadelphia Convention, failed to confront the greatest colonial power imbalances, particularly those between men and women and between whites and blacks. Conservative sensibilities about the subordinate place of women and blacks, along with laws meant to retain existing hierarchies, diminished the welfare of well over half the country's residents. From the perspective of groups who were excluded from politics, majority rule was not so cheery.[12]

The problem with republican ideals was not so much the framework of revolutionary ideology. The disconnect between ideals and practices resulted from an unwillingness to alter colonial power structures. The enlightened view of equal liberty, to which the framers committed the country, became a part of the framework of American culture. Much of the task of putting principle into practice was left to future generations.

Of the many documents revolutionary pamphleteers produced, none more elegantly distilled the convictions of the day than the Declaration of Independence. The Continental Congress appointed a committee to draft it on June 7, 1776, in response to Richard Henry Lee's motion, which John Adams seconded. The committee included Adams, who was from Massachusetts, Benjamin Franklin of Pennsylvania, Roger Sherman of Connecticut, Thomas Jefferson of Virginia, and Robert R. Livingston of New York. The principle task of writing the manifesto fell on the thirty-three-year-old Jefferson. He understood his directive "not to find out new principles, or new arguments, never before thought of, not merely to say things which had never been said before" but to express widely held convictions of "the American mind."[13]

The Declaration relied on an ethical theory to explain the need for rupture with England. The manifesto took for granted the self-evidence of natural human equality. It condemned despotic rule for being imposed on subjects without their consent. The people had no obligation to remain the subjects of a government that infringed on their inalienable rights of life, liberty, and the pursuit of happiness. A litany of accusations against George III followed. They were meant to show that the king's despotism had forced the colonists' hand, leaving them with no choice but to break from the Mother Country. The Declaration asserted that a divine natural order granted everyone equal and inalienable rights. The power of government was derived from the people, who could overthrow any authority that failed to safeguard their happiness and, then, could form a new state.[14]

On the subject of equally inalienable rights, the Declaration differed from the language of several state constitutions only insofar as it was explicitly inspired by theism. The Virginia Constitution of 1776 asserted that "all men are by nature equally free and independent, and have certain inherent rights, of which, when they enter into a state of society, they cannot, by any compact, deprive or divest their posterity; namely, the enjoyment of life and liberty, with the means of acquiring and possessing property, and pursuing and obtaining happiness and safety." The same year Pennsylvania's constitution similarly declared "That all men are born equally free and independent, and have certain natural, inherent and inalienable rights, amongst which are, the enjoying and defending life and liberty, acquiring, possessing and protecting

property, and pursuing and obtaining happiness and safety." And the constitutions of Massachusetts and Vermont began with similar assertions.[15]

The framers' embrace of human equality diverged sharply from their
failure to jointly condemn colonial slavery for its harmful effect on the common good. Massachusetts Colony Governor Thomas Hutchinson, an active
British Loyalist, wanted to ask "the Delegates of Maryland, Virginia, and the
Carolinas, how their Constituents justify the depriving more than an hundred
thousand Africans of their rights to liberty, and *the pursuit of happiness,* and in
some degree to their lives, if these rights are so absolutely unalienable."[16]

Even the Declaration of Independence, with its bold assertion of coequal
rights, lacked any explicit censure against slavery or the slave trade. This was
no mere oversight. Jefferson's original draft of the Declaration had accused
King George of acting "against human nature itself" by keeping open an
international slave trade that violated the "rights of life and liberty in the
persons of a distant people." When South Carolina objected to that clause,
the Continental Congress excised it from the final draft.[17]

This wavering on matters of principle did not efface the Declaration's
vision for creating a nation dedicated to preserving liberal equality. Its doctrine, as Samuel Adams said nearly thirty years after the states ratified it,
became part of "the political creed of the United States." That creed prevented tyranny and committed the national government to achieving the
common good instead of "the profit, honor or private interest of any one
man, family, or class of men."[18]

The human rights implications of the Declaration were profound for any
future generations willing to put the creed into legal operation. The ethical
perspective of the manifesto demanded national self-evaluation and self-
criticism in response to America's statement of purpose. Its chief weakness lay
in the lack of any enforcement mechanism.

The Preamble to the Constitution reiterated the framers' perspective on
the public good and freedom but excluded the Declaration's statement on
equality. Madison later explained that while the "perfect equality of mankind
. . . to be sure is an absolute truth, yet it is not absolutely necessary to be
inserted at the head of a constitution."[19] Although in legal terms, neither the
Declaration nor the Preamble dictated passage of any particular law, instigated any police action, or mandated the interpretation of any case, they
did provide all three branches of government a sense of normative purpose.
They also served as measuring rods against which the people could evaluate
whether their government acted for the overall welfare. But because they were

no more than statements of purpose, absent the promulgation of civil rights statutes, liberty and equality could be ignored in favor of personal gain and outright exploitation.

The country that professed its devotion to universal equality found excuses for the misappropriation of slave labor. Where elective franchise and political office were said to be critical for protecting individual rights, states kept women and indigents from voting. The principles found in the Declaration and Preamble said something about America's expectation for itself, but oaths about national values little benefited those who were under an immediate yoke of subordination.

Government for a Liberal Equality

A lack of legal protection against overt racial and gender discrimination was irreconcilable with the notion that government aimed to protect each person's equal share of liberty. Even in a state of nature, that hypothetical place that existed before the formation of government, morality rejected the freedom of individuals to violate the natural rights of others. The Reverend Judah Champion depicted a natural world, before governments were formed, where no one was superior to anyone else. Civil order became necessary because the enjoyment of rights was precarious where each person was answerable only to himself. The reason every person enjoyed the same natural rights, Hamilton postulated, was that each shared a rational faculty.[20]

According to another contemporary of the Revolution, people chose representatives who could better further their happiness than they could themselves in a state of nature. Free people, unlike slaves, could be governed only by those in whom they vested the authority to make public decisions. Policymakers lacked authority to trample the "equal impartial liberty, which is the property of all men from their birth as the gift of their Creator." The very reason why "equally free and independent" men join a constitutional government, Virginia maintained in its June 1776 Declaration of Rights, was to protect the personal freedoms, especially the right to own property.[21]

The purpose of constitutional government, Samuel Adams wrote anonymously in the *Boston Gazette*, was to protect "equality to the most extensive degree." He recognized that residents had to subject themselves to the government so long as it did not exercise its power oppressively. Another article, published in the *Virginia Gazette* before the Revolution under the pseudonym Philanthropos, defended the restrictive use of democratic government "to pursue such measures as conduce to the prosperity of the whole." Some self-sacrifice was necessary for the greater good to make rights more secure than they could be in a state of nature. Submission to laws promulgated by elected officials was necessary for the efficient functioning of government. To avoid aristocratic despotism, Americans thought to create a meritocractic government so that even persons who were born in humble circumstances could one day take the reins of power.[22]

This aspiration was naive in a culture where persons of color, women, and even white men without property were excluded from holding political offices. To their credit, many states began creating public schools to reduce disparities between the rich and the poor. Knowing that formal education enabled people to "guard against *slavery*," colonists began funding schools and colleges. Promoting education was essential to guarding against the abuse of social station. Since early theorists believed that government without popular consent was despotic, decisionmaking had to be diffused throughout an educated population.[23]

North Carolina established schools and provided public funding for teachers; Pennsylvania ordered each county to create a school, paid teachers salaries adequate for them to "instruct youth at low prices," and founded a university; and Vermont was even more specific, requiring each town to have a school that taught students at a low price, each county to have at least one grammar school, and the state to have at least one university. The New Hampshire Constitution best explained why public schools were essential to an open society: They disseminated "knowledge and learning," thereby conducing to increased "opportunities and advantages . . . through the various parts of the country" needed for the "preservation of free government."[24]

The vision of informed participation did not extend, however, to blacks and women, whose school enrollment was often proscribed by law or custom. With an elite group making the key political decisions, the contemporary gender and racial stratifications remained intact. Laws as well as customs denied blacks particularly the opportunity to stand on "an equal Footing with the white People," giving them "no Inducement" to exercise their natural capacities. As John Wesley, the founder of Methodism, realized, it was the lack of opportunity, not natural inferiority, that stifled potential.[25]

The welfare of the whole could not prosper where the interests of entire segments of the population were undermined. In theory, representative government had beneficent obligations to everyone, but the revolutionaries systematically provided for the rights of propertied white men, while they gave only partial provision for minorities and women to flourish and contribute their talents to the nascent republic. Neither the natural sciences nor government could achieve their full potential where input was limited by arbitrary categories having nothing to do with natural potential.

Property Interests

Colonists expressed concern about the consequences of economic inequality far more often than about the status of minorities and women. "Whenever there is [*sic*] in any country, uncultivated lands and unemployed poor," Jefferson wrote Madison, "it is clear that the laws of property have been so far extended as to violate natural right." Benjamin Rush thought it fair to "promote that equitable distribution of property" by limiting slavery in southern colonies.[26]

Federalists claimed that united states would be better equipped to end aristocratic rule. Expanding the nation, explained Madison in the tenth *Federalist*, would make it more difficult for economic factions to organize against the interests of politically weaker individuals. Representatives with diverse constituents, he predicted, would more likely act for the public good than be beholden to factions. His view was predicated on the presumption that political parties would have little role in American politics. This proved to be inaccurate, particularly by the middle of George Washington's first presidential term, when the supporters of Thomas Jefferson split sharply with those of Alexander Hamilton. In the political order that emerged, parties were, indeed, beholden to the interests of the electorate, but the electorate was only a sliver of the population. And that sliver favored the protection of property rights, which only part of the American population enjoyed.

The established order of property ownership resulted in the very economic factionalism that the tenth *Federalist* expected the Constitution would solve. That is not to say, with Charles Beard, that the driving force of revolution was economic. To the contrary, the stratified order that emerged undermined the common good heralded by natural-rights principles. John Adams typified affinity to the "positive Passion for the public good" for which "private Pleasures, Passions and Interests . . . when they stand in Competition with the Rights of Society" had to be sacrificed.[27]

The willingness to overlook a large segment of the population's interest in life and liberty rested, in no small part, on the revolutionaries' fixation on the right to property. In this, John Locke's broad definition influenced them but was not identical to dominant colonial thought. Locke distinguished between "property" and "estate" in a way that the framers of the Constitution did not: " 'Tis not without reason," wrote Locke in the *Second Treatise on Government*, "that he seeks out, and is willing to joyn in Society with others who are already united, or have a mind to unite for the mutual *Preservation* of their Lives, Liberties and Estates, which I call by the general Name, *Property*."[28] The legislature's duty was to make this broad category of property secure for the common good.[29]

Debates during the Constitutional Convention likewise assumed government's primary obligation to protect property and public safety.[30] The American use of "property," however, was closer to Locke's "estate." The notion was that freedom could be enjoyed only by people who could use, possess, dispose of, or rent their real and personal investments. Those who lacked such a privilege were literally or figuratively slaves, beholden to the will of others. In this vein, a sermonizer confidently preached, "PROPERTY is a blessing when accompanied with liberty; then it renders life comfortable and pleasant; but to be stript of all we can call our own, and be dependent upon others for our support and subsistence, must needs be very disagreeable: 'tis but the life of a slave, and but half living at best." Property, then, was essential to the enjoyment of the full range of freedoms.[31]

The condemnation of Britain over various tax laws, such as the Stamp Act or the Townshend Duties, also took its cue from Locke's insistence that the government raise no "*Taxes* on the Property of the People, *without the Consent of the People,* given by themselves, or their Deputies." Throughout the 1760s the colonists denounced the British Parliament, insisting "that they who are taxed at pleasure by others, cannot possibly have any property . . . can have no freedom, but are indeed reduced to the most abject slavery."[32]

This led to an exaggerated emphasis on property. To many framers, legal protections of that interest became of greater consequence for the common good than protections on life and liberty. An anonymous author in 1768 explained that when people joined to form civil communities, "*property* became unequally divided among them"; from that point, they had a right to possess whatever of it they could "acquire by the laws of a free country; and the principle on which this is founded, is the common good of mankind."[33] Within this framework, it was easier to protect existing property interests, including those in slaves, than to alter discriminatory social structures. Absolute proprietary rights had a tendency to overshadow human rights. And since property ownership went along with the right to vote, much of the population emerged after the Revolution without the freedom to exercise that franchise.[34] In the case of African slaves and some Native Americans, slave-holders thought of them as property to be exploited for the sake of the betterment of owners' lives. These groups lacked the same right to purchase and alienate property; consequently, they were unable to share in the common good of freedom.

Voting Rights

Property and caste stood at the heart of colonial voting restrictions. Nearly everywhere, voting was limited to white, propertied men. For people of that era, only persons with property had adequate interest in the state to cast their vote. Thus property, which existed as a state-protected institution, not liberty, life, or happiness, which existed in a state of nature, was the means to political personhood. Seven colonies—New Hampshire, Rhode Island, New York, New Jersey, Virginia, North Carolina, and Georgia—predicated suffrage on the possession of real estate, while the others also granted the vote to male taxpayers or those with a set minimum amount of personal property. Other groups, like women, juveniles, blacks, Native Americans, Jews, Catholics, and indentured servants, were explicitly excluded from casting ballots.[35]

Lack of representation in the British Parliament had been the rallying issue in the colonies. Taxation, in and of itself, was not the problem, explained a contributor to the October 3, 1765, *Georgia Gazette:* "It is the unconstitutional manner of imposing it, that is the great subject of uneasiness to the colonies." British and colonial interests were not always identical, Daniel Dulany explained, giving rise to the concern that "even acts, oppressive and injurious to the colonies . . . might become popular in *England,* from the promise or expectation, that the very measures which depressed the colonies, would give ease to the inhabitants of *Great Britain.*" Self-government, in contrast, assured that the interest of legislators and the electorate were "inseparably interwoven."[36]

After the Revolution, voting laws eased to allow for greater political participation. Nine of thirteen states changed their freehold systems. The norm was to allow taxpayers to vote, regardless of whether they paid taxes on real or personal property. New York even allowed renters of land and houses to vote, not merely the owners. Free blacks with $250 worth of property to pay taxes on could vote there, but few were able to meet that requirement. In 1825 of the 12,500 blacks living in New York City, which then occupied only the island of Manhattan, just sixteen were eligible to vote.[37]

The small number of eligible voters who actually cast votes in the young republic indicates that ordinary Americans, unlike their leadership, placed less import on self-representation. Few adult white men in America actually exercised that privilege. In 1778 and 1780, when the Massachusetts legislature submitted draft state constitutions to citizens, and in 1779, when it asked "whether they would choose" at that time "to have a new government," only about a fourth of the 16 percent eligible to vote cast ballots. In 1778, 120 towns did not even bother to submit returns. According to the historian J. Franklin Jameson's detailed study, from 1780 to 1789 only about 3 percent of the Massachusetts population actually cast ballots even though at the close of the colonial period 16 percent of the population was eligible to vote. Voting in Virginia was similarly sparse. In the late 1780s, when such important matters as the ratification of the United States Constitution were decided, only about 6 percent of the white population voted. Voting in America was a local matter; these figures cannot simply be extended to the nation as a whole. Nevertheless, widespread apathy and arbitrary disqualification from suffrage appear to have been the norm. It must also be borne in mind, however, that the low turnout in those days was sometimes attributable not to apathy but to the difficulty of traveling to polling stations, especially on rural roads during inclement weather.[38]

With such a small segment of the population eligible, or even interested enough, to vote, the claim that the People, rather than a relatively elite group, wanted to end taxation without representation is less convincing. Taken to its logical conclusion, Hamilton's claim that freedom and slavery differ only in that free people consent to laws governing them while slaves do not seemed to mean that most Americans were slaves. The majority of the population either lacked a political voice or neglected to exercise it. If the colonists needed a say in the British Parliament to prevent England from acting against their interests, so too did blacks, Native Americans, Jews, Catholics, and women. These groups' concerns were often discounted when it best suited the voting public.

Office holding was even less participatory than voting. State and national public officials tended to have enough money to campaign without party support, time to travel great distances, and wherewithal to leave farms with overseers, wives, or slaves. The nature of eighteenth-century representation belied the claim of J. C. Jones, delegate to the Massachusetts Convention for the ratification of the Constitution: "To say that the power may be abused, is saying what will apply to all *power*. The federal representatives will represent *the people*; they will be *the people*; and it is not *probable* they will abuse themselves." Jones's fellow delegate Samuel Stillman also reassured the convention that the national congress would be made up of "men of our own choice." They would be attentive to their constituents' good in the hope of being reelected.[39]

The politicians of that age were committed to representative principles, but they often relied on little more than personal experience, with all its limitations of upbringing, knowledge, and status, to act on behalf of groups whose interests were sometimes categorically opposed to their own. In the absence of democratic representation, legislatures sometimes enacted discriminatory laws and framers of the original Constitution included several provisions against the welfare of the whole.

CHAPTER TWO

Constitutional Republic of Equals?

The ideals expressed by the Declaration of Independence fed expectations that each American's fundamental rights would be equally protected. Many contemporaries understood that justifications for the American Revolution were irreconcilable with persistent colonial slavery. Their view that the British Parliament's taxation was despotic forced them to evaluate their own conduct toward African slaves. Talk of equality and representation made slavery an aberration where it had been a norm for more than a century. The revolutionaries' justification for independence was not in keeping with the exploitation of human chattel and the enforcement of slave codes.

For slaves, the struggle for freedom was even more urgent than it was for white colonists who, like Patrick Henry, preferred death to a life of political bondage. No matter how heavy the yoke of British oppression, it was overshadowed by the deprivations imposed on slaves. British colonial slavery developed as an exploitation of cheap, uneducated labor and the agricultural practice of exhausting farmland rather than using it efficiently. Indentured European servants worked side by side with African and Native American slaves from the seventeenth to the early eighteenth century. Mid-eighteenth-century periodicals carried numerous awards for the capture of English, Scottish, and Irish indentured servants along with those seeking the return of black slaves.[1]

By the Revolution, slavery had been racialized. Hereditary slavery targeted blacks as no other race. With improved labor conditions in late-seventeenth-century England, the American colonies experienced a shortage of European indentured servants, and an abundance of imported African captives led to the flourishing of slavery. By the end of 1730 black slaves had replaced white servants in the Chesapeake. The change was also pronounced in South Carolina, where planters found slaves experienced in rice production. The black population there rose from 17 percent of the whole in 1680 to 70 percent in 1720. In 1680 blacks made up about 7 percent of the combined population of Virginia, Maryland, South Carolina, and North Carolina. By 1730 blacks constituted nearly 22 percent of those states' population. This proportion was representative of the black population in the colonies as a whole, which increased from about 15 percent in 1720 to 21 percent in 1770.[2]

Slaves were treated as property. Infants and adults were subject to discretionary sales by owners, who had the legal right to act out of economic self-interest. Advertisements often indicated no more than a passing inclination to sell family members together, but a readiness to sell them apart. Racial stratification abrogated even the bonds of familial affection. The business dealings of slave importers read like transactions in cattle. William Vernon, for instance, a friend of John Adams's and later first secretary of the navy, ordered the master of his slave ship not to purchase "old slaves, neither very Small, as those under four foot two inches high," and demanded the captain to be "careful of giving your slaves good Diet." At auction, slaves were manhandled for physical deformities. Once on plantations, they were treated like beasts of burden. Overseers of work, who were both black and white, were "a cruel Set of Fellows, who either have very little Humanity in their Composition, or know not how to exercise it," wrote an observer during his travels through Maryland in 1777. The *Boston Gazette* from the mid-eighteenth-century also indicated the extent to which African slaves were thought of as property. One advertisement from January 7, 1735, was for the sale of two "Negro Men and a Boy. . . . Likewise . . . super-fine . . . Tea. . . . Together with Rugs, Blankets." The *Virginia Gazette* from December 11, 1766, advertised an estate of "Hogs, Horses, Cattle, Sheep, Houshold and Kitchen Furniture, and several choice SLAVES."[3]

The sense of superiority colonists expressed in the early eighteenth century contributed to the growth of slavery. Thinking themselves justified by religion, culture, and biology, they enacted slave codes. The laws of South Carolina were representative of other colonies' regulations. A 1712 statute prohibited slaves from freely traveling outside their masters' plantations without express permission or in the company of whites. In the same year, another South Carolina statute, which called Africans "barbarous, wild, and savage," punished the murderers of blacks and slaves by a monetary fine but imposed no jail time for the crime.[4]

Laws prohibiting interracial marriages, which were codified throughout the colonies, indicated an all too common aversion to blacks. Some punishments for intermarriage were even more severe than those for killing free or enslaved blacks. Virginia, as early as 1691, enacted a law "for prevention of that abominable mixture and spurious issue . . . by negroes, mulattoes, and Indians intermarrying with . . . white women." An act of 1705 confined white men and women to jail for intermarrying "with a negro or mulatto man or woman." In September 1664 the Maryland Assembly found that "free borne English women forgettfull of their free Condicôn and to the disgrace of our Nation doe intermarry with Negro Slaues." The children of such a union were to be enslaved until their thirtieth year. Any white woman found violating Maryland's sense of marital decency had to serve her husband's master for a life term. The law was appended in 1717 to prevent intermarriages between whites and free blacks. In the latter circumstances, black spouses became lifelong slaves, while white spouses were relegated to servitude for seven years. The law in Pennsylvania in 1726 declared that any black partner of such a union would be enslaved, confined the white spouse for seven years of servitude, made their children servants until their thirty-first year, and even fined anyone officiating their intermarriage. In the North, an early-eighteenth-century Massachusetts law made intermarried couples subject to monetary fine.[5]

The cruelty of chattel slavery did not go unnoticed to a generation given to the study of representative government. To them slavery represented the forced deprivation of natural freedoms. Human bondage treated individuals as physical objects who lacked any of the natural equality of humanity. The inconsistency of slavery with the protests against colonial servitude proved to be the greatest infraction against revolutionary principles.

Denouncing Political Servitude

During the seventeenth century, "slavery" signified a variety of oppressive behaviors. The word referred to more types of oppression than it does today. Besides its obvious reference to chattel servitude, its most common use around 1776 was for the exercise of political power without consent of the governed. The enslaved were forced to act "according to the arbitrary will and Pleasure of another." In this sense, slavery appeared repeatedly in discourse on the nature of legitimate government. Politically powerful despots could enslave nations, just as petty despots could enslave individuals. Joseph Hawley, a member of the Massachusetts committee to the Provincial Congress, explained that a relationship between different parts of a community can resemble masters' relationships to their servants because "an individual who has the absolute right to direct the conduct, dispose of the property, and command the services of another, is, with propriety, called a master." In support of the Revolution, a foreigner wrote that a state "is in *slavery*" unless the people elect their representatives. Moses Mather explained that being deprived of political participation left the colonists without "security against tyranny" that was aimed at divesting them of liberty and property.[6]

The Revolution challenged the perceived British attempt to enslave the colonists through a series of oppressive laws. Parliamentary passage of the Tea Act (1773), the Boston Port Act (1774), and the Massachusetts Government Act (1774) heightened fears of imperial dominance. From the colonists' perspective, theirs was not simply a dispute with the Mother Country—a disagreement about the price of stamps, tea, or even shipping rights—but a struggle to maintain control over their affairs. Keeping them from the reins of government was a bald-faced intrusion against their natural rights.

Readily available pamphlets, newspapers, and books spread passionate calumny from one colony to another and one city to the next. With a grief-stricken plume, the Massachusetts attorney Josiah Quincy, Jr., wailed, "Britons are our oppressors—I speak it with shame—I speak it with indignation—we are slaves." With less shrill but like exaggeration, Stephen Hopkins, a signer of the Declaration of Independence, equated the lot of colonists being subject to a tax levied without their consent to "the miserable condition of slaves." John Dickinson, who later manumitted all thirty-seven of his slaves, wrote this powerfully influential syllogism: "*Those* who are *taxed* without their own consent, expressed by themselves or their representatives, are *slaves. We are taxed* without our own consent, expressed by ourselves or our representatives. *We* are therefore—SLAVES." George Washington too thought the Parliament was "trampling upon the valuable rights of Americans" rather than acting in furtherance of justice.[7]

Outrage against Chattel Slavery

The harms countrymen committed against chattel slaves made accusations against the British seem more trivial and less convincing. In opposing the Boston Port Act, John Allen demonstrated his evenhandedness by denouncing slaveholders, calling them "trifling patriots" and "pretended votaries for Freedom" who trampled on the natural rights and privileges of Africans even as they made a "vain parade of being advocates of the liberties of mankind."

He further pointed out that a duty on tea was of far smaller consequence than the bondage of captivity. A 1770 Philadelphia Grand Jury indictment against the British Parliament seems cast in rhetorical terms that should be turned on the owners of human laborers: "What slavery can be more compleat, more miserable, more disgraceful, than that lot of a people, where justice is administered, government carried on and a standing army maintained at the expence of the people, & yet without the least dependance upon them?"[8] By equating their condition to slavery, the wealthy, educated, and mobile group who led the Revolution came face to face with the arbitrary conditions they imposed or tolerated to be imposed against persons of African descent.

Blacks experienced proportionately greater deprivation on their rights than whites. They were excluded from formal political processes and could not consent to the imposed governing structure. In 1777 a group of Massachusetts black petitioners, who had absorbed the revolutionary mentality along with their countrymen, petitioned the legislature to "be Restored to the Enjoyments of that which is the Naturel Right of all men" lest "the Inhabitance of this States No longer [be] chargeable with the inconsistancey of acting themselves the part which they condem and oppose in others." In another petition "A Son of Africa" bemoaned the nearsightedness of denouncing Great Britain but doing nothing to end the enslavement of Africans, whom God, "by the law of nature, gave everything . . . equally alike to everyman richly to enjoy."[9]

Groups of black petitioners relied on revolutionary ideals to press their case. They shared the revolutionary certainty that liberty was essential to their happiness and that they were born equal but forcefully deprived of their rights. Black petitioners from New Hampshire reasoned that since "freedom is an inherent right of the human species" then slavery must be a detestable form of tyranny. Another group, writing in the early 1770s to Massachusetts Governor Thomas Hutchinson, apprehended that they had "in comon with other men a naturel right to be free and without molestation to injoy" their property. Writing in the same decade, "a Great Number of Blackes" from Massachusetts asserted their common claim on the "natural right to our freedoms" without being "unjustly dragged" away from families and friends into slavery. Another petition decried the slavery of New England states: "We have no Property! We have no Wives! No Children! We have no City! No Country." On June 14, 1775, black petitioners from Bristol and Worcester, Massachusetts, were able to get a resolution from a convention held at Worcester. "That we abhor the enslaving of any of the human race, and particularly of the negroes in this country, and that whenever there shall be a door opened, or opportunity present for anything to be done towards the emancipation of the negroes, we will use our influence and endeavor that such a thing may be brought about."[10]

These sentiments seem to have been shared by a large number of white colonists. Worcester had instructed its representative to the Massachusetts General Court, the state's legislature, to use his "influence to obtain a law to put an end to that unchristian and impolitic practice of making slaves of human species in this province." On January 12, 1775, a group from Darien County, Georgia, bristled at the notion that the colonial struggle should be thought in pragmatic terms: "To show the world that we are not influenced by any contracted or interested motives, but a general philosophy for all mankind, of whatever climate, language, or complexion, we hereby declare our disapprobation and abhorrence of the unnatural practice of Slavery in America."[11]

Fourth of July orations throughout the country made reference to such sentiments as a matter of course. A Philadelphia newspaper recounted that two of the 1792 Independence Day toasts were for "The daughters of America" and "The people of Africa." The next year, the same paper transcribed the Order of Cincinnati's Independence Day toast to the "human race—may the great family of mankind without distinction of countries or colours, be united . . . and enjoy liberty as a common inheritance." In a later year, celebrating the holiday in Maryland, a toast contained the message that as slavery was "Contrary to the declaration that 'all men are created equal,' may Congress consider the necessity of an immediate eradication of this evil."[12]

Many of the most significant revolutionary leaders drew attention to the incongruity between American demands for freedom and their rationales for the tyrannies of slavery. Hamilton, for instance, wrote that "no reason can be assigned why one man should exercise any power, or preeminence over his fellow creatures more than another; unless they have voluntarily vested him with it." Thomas Paine, exhibiting a knack for penetrating brevity in his first published article, entreated Americans to consider "with what consistency, or decency they complain so loudly of attempts to enslave them, while they hold so many hundred thousands in slavery; and annually enslave many thousands more, without any pretence of authority, or claim upon them."[13]

James Otis, in 1764 when he was arguably the most influential Massachusetts agitator against colonial rule, mocked the racism that went hand in hand with slavery: so "shocking violation of the law of nature" could never be excused because Africans have "short curl'd hair . . . instead of Christian hair, as tis called by those, whose hearts, are as hard as the nether millstone." Nor could justification for it "be drawn from a flat nose and a long or a short face."

He viewed the institution of slavery as a despoiler of civilization that prefers the interests of petty tyrants to the value of liberty. In another publication, Otis mocked the paradox of opposing the Stamp Act while leaving slavery intact: "I affirm, and that on the best information, the Sun rises and sets every day in the sight of five millions of his majesty's American subjects, white, brown and black." The theologian Samuel Hopkins, who after the Revolution proved critical to abolishing slavery in Rhode Island, was equally indignant in his call for emancipation. Denouncing the "shocking, the intolerable inconsistence" of embracing liberty while "at the same time making slaves of many thousands of our brethren, who have as good a right to liberty as ourselves, and to whom it is as sweet as it is to us, and the contrary as dreadful!" The commerce in humans was against nature, wrote Abraham Booth, because everyone, whether African or European, has an "equal claim to personal liberty with any man upon earth." Everyone, therefore, has a common stock of human rights. To think otherwise would fly in the face of founding principle that "all men are created equal."[14]

Each slave, wrote Richard Wells, "carries about him the strongest proofs in nature of his *original rights.*" Slavery was incompatible with the proposition that "All *the inhabitants of America* are entitled to the privileges of the inhabitants of Great-Britain." So many people shared Wells's views that on April 14, 1775, five days before the battles of Lexington and Concord, the first antislavery society was born. In 1785 the New York Society for Promoting the Manumission of Slaves was organized, with John Jay as its president. In 1792 similar societies operated in Delaware, Rhode Island, Connecticut, New Jersey, Maryland, and Virginia. The 1794 delegates to the Abolition Society decried the illogic of a republic that zealously advocated freedom to tolerate "in its bosom a body of slaves."[15]

Paine, on March 8, 1775, just a month before he played an important part in the first antislavery society's formation, bluntly asked Americans to consider "with what consistency, or decency they complain so loudly of attempts to enslave them, while they hold so many hundred thousands in slavery; and annually enslave many thousands more, without any pretence of authority, or claim upon them?" The Quaker Anthony Benezet was as poignant at using religious arguments as Paine was at using secular ones. Back in the 1760s, Benezet, who was one of the abolitionists' forerunners, related people's natural equality to their identity as a "species." None was naturally superior since the "black-skin'd and the white-skin'd" were "all of the human Race."[16]

Benezet not only dispelled the notion that slavery was a benevolent institution but further reflected on how to free those Africans who had been enslaved. He realized that without receiving some aid after their liberation, former slaves would be unable to compete with other free persons in the job market. Therefore he recommended that both adults and children receive adequate instruction to become productive members of the community. Seeking to calm the fears of whites about the behavior of free blacks, Benezet explained how liberation would help government achieve security and welfare: the tax burden would be eased because the obligation to pay taxes would fall on everyone, the trades and arts would advance, and productivity would increase since more vacant land would be cultivated. Abolition therefore would benefit the general welfare. Liberation meant much more than just ending obligatory labor; it required colonists to grant blacks the opportunity to participate in the privileges of equal citizenship.[17]

Given the broad consensus that slavery lacked any legitimacy, it is no surprise, as the historian Winthrop D. Jordan summarized, that in the years preceding the Revolution a general impression prevailed that slavery was a "communal sin." Benjamin Rush mentioned this collective strain of thought in a letter to Granville Sharp, a British abolitionist. "The cause of African freedom in America," Rush wrote in 1774, "continues to gain ground." He expected slavery in America to end within forty years. That view, unfortunately, wound up being overoptimistic. Another ninety years intervened before a constitutional amendment ended legalized slavery.[18]

Even the southern vanguard of the Revolution realized the anomaly between liberty's cause and the inequitable institution it chose to perpetuate. Patrick Henry, for one, acknowledged his own hypocrisy after scrutinizing one of Benezet's abolitionist tracts:

> Is it not amazing, that at a time when the rights of Humanity are defined & understood with precision in a Country above all others fond of Liberty: that . . . we find Men, professing a Religion the most humane, mild, meek, gentle & generous, adopting a Principle as repugnant to humanity. . . . Would any one believe that I am Master of Slaves of my own purchase! I am drawn along by the general Inconvenience of living without them; I will not, I cannot justify it. . . . I believe a time will come when an opportunity will be offered to abolish this lamentable Evil.

Little could Henry know that the "lamentable Evil" would be abolished only after a bloody civil war. Thomas Jefferson also recognized the incongruity of slavery with the Age of Revolution. Jefferson, indeed, had some premonition about the national catastrophe that slavery could catalyze, believing that it was destroying the people's morals.[19]

With the passage of time, Jefferson grew increasingly indifferent about the plight of slaves. His changed attitude was indicative of the country's shift from liberal ideals. Writing during the heyday of American expectations, Jefferson had wanted to end the importation of slaves into the colonies and follow that with the "abolition of domestic slavery." In 1776, the same year his draft Declaration of Independence proposed condemning King George for the slave trade, Jefferson's second and third drafts of the Virginia Constitution contained a provision that "no person hereafter coming into this country shall be held in slavery under any pretext whatever." Jefferson, like his fellow slaveholder George Mason, retained his slaves during and after the Revolution, even while admitting that every "master of slaves is born a petty tyrant."[20]

It was this lack of integrity to principle that gave opponents of the Revolution an occasion for criticism. John Mein, a British Loyalist, pointed out the disingenuousness of Bostonians who grounded their struggle in the immutable laws of nature while they lived in a town where two thousand out of fifteen thousand inhabitants were black slaves. The evident contradiction evoked the overstated disdain of Samuel Johnson, an English lexicographer and opponent of colonial independence. As he saw it, the "loudest yelps for liberty" were heard from "drivers of Negroes."[21]

Thirty-eight years after independence, Jefferson had become complacent in the oppression that, by then, only a constitutional amendment could eliminate. In 1814, writing to Edward Coles, who would manumit his slaves and become the antislavery governor of Illinois, Jefferson acknowledged that "the flame of liberty" that he had hoped would spark in the younger generation, leading to a popular movement against slavery, had failed to ignite. Jefferson's indifference to the plight of slaves was stark. Despite his avowed disappointment at this shortcoming of the Revolution, Jefferson counseled Coles not to free his slaves. The degeneration from idealism to cold resignation, complicity, and participation typified a political arrangement willing to sacrifice the interests of slaves for creature comfort and domestic tranquility.[22]

Not all those who helped achieve independence became apathetic about its potentials. Coles is just one example of those who showed their integrity by manumitting slaves. General William Whipple, a veteran of the battle of Saratoga who also served as a delegate to the Continental Congress from New Hampshire, likewise acted on the logic of natural-rights principles. His slave, Prince, had been in combat and was even an oarsman on George Washington's boat as it made its way through the icy Delaware River during a Christmas storm in 1776. In 1777, Prince said, "*You* are going to fight for your *liberty*, but I have none to fight for." These words cut Whipple to the quick, and he immediately freed the slave.[23] Among the great personages of the day, George Washington, John Randolph, and Robert Carter III provided for their slaves' freedom by will.

Washington is said to have been a master who cared for sick slaves and ordered overseers to be humane. He emancipated several hundred of his own slaves at death, but he was unable to free his wife's dower slaves. Washington bequeathed that elderly freed persons be given pensions, he provided that others be taught to read and write (even though Virginia laws prohibited educating blacks), and he paid slaves who remained on his estate for their work.[24] Slavery was so embedded in Virginia, however, that Washington's nephew and estate executor, Bushrod Washington, who was then a Supreme Court justice, carried out only part of his uncle's will, selling some of the slaves instead.[25]

Individual acts of manumission and kindness achieved only small-scale reform. Free blacks fared little better than slaves; a former general of the Continental Army wrote that in Virginia "it is not only the slave who is beneath his master, it is the negro who is beneath the white man."[26] Northern states, unlike those in the South, used coordinated policy to end slavery; meanwhile, the Constitution ensnared the entire nation in the net of slaveholding.

Early Antislavery Efforts

Before the Revolution, slavery was legal in all thirteen colonies. The nation's embrace of principled discourse during the revolutionary period led to several antislavery efforts. In 1774 the Continental Congress required that the importation of slaves cease after December 1, 1775, but it lacked the power to enforce the decree. The historian and sociologist W. E. B. Du Bois pointed out that the colonists' motives for ending the trade were complex, including a genuine commitment to the philosophy of freedom in the northern and middle states, fear of slave insurrections fomented by newly arrived Africans, domestic slave breeders' economic self-interests, and a strategic decision to harm British commerce. The Northwest Ordinance of 1787 prohibited the slave trade, slavery, and involuntary servitude from spreading into a territory that includes present-day Ohio, Indiana, Illinois, Michigan, and Wisconsin. Yet it was an imperfect provision that contained an article allowing masters to lawfully reclaim fugitive slaves or indentured servants who fled there.[27]

Some individual states also ended slave importation. Rhode Island in 1774 restricted the slave trade, prefacing the law with the statement that "those who are desirous of enjoying all the advantages of liberty themselves, should be willing to extend personal liberty to others." That assertion was only partly sincere since the state continued to allow slave traders who were not able to dispose of their cargo in the West Indies to bring it to Rhode Island, as long as they reexported it within a year. Connecticut in the same year passed a statute prohibiting slave importation, and Delaware (1776), Virginia (1778), and Maryland (1783) followed suit. As for South Carolina (1787) and North Carolina (1786), they made importation more difficult but manifested no fundamental aversion to it.[28]

Northern states' decisions to abolish slavery were of even more import. The 1777 Vermont Constitution outlawed slavery because "all men are born equally free and independent, and have certain natural, inherent and unalienable rights, amongst which are the enjoying and defending life and liberty; acquiring, possessing and protecting property, and pursuing and obtaining happiness and safety." The New Hampshire Bill of Rights seems to have been the primary legal means for ending slavery there in 1784. It provided that the natural rights to life, liberty, and property "shall not be denied or abridged by this state on account of race, creed, color, sex or national origin." In Massachusetts, Superior Court Chief Justice William Cushing decreed slavery to be unconstitutional and against principles of natural rights, considering all men to be born free and equal. Those states' commitments made tangible the principles of the Declaration of Independence.[29]

In other northern states, change came more slowly. A gradual abolition law went into effect in Pennsylvania in 1780. Benezet, who lived to see its passage, could claim no more than partial success for his years of effort to achieve immediate emancipation. Rhode Island and Connecticut enacted similar laws in 1784, New York in 1799, and New Jersey in 1804. New York and New Jersey took the extra step of providing for the support of abandoned slave children. Gradualism aimed at minimal intrusion on present owners' interests while granting no one immediate reprieve from what was recognized to be reprehensible practice.[30] The closest measures to abolition in the South, though woefully short of revolutionary aims, were the 1780s and 1790s legal relaxations in Virginia, Maryland, and Delaware that allowed masters to manumit their slaves, so long as they were willing to vouch that the freed persons would not become public wards.

Lacking the political power to make any meaningful change, former slaves emerged from a lowly state without compensation and with few opportunities. After the Revolution, the country came to a historical moment that might have led it to recognize universal rights; instead, it placated slave interests in the interest of constitutional union.[31]

Constitutional Compromise

Despite a steady outcry against slavery and the trend of northern and middle states to abolish the institution, the Philadelphia Constitutional Convention of 1787 drafted an instrument more considerate of southern economic interests and racial sensibilities than it was principled. The founders achieved union and security at the cost of countenanced tyranny. South Carolina and Georgia delegates demanded that the Constitution include protections for slavery, and the other colonies capitulated. Slavery became a constitutionally recognized form of property.

The Constitution nowhere used "slave" or "slavery"; instead it recognized the right to own humans through several euphemisms—"person held to Service or Labour," "such persons," and "other persons." Unlike the Continental Congress, the Constitutional Convention decided against an outright prohibition of the slave trade. The Slave Importation Clause placed a twenty-year moratorium on any national prohibition against the international slave trade. The moratorium was so important to achieving colonial union that to reassure states actively engaged in the trade that their interests would not suffer excessively, article V of the Constitution prohibited Congress from amending the Importation Clause. Protecting the trade was critical to South Carolina and Georgia, declared Charles Cotesworth Pinckney, because without the resupply of fresh slaves they would be unable to compete economically. Achieving equality, for Pinckney, meant establishing a confederation for the commercial advantage of each member state. Jonathan Rutledge, also from South Carolina, echoed Pinckney's insistent demand.[32]

Most Northerners either acquiesced silently or relied on strained reasoning to explain their support for the proposal. Connecticut delegate Oliver Ellsworth, an otherwise astute constitutional theorist who was a member of the Committee of Detail, illogically claimed that the Importation Clause would pave the way to abolition. He, like many of his fellow delegates, believed that the "morality or wisdom" of slavery should be left to each state.

Some of the Upper South's opposition to the clause was driven not by antislavery sentiments but by the desire to increase the value of domestic slaves. In opposing ratification of the Constitution, George Mason, for one, argued that slave importation was "infamous" and detestable. He reminded fellow Virginians that Great Britain's support for it "was one of the great causes of our separation." Augmenting "slaves weakens the states; and such a trade is diabolical in itself, and disgraceful to mankind." Mason's aversion to human chattel, however, seemingly went no further than importation. He owned three hundred slaves himself and was upset that the Constitution did not secure "the property of the slaves we have already." Ellsworth, and other contemporaries, claimed that Mason's opposition was based on his interest in maintaining high prices for domestically sold slaves, which the importation of Africans was likely to depress.[33]

Not all opponents of the slave trade were so calculating. Many Antifederalists were more authentic in opposing the Constitution's ratification because it, in effect, sanctioned the international trade in human cargo. One tract drew attention to the plight of kidnapped Africans. What man, the author rhetorically asked, would allow sons and daughters to be torn from him and doomed to hereditary slavery? The argument gave no credence to the claim that the importation of slaves was critical to Georgia and South Carolina to recoup their residents' property losses from the War of Independence. No person could be the property of another since each was the proprietor of himself alone; therefore no one had any basis for claiming compensation for the loss of slaves. Joshua Altherton, at the New Hampshire ratifying convention, proclaimed that having the Importation Clause in the Constitution would make all states "*consenters to,* and *partakers in,* the sin and guilt of this abominable traffic." The slave trade was, in fact, not exclusively a southern business. New Englanders and New Yorkers also participated in shipping ventures across the Atlantic.[34]

The long-term political fallout from a second provision—the Three-Fifths Clause—was more significant than the backlash from the Importation Clause. The former clause augmented slave states' federal representation by counting three-fifths of their slaves for apportioning seats to the U.S. House of Representatives. Southern delegates to the Constitutional Convention had wanted an even more favorable provision but were unable to muster enough votes for it. Pinckney and Pierce Butler, another South Carolina delegate, sought to count blacks and whites equally for representation, while granting blacks no opportunity for participating in elective politics. North Carolina delegate William R. Davie held equally strong convictions. He asserted that North Carolina "would never confederate on any terms" unless, at a minimum, the three-fifths formula was adopted. Speaking on behalf of Virginia, Governor Edmund J. Randolph chimed in for the adoption of the clause as a means of protecting property in slaves.[35]

In opposition to the strong-arm tactics of the Deep South, James Wilson of Pennsylvania pointed out the absurdity of using slave property for representation but counting no other chattel—like cows, rakes, and carriages—for that purpose. Another Pennsylvania representative to the convention, Gouverneur Morris, was more acerbic in his criticism. He refused to encourage those who profited from the slave trade "by allowing them a representation for their Negroes." Relying on natural-rights principles, he reeled at the idea that any "inhabitant of Georgia and S.C. who goes to the coast of Africa, and in defiance of the most sacred laws of humanity tears away his fellow creatures from their dearest connections and dam[n]s them to the most cruel bondages, shall have more votes in a Govt. Instituted for protection of the rights of mankind, than the citizen of Pa. or N. Jersey who views with a laudable horror, so nefarious a practice." Morris regarded slavery as a vestige of aristocracy that the proposed clause would require the North to defend militarily.[36]

No other Northern delegate was as principled in his opposition to the Three-Fifths Clause as Morris. Most favored its adoption to the alternative, disunion, and saw concession to slave power as a necessary means of gaining southern concessions. Roger Sherman of Connecticut similarly considered the slave trade "iniquitous" but refused to vote against the passage of the clause.[37]

Southerners benefited from the Three-Fifths Clause as early as the first national election, gaining disproportionate federal power in the House of Representatives. The South had a collective political interest in protecting the institution. That put it at odds with the North, distinguishing the welfare of the two regions from the nation's inception. By 1803 the South had three more representatives in Congress and twenty-one more electoral college votes for the presidency than the North, even though New York and New England had some sixty thousand more free inhabitants than the entire South. Southern gains through the Louisiana Purchase further increased this political imbalance. The representative majority gave southerners and their allies the power to offer proslavery bills for congressional debate and the numbers to enact them into law.[38]

The Three-Fifths Clause also influenced the outcome of presidential elections. Article II, section 1, clause 2 of the Constitution granted each state presidential electors whose number was equal to the state's combined senators and representatives. The electors played a decisive role both in placing slaveholders, rather than antislavery advocates, into the executive branch (as happened in 1800, when Thomas Jefferson defeated John Adams for the presidency), and in seating northerners willing to placate the slave South (as was the case with James Buchanan's victory in 1856 over John C. Frémont, the Republican candidate).[39]

Other constitutional provisions guarded slaveholders against recalcitrant slaves and required federal action in maintaining the peculiar institution. The Insurrection Clause gave Congress the power to call up the militia to suppress revolts, including slave rebellions such as the Nat Turner Rebellion. Another constitutional provision, the Fugitive Slave Clause, made "the whole land one vast hunting ground for men," in the words of Frederick Douglass, making felons out of persons who broke the fetters of slavery. Not a single representative at the Constitutional Convention voted against passage of the Fugitive Slave Clause. Before the Thirteenth Amendment went into effect, that clause, coupled with enabling legislation, required that fugitives be returned "on demand" and prohibited free states from liberating them. The amendment provision in article V of the Constitution required the support of two-thirds of both congressional houses to propose an amendment and three-fourths of state legislatures or conventions to ratify it. Before the Civil War, any proposed antislavery amendment would have been doomed because so many congressmen represented slave states. In 1860, on the threshold of war, slavery was legal in fifteen of the thirty-three states of the Union.[40]

From the country's founding, persons of African descent confronted systematic barriers against their upward mobility. The framers of the Constitution broke the British yoke of bondage and immediately crafted provisions to keep blacks from enjoying the benefits of civil liberty. Nor were they the only group denied the right to participate in self-government.

Women in the New Republic

Besides capitulating to slavery, another of the revolutionaries' great failures was their unwillingness to end the subordination of women. The popular press of the day was replete with images of women as helpmates whose place was in the home, and out of public life. A Connecticut observer's view in 1786 was typical, asserting in a patronizing tone that the "chief object of a woman's attention ought to be domestic economy and domestic happiness." Her role was to attend to "family cares, so that her husband may be at full liberty to pursue business." An earlier author had been even more cavalier toward women's abilities, writing that a married couple "are yoak-fellows in mutuall familiaritie, not in equall authoritie. . . . If therefore he will one thing, and she another, she may not thinke to haue an equall right and power. She must giue place and yeeld."[41]

Women were perceived as the legal wards of male family members. They did not need the same legal rights as men since their husbands, fathers, or brothers looked after their best interests. "Let the Women . . . not regret the Want of Liberty," counseled an anonymous author; rather, they should extol their subordination and "praise that Precaution which is taken to supply them with all they want." Another wrote that a woman should be happy with her lowly status since it kept her "free from care, and free from woe," secure at every stage in life that a man was "her guardian-god below."[42]

Some contemporaries realized that this line of reasoning was not in keeping with American republicanism. One of the giants in the pantheon of revolutionaries, James Otis, was a proponent of women's rights. His influential pamphlet *The Rights of the British Colonies Asserted and Proved,* written shortly before his mental breakdown, recognized the inconsistency between a social compact founded on the consent of equals and the colonial treatment of women. In a state of nature, he asked rhetorically, would "not apple women and orange girls [have] as good a right to give their respectable suffrages for a new king?" In this vein, an article appearing in *American Museum,* a late-eighteenth-century magazine, painted a picture of wretchedness because "women seem as totally to be edged out of all employment" and forced to be "dependent almost entirely on their husbands." A lady, in the same magazine, wrote:

> How wretched is poor woman's fate! . . .
> Subject to man in ev'ry state, . . .
> In youth, a father's stern command, . . .
> A lordly brother watchful stands, . . .
> The tyrant husband next appears, . . .
> That man, vain man, should bear the sway,
> To slavish chains add slavish mind,
> That I may thus your will obey.[43]

This assault on the status quo came at a time when Americans were reexamining their political values based on revolutionary notions of liberal equality. The unfortunate truth, however, is that most contemporary writers did not even address the disconnect between women's treatment and the purposes of representative government. Despite this oversight, women's lives improved, although at a snail's pace. Many colonies began extending a variety of personal, economic, and political rights to women. Females gained lasting freedoms in states like Pennsylvania, New York, Maryland, and Virginia, which granted them the right to file for divorce. Laws abolishing primogeniture, which had given the eldest son a double share of inheritance, helped decedents' daughters and younger sons. Other state laws extended identical inheritance rights to the daughters and sons of persons who died intestate, without having executed a will. There continued to be a disparity between the treatment of married and unmarried women in such states as Georgia, where the eldest daughter's right to intestate succession was based on being unmarried and landless. Only a *feme sole*—a spinster or a widow—had legal rights to convey property, be party to lawsuits, enter into contracts, and execute wills.[44]

A married woman, *feme covert*, remained riddled with restrictions against alienating title to property without first obtaining her husband's consent. This incapacity affected most women in colonial times since few were willing to suffer the social stigma of spinsterhood. Laws on property ownership varied significantly between states. In Connecticut after 1723 and in some southern states, such as South Carolina, Virginia, and Maryland, married women could inherit property. An heiress's husband could not then sell without her written consent. To avoid private coercion, those states further required the wife's verbal attestation before a justice of the peace. Massachusetts, on the other hand, allowed husbands to alienate wives' property with only written consent, leaving uncertain whether her consent was given freely, provided under duress, or fraudulently obtained. Even women who retained ownership over land were typically obligated to transmit profits from that interest to their husbands. Technical legal handicaps on married women were not always strictly enforced, indicating a realization of their harmful effect on both individuals and the economy. Courts of equity could ameliorate statutory and common law inequality by crafting opinions based on individual cases rather than relying on the lack of parity endemic to the law.[45]

With few exceptions, like the New Yorkers Mary Spratt and Ann Elizabeth Schuyler, each of whom was a widowed merchant with extensive business contacts, women had even less control of business matters than of estates.[46] Married women typically could carry on commercial transactions only with their husbands' consent because they owned no personal property to offer in consideration for entering into contractual obligations.

The handicaps women faced in owning private property and in contracting paled in comparison with the barriers they confronted on participating politically. Since the seventeenth century, colonial laws had rendered women, irrespective of their marital status, about as devoid of public power as children.[47]

Women's participation in various facets of the Revolution—from giving logistical support to sharing military intelligence and taking care of estates—made them ever more aware of their precarious legal status. During the struggle for independence, battles, political maneuvers, and governance became the conversation of women in parlors just as it was of men in the halls of Congress. Eliza Wilkinson asserted, during the British invasion of South Carolina, where she lived, that "none were greater politicians than the several knots of ladies" who put aside "all trifling discourse of fashions . . . and . . . commenced perfect statesmen."[48]

Women's inability to participate in formal politics remained the norm even after states ratified the Constitution. Women connected to well-known politicos, such as Abigail Adams, whose husband became the second president of the United States, and Hannah Lee Corbin, Richard Henry Lee's sister, tried using letters to sway the political process. Adams unsuccessfully pleaded that, in founding a new country, her husband and his fellow delegates to the Continental Congress not forget ladies' rights. Corbin pointed out that women had been excluded from full participation in the Revolution. She decried the hypocrisy between requiring politically disempowered widows to pay taxes and the revolutionaries' aversion to taxation without representation. Most women, like Wilkinson, were forced to be so discreet at giving political advice as to become virtually invisible because of the stereotype that they were good only at "spinning and household affairs."[49]

In the period immediately following the Revolution, only New Jersey granted women franchise. The state's Provincial Congress passed a law in 1776 granting the vote to "every person" who had lived in New Jersey for a year and whose estate was worth fifty pounds. The general election law of 1783 reiterated this qualification, making "all Inhabitants of this State of full Age, who are worth *Fifty Pounds*" eligible to vote for public officials. That legal formula left uncertain whether women and blacks, including slaves and servants, were eligible to vote. Many women relied on the open-ended language to cast ballots.

Meanwhile, opponents waged a persistent campaign against the continued inclusion of these historically disempowered groups. William Griffith exploited stereotype in his quest for reform, insisting that "women, generally, are neither, by nature, nor habit, nor education, nor by their necessary condition in society, fitted to perform this duty." The fraudulent results of an 1807 referendum, for which data indicated that women were partly culpable, provided an excuse for disallowing foreigners, "females, and persons of color, or negroes to vote in elections." For more than a century thereafter, until 1920, when the Nineteenth Amendment was ratified, only white men could vote in New Jersey.[50]

The notion that women should not enjoy the right to vote because of their lack of habit for independent thought, lack of formal education, and inferior social standing levied blame for legal and cultural chauvinism of the day. For women, as for their male counterparts, increased educational opportunities allowed them to gain the skills essential for participating in industry, the economy, and the affairs of their communities.

Before the revolution, girls' education was rudimentary. "Dame-schools" provided literacy education to young girls. Wealthy girls sometimes went onto "adventure schools" that offered some advanced training in language or in ornamental skills. These schools were of variable quality because individuals with divergent talents ran them, commonly from their own homes. At the same time, excellent schools like Harvard, Yale, and Princeton made advanced education available for boys.

Many women craved education. In 1790, two years before Mary Wollstonecraft's *Vindication of the Rights of Women,* Judith Sargent Murray published *On the Equality of the Sexes.* Both works signaled that human equality, which was the logical outgrowth of natural-rights rhetoric, applied to women. Murray, who was married to the founder of American Universalism, denounced the inequality of forcing females into a secondary role from childhood. Their brothers were "taught to aspire," while girls were "early confined and limited." This policy stifled the potential of capable people because so many men regarded woman to be "an inferiour soul" and aggrandized their own capabilities to be unmatchable by women.[51]

The physician and politician Benjamin Rush was among the early visionaries of female education. While unable to entirely shed the paternalism of his time, he understood that the amassing of wealth in America required women to be "stewards, and guardians of their husbands' property." He advocated teaching females literature, grammar, calligraphy, bookkeeping, geography, music, dance, and religion. Broad-based knowledge benefited not only students but the public as well. Given the "equal share that every citizen has in the liberty, and the possible share he may have in the government of our country," women would need to be educated in order to instruct "their sons in the principles of liberty and government."[52]

The development of a public school system shortly after the Revolution helped boys and girls advance. By 1783 girls older than ten years of age attended common schools alongside boys. An early historian of the period wrote of the social harm of earlier female exclusion: "I contended that science would never reach its acme, while the influential half of our race, to whom the training of the rising generation is committed, were left in ignorance of it." Shortly thereafter, when advanced private academies opened, they allowed females to "promote their own happiness, as well as that of others; whether the scene of their labors was the nursery, the kitchen, the parlor, or the wider sphere of public and extensive plans of benevolence." These institutions attracted great teachers, including Timothy Dwight, who went on to be the president of Yale. He taught at a nationally renowned academy where girls and boys were assigned the same advanced studies. Noah Webster, who is best known for his *American Dictionary of the English Language,* was also for a time a schoolmaster who advocated equal education opportunity for females. The efforts to cultivate women's intellect paid off with a significant increase in female literacy during the early stage of the Republic.[53]

Educational changes were incremental but critical to the common good so often mentioned in contemporary pamphlets. Discrimination against women harmed individuals first but had repercussions on society as a whole. Revolutionary literature repeatedly asserted the need for governmental protections of individual liberties for overall welfare. The basic idea was that personal deprivations divested society of talents necessary for national growth and production. Women's inability to contract, for instance, hindered capitalism by reducing the number of investors, suppliers, and producers. The changes in women's status were not predicated purely on economic necessity. The supporters of female education understood the personal and familial need for both genders to be educated. They also realized how much the economy, government, and science could benefit by providing females with a more nearly equal share of opportunities.

Toward a Bill of Rights

While the advancement of women's rights was only a peripheral issue for most revolutionaries, the promotion of individual rights was a central point of dispute that energized the Antifederalist opposition to the Constitution. The original Constitution did not contain a bill of rights because the Federalist framers were certain that a representative government would protect the people's natural rights, especially their right to property. They thought that a bill of rights was unnecessary to a republic that relied on representatives to work for the people's common good. In the words of future Supreme Court Chief Justice Oliver Ellsworth, a declaration of them was "insignificant" because "all the power of government now has is a grant *from the people.*"

Hamilton explained, in *The Federalist* no. 84, that in the past bills of rights had been grants from kings to their subjects. Such grants were unnecessary in America, where the power of government came from the people, who "surrender nothing" of their inalienable rights and therefore need not explicitly reserve any part of them. James Wilson proudly distinguished British citizens' need for a declaration of rights and the American citizens' implicit retention of rights against governmental interference: the Magna Carta regarded the declared liberties to be "the gift or grant of the king"; on the other hand, the Constitution was a grant of power to government from the people who would not part with their natural liberties. Thomas Hartley explained further that since the people delegated power to government through the Constitution, "whatever portion of those natural rights we did not transfer to the government was still reserved and retained by the people." During the North Carolina ratification convention, a participant argued that "if there be certain rights which never can, nor ought to be given up, these rights cannot be said to be given away, merely because we have omitted to say that we have not given them up."[54]

Some of the founders were also concerned that the implication of constitutionally enumerating rights would be that the list was exhaustive. Pennsylvania Supreme Court Justice Thomas McKean worried about an "inconveniency and danger if there was any defect in the attempt to enumerate the privileges of the people." This would stifle the rational development of thought on the extent to which human liberties limit governmental authority. A bill of rights attempting to enumerate an exhaustive list of natural rights would be counterproductive, Rush urged the Pennsylvania Convention, since "our rights are not yet all known."[55]

With that said, the original Constitution did not entirely shy away from explicit protections for rights. It secured criminal jury trials, prohibited the enactment of ex post facto laws, provided that citizens of each state would enjoy all the privileges and immunities afforded to citizens of the other states, prohibited religious oaths as qualifications for political office, and made the writ of habeas corpus available under ordinary circumstances.[56]

The framers' early aversion to an enumerated bill of rights in preference for an unspecified and rationally determinable set of natural rights eventually gave way to Antifederalist criticism. The change of attitude appeared in correspondence between James Madison and Thomas Jefferson. These letters demonstrate that though Madison became the principal architect of the Bill of Rights, he was initially a reluctant designer.[57]

Their communication on the subject began with Jefferson expressing so much concern over the failure of delegates to include a bill of rights in the Constitution that he hoped "that the nine first [state] conventions may receive, and the four last reject it. The former will secure it finally; while the latter will oblige them to offer a declaration of rights in order to complete the union." In his response to Jefferson, Madison cautiously endorsed amending the Constitution to add a bill of rights but indicated that he thought such a bill to be extraneous. He had never found its omission from the Constitution to be a material defect "nor been anxious to supply it even by *subsequent* amendment, for any other reason than that it is anxiously desired by others." He thought amending the Constitution to be relatively unimportant because the people had retained their rights when they granted the federal government power. But another reason underlay Madison's skepticism.

He had come to understand, he continued in his letter to Jefferson, that a bill of rights would place restrictions against legislative abuses but would be inoperative against powerful majorities, which he thought posed the greatest risk of abuse. Madison returned to this theme in the House of Representatives, during a speech meant to bolster support for amending the Constitution. He explained his worry that a bill of rights would ignore "that quarter where the greatest danger lies." That threat is "not found in either the executive or legislative departments of government, but in the body of the people, operating by the majority against the minority." Despite Madison's recognition of this substantial oversight, reviewing how state bills of rights prevented governmental abuse had convinced him that "altho' some of them are rather unimportant, yet, upon the whole, they will have a salutary tendency." He, therefore, acknowledged that it was "not entirely without foundation" that a bill of rights would help counteract dangerous interests and passions. Furthermore, "Altho' it be generally true as above stated that the danger of oppression lies in the interested majorities of the people rather than in usurped acts of the Government, yet there may be occasions on which the evil may spring from the latter sources; and on such, a bill of rights will be a good ground for an appeal to the sense of the community."[58] The lack of constitutional protection against majoritarian and individual discrimination would plague the country, from the business exploitation of labor to the racialist abuse of slaves. The lack of protection against gender discrimination allowed men to become domestic despots who were unanswerable for inequality in any private or public institution, from businesses to schools.

Despite these glaring shortcoming, the Bill of Rights became a landmark

protection of civil rights. The rights to freedom of the press, worship, association, life, liberty, and property were no longer dependent on the uncertainties
of democratic politics. At least on paper, these and other liberties became
immune from political battles about natural rights or reasonable government
action that would inevitably play out in the national arena. A powerful majority able to garner most of the vote would be unable to intrude on the values
the Bill of Rights espoused. Yet even as an instrument against political majorities, that amendment to the Constitution proved to be of limited value since
prior to post–Civil War Reconstruction, the Bill applied only to the federal
government. This limitation left the vast majority of controversies about
fundamental rights at the discretion of individual states, some of which found
race, religion, and gender to be relevant disqualifications from civil rights
protections.

The Bill of Rights rested philosophically on a coupling of liberty and
equality that was commonly accepted during the revolutionary period. While
the Bill did not explicitly mention "equality," it was premised on the notion
that all Americans have the same natural liberties, which government has no
authority to infringe. Nothing in it explicitly limited provisions by race or
gender. The reality, however, was that all Americans had only a claim to like
treatment, but that local and national prejudices kept many from enjoying the
range of opportunities that national citizenship afforded. By excluding many
Americans from the Bill of Rights' protections, the framers catapulted the
country into sectional conflict.

That the framers did not do all they could to end arbitrary barriers is an
understatement. The steps that they did take were nevertheless significant for
securing personal rights for the greater good. Their inability to overcome the
prejudices of their times qualifies the extent of their achievements but in no
way undermines the legacy they left future generations to build upon.

CHAPTER THREE

The Controversy about Slavery

The Revolution failed to bring about the relief from slavery many contemporaries had expected. In theory, the framers had formed a government for safeguarding personal liberties to better the common good. Exploiting labor for the sake of agronomic success, however, became of greater import than civil rights when, about the time of the War of 1812, southern sugar and cotton belts began realizing greatly increased profits.[1] The dissemination of antislavery thought, by Quakers and some orders of Methodists, Baptists, and Presbyterians, was too small in scale to make a dent in American attitudes. Southern society became increasingly dependent on slavery as an economic and cultural institution. The nation came to accept the anomaly of racial oppression for the sake of sectional balance.

The founding generation had planted the seeds of a moral dilemma. With manumission in the North, prohibition against slavery in the Ohio territory, and cessation of the slave trade, slavery became mainly confined to the South. Slavery was considered a domestic institution that the federal government could regulate only in the territories, if at all, not within states. Slavers commanded a strong share of American commerce and political power. Undaunted by this clout, a vocal group of abolitionists, who insisted on immediately securing coequal rights for Americans, became increasingly well organized.

Unabated Slavery and Racism

After the Revolution, slavery retained a stronghold in the United States despite the country's decisive stand against authoritarianism. Contemporary writers thought it was a temporary institution. As the years passed, timesaving inventions, such as Eli Whitney's cotton gin and Henry Ogden "Hodgen" Holmes's sawtooth gin, both of which were patented in the 1790s, made slave labor more profitable and slaveholding more enticing. Slave prices doubled, making manumission a more costly proposition. Spreading the institution geographically was a crafty way of increasing political power. In the South, what had been a burgeoning antislavery movement withered, and in the North, willing entrepreneurs provided manufacturing markets for slave labor. The exploitation of humans required a new mentality, one that attributed sinful wickedness, inferiority, and perversity to blacks. Slave codes were increasingly severe and elaborate. Laws treated slaves as property and denied free blacks the privileges and immunities of citizenship.

Slave codes gave legal sanction to a hideously degrading system. Laws prohibited education, established clothing etiquette, limited the associational rights of religious groups, restricted movement, denied property ownership, and disenfranchised.

To enforce these codes, states like South Carolina and Virginia created separate courts in which criminal procedures were sparse; for instance, they typically did not provide for trial by jury and usually were more expeditious than they were thorough: grand juries served as arms of local prejudices, the slaves' guilt was typically assumed, appeal was either extremely limited or unavailable, no record was maintained, and punishment was harsh.[2] Only the most serious slave crimes, such as rape and murder, were heard in circuit courts. At the same time, the human rights of blacks were so devalued that until 1821 South Carolina subjected whites who murdered blacks to only a fine. (Thereafter the state followed the general trend by making the crime a capital offense.) In other circumstances courts, as those in South Carolina and North Carolina, typically found slaves had no standing to sue.

The whimsical actions of slaveholders and overseers made slave life precarious because habits and local mores were unreviewable in courts. Theodore D. Weld gathered factual information from eyewitness accounts finding that "American slaveholders possess a power over their slaves which is virtually absolute" and rife for abuse. Thomas Jefferson traced the "worst of passions" and "odious particularities" of slaveholders to callous habits they picked up from their parents during childhood. A Georgia resident was shocked at how much power her young daughter commanded over slaves, "learning to rule despotically . . . fellow creatures before the first lesson of self-government has been well spelt over." Without any legal oversight, slaveholders chose slaves' names, picked their marriage partners, set their work and sleep schedules, dictated maternity leave, chose clothing, meted out punishment, controlled gatherings, and guided a plethora of life's minutiae. Overseers, white and black, were empowered by masters. They in turn doled out whippings, jailed slaves in what amounted to dungeons, and took away holiday privileges.[3]

Family relationships were beholden to masters. Spouses could be sold separately, as could parents and children. Virginia, North Carolina, South Carolina, Tennessee, Arkansas, and Texas had no minimum age for children to be sold apart from mothers. Ten- and twelve-year-olds were commonly dealt alone, and even infants were periodically wrenched from mothers. Masters also created many temporary familial ruptures. They rented out slaves, assigned them to work at different plantations, and gave them assignments that interfered with family plans.

Slaves were unable to formally marry, since marriage was a contractual relationship and they were barred from entering into contracts. Their length of cohabitation was subject to forces outside their control. Sexual relations between masters and female slaves resulted in racially mixed slaves. In some cases masters fathered children whom they later sold. One account concerned an owner in New Jersey, where emancipation was gradual, who "had three negresses, by each of whom he had children; and whenever he could dispose of these his own offspring, he sold them, in the same manner as he would have disposed of his hogs!"[4]

Whites were aware that their slaves, like any other person in bondage, thirsted for freedom. They consequently lived in fear of slave insurrections, realizing that the human spirit rebelled against captivity. Slave states created an internal enemy without whose labor their economies would have been depressed but whose labor they allowed to be exploited without proper compensation.[5]

Slavery relied on civil practices that went well beyond the control of labor for maintaining a racially disjunct society. Slaves were often assigned dangerous tasks with high morbidity rates, such as clearing swamp lands, because not enough white laborers were willing to do them. The South Carolinian Charles Cotesworth Pinckney argued that the federal government should protect slavery because African laborers were the only ones biologically capable of cultivating his state's swampy flats. He and others speculated that blacks were better adapted to that "pestilent atmosphere."[6]

These beliefs were indicative of the racial stereotypes that grew along with slavery. Every white man could feel himself superior, regardless of his social station and education, because his race made it possible to one day own slaves or at least enjoy the privileges of citizenship. Even a poor man, wrote Judge N. Beverley Tucker, wanted to protect property rights in slaves: "though he has none as yet, he has the purpose and the hope to be rich."[7] Whatever antagonism might have arisen from wealth and power disparities and between land owners and poor farmers was lessened by the mutual need to prevent slave insurrections.

Slavery reduced differences between labor and capital. A Georgia jurist, Thomas R. R. Cobb, and others popularized the notion that racial suprema-cism was necessary to achieve "republican equality." By relegating the most menial tasks to blacks, "the poorest meets the richest as an equal" since "it matters not that he is no slaveholder; he is not of the inferior race; he is a freeborn citizen." In 1856 Robert Toombs, who later became secretary of state of the Confederacy, argued that at the foundation of "our republican system" were "the perfect equality of the superior race, and the legal subordination of the inferior." Speaking in the House, Representative Henry A. Wise of Vir-ginia warned that if slavery broke down, "you would with the same blow destroy the great Democratic principle of equality among men."[8]

Eventually, the system weakened of its own aristocratic character. Non-slaveholding farmers in border states, particularly in Kentucky, Delaware, Maryland, and Virginia, where the institution was not as pervasive as in the deep South, came to realize that plantations had an unfair competitive edge. The author of an 1849 article wrote heatedly of slaveholding plantations taking away jobs from "poor white men who must depend upon that kind of labor to make their living. . . . The abominable system of black slavery does this; for, were it not for this, these rich landholders would be bound to sell some of their lands, or let tenants or renters farm it, and thus divide the spoils."[9]

Such opposition to slavery, based on white self-interest rather than fun-damental principles, did not rein in the institution. The number of blacks in America increased, and freedom for them was both elusive and uncertain. At the outbreak of the Civil War, only 476,748 of 4,427,259 blacks were free.[10] Even those who were nominally free often lived at the sufferance of whites since they lacked citizenship rights.

Racial tensions were also endemic to the relationship between whites and free blacks. Nearly all slave states had laws similar to an 1806 Virginia statute that required manumitted blacks to leave the state twelve months after gain-ing freedom and never to reenter. Since enforcement of the law was lax in Virginia, laws of 1815, 1819, and 1837 allowed counties to grant freed blacks exemptions. This left blacks in a precarious state of uncertainty about their future residency. At the whim of a county official, they could be reenslaved for overstaying their welcome. An 1831 Tennessee law likewise allowed for the manumission only of persons who could be "forthwith transported from the state." Tennessee periodically relaxed and reinstated this requirement. Any praise Maryland might have warranted from its fairly high rate of manumission must be tempered by its prohibition against black entry. Thus manumitted blacks faced hardships both in remaining in their state of origin and in finding a home elsewhere. The movement of free blacks was monitored throughout the South. They were required to register in cities like Richmond. Upon demand they were required to produce paperwork to prove their status. Without it, just because of the pigment of their skin, free people could be fined and required to perform hard labor.[11]

Employment discrimination forced most free blacks to work as low-paid laborers and domestics; few enjoyed high earnings as shopkeepers or artisans. Bans on some professions limited blacks' choices of occupation altogether. While opportunities were few, serious consequences attended inactivity. Any Delaware free black whom authorities deemed to be idle was subject to forced labor, as were blacks convicted of property crimes, which included breaches of contract. For a time, free blacks could vote in Tennessee, North Carolina, and parts of Louisiana, but the former two states withdrew that privilege in 1830, and in Louisiana the Code Noir prohibited free blacks from voting and holding public office as of 1724.

Nor were blacks from foreign countries spared the sting of local prejudices. The port states of South Carolina, North Carolina, Alabama, Louisiana, Georgia, Florida, and Mississippi adopted Negro seamen acts that prohibited sailors from leaving ships on threat of incarceration. International agreements did not prevent states from enforcing these acts. Great Britain protested the arrest of its seamen under the South Carolina Negro Seaman Act of 1822. The statute required that free black sailors be jailed throughout the duration of their stay. In one instance a seaman sued for his freedom, and on his behalf the Britain consul argued that the Seaman Act interfered with the 1815 U.S.-British commercial treaty. Supreme Court Justice William Johnson, who heard the case as a designated circuit court judge, stated in dicta that the act was unconstitutional. South Carolina deemed Johnson's view to be unenforceable and continued imprisoning foreign seamen.[12]

The two sections of the country were moving in different directions with regard to slavery, but exclusionary laws were common to both. The North abolished slavery, either immediately or gradually, but it retained many of the prejudices that formally sustained the institution. Alexis de Tocqueville, during the course of his travelogue research on democracy in American, remarked that northern racial prejudice was even worse than that he had encountered in the South. While his observation was anecdotal, travel and residency restrictions gave it some support. Oregon joined the Union in 1859 with a constitution that prohibited blacks from entering the state. Those who already lived there could not own real property, enter into a contract, file a lawsuit, or vote. The Illinois Constitution of 1848, which also prohibited free blacks from entering the state, might have served as Oregon's model. To enforce that provision, Illinois enacted a statute in 1853 that made it a misdemeanor for blacks to enter the state for the purpose of residing there. Those who were convicted but unable to pay the $100 to $500 fine were to be sold into forced labor. Ohio, as of 1803, offered a prototype for these statutes. It allowed blacks to enter only if they could deposit a prohibitive $500 bond of good behavior. Once they entered, black children were forbidden from enrolling in schools, although unlike southern states, Ohio permitted them to obtain other means of instruction. So the North moralized with the South while refusing to treat blacks as equal citizens.[13]

Colonization Efforts

The colonization movement used benevolent-sounding rhetoric about freeing slaves. Its principle aim, however, was not to secure blacks' civil rights but to expel them. In December 1816 the Virginia legislature requested that the governor contact President James Madison to obtain territory outside the United States for colonizing the state's free black population. The American Colonization Society, which held its first meeting on December 21, 1816, began a national effort that succeeded in founding the country of Liberia in western Africa in 1822. Many of the most prominent men of the age, including George Washington, Jefferson, Bushrod Washington, Henry Clay, Madison, John Marshall, and Andrew Jackson joined the American Colonization Society. The presence of so many slave owners within its ranks was indicative of the society's tolerance of the institution. It advocated compensating those slaveholders who manumitted slaves. Yet it was decisively opposed to complete emancipation. At the society's inaugural meeting, Clay reassured southerners that, being a slaveholder himself, he "considered that species of property as inviolable as any other in the country." The society, he declared, had no intention of "in any manner" interfering with slave ownership. He did assure

free blacks that they would not be forcefully removed, but that was no indication that the society advocated equality for those who remained. Shortly after
Clay delivered his remarks, General Robert C. Harper gave voice to the
animating desire of "ridding us of a population for the most part idle and
useless." Colonization would not alleviate discrimination or end slavery, but,
as Clay explained in 1829, it would reduce the risk that freemen might foment
"the carnage and the crimes" of slave revolts.[14]

Many blacks denounced the colonization plan publicly, understanding it
to be contrary to their well-being. Protests against colonization began almost
at the society's inception. Free blacks living near Washington, D.C., met in
Georgetown days after the society's first meeting to proclaim that they would
refuse colonization anywhere outside the United States. In 1818 a committee of
free blacks from Philadelphia asserted their rights to House Representative
Joseph Hopkins: "Our ancestors," wrote the petitioners, "were, though not
from choice, the first cultivators of the wilds of America, and we, their
descendants, claim a right to share in the blessings of her luxuriant soil which
their blood and sweat manured." Lewis Woodson, a black operator of the
Underground Railroad in southern Ohio, thought colonizing as a viable
option absurd since "we never asked for it—we never wanted it; neither will we
ever go to it." Against the "pretensions of the American Colonization Society,"
a group of blacks from Baltimore wrote on March 21, 1831, that since they had
been born and raised in America, this was their "true and appropriate home."
A meeting conducted at a black church in Hartford, Connecticut, resolved
that "we have committed no crime worthy of banishment, and that we will
resist all attempts of the Colonization Society to banish us from this our native
land." Samuel Cornish, the black editor of *Rights of All,* a New York weekly,
wrote that America should be just to its black population rather than returning
blacks to Africa. A group from Brooklyn demanded just treatment instead of
the society's "gratuitous" scheme: "We are *men,* . . . we are *brethren,* . . . we are
countrymen and *fellow-citizens,* and demand an equal share of protection from
our federal government with any other class of citizens in the community."[15]
The Colonization Society never allied itself to the abolitionist movement,
maintaining through the 1850s the inviolability of slave property.

Proslavery Defense

The American Colonization Society's attempt to rid the country of African
Americans under the banner of "antislavery" was a whitewashing of society's

unremitting racial inequality and slavery. The positive-good theory came into its own during the 1820s, describing slavery as legally, morally, socially, and culturally good. Harnessing earlier ideas, the theory presented them in a systematic manner. As early as 1807 Georgia Representative Peter Early presumed that "a large majority" of southern people supported slavery and "do not consider it even an evil." The popularity of proslavery thought drove antislavery advocates out of the South. Religious, social, and economic institutions came to the defense of human bondage.[16]

In the minds of planters, God himself had made Africans subordinate to them. The earliest justification for slavery in the colonies was biblically based. A popular myth, dating to the sixteenth century, attributed slavery to Noah's curse against one of his sons, Ham. George Best, a British explorer, posited that God cursed Ham's son, ordaining that Canaan and "all his posteritie after him should be black and lothsome." According to this perspective, slavery was God's punishment for an ancestor's sins.[17]

Religious excuses for slavery continued to grip the popular imagination throughout the antebellum years. For the minions who believed it, including Alexander H. Stephens, the vice president of the Confederacy, slavery was "best, not only for the superior, but for the inferior race" and "in conformity with the ordinance of the Creator." The weak religious apology for slavery drew attention to the lack of biblical proscription against it. The stronger apologetics, such as *Scriptural and Statistical Views in Favor of Slavery,* located New and Old Testament passages, like Paul's instructions to the Corinthians (chapter 12) or to Philemon, approving the institution. Perpetuating "the institution of domestic slavery," Benjamin M. Palmer instructed parishioners from the pulpit, is a "duty. . . . We hold this trust from God."[18]

The paternalist argument, by contrast, was secular in nature. It regarded blacks to be a docile and childlike race in need of stern supervision. A Floridian plantation holder regarded slavery to be superior to white labor. "Negroes are safe, permanent, productive and growing property, and easily governed," he wrote. The planter provided them with "clothing, implements of husbandry," unlike the free white man who commonly "consumes all his earnings" and suffers from "cold, hunger, and want of employment." Paternalism depicted blacks as pitiful creatures whom whites had enslaved for their own good. Whites and blacks were so different, wrote a Boston pastor of his 1854 travels in the South, that the races can live together only "by the entire subordination of one to the other." To him, blacks were so juvenile that, if freed, they would "fall a prey to avarice, suffer oppression and grievous wrongs, [and] encounter the

rivalry of white immigrants." This self-proclaimed "ardent friend of the colored race" regarded it essential for the "stronger race" to protect blacks for their
own good. An Episcopalian bishop from Vermont shared this impression,
thinking masters to be more capable of benefiting blacks than they could
themselves.[19]

This perspective considered manumission without colonization to be
fraught with peril, since free blacks "were inherently shiftless and idle, prone
to criminality, and incapable of improvement." Blacks could never be the
equals of whites, according to this view; thus education could never alter their
base drives. In turn, the argument justified legal favoritism of whites and the
unequal treatment of blacks in education and labor. The fixation on black
physicality went hand in hand with the denial of their intellect. The reigning
thought was that Africans were less cerebrally evolved but physiologically
stronger than whites.[20]

The affections in the races supposedly differed as much as their intelligence. Blacks were said to lack whites' concern for their children. That
supposition was a balm for slave traders' consciences, even though they knew
from experience that parents and spouses often wailed at slave markets. The
myth also made all black men into lustful rapists, against whom white women
had to be guarded via capital punishment, and black women wenches, the
seducers of their masters, who were merely unwilling participants in adultery
and fornication.[21]

Planters' and poor whites' aversion to blacks was driven by a science that
compared brain sizes and contrasted the anthropological achievements of
races. The movement was just one example of how pseudoscientists can
manipulate knowledge to perpetuate the subjugation of an entire group of
people. Early writings identified Africans as being evolutionarily between
whites and monkeys. An anonymous author in 1773 divided Africans into five
categories: "1st, Negroes, 2d, Ourang Outangs, 3d, Apes, 4th, Baboons, and
5th, Monkeys. . . . There never was a civilized nation of any other complexion
than *white*." A year later Edward Long, who was an established Jamaican
planter and slaver, created a remarkably misleading picture, claiming, for
example, that orangutans copulate with African women: "The amorous inter-
course between them may be frequent . . . and it is certain, that both races
agree perfectly well in lasciviousness of disposition." Only their outward
appearance was comparable to whites, according to Long; otherwise, they
were "incestuous, savage, cruel, and vindictive."[22]

By the nineteenth century, increasingly scientific-sounding terms and

methods sought to explain away inequality in a country supposedly mindful
of equal natural rights. What is surprising is how long these eighteenth-
century ideas lingered. Samuel Cartright maintained in 1857 that blacks were
a "different species from the man of Europe or Asia," one close to simians;
Louis Agassiz, a Harvard professor of zoology, claimed that a black child
could not develop intellectually beyond white boyhood because his brain
"bears a striking resemblance . . . to the brain of an ourang-outang." His views
were incorporated into the defense of slavery. Based on cranial studies, Josiah
C. Nott, a physician and ethnologist, declared that "the Almighty in his
wisdom has peopled our vast planet" with "races of species originally and
radically distinct." Neither could the "permanence of moral and intellectual
peculiarities of types be denied." Another medical doctor, John H. Van Evrie,
wrote that the Caucasian "is the most superior" and the Negro "the most
inferior—and between these extremes of humanity are the intermediate races.
. . . Color is the standard and the test of the specific character, revealing the
inner nature and actual capabilities of the race." The brains of whites, he
continued, are capable of elevated reasoning, while those of blacks are feebler
and "endowed with strength and acuteness of the external senses."[23]

Prominent scientists and politicians strengthened the rationalization for
perpetuating slavery. With the aid of supremacist reasoning, natural rights
became associated, in the statements of slavery's supporters, only with the
white race. Equality became intraracial, with racial inequality but one of the
natural differences. Various races had different talents, abilities, and strengths;
and race turned out to be a legitimized determinant to citizenship. Democracy
was a system of governance among white equals. In this monolithic form of
democracy, liberty took on racial characteristics. *"He is in the enjoyment of
freedom, whatever his condition, who is suffered to occupy his proper place. He only,
is the slave, who is forced into a position in society which is below the claim of his
intellect and moral."*[24]

The notion that men were born equal was said by some to be an abstrac-
tion or a characterization of the universal helplessness of babes, not a condition of people living in civilized countries. Equality was conceived in the
narrowest of terms. "In the South all men are equal," said Senator Albert G.
Brown, during debates on the Kansas-Nebraska Bill. "I mean, of course,
white men; negroes are not men, within the meaning of the Declaration. If
they were, Madison, and Jefferson, and Washington, all of whom lived and
died slaveholders, never could have made it, for they never regarded negroes
as their equals." Some southerners began to mock the literal meaning of the

Declaration, refusing to accept an inclusive interpretation. William G. Simms, a popular novelist and a defender of slavery, pointed out that life, liberty, and property were all alienable: rapists were put to death, thieves were locked up in prisons, and property was taken to repay debts. The inalienability of rights, in his mind, turned out to be a mere piece of rhetoric, useful, perhaps, as a tool against the British, but ultimately fictitious.[25]

While southerners often showed little enthusiasm for the Declaration, they found support for their position in the Constitution. Civil rights had been left in the hands of states rather than under national control, and the federal government stayed out of the field, except when federal troops were needed to put down slave revolts, as occurred with the Denmark Vesey (1822) and Nat Turner (1831) rebellions. The multiple clauses of the Constitution that protected the institution, including the Three-Fifths, Insurrection, and Importation Clauses, indicated to the defenders of slavery that the framers had tried to make it unassailable. Since officials in all three branches of federal government were sworn to upholding the Constitution, which protected slavery, they were obligated to protect the institution. In the slave states, social-compact theory came to be identified with a government that whites had created for advancing the property interests of others of their type. Some based that view on the incontrovertible fact that many of the framers continued to own slaves even after ratification of the Constitution. This constitutional doctrine, coupled with the sociological and scientific views that the two races were different intellectually and physically, provided excuses for depriving blacks of political, social, and educational opportunities.

Constitutional theory was put to work in the field of politics. The best-known expositor of the proslavery position was John C. Calhoun. His influential Parkenham letter concerning the annexation of Texas, which he wrote as secretary of state of the United States, identified slavery as "in reality a political institution, essential to the peace, safety, and prosperity of those States of the Union in which it exists." On his account blacks had no place in governance, a theme that several authors adapted. During an 1845 debate on slavery, held in Cincinnati, a speaker conceded that he supported gradual emancipation and colonization but went on to say that present circumstances made slaveholding a justifiable relationship. He would not countenance blacks being manumitted and allowed to participate in democratic politics. If they became governors, legislators, and judges, the administration of government would fall into "the hands of degraded men, wholly ignorant of the principles of law and government." James K. Paulding, onetime secretary of the navy, likewise stood democracy on its head. A country with a "nearly equal number of whites and free blacks, enjoying the same political rights," would find "peace and harmony" highly improbable or impossible. Paulding defended slavery because he feared that if blacks came to power they would abuse the state to "suit their own wayward purposes," having no concept of governance and wreaking revenge against "their ancient masters."[26]

Proslavery thought was at once a symptom and a cause of the gnawing wound that America had inflicted on itself. The interests of African Americans were sacrificed on the altar of property rights. Laws restricting education, employment, and familial autonomy depressed millions of people and limited their ability to contribute to the nation's economic, cultural, and political betterment. Slavery evidenced an abandonment of national principles, not a lack of them. Restrictions on political rights were diametrically opposed to the very purposes of the Revolution.

In a land established to safeguard the equal right to live freely, proslavery arguments constituted a means for justifying arbitrary preferences based on racial ancestry. Maintaining black subordination became more important than adhering to constitutional values like free speech. For a time, the "gag rule" forbade antislavery petitions even from being heard or discussed in Congress, and postmasters confiscated abolitionist literature. No such limitations bridled the dissemination of proslavery views. Abolitionists turned to the North to achieve reform, but even there they met entrenched opposition.

Abolitionist Commitments

Abolitionists set out on an unqualified mission to end slavery. Regardless of the approach they took—be it moral, evangelical, or political—abolitionists refused to wait patiently for slavery's demise. Nothing less would satisfy blacks like Frederick Douglass and whites like William Lloyd Garrison and Charles Sumner than the total and immediate end to the institution; as far as they were concerned, the gradualism and deference of colonizers was just as unacceptable as the institution itself. Further, the Declaration of Independence was the cornerstone of a government committed to protecting individual rights for the entire populace, regardless of race. Some abolitionist groups agreed with proslavery theory insofar as both thought that the Constitution protected slavery. Those abolitionists located the self-evident truths of equal freedom in the Declaration. A different abolitionist group interpreted the Constitution to include legal empowerments against slavery. Both groups retained a revolutionary passion for liberty and equality and decried the abuse of power and oppression.

Abolitionists retained the ideology of fundamental rights and the anti-slavery views of revolutionaries like Benjamin Rush and James Otis. Yet post-1830 abolitionism was of an entirely different character. Refusing to be genteel, it opted for knocking down barriers rather than taking them apart one cornerstone at a time. In 1831, two wealthy dry-goods merchants, Arthur and Lewis Tappan, began funding the American Anti-Slavery Society. On New Year's Day of the same year, twenty-six-year-old William Lloyd Garrison set to publishing his weekly, *Liberator*. Garrison helped draft the society's inaugural platform, in 1833, declaring its dedication to the "Temple of Freedom" established by the "band of patriots," but renouncing their concessions to slavery. The founders' grievances were "trifling in comparison with the wrongs and sufferings" of enslaved persons. Drafters of this early document still tried to be affable, retaining the notion that "*under the present national compact*" Congress could only prevent interstate or territorial slavery, but states had exclusive jurisdiction over slavery within their borders.[27]

So great was the trailblazers' faith in the power of moral suasion that in 1833 Theodore Weld could write, "Abolition is very unpopular in New York and New England; but mark my word, two years will make an overturning from the bottom." Eventually the abolitionist movement spread its message nationally through pamphlets, speaking tours, sermons, two national associations, and local antislavery societies.[28]

The movement then took a more radical trail, setting itself firmly against gradualism. Unlike the colonizationists, abolitionists refused to acknowledge that slaveholders had any property rights in humans, and spoke rather of "our common nature." The Unitarian leader W. E. Channing explained in 1835 that the abolitionists' argument rested on the Declaration of Independence's assertion of "the indestructible rights of every human being." Each person was "born to be free," and the desire for wealth, especially in human capital, could never trump individual rights. Slavery was inimical because it stripped "man of the fundamental right to inquire into, consult, and seek his own happiness." Slavery reduced people to property, suppressing their humanity and depriving them of meaningful opportunities. The National Anti-Slavery Convention of 1857 continued relying on "the self-evident truths of the Declaration of Independence . . . and in the Golden Rule of the Gospel—nothing more, nothing less." The abolitionists in Congress echoed the same sentiments. During the debates on the Kansas-Nebraska Bill, Senator Charles

Sumner asserted that "slavery is an infraction of the immutable law of nature, and, as such, cannot be considered a natural incident to any sovereignty, especially in a country which has solemnly declared, in its Declaration of Independence, the inalienable right of all men to life, *liberty*, and the pursuit of happiness." Weld's *American Slavery as It Is* showed through many examples that slaveholders plundered slaves' "bodies and minds, their time and liberty and earnings, their free speech and rights of conscience, their right to acquire knowledge, and property, and reputation."[29]

The Preamble to the Constitution also served as a starting point for legal arguments against slavery. Congress's transparent protection of slavery violated the General Welfare Clause. Impartial laws were necessary to stop the exploitation of millions of laborers.[30]

Abolitionists regarded the Declaration and Preamble as implicit mandates to immediately end slavery. Gradualism would only "perpetuate what we aim to destroy." As James McPherson has pointed out, the willingness to work to end slavery immediately and unconditionally was an essential component of the movement. The failure of gradualism during the revolutionary period made a firm-minded approach more convincing. Abolitionism drew attention to the immorality of slavery and individuals who tolerated it. This was a radical departure from the past placation of slaveholders and their congressional and business supporters. The argument was not simplistic in demanding liberty. The immediate needs of the to-be-freed were consistently discussed, but many of the details of liberation were only sketchily explored, presumably leaving lawmakers the task of filling them in.[31]

Immediate abolitionism had been in the wind for years, even in statements linking it to colonization. George Bourne, who deeply influenced Garrison, gave immediatism religious connotation in 1816, asserting that it is Satan who "advises the adoption of *prudent and moderate reform.*" Elizabeth Heyrick, in 1824, was the first to systematically expound the theory in *Immediate, Not Gradual Abolitionism.* Mere liberation, she wrote, would not be enough; instead, an equitable plan had to be worked out to recompense the slave for "his compulsory, unremunerated labor, under the lash of the cart whip." But hers was only a short pamphlet that needed future elaboration. To that end, Garrison, who had read it, succinctly expressed the abolitionist decision to press for immediate change: "In demanding equal and exact justice, we may get partial redress; in asking for the whole that is due us, we may get a part; in advocating the immediate, we may succeed in procuring the speedy abolition of slavery. But, if we demand any thing short of justice, we shall recover no damages; if we ask for a part, we shall get nothing; if we advocate gradual abolition, we shall perpetuate what we aim to destroy, and proclaim that the self-evident truths which are set forth in the Declaration of Independence are self-evident lies!" Others were even more explicit in explaining their meaning.[32]

Immediate emancipation, wrote Amos A. Phelps, placed demands on a slaveholder to free people he exploited as property and "instead of turning them adrift on society, uncared for, he should offer to employ them as free hired laborers, giving them, however, liberty of choice whether to remain in his service or not." The community's obligation was to treat them "as subjects of equal law" and to provide them with equitable and due legal process. The New England Anti-Slavery Society committed itself to obtaining for "free people of color . . . equal civil and political rights and privileges with the whites." The need for legal transformation, not merely individual reform, appeared time and again. The holders of slaves, wrote the Western Reserve professor Elizur Wright, Jr., were obligated to restore to blacks the earnings they had kept from them. The legislature's duty was to provide blacks with "the full protection of law."[33]

The consuming issue of the age was slavery, but the extensive participation of women in the abolitionist movement brought attention to the multi-layered injustices to which they themselves were systematically subjected. Women's educational, marital, commercial, and proprietary opportunities were restricted through legal sanctions and social strictures. Many abolitionists extended their advocacy of liberal equality beyond blacks.

In some cases, whole families were committed to abolitionism and feminism. The Quaker couple Lucretia Mott, who called the Seneca Falls Women's Rights Convention of 1848, and James Mott had been abolitionists from the movement's inception; Elizabeth Cady Stanton, who helped organize and hosted the convention, was the cousin of the antislavery congressman Gerrit Smith; and Susan B. Anthony's father entertained the likes of Garrison and Douglass. On the other hand, Lucy Stone, another critical proponent of women's suffrage, rebelled against her father's notions of male domination.

These and thousands of other female abolitionists were intrinsic to the cause, distributing petitions, lobbying Congress, organizing, lecturing, writing, and editing. By 1838 hundreds of women's antislavery societies, with more than six thousand members, worked to end the unequal treatment of women, in both the domestic and the public sphere. Catherine E. Beecher helped explain the connection between the movements: "These rights may be wrested from the slave, but they cannot be alienated. . . . Now if rights are founded in the nature of our moral being, then the mere circumstance of sex does not give to man higher rights and responsibilities, than to woman."[34] Black women like Sojourner Truth needed no explanation about the connection between feminism and abolitionism, having a personal stake in both. A group of abolitionist women in Fall River, Massachusetts, worked for the day when the "black man would stand erect by the side of his white brother, and the black woman would [be] restored to women's rights and privileges."[35]

Progressive women found principled males eager to help them get their equal share. Theodore Parker, for instance, hid the black abolitionist Ellen Craft while she was a fugitive and then helped her escape to Canada. Wendell Phillips pointedly advocated women's suffrage, excoriated unequal treatment of women under law, and demanded that they receive equal pay.

Men and women worked side by side to end women's subordination and abolish slavery. Weld and the Grimké sisters—Sarah and Weld's wife, Angelina—put their passion for justice into practice. In Cincinnati they opened schools for "colored people" that taught a variety of subjects, including grammar, geography, arithmetic, and science. They also worked at opening a multiracial library and a reading room. Others placed responsibility for educating slaves on those who had previously held them in bondage. The attempt to educate blacks met with fierce resistance. At the heart of this opposition was the fear that fair and equal treatment of blacks would lead to unwanted social contact with them and to the amalgamation of the races. The Lane Theological Seminary tried to discipline Weld and other students for their role in openly educating Cincinnati blacks, voicing their support for immediate abolition, and eating and otherwise communing with black families. The students, in turn, withdrew from the school and enrolled in Oberlin College, also located in Ohio. In his native state of Kentucky, James G. Birney, who had himself once been a slave owner, encountered "the reign of terror" that forced almost all Sunday school programs for blacks to close.[36]

Mob violence became part of the experience that abolitionists expected, even in cities with liberal traditions like Boston. Stones, bricks, eggs, sticks, and occasional arson did not deter them. They held to uncompromising abolitionist principles, unafraid to "lie upon rack—and clasp the faggot—and tread with steady step the scaffold," as Weld described his commitment after being the victim of a mob in Troy, New York. The South's reaction to abolitionists was increasingly entrenched dogmatism coupled with a demand for more federal compromises to assure the continued vitality of slavery against these firebrands.[37]

While abolitionists agreed in seeking education, an immediate end to slavery, and the equal protection of laws for blacks, they differed in their constitutional interpretations. The most controversial camp was under Garrison's leadership. With its even more polished spokesman, Phillips, an attorney who would briefly break with Garrison in 1865, this group denounced the Constitution's compromises with slave interests. They eschewed politics, refusing to dull their demands for elective reward. Theirs was a moral and religious crusade to restore blacks' and women's equal rights. Sarah Grimké and Truth added their voices to this group's decision to avoid public office until civil rights, among which they counted the right to vote, received universal protection. Seeing no hope of achieving the necessary reform within the existing federal system, they demanded that the North separate from the South. Their aversion for the Constitution was best reflected by Garrison's July 4, 1854, speech, when he burned the Constitution, calling it "a covenant with death and an agreement with hell." The proslavery clauses of the Constitution, as Phillips pointed out in response to the political abolitionist Lysander Spooner, could be disarmed only by an amendment. With no change to the Constitution, Garrisonians like the physician and abolitionist Henry I. Bowditch clung to John Quincy Adams's statement that calling the United States a democracy was insulting to mankind because its slave-protecting clauses made "the preservation, propagation, and perpetuation of slavery, the vital and animating spirit of the national government."[38]

Another group of abolitionists, led by the likes of Spooner, Douglass, Alvan Stewart, Gerrit Smith, and Lewis Tappan, held a very different constitutional view from the Garrisonians'. According to these radical political abolitionists, as they called themselves, the institution violated numerous provisions of the Constitution. They regarded the Constitution as a safeguard of self-evident, universal rights. At the Radical Political Abolitionist Convention of 1855, they also voiced opposition to dissolving the Union, advocating instead for either a constitutional amendment or statutory enactment of abolition, since "the Constitution" already "provides amply for liberation, but makes no provision for dissolution." From their perspective, "the general structure of the Federal Constitution, as well as its particular provisions, preclude [*sic*] the legal existence of slavery, forbid the States to maintain it, provide for the liberation of the enslaved, and authorize and require, at the hand of the Federal Government, its suppression."

Political radicals considered the Due Process Clause of the Fifth Amendment one constitutional source of protections against slavery. Those who enslaved Africans had infringed on their liberty interests without the due process of law. The aristocratic order of "slaveocracy," they further argued, violated the prohibition against granting titles of nobility. The federal government had both the power and duty to abolish slavery. By doing so, Congress would "provide for the common defense, promote the general welfare, and *secure the blessings of liberty.*"[39]

Radicals thought that the framers had been unable to agree on a federal compact that directly abolished slavery, so had settled for provisions giving Congress the authority to pass laws consistent with natural law. The revolutionaries, wrote George Mellen and Joel Tiffany, provided constitutional means for ending slavery, having a fresh memory of the battle for their own liberties, only recently won from British political slavery. The Preamble, for instance, gave Congress the power "to provide for the common defence and general welfare." Since Congress could use that clause to authorize the purchase of Louisiana, Florida, and California and the annexation of Texas, argued Spooner, it could also rely on it to end slavery. Others asserted that the Preamble, whose express object was "to secure the blessings of liberty," was a temple of freedom, "not a den of Slavery." That guarantee was for the "people," which were not distinguished by race, to "establish justice," while slavery was a great injustice. According to article I, section 8, Congress could collect taxes to provide for the general welfare. Slavery was opposed to the general welfare, in light of "the necessary evils slavery must and does bring in its course, such as ignorance, dissipation, vice, immorality. . . . [Furthermore,] the arts, sciences, manufactures, even agriculture, declines [*sic*] under its withering influences." Congress could use its taxing power to end these harms against the general welfare.[40]

Blacks, whether free or slave, political radicals thought, were citizens, like any other persons born in the United States. No state could take away their national citizenship rights, and the federal government retained power to protect its citizens' natural rights. The federal government, for instance, could secure the rights to personal liberty and property ownership, since these were privileges and immunities of national citizenship. As citizens, blacks were eligible for every public office, including the presidency of the United States, since the Constitution contained no racial eligibility. The national polity, in accordance with article IV, guaranteed to each state a republican government, which was defined to protect the equal rights of everyone to freedom and property. States could not maintain slaves against federal statutes because states lacked any authority to violate the "inalienable rights for the protection of which both the State and National Governments were organized." Blacks were denied a republican government because they, like women and Native Americans, were politically unrepresented. This, Stewart and others argued, meant that the United States could end slavery in all states. Without federal protections, he explained, blacks were denied any of the rights secured under the Bill of Rights, including the right to jury trials in fugitive slave cases.[41]

The most difficult clauses for radical political abolitionists to explain were those that Garrisonians considered to be proslavery. Radical arguments on these points were the most strained. According to Smith's perspective, the Importation Clause did not perpetuate the slave trade; instead, it was the means by which Congress could end it. On the Three-Fifths Clause, Smith dismissed the notion that slaves, since they could not vote, should not be counted in apportioning representatives. He pointed out that other groups who were counted for apportionment, including women and white men without property, were also disenfranchised. He thus thought not counting slaves at all would be a greater injustice that counting them only partly. The Fugitive Slave Clause, he thought, was not about slavery but about the right of parents to pursue their children and masters their apprentices. Given southern use of these clauses to strengthen slavery, Smith's arguments were a stretch.[42]

A third group, which gained the support of politicians like Birney and Salmon P. Chase, is better characterized as antislavery than abolitionist. This political movement sought to prevent the spread of slavery, but it was deferential to the existing order in slave states. Theirs was a campaign not for the immediate end of all slavery, wherever it existed, but against the spread of slavery to United States territories. This faction, along with some radical abolitionists, morphed from the Liberty Party (1840) to the Free Soil Party (1848), finally ending up as the Republican Party (1854), under whose aegis Abraham Lincoln helped capture the presidency.

Such political concessions were unacceptable to both Garrisonian and radical abolitionists; however, the distinctions between political antislavery advocates and abolitionists were less pronounced than their mutual differences with antislavery colonizationists. Abolitionists all wanted one thing, an immediate end to slavery. They were uncompromising in this mission. The political movement also wanted to ban slavery but thought some temporary, negotiated settlement with the South was necessary for national unity. Politicians tended to make some concessions, believing that with time slavery would wither of its own accord because it was economically wasteful and contrary to the nation's core commitments. Colonizationists, some of whom owned slaves, tolerated slavery, all the while arguing that the expulsion of blacks would help them enjoy equality among those of their race. Proslavery advocates explicitly regarded any talk of ending slavery offensive to their supremacist sensibilities.

By the middle of the nineteenth century, proslavery advocates had gained the upper hand in Congress. They compelled the nation into a series of compromises that stretched the geographic limitations of where slavery could be compelled until, after the United States Supreme Court's *Dred Scott* decision, the institution threatened to gain a foothold throughout the United States.

CHAPTER FOUR

Sectional Compromise and National Conflict

D ebates about the constitutionality of slavery were no asides. They probed the central question of the day, whether a federal republic that on the one hand guaranteed individual rights but whose Constitution, on the other, contained clauses used to augment slaveholders' political power could remain intact. Beginning with the Missouri Compromise of 1820, the South and North pursued alternatives to belligerence. They all proved to be stopgaps that perpetuated the misery of millions of Americans coping with slavery.

Truces over slavery were tested repeatedly. Southern demands for more land to extend political power did not stop at Missouri. During the early nineteenth century, the nation confronted its constitutional heritage through a series of debates about extending slavery into the western territories. The revolutionary generation had founded the country on principles that would carry the abolitionists from being a reviled minority in the 1830s to the heights of national power. The decision to protect slavery for the sake of national unity was of temporary use, leading eventually to the cataclysm of civil war.

Where natural rights had defined the progressive philosophy of the revolutionary period, the period of compromise was marked by racial politics. The dominant trend in the country was from conceiving rights as universal and absolute to thinking of them as relative. Racial and gender legal qualifications were emblematic of how culturally embedded supremacist conceptions of humanity were. The relatively small number of abolitionists and feminists throve on ideals, but their successes were few. The tide of reform seemed to be increasing slavery's foothold and moving it westward, especially after the *Dred Scott* Supreme Court decision. The national self-destructiveness of sectional conflict came to a head with the Civil War, and then, at least briefly, the country seemed to realize how harmful inequality had been all along.

Debating the Missouri Compromise: A Missed Opportunity

Congress could have ended the spread of slavery in 1819 when it began debating Missouri's proposal to form a constitution and join the Union as a state. Missouri had been part of the land that the Jefferson administration acquired through the Louisiana Purchase in 1803. During debate on the statehood bill, New York Representative James Tallmadge, Jr., offered an amendment that would have conditioned entry into the Union on gradual emancipation to those then enslaved in the Missouri Territory and freedom for everyone born after statehood. When this proposal failed to gain enough support, Tallmadge, who later became president of New York University, altered his proposed amendment to prohibit any further introduction of slaves into Missouri and to mandate manumission, at the age of twenty-five, for any slave children born after the state's admission.

At the time of Missouri's admission, it had only 66,586 inhabitants, of whom 347 were free blacks and 10,222 were slaves. To the slave states, Missouri's future status was crucial for gaining additional congressional seats. They realized that as the state's population grew, the electorate would be apportioned additional representatives. The southern block could thereby gain more votes in the House of Representatives.

The Tallmadge amendment became a fulcrum of contention because, if passed, it could have prevented Missouri from entering the Union as a slave state. To Tallmadge the issue was important enough to enter the eye of the developing storm: "If a dissolution of the Union must take place, let it be so! If civil war, which gentlemen so much threaten, must come, I can only say, let it come." Tallmadge's dire statement was ahead of its time. For Jefferson, too, the Missouri controversy portended a terrifying threat to the country's existence that awoke him like a "bell in the night" from the repose of domestic tranquility.[1]

Senator Rufus King, one of Tallmadge's antislavery supporters, argued that the Constitution allowed Congress to condition the admission of a new state on its forming a republican government. Slavery was incompatible with republican institutions; therefore, King concluded, Congress could condition admission on Missouri's abolition of slavery. Others, like Senator Benjamin Ruggles of Ohio, said that slavery contradicted republican principles enshrined in the Declaration of Independence. Representative Timothy Fuller of Massachusetts likewise argued that the Declaration's assertion of self-evident truths about inalienable rights meant that a republican state was incompatible with slavery. "Since . . . it cannot be denied that slaves are men, it follows that they are in a purely republican government born free, and are entitled to liberty and the pursuit of happiness." In response, slavery supporters said that Fuller's remarks implied that southern states were not republican. To his critics he conceded that the Constitution had allowed states with slaves to retain them until "they should think it proper or safe to conform to the pure principle of abolishing slavery."[2]

The statements of New Hampshire Representative Arthur Livermore evinced disgust with slavery. He supported Tallmadge because "the light of science and of religion is utterly excluded" by laws prohibiting slave education and public worship. The sympathies of "slaves are disregarded; mothers and children are sold and separated. . . . The proposition before us goes only to prevent our citizens from making slaves of such as have a right to freedom." This was an opportunity to "prevent the growth of a sin which sits heavy on the soul of every one of us."[3]

Congress could act in a federal system only on the basis of its constitutional authority. The supporters of the Tallmadge amendment also relied on the constitutional section granting Congress the power to "make all needful rules and regulations respecting the territories" (article IV, section 3). To them, that meant that Congress could proscribe the conditions for a territory to be admitted into the Union as a state. Congress had exercised that power in 1802 to demand that Ohio adopt an ordinance against slavery and involuntary servitude as a precondition for admission. Different requirements had been placed on Indiana, Illinois, and Mississippi. Thus the Tallmadge amendment was not unprecedented.

Missouri Bill debate participants understood that they were at the threshold of a great decision. Representative John W. Taylor of New York, who would soon become speaker of the House, argued that a vote on the Tallmadge amendment would "determine whether the high destinies of this region, and of these generations, shall be fulfilled, or whether we shall defeat them by permitting slavery, with all its baleful consequences, to inherit the land." He called on fellow congressmen to put American "principles into practice." Taylor derided House Speaker Henry Clay's assurances that Missouri slaveholders would make sure that their property was well clothed, well fed, and sheltered. He characterized Clay's benevolence as "counterfeit, . . .

that humanity . . . which saves a finger to-day, but amputates the arm to-morrow." Senator David L. Morril of New Hampshire, who later became his state's governor, seconded Taylor's words: "We boast of our liberties; we call ourselves a nation of freemen; we delight to hear our children" speak of "the freedom, the liberty, equality, and republicanism of our country; we teach them in their infancy, that these sentiments may grow. . . . We chant them in our songs; we prefix them in our books; we inscribe them in our temples; we present them in our halls; shall we abandon and deny them? . . . Forbid it ye guardians of the people's rights!"[4] These passionately held principles spoke of unfulfilled personal and national commitments.

On the other side of the debate were those who argued that Congress had only the authority to decide whether to admit a state, not the authority to decide for its inhabitants what constituted a republican government. Southerners like Virginia Representative Philip P. Barbour, who went on to be a justice of the United States Supreme Court, and Maryland Senator William Pinkney argued that entering states could decide for themselves on a form of government. The federal government could not interfere in those decisions; otherwise, the resulting Union would be unequal in its treatment of citizens. A prohibition on the importation of domestic slaves into Missouri would infringe on southerners' constitutional privilege of moving to that state. Furthermore, opponents of the Tallmadge amendment warned, if Congress could define the nature of republican government, it could abolish slavery in states already admitted.[5]

The Tallmadge amendment went down to defeat in the Senate, even though the House approved it. A compromise was eventually reached, based on the proposal of Illinois Senator Jesse B. Thomas. Other than in the state of Missouri, which was allowed to become a state without any bars on slavery, the institution was "forever prohibited" above the latitude of 36 degrees, 30 minutes, the southern boundary of Missouri. The agreement also provided that Maine, which had also applied for admission, would come into the Union as a free state. This was important to retain Senate equality of power between the two sections.

Testing National Power

The Missouri Compromise briefly put sectional conflict to rest. The truce was temporary as the South continued agitating for the sovereign right to act against federal mandate. States' rights advocates often relied on Jefferson's

Kentucky Resolution, which he wrote as vice president. In the decades that followed, the resolution became a primary source for the nullification theory of exclusive state authority over local matters, including slavery. "Every State," Jefferson wrote, "has a natural right . . . to nullify of [its] own authority all assumptions of power by others within [its] limits." Robert J. Turnbull also won a large following, especially in South Carolina, with his *Crisis; or, Essays on the Usurpations of the Federal Government* (1827). Turnbull saw a gulf between the North's and South's economic interests and opposed nationalism as an unconstitutional step toward the abolition of slavery. While Turnbull did not use the word "nullification," he advocated "firm resistance" against the national efforts.[6]

In 1833, during the Nullification Crisis, South Carolina relied on these theories to challenge federal laws it considered to be overreaching into its commercial sphere. Central to the dispute between that state and President Andrew Jackson's administration were two nationwide tariffs, of 1828 and 1832, regulating the importation of goods that benefited northern manufacturers and southern capitalists but hurt southern planters. South Carolina, which was a planter society where only 10 percent of the population was eligible to vote, threatened to nullify the tariffs. It even readied a militia to repel federal forces. The crisis was defused only after Senator Henry Clay orchestrated a tariff-reduction compromise.[7]

On its most consequential level, the crisis helped John Calhoun place slavery in a state nullification context that would be repeated at the start of the Civil War. Nine months after he resigned from the vice presidency because of his opposition to the tariff, Calhoun described it as the "occasion, rather than the real cause of the present unhappy state of things." At bottom, Calhoun wrote in a letter, was the question of whether the federal government could interfere with the "peculiar domestick institutions of the Southern States, and the consequent direction which that and her soil and climate have given to her industry, has placed them in regard to taxation and appropriation in opposite relation to the majority of the Union; against the danger of which, if there be no protective power in the reserved rights of the states, they must in the end be forced to rebel, or submit to have . . . their domestick institutions exhausted by Colonization and other schemes." Just as Jefferson was alarmed that slavery was the source of the controversy that led to the Missouri Compromise, Madison foresaw that the South Carolina crisis could lead to "nullification, secession, and disunion in the southern States."[8]

No compromise could end so contentious an issue as whether slaves were a legitimate form of property or oppressed people denied their natural rights. With the passing of years, for the North slavery remained a moral issue, while for the South it was a matter of economics and self-determination. Northern aversion to slavery, however, was not identical to the equality efforts of Garrisonians and radical political abolitionists. The emphasis for a majority of northern politicians was on arresting the spread of slavery, not on abolishing it immediately. Furthermore, many in the antislavery camp regarded the western territories to be bastions for white labor to flourish without the disturbance of black competition. Pennsylvania Representative David Wilmot, for instance, made clear that he was pleading "the cause of the rights of white freemen. I would preserve for free white labor a fair country, a rich inheritance, where the sons of toil of my own race and own color, can live without the disgrace which association with negro slavery brings upon free labor."[9]

This same Wilmot, during his first term in the House of Representatives, made a historic demand to prevent slave expansion into the North during the Mexican-American War. Shortly after the start of hostilities, in 1846, President James Polk requested that Congress allocate the executive branch $2 million to sue for peace. The Whigs in Congress, like Hugh White of New York, did not trust the president to use these resources without further instruction from Congress. White and others thought Polk had "projected, planned, and provoked" the war to gain additional lands for spreading slavery. Rather than putting the allocation matter to a vote, Wilmot proposed an amendment, which came to be known as the Wilmot Proviso, incorporating the language of the Northwest Ordinance. His amendment predicated allocation of the money on the condition that no slavery or involuntary servitude, except for a criminal conviction, be established on territory that the president might acquire with it. Wilmot was by no means an abolitionist. He had earlier voted for the annexation of Texas and against the exclusion of slavery there. He took a position that the Free Soil Party would come to adopt: slavery was bad and should not be allowed to spread, but the federal government lacked the power to interfere with southern states' sovereign prerogative over it.

While his amendment never became law—indeed, in the next year Polk got a $3 million allocation without any conditions attached to its use—Wilmot set off a lasting debate. When Mexico ceded land in 1848 to the United States, for $15 million through the Treaty of Guadalupe Hidalgo, the decision of whether to allow slavery to spread there became even more pressing. The eventual acquisition of one and a quarter billion square miles of land, increasing the area of the United States by a whopping 73 percent, threw the country into careening debates about how to deal with slavery.[10]

The Compromise of 1850: Temporary Consensus

After the Mexican-American War the permanent truce that the United States expected to achieve through the Missouri Compromise became even more elusive. Antagonism between sections surrounded the debate about dealing with land acquired through the Mexican Cession. That land had been free soil under Mexican law, and the debate grew over whether it should remain free after the change in sovereignty. At its core the question was whether Congress in 1850 would work to gradually eliminate slavery or whether it would seize the opportunity to expand it. Many wondered whether Americans, having won an expanse of fertile land, would spread liberty and equality there or diminish the rights that Mexico had recognized.

Proslavery congressmen considered Mexican law irrelevant after the Treaty of Guadalupe Hidalgo. Planters worried that admitting only free states was the North's attempt to change the polarity of U.S. politics and, eventually, to abolish slavery altogether. This made them concerned for both their financial stake in slavery and their social and political stations.

The most pressing issues before Congress were whether California should be admitted with a constitution prohibiting slavery, where to place the Texas–New Mexico boundary, whether New Mexico and Utah should be organized as free territories, what the future status of slavery in the District of Columbia should be, and how to amend the fugitive slave law. Numerous congressmen floated proposals to resolve these matters, but none gained enough support to pass.[11]

The seventy-three-year-old Senator Henry Clay proposed an omnibus solution that was composed of several seemingly unrelated bills. Its most controversial provision required the federal government to join in the recovery of fugitive slaves.

Even though Clay claimed to be "no friend of slavery," he preferred "the liberty of my own country to that of any other people, and the liberty of my own race to that of any other race." Just a short time before, he had suffered one of the greatest defeats of his long political career, losing the Whig presidential candidacy to Zachary Taylor, but his passion for the Union was unwavering. An even worse insult to Clay was President Taylor's adamant refusal to back his proposal. Taylor believed it the work of a cabal, headed by his former son-in-law and future Confederate president Jefferson Davis, determined to secede from the Union unless the federal government agreed to extend slavery to the Pacific Ocean.

The omnibus bill's prospects of success improved when Taylor died of acute gastroenteritis. After his vice president, Millard Fillmore, was sworn in as president, he determinedly backed Clay's plan. This, the states' rights supporters thought, would increase the likelihood of passing all the bills as a single legislative package, for the "the peace, concord, and harmony of the Union," in contrast to the uncertain support each might receive separately. With the backing of the influential Senator Daniel Webster, the bill gained the support of an even bigger block of votes.[12]

A thirty-seven-year-old first-term senator from Illinois, Stephen A. Douglas, put the fine touches on Clay's work. Douglas, working from the Democratic Party side of the aisle, wanted to achieve the same results as Clay, who was a Whig. Rather than seeking compromise votes on the entire omnibus provision, however, Douglas separated its parts. He was able to get a Senate majority for each component, patching together a variety of voting blocks. The House, which had taken part in shaping the measures before the Senate voted on them, then passed all parts of the Compromise of 1850, and Fillmore signed it into law. The compromise's primary purpose was to defuse sectional tensions about slavery. The resulting five statutes admitted California into the Union as a nonslave state; resolved the border dispute between slaveholding Texas and the New Mexico territory, in part by requiring the federal government to pay Texas's $10 million preannexation debt; allowed New Mexico and Utah to decide whether to make slavery legal and provided that either could eventually be admitted as a free or slave state; abolished the slave trade, but not slavery, in the District of Columbia; and refined provisions for the capture and return of fugitive slaves.[13]

The Fugitive Act of 1850 was not the first attempt to prevent slaves from escaping north to claim their freedom. Article IV of the Constitution provided that anyone who was "held to Service or Labour" under the laws of one state and escaped into another "shall be delivered up on Claim of the Party to whom such Service or Labour may be due." To enforce that provision, the first government of the United States, under the leadership of President Washington, passed the Fugitive Slave Act of 1793.

The 1793 federal law allowed slaveholders or their agents to seize slaves and file lawsuits in either federal or state court. A judge or magistrate was to examine proof of ownership through oral or affidavit evidence and, when appropriate, to grant certificates for removing fugitives. Anyone who obstructed the seizure or removal was subject to a hefty $500 civil fine. The act included no mention of habeas corpus, jury trials, or due process.[14] The slave-trading industry owed its legal status to this act, but its work often proceeded extrajudicially, through kidnapping, because the law legitimized slaveholders' rights above those of slaves. Free blacks were also sometimes the victims of indiscriminate posses. Even when cases got to court, identifications were questionable, especially when they were based on affidavits rather than live testimony.

Several states sought to remedy these human rights violations, realizing that they constituted an affront to the human decency for which government was formed. Personal liberty laws, such as an 1826 Pennsylvania statute, provided some of the judicial safeguards that the federal law lacked. The Supreme Court of the United States reviewed that law in *Prigg v. Pennsylvania* (1842).[15] The appeal arose when a jury convicted a slave catcher under the Pennsylvania Personal Liberty Act of 1826 for kidnapping an alleged runaway slave and her children and returning them to Maryland. The Supreme Court found the 1793 Fugitive Slave Act to be constitutional and struck the Pennsylvania law as an unlawful usurpation of federal law. The Court protected slave holders' rights to the detriment of fugitives.

There was a slight upside, however. *Prigg* found that recapture was a federal responsibility that neither the state nor its officers had to participate in. Chief Justice Roger B. Taney, writing a concurrence, was significantly more amenable to the proslavery argument. Unlike the majority, he believed the act of 1793 required states to assist in the recapture. Justice John McLean's sentiments, which he expressed in a separate concurrence, were very different. He thought it a given that the federal government could not regulate the conduct of state courts and that free states like Pennsylvania could pass laws prohibiting their agents from participating in the removal of fugitives.

In the flurry of antislavery activity that followed *Prigg,* Massachusetts, Vermont, Connecticut, Illinois, New Hampshire, Pennsylvania, and Rhode Island passed personal liberty laws using the Court's limitation on federal coercion to provide runaways with state protections. Massachusetts's law of 1843, known as Latimer's Law after a fugitive named George Latimer, is representative of this trend. This earliest response to *Prigg* prohibited state judges from granting certificates in cases arising under the Fugitive Slave Act of 1793. Government agents were prohibited from arresting or using a public building to detain any alleged fugitive. Violators were subject to criminal penalties. Vermont passed one of the most effective acts of this type, on November 1, 1843. The state's senate later explained the law's connection to United States civil rights history: "Born of a resistance to arbitrary power . . . her first voice a declaration of the equal rights of man—how could her people be otherwise than haters of slavery." Vermont afforded alleged fugitives the right to a jury trial and state-provided defense attorneys. Pennsylvania also demonstrated a continuing commitment to civil liberty by revising its personal liberty law in 1847. Among other provisions, the act made kidnapping runaways punishable by a fine and five to twelve years of hard labor, prohibited state judges and justices of the peace from hearing fugitive slave cases, gave judges the power to issue writs of habeas corpus for persons who were detained, and prohibited the use of state jails to further the capture.[16]

The Fugitive Slave Act of 1850 was meant to fill the loophole for aiding runaways. The 1850 law was stringent and offensive to northern states' sense of sovereignty and individual rights. In order to establish title, live witnesses were no longer required; claimants needed only to swear out written affidavits, and this ex parte information sufficed to establish a cause of action; pursuing owners could recapture fugitives without resorting to formal hearings or jury trials; and specially appointed federal commissioners were granted authority to determine cases "in a summary manner." At the end of abbreviated hearings, without due process protections and without giving the alleged fugitive an opportunity to offer a defense, the commissioner could issue certificates immediately sending the respondent to a life of slavery. In a provision that privileged reenslavement, commissioners who found respondents were runaways received ten dollars, while those who set them free were paid five dollars. Not only were marshals and deputies under obligation to participate in recapture, on penalty of a fine, but the law also required that upon demand members of the public join a posse in the manhunt. Anyone who knowingly or willfully obstructed the effort was subject to a one thousand–dollar fine. Persons who hid or aided fugitives could be also fined one thousand dollars and imprisoned for up to six months.[17]

A new set of state personal liberty laws were enacted after the Fugitive Slave Act of 1850 in an effort to help captured persons despite the *Prigg* decision. These varied from state to state, but they typically prohibited the use of state jails, punished anyone seizing another for enslavement, and prohibited state judges from assisting would-be slave recapturers. In Vermont's case, any slave that set foot there was free.[18]

The constitutional opposition to the 1850 act rested on the Fifth Amendment's guarantee against the deprivation of life, liberty, or property without due process; the Seventh Amendment's guarantee of trial by jury; and the article I, section 9, clause 2 prohibition against suspension of the writ of habeas corpus. But the existence of constitutional clauses that protected slavery, especially the Fugitive Slave Clause, and the supremacy of federal law weakened contrary arguments.

In its revised form, the law took an enormous human toll. Free blacks as well as fugitives feared being dragged into slavery. In 1851 a Madison, Indiana, man named Mitchum was forcefully separated from his family and sent to a man who claimed he had escaped nineteen years earlier. On another occasion, witnesses saw a bloodied man running from a building yelling that he would not be taken alive. He jumped into a river but emerged when the pursuing posse, with a U.S. marshal at its head, brandished a weapon.[19]

Popular opposition by whites to the Fugitive Slave Act of 1850 showed a willingness to stand up to despotism at personal risk. The Underground Railroad became more active in whisking runaways to Canada. Rescues took various forms. Fugitives often fled to Chicago, where the Illinois Underground Railroad ended. A large crowd gathered in 1851 around a Chicago courthouse during the trial of Moses Johnson, ready to rescue him if the court ruled against his freedom. Only Johnson's acquittal defused the unrest. The Underground Railroad also became more active in Ohio, where fugitives traveled by night and were kept safe in homes by day, typically hiding indoors no later than nightfall to prevent detection. Harriet Tubman, with underground stations from Maryland to New York, Albany, Troy, Schenectady, and all the way into Canada, risked her life to help others make their way north to safety. Some found violence preferable to peaceful resistance. In 1851 a slave catcher lost his life in Christiana, Pennsylvania, while attempting to capture four persons pursuant to fugitive slave warrants. Boston showed particular zeal, under the leadership of abolitionists like Theodore Parker, who personally spirited away the fugitives William and Ellen Craft. Black activists living there were also active, on one occasion rescuing a man known as Shadrach in the midst of a court proceeding.[20]

These acts of opposition had no effect on the Supreme Court. Taney upheld the constitutionality of the Fugitive Slave Act of 1850 in *Ableman v. Booth* (1858). The case arose when the Wisconsin Supreme Court found the 1850 act unconstitutional and twice issued writs of habeas corpus to intervene on behalf a fugitive named Booth. The U.S. Supreme Court, however, reversed the Wisconsin decision, holding that state judges had no authority to oppose a federal court order by issuing writs of habeas corpus.[21] The Court had taken the country in the direction of protecting property over individual rights.

Kansas-Nebraska Act: Consensus on Popular Sovereignty

Congress passed the Kansas-Nebraska Act in 1854, the year of the kidnapping leading up to the *Ableman* decision. Senator Stephen A. Douglas sponsored the initiating bill, proposing popular sovereignty to decide the matter of slavery in an unorganized territory lying west of Iowa and Missouri and north of 36 degrees, 30 minutes, the parallel above which the Missouri Compromise of 1820 had "forever prohibited" slavery. The United States had acquired the vast majority of that land through the Louisiana Purchase. Douglas argued that under the Constitution, territories could decide democratically whether to legalize slavery. The right to vote on whether slavery was a legitimate form of property downplayed contrary human rights principles. Abraham Lincoln, a former one-term Whig congressman from Illinois, asserted in 1854 that Douglas's aims were inconsistent with most of humanity's condemnation of slavery as "a great moral wrong." Lincoln called for a return to the Declaration of Independence's "fundamental principles of civil liberty."[22]

Inadvertently, Douglas set the country careening toward a civil war. In large part, he was driven by personal ambition. He expected in return for opening additional territory to slavery that the South would support his bid for the Democratic presidential ticket of 1856. Douglas also had a financial stake in having slavery in the territory. He had dreamed for nearly a decade of opening a railroad route, running partly through land in which he had invested heavily, at the head of Lake Superior and Chicago. He could not, however, get southern support to incorporate the territory without his willingness, as the chairman of the Committee on the Territories, to make the spread of slavery possible there. Southerners became willing to incorporate Nebraska only after Kentucky Senator Archibald Dixon offered an amendment to Douglas's original bill that explicitly repealed the Missouri Compromise. The barbs of slavery once again opened the festering wound of an ailing nation that, time and again, returned to the same wrenching debate.[23]

Thus even though numerous factors entered into the debates over the organization of Kansas and Nebraska, it was the question of slavery that drove them. Douglas professed allegiance to the same doctrine of nonintervention that in 1850 had facilitated the admission of Utah and New Mexico into the

Union. The premise that slavery could be democratically imported into the territories was predicated on concern for equal self-determination that extended no further than whites and devalued the concerns of the rest of humanity. Some congressional opponents of Douglas's popular sovereignty plan were disquieted only by white labor's ability to compete for jobs, but others impugned the scheme for inevitably extending human suffering. The "Appeal of Independent Democrats" was the most influential of the latter statements. This joint effort of three longtime opponents of slavery, Representative Joshua R. Giddings and Senators Charles Sumner and Salmon P. Chase, set off a firestorm in Congress and free states. Three congressmen, including Gerrit Smith, joined them. The Kansas-Nebraska Bill, they asserted, was not only a gross violation of the Missouri Compromise but an attempt to convert Nebraska "into a dreary region of despotism." They evoked national principles: "We entreat you to be mindful of that fundamental maxim of Democracy—EQUAL RIGHTS AND EXACT JUSTICE FOR ALL MEN. Do not submit to become agents in extending legalized oppression and systematized injustice." Sumner, on the Senate floor, explained that he opposed local sovereignty because the will of the majority could never legitimize slavery, which was "an infraction of the immutable law of nature, especially in a country which has solemnly declared, in its Declaration of Independence, the inalienable right of all men to life, *liberty*, and the pursuit of happiness." Senator William H. Seward warned that slavery would continue to rear its head and could not diminish the North's "old, traditional, hereditary sentiment" for freedom.[24]

Dred Scott: Devaluing Citizenship and Limiting Congress

The Kansas-Nebraska Act made popular sovereignty over slavery the rule throughout the territories. Congress and the president had failed to stop the spiral of sectional conflict; what remained for the Supreme Court, the final interpreter of the Constitution, to decide was whether the United States had the authority to prohibit slavery in the territories and whether their inhabitants could vote to bar slavery. The Court's decision on this matter, *Dred Scott v. Sandford* (1857), made clear that the Supreme Court could not be a neutral arbiter, intellectually removed from the passions of its era.[25] Like every other institution, it was infused with politics, and its opinions required the justices to pick a side of the political question and to couch their decisions in constitutional terms.

Dred Scott's fate offered a glance into how congressionally finagled compromises failed to stem the growth of slavery. Indeed, it was the unwillingness of the Constitution's framers to take firm steps against the institution that allowed later generations to choose their own direction, and the majority chose to extend slavery. The Supreme Court, when it found the opportunity to render an opinion on the expansion of slavery into the territories, was even more zealous than Congress and the president had been in preserving private property rights that, by their very nature, reduced individuals to mere commodities.

Scott lived on free land for the first time in 1834, when his holder, an army physician named John Emerson, was sent to Fort Armstrong in Rock Island, Illinois. In 1836, when Fort Armstrong closed, Scott accompanied Emerson to his new assignment in Fort Snelling, located in the northern part of the Louisiana Purchase, then known as the Wisconsin Territory and now part of the state of Minnesota. That territory was free by virtue of the Missouri Compromise. While at Fort Snelling, Scott married, something he could not have lawfully done in any southern state. From there, Emerson was transferred to St. Louise, Missouri, and then to Louisiana. When Emerson died, in 1843, Scott was bequeathed to Emerson's wife, the former Eliza Irene Sanford. Shortly thereafter, in 1846, the year Wilmot introduced his proviso, Scott brought suit in a state court for his freedom against Emerson's widow, whom he claimed beat him. While he won his freedom at the trial level, he lost it after Irene Emerson's appeal to the Supreme Court of Missouri.

That would have ended the case, but by a strange twist of events, Irene Emerson married an abolitionist, Dr. Calvin C. Chaffee, who was later elected to Congress, and she moved to live with him in Massachusetts. She left Scott to live in St. Louis, under the ownership of her brother, John Sanford, a citizen of New York and administrator of his deceased brother-in-law's estate. This provided a new defendant against whom Scott filed suit in federal court on the basis of diversity jurisdiction, which requires that the plaintiff and defendant be citizens of different states. After the district court found that it had jurisdiction and entered a judgment in favor of Sanford, Scott appealed to the Supreme Court of the United States.[26]

The justices who heard the case seemed to be a sectionally balanced bunch, with five southerners and four northerners; nevertheless, at least seven of them—everyone except Justices McLean of Ohio and Benjamin R. Curtis of Massachusetts—had markedly southern leanings on the issue of slavery. Chief Justice Taney of Maryland had a long list of seemingly enlightened accomplishments. He had freed his slaves and even provided a monthly pension to those who were too old to work. He helped a free black to purchase his wife by fronting him the money, though he did bind him until the money was repaid. In any case, these were not signs of opposition to the institution of slavery. As an attorney general under President Andrew Jackson, Taney declared, "The African race in the United States even when free, are every where a degraded class, and exercise no political influence. The privileges they are allowed to enjoy, are accorded to them as a matter of kindness and benevolence rather than of right." We have seen his markedly proslavery stance in the concurrence to *Prigg* and the opinion in *Ableman*. Justice John A. Campbell of Alabama had also manumitted his slaves but was so passionately prosouthern that at the outbreak of the Civil War he quit the Supreme Court to become the assistant secretary of war to the Confederate government. The other three southerners, Justices James M. Wayne of Georgia, Peter V. Daniel of Virginia, and John Catron of Tennessee, were slave owners, and therefore had an indirect interest in the outcome of *Dred Scott*. The two northerners besides McLean and Curtis were committed to Democratic appeasement of southerners. Justice Samuel Nelson of New York winked at slave trading in New York, and, like Justice Robert C. Grier of Pennsylvania, while acting as a designated circuit justice, repeatedly enforced the Fugitive Slave Acts of 1793 and 1850 and counseled against the risks of resistance.[27]

Taney wrote a fractured opinion for the Court. Six other justices joined him in finding that Scott was not free, but each of them decided to write a separate concurrence to explain his reasoning. The first part of Taney's opinion denied that Scott was a citizen of any state or of the United States. The chief justice claimed that the framers intended neither slaves nor any of their free descendants to be citizens. When the Constitution was ratified, blacks were "considered a subordinate and inferior class of beings, who had been subjugated by the dominant race" and lacked citizenship in all states. Taney adopted the proslavery argument that the Declaration's assertion that "all men are created equal" had nothing to do with blacks. For Scott, this meant that he could not sue for his freedom in federal court on the basis of diversity of citizenship. For blacks, it meant that they lacked any of the privilege and immunities of national citizens.

Justice Curtis's dissent dug its claws into Taney's opinion and showed it to be based on false premises. At the time of the founding, blacks had been citizens of several states—New Hampshire, Massachusetts, New York, New Jersey, and North Carolina—that had granted them the right to vote. When the Union was formed, blacks obtained national citizenship by virtue of their state citizenship. The limiting factor of Curtis's argument was that if a state did not grant a class of persons citizenship, they could never be citizens of the United States.

For its contemporaries, the more incendiary part of Taney's opinion dealt with the merits of Scott's case. His decision on the plaintiff's citizenship should have led to the conclusion that the Court lacked any power to render a decision on the merits. After all, if diversity jurisdiction was absent, the Court lacked the authority to adjudicate the dispute of the litigation. But Taney was determined to try to resolve decades of sectional conflict in one fell swoop. The Missouri Compromise, he asserted, violated the substantive due process rights of slave owners under the Fifth Amendment to enjoy their property in all parts of the United States, including the territories. Congress had extensive powers over the territories, Taney further wrote, and both Wayne and Catron agreed. But those powers, Taney went on, were limited by the Fifth Amendment's prohibition against the deprivation of property without due process. Thus the Compromise had been an unconstitutional exercise of congressional authority. Scott could never have become free because, according to Taney, Congress could not invade slaveholders' property right to own human chattel. Catron in his concurrence saw the abuse in the violation of the Louisiana Purchase treaty, which, he claimed, required the continuation of slavery in the territory.

Other justices who joined the majority opinion saw things differently. Daniel and Campbell understood Congress's power in the territories to be limited. Daniel asserted that the Missouri Compromise was void because the Constitution specifically recognized slave property, and its owners could not be excluded from the territories. Campbell argued that the framers never meant to give Congress the power to legislate the territories' internal politics. Nelson also regarded this as a conflict-of-laws issue but thought that since Scott was a resident of St. Louis, the slave law of Missouri should be used to resolved the case. Grier agreed with Nelson on the jurisdictional matter and with Taney on the unconstitutionality of the Compromise.

The two dissents argued that the Missouri Compromise was a proper use of authority. Whether slavery should be permitted in the Missouri Territory, wrote Curtis, was a political question that was beyond the scope of judicial review. The Louisiana treaty, wrote McLean, could not forever bind the United States' dealings with slavery. It might have applied to all slaves at the time the United States made the agreement, but in 1820 there remained no outstanding issues that would limit congressional action.

Although the Court's majority refused to acknowledge he was a person with rights, Dred Scott did gain his freedom. Peter Blow, whose father had sold Scott to Emerson, bought Scott's freedom.

The *Dred Scott* decision itself, with its holding on citizenship and the Missouri Compromise, only exacerbated sectional tension. The Court had tried to play a mediating role in politics, but it was unable to achieve even internal unanimity. The little that the seven justices who wrote against Scott's freedom were able to agree upon placed the basic value of liberal equality at odds with the Constitution. They subordinated life and liberty to property interests. Taney's reliance on Fifth Amendment property rights put in doubt whether free states that prohibited the use of slave labor within their borders were violating the Constitution. The dissents regarded the majority's arguments to be inaccurate. *Dred Scott* was met with a scathing attack from the fledgling Republican Party.

As Mark Graber has recently pointed out, Chief Justice Taney's judicial attempt to resolve sectional conflict proved to be as ineffective as congressional compromises had been.[28] The negative reaction to *Dred Scott* further polarized the country. Abraham Lincoln, for one, regarded the opinion to be a grave threat to the North and to democracy in general. His well-known 1858 "House Divided" speech expressed concern about the opinions implications: "We shall *lie down* pleasantly dreaming that the people of Missouri are on the verge of making their state *free;* and we shall *awake* to the *reality,* instead, that the *Supreme* Court has made *Illinois* a *slave* state."[29] The South, on the other hand, and its northern Democratic Party supporters, like President James Buchanan, applauded the decision and became more resolute in their support for slavery. The opinion also made supporters of slavery more aggressive toward the North. Now that the nation's highest court had sided with them, they became increasingly indignant about antislavery moralizing.

Lincoln's presidential victory in 1860 was a call to arms in the South. He was, after all, the head of the Republican Party, whose platform called for the abolition of slavery in the territories. South Carolina, which had instigated the nullification controversy in 1833, again took the lead, publishing the Declaration of Causes for secession. That document declared that "the Union heretofore existing between this State and the other States of North America is dissolved." No economic grievances were mentioned; the Declaration of Causes indicted nonslaveholding states for denouncing "as sinful the institution of Slavery; they have permitted the open establishment among them of societies, whose avowed object is to disturb the peace of and eloign the property of the citizens of other States."[30] No sectional compromises could resolve the issue of slavery because they all perpetuated an institution at odds with the nation's self-image. The Civil War began at a time when the presidency was held by a person who was willing to prevent disunion and committed to halting the spread of slavery.

CHAPTER FIVE

Reconstructing the American Dream

B y 1861 slavery was deeply entrenched in the United States. Even among the institution's opponents, few called for its immediate aboli-tion. Most would have been satisfied to prevent its expansion into the American territories. When the South seceded from the Union, the nation was jarred from its complacent attitude. As the Civil War dragged on, victory became increasingly linked with permanent and uncompensated abolition.

After the war, newly ratified constitutional amendments provided the federal government with an increased mandate to protect fundamental rights. The Thirteenth Amendment reversed *Dred Scott,* abolishing slavery and giv-ing Congress discretionary power to end any remaining incidents of involun-tary servitude. Reconstruction efforts, however, met significant resistance from President Andrew Johnson. In response to his repeated vetoes, the Fourteenth Amendment explicitly guaranteed the rights of citizens to due process and the equal protection of laws. And the Fifteenth Amendment increased political participation.

For a brief period of time, the Radical Republicans who had taken the reins of national power valiantly tried to build an inclusive society. After Reconstruction, however, it became clear that their efforts to end racial dis-crimination were only partly successful.

Growth of a Leader: Abraham Lincoln

Lincoln opposed slavery throughout his adulthood. In May 1831, at the age of twenty-two, he witnessed "negroes in chains—whipped and scourged." Walking with two other friends, he saw a slave woman groped on an auction block. He then announced his intent to hit hard at slavery. In the Illinois legislature he publicly stated in 1837 that slavery was an injustice and bad policy. To a Cincinnati audience on May 6, 1842, he declared that a true democracy could not deny blacks the right to suffrage. "All legal distinction between individuals of the same community, founded in any such circum-stances as color, origin, and the like, are hostile to the genius of our insti-tutions, and incompatible with the true history of American liberty. Slav-ery and oppression must cease, or American liberty must perish." During his one term in the House of Representatives, Lincoln voted for the Wilmot Proviso, which would have prohibited slavery in lands Mexico ceded after the Mexican-American War. Then in 1849 he unsuccessfully moved that a House committee report a bill for the gradual and compensated emancipation of slaves in the District of Columbia.[1]

He dropped out of national politics until strong sentiments against the Kansas-Nebraska Act drove him back to it. At that point, he resorted to the political expedient of renouncing slavery in the territories while announcing his unwillingness to interfere with it in the southern states. In October 1854, while stumping for legislators opposed to the act, Lincoln debated Senator Stephen A. Douglas, the principal architect of the law, in Springfield and Peoria, Illinois.

In Peoria, Lincoln asserted that at the core of civil rights protections was the American high regard for human nature. The repeal of the Missouri Compromise by the Kansas-Nebraska Act could not legitimize slavery. The Declaration of Independence made natural equality a basic article of Ameri-can identity that was averse to enslaving fellow persons. Every member of the polity deserved "an equal voice in the government," said Lincoln, maintain-ing his earlier view on self-determination. He would not, however, take the morally unequivocal stances of Charles Sumner, Wendell Phillips, and Fred-erick Douglass. Instead, Lincoln made statements to bring in votes: "Let it not be said that I am contending for the establishment of political and social equality between the whites and blacks." As a solution to slavery he preferred deporting freed blacks to Liberia and now opposed abolishing the institution in the District of Columbia, even though he thought the Constitution granted Congress the power to do so. Furthermore, a fugitive slave law that provided adequate protections against the kidnapping of free blacks would have met Lincoln's constitutional frame of reference. These political state-ments were out of step with many in the Republican Party, which Lincoln joined in 1856.

His views differed even more from those of Garrisonian abolitionists,

who were uncompromising about universal, immediate freedom. Garrisonians' refusal to make any concessions to the prejudices of the white majority
kept them out of politics. They preferred disunion to gaining votes by aban-
doning equality principles. The Lincoln of the 1850s, on the other hand,
emphasized his affinity to national unity above his sincere hatred of slavery: "I
would consent to the extension of it rather than see the Union dissolved, just
as I would consent to any great evil to avoid a greater one." During his
presidency, before issuing the Emancipation Proclamation, Lincoln continued to believe that national unity should not be sacrificed for the sake of
abolition. Despite his legalisms and political preferences, he worked ar-
duously against slavery. Nor did he give credence to white claims of superiority based on color, intellect, and interest, as he made clear in another 1854
statement, recognizing that white self-aggrandizements were just as unsub-
stantiated as black ones would be.[2]

In public, especially during his run for the Senate in 1858, Lincoln continued to attack slavery but called only for its gradual demise. The contest was
for Douglas's Senate seat. Their debate often returned to slavery, as did so
many political conversations of the day. To join the Senate, Lincoln needed to
win the support of a southern Illinois electorate that often supported Douglas's overt racism. In one oratorical flourish, Douglas asked the audience,
"Now, I ask you, are you in favor of conferring upon the negro the rights and
privileges of citizenship?" "No, no," replied the audience. Douglas drew a
picture of abolition amounting to an open floodgate of blacks flowing into
Illinois. He blamed Lincoln, and other so-called Black Republicans, for seeking to include blacks on juries and in government. Douglas received a warm
reception from an audience who worried that blacks would take their jobs and
dilute their political voice. "For one," Douglas assured them, "I am opposed
to negro citizenship in any form." This reference to the *Dred Scott* decision
drew cheers. "I believe that this government was made on the white basis," he
said, to which the crowd shouted, "Good." "I believe it was made by white
men for the benefit of white men and their posterity forever, and I am in favor
of confining the citizenship to white men—men of European birth and European descent, instead of conferring it upon Negroes and Indians, and other
inferior races."[3]

Lincoln's response to Douglas set him apart from abolitionists like Elijah
P. Lovejoy and Joshua R. Giddings. Unlike them, Lincoln was willing to
adopt office-seeking rhetoric as a means of ending the "monstrous injustice"
of slavery. In order to curry political support, Lincoln was willing to indulge

his audience. He first asserted the continued vitality of "all the natural rights enumerated in the Declaration of Independence, the right to life, liberty, and the pursuit of happiness." He agreed with Douglas that blacks were "not my equal in many respects" but went on to qualify his answer with "certainly not in color, perhaps not in moral or intellectual endowment." This left Lincoln with the latitude to argue on behalf of black labor and property rights: "In the right to eat the bread, without leave of anybody else, which his own hand earns, he is my equal and the equal of Judge Douglas, and the equal of every living man." Lincoln lost the 1858 bid for Senate despite his conciliatory language; on the other hand, had he expressed an immediatist position during his debates with Douglas, Lincoln might have committed political suicide and never have become the "Great Emancipator."[4]

According to one study, the unifying theme of Lincoln's 175 speeches from 1854 until his nomination for president in 1860 was opposition to the expansion of slavery. Throughout that time, he maintained a moderate enough rhetoric to make him a viable presidential candidate. But even his approach of not obtruding on the existing forced labor customs of the South while deriding the institution of slavery was too radical for the majority of the country. Despite his moderation, Lincoln's presidential victory in 1860, with only 40 percent of the popular vote, was possible only because a political schism between the supporters of Douglas and of John C. Breckinridge fractured the Democratic Party.[5]

Secession embroiled the nation almost immediately upon Lincoln's election to the executive mansion. True to his youthful attempts at compromise, the president tried to move slowly on the most divisive of national issues. He backed an amendment to the Constitution, which both houses of Congress passed for state ratification, that would have prohibited changes "to the Constitution which will authorize or give Congress the power to abolish or interfere" with state slavery laws. Three states—Ohio and Maryland by state conventions and Illinois by constitutional convention—eventually ratified the amendment. The Confederate guns that fired at Fort Sumter on April 12, heralding the beginning of the Civil War, stunted the ratification process and quieted the conventional wisdom that appeasement would maintain intersectional harmony.[6]

Even with deaths mounting on both sides of the struggle, Lincoln's first reaction was to continue on Clay's compromising path. The newly elected president attempted to avoid further splitting the country. During the early months of the war, Lincoln showed more caution than some of the generals under his command. For instance, Major General John C. Frémont issued a military proclamation on August 30, 1861, to free the slaves of Missouri's Confederates. Lincoln ordered Frémont to alter his edict and to rely instead on Congress's Confiscation Act of August 6 authorizing the taking of property, including slaves, used for insurrection.[7]

Lincoln wanted to lead any executive branch efforts rather than have his generals dictate the pace. On March 6, 1862, he proposed a joint congressional resolution for a gradual and compensated emancipation. His proposal, like any other to pay for slaves, was objectionable to abolitionists since it implicitly recognized slavery as a legitimate form of property whose loss had to be compensated. Congress, on the other hand, had no qualm about acceding to the president's request, passing the measure on April 10, 1862.[8]

Before Lincoln could act on his new power, General David Hunter issued a May 9 resolution forever freeing slaves in areas under his command in Georgia, Florida, and South Carolina. But Lincoln nullified Hunter's incentive, still hoping to end the conflict solely through negotiation.[9]

On July 12, at a White House meeting, the president tried to convince congressmen from Delaware, Maryland, western Virginia, Kentucky, and Missouri to accept his gradual compensation plan. After being frustrated in that attempt, Lincoln finally realized that slaveholders had such a consuming interest in maintaining their ownership interests that unilateral action would be essential to Union victory.[10]

Congress kept charging ahead of the president. In a show of support for Frémont and Hunter, it passed the Second Confiscation Act of July 17, 1862, declaring that the escaped and captured slaves of anyone involved in the rebellion were "forever free." Perpetual freedom was also decreed on any land occupied by the Union that had formerly been under the charge of the Confederacy. The same day, the Militia Act authorized the president to use the ex-slaves of Confederates to suppress the rebellion and granted them and their families freedom. Legislators also abolished slavery in the territories and freed slaves in the District of Columbia. Though these gains were substantial, they were all framed in terms of military necessity rather than as a civil duty to safeguard blacks' natural freedoms.[11]

Lincoln's views on slavery never assumed radical form, but through the war years he became increasingly intolerant of political bargains with the supporters of slavery. At the early stages of the war, Lincoln relied on Congress to end slavery in areas under military rule. He was, at first, careful not to alienate slaveholders in Kentucky, Missouri, Delaware, and Maryland, which had not joined the Confederacy. His primary concern then was keeping the Union intact, as he made clear in an August 22, 1862, letter to the *New York Tribune* editor, Horace Greeley. Yet his statement on the priority of saving the Union fell on deaf ears. Unlike former Senator Henry Clay, a slaveholder himself who had struggled to find a middle ground between the North and South during the Compromises of 1820 and 1850, Lincoln began contemplating the possibility of achieving his lifelong dream to end slavery. He was willing to make it a reality only if ending the institution would help save the Union.[12]

On July 13, the same day Lincoln received the negative response from the border-state delegation, he met with Secretary of the Navy Gideon Welles and Secretary of State William H. Seward and told them that he was finished negotiating on slavery. Lincoln had decided that if the war dragged on, liberating slaves would be both a "necessity and a duty on our part." Military victory depended on it. The obligation arose under the Declaration of Independence. This decision was a significant departure for Lincoln, who had previously told the cabinet that the federal government lacked any constitutional authority for "emancipation or interference with slavery in the States." When Lincoln presented the proposal to the cabinet on July 22, only Postmaster General Montgomery Blair cautioned against issuing it, fearing that it would bring defeat to Republicans in the 1864 presidential election. Seward approved of the measure, but observed that at a time when the North had suffered a string of defeats, the public could view the Proclamation as "consequent upon our repeated reverses." This consideration had eluded Lincoln, and he decided to wait for significant "military success, instead of issuing it" on the heels of the "greatest disasters of war."[13]

For slaves who lived within the Confederacy, it may have been better that Lincoln held off the Proclamation. They could, to a limited extent, already rely on the Second Confiscation Act, which as of July 17 had declared them to be forever free. The first draft of the Emancipation Proclamation, which Lincoln had been ready to issue after the cabinet meeting, provided only for gradual compensated manumission. That version would have put into doubt the federal government's determination that slavery violated fundamental rights that no property interests could infringe. The added time between his meeting with cabinet members and the issuing of the Proclamation allowed Lincoln to alter it periodically.

After a Union victory at Antietam on September 17, 1862, Lincoln decided to move ahead with greater certainty. He again consulted his cabinet, then issued the Emancipation Proclamation on January 1, 1863. The final version had no mention of compensation to slaveholders; rather, it provided that "all persons held as slaves within any State or designated part of the State, the people whereof shall be in rebellion against the United States, shall be then, thenceforward, and forever free." The Proclamation also demonstrated Lincoln's matured understanding that colonization would be an injustice to blacks, especially those who had fought in the Union ranks. Black rejection of the colonization plan, which he had proposed as recently as August 14, 1862, informed him that he was asking the victims of injustice to give up their homes for an uncertain promise of distant democracy.[14]

Lincoln had finally come to understand that the chief aim of the Civil War had to be ending the suffering of individual slaves and living up to the ideals the country had first espoused during the American Revolution. The Proclamation was also a critical tool for recruiting black soldiers because it evinced the country's commitment to freedom. Eventually, more than 179,000 black men enlisted to fight for their own future and for the common good of a country united by the pursuit of equality. Lincoln had used the military necessity to do what he considered to be just, to put slavery on the run. At the conclusion of the Proclamation, he explained that he "sincerely believed" it "to be an act of justice, warranted by the Constitution, upon military necessity." The Proclamation left the impression that the chief aim of keeping the Union intact was putting an end to slavery. Lincoln must have realized the profound novelty of the Proclamation to a nation whose federalist system, with a dual national and state sovereignty, had left civil rights in state hands. Here was a federal mandate that refused to recognize that state laws about the ownership of slaves could trump the intrinsic fairness of liberating people who had been exploited for centuries without political recourse. The Proclamation hit at the South's most important property with uncompromising national resolve.

The Proclamation focused the war on a clear moral objective. Lincoln believed that the Constitution limited his military authority as commander in chief to freeing slaves who were residing in states that were in rebellion. The Proclamation left slavery untouched in the loyal border states—Delaware, Maryland, Kentucky, and Missouri—and several enumerated places: Virginia counties that within a year would become West Virginia; parts of eastern Virginia, including Norfolk; several parishes of Louisiana, including New Orleans; and Tennessee, which was already under Union control. Still, it freed significantly more persons than the Second Confiscation Act, which extended only to the slaves of persons participating in the Confederate Army or government.

The Proclamation's primary import was as an articulation of the resolve to end slavery. It was only a first step, but as sure a death blow to chattel slavery as the Declaration of Independence had been to political slavery. While many slaves did not hear of the Emancipation Proclamation, those who did were emboldened to escape and in turn encouraged others.

Advocates of civil rights did not achieve the victory they had dreamed of from the Proclamation; nevertheless, it offered hope to hundreds of thousands of people who began to see light at the end of a 250-year-long tunnel of government-supported tyranny. It rejuvenated abolitionists, who reaped some success after decades of frustrating advocacy, though reaction to the Proclamation was not uniformly supported by those who had been committed to antislavery efforts.

Lincoln drew attention to the monumental nature of the Proclamation by handing the pen to one of the leaders of radicalism, Senator Sumner. Outside Congress, Douglass called the Proclamation's issuance "the greatest event of our nation's history if not the greatest event of the century." But he cautioned that "slavery was not declared abolished everywhere in the Republic." Samuel May, Jr., also felt a sense of elation coupled with concern, saying that he would not "stop to criticize now, and say this freedom ought (as indeed it ought) to have been made immediate, that it ought to have been proclaimed (as it ought) seventeen months ago. . . . I cannot stop to dwell on these. Joy, gratitude, thanksgiving, renewed hope and courage fill my soul." William Lloyd Garrison was initially cautious, because he had hoped that the end of slavery would come immediately and everywhere, but he soon came to regard Lincoln as the only realistic prospect for abolitionist reform. The Proclamation, as Garrison saw it, was an unequivocal national decision in favor of "equal rights." The split between Garrison and Wendell Phillips arose partly over Lincoln's role in emancipation. Phillips thought that Lincoln remained ready to abandon blacks and the Emancipation Proclamation if this would promote national unity. Phillips was unsatisfied with anything short of an amendment guaranteeing that the national obligation to secure equal rights was beyond the reach of politics. For Phillips, the Proclamation had freed "the slaves but [ignored] the negro."[15]

Most of the Proclamation's states' rights opponents found different cause to attack it. The Illinois legislature declared it to be a "giant usurpation" and a "revolution in the social organization of Southern States." The Confederacy looked upon the Proclamation as an act of total war. President Jefferson Davis of the Confederacy construed Lincoln's proclamation as an incitement to slave insurrection, aimed at unleashing an internal southern enemy.[16]

The Thirteenth Amendment

Once Lincoln decided to abandon the go-slow approach to freedom, he unhinged himself from the obligation to consult the South about the pace of civil rights reform. During the presidential campaign of 1864, Lincoln endorsed an amendment ending slavery. He influenced the process of abolition by putting it on the Republican Party agenda and gaining the support of key Democrats. Lincoln had taken a risk for freedom. His decision to stop placating the South inflamed John Wilkes Booth and led to his assassination.[17]

Congress began initiating civil rights efforts even before the Constitution was modified. Before the ratification of the Thirteenth Amendment, legislators had twice (1864 and 1865) prohibited discrimination on Washington, D.C., streetcars. Both statutes demonstrated an aversion to segregation because it burdened American citizenship with racial handicaps. The Supreme Court later found that the two laws were Congress's decision that "the colored and white race, in the use of the cars, be placed on an equality."[18]

The effort for a constitutional commitment to make slavery illegal began shortly after Lincoln issued the Proclamation. On December 14, 1863, Representatives James M. Ashley and James Wilson proposed separate constitutional amendments abolishing slavery. After some tinkering, the Senate Judiciary Committee adopted language that states later ratified, making it the Thirteenth Amendment to the United States Constitution: "Section 1. Neither slavery nor involuntary servitude, except as a punishment for crime whereof the party shall have been duly convicted, shall exist in the United States, or any place subject to their jurisdiction. Section 2. Congress shall have power to enforce this article by appropriate legislation." The amendment's first section was a prohibition against despotic private and state conduct, while the second section was a grant of national authority.

Sumner had wanted the amendment to provide that "all persons are equal before the law." That proposed language was not adopted because Radical Republicans like Senator Jacob Howard already thought equality to be intrinsic to abolition. Along the same lines, Congressman Isaac Arnold, one of Lincoln's confidants, asserted that the amendment would make "*equality be-*

fore the law . . . the great cornerstone" of government. It became apparent only later that Congress made the amendment less effective by excising Sumner's wording. The equality language could have provided Congress with a clearer mandate to end discriminatory practices, such as operating segregated public facilities.[19]

During congressional debates, even the sincerest supporters of abolitionism focused on the limits of congressional authority more than on defining the rights Congress would be able to protect. Visionary statements tended to be generalities because, so the thought went, the specifics could be worked out after ratification, through the legislative process. Senator James Harlan of Iowa, whose daughter married Robert Todd Lincoln, was keen on the amendment, believing that it would enable Congress to end state and local prohibitions against blacks serving on juries, owning property, and marrying. Senator Henry Wilson of Massachusetts, who considered slavery a system of racial subjugation and wrote a book on the subject, thought the amendment would change American racial practices. If incorporated into the Constitution, he declared, the amendment would "obliterate the last lingering vestiges of the slave system; its chattelizing, degrading, and bloody codes; its dark, malignant, barbarizing spirit; all it was and is, everything connected with it or pertaining to it."[20]

Wilson and other Radical Republicans emerged from the abolitionist tradition of relying on the Declaration of Independence and Preamble to the Constitution. An amendment to the Constitution would provide inviolable rights to all races on an equal footing. Americans expected "a practical application of that self-evident truth that [all men] are endowed by their creator with certain unalienable rights." They planned to use the proposed amendment's enforcement provision to pass laws furthering the Preamble's guarantees of life, liberty, and the general welfare. Illinois Representative Ebon C. Ingersoll, who was elected to fill Owen Lovejoy's seat, thought that only when people could freely benefit from their labors and enjoy marital rights were they "in a state of freedom." To his mind, the proposed amendment would not only free slaves: it would also apply to "the seven millions of poor white people" whom "slavery . . . kept . . . in ignorance, in poverty and in degradation."[21]

The amendment gave Congress the authority to end private and public acts associated with slavery. This scheme altered the working relationship between states and the federal government. The new provision to the Constitution precluded the states from violating nationally recognized civil rights.

Republicans made the decision that "a free nation" would be "untarnished by aught inconsistent with freedom." Individual rights had to be protected equally throughout the entire country. The source of those rights was the "great charter of liberty given to them by the American people." Passage of the amendment, said a Pennsylvania representative, would give each citizen, regardless of his social station, fundamental rights and immunities, including the rights to enter into a contract; sue; testify in court; and inherit, purchase, lease, hold, and convey real property. This view overlapped with those of others, like Senator Harlan's and Iowa Representative John A. Kasson's. They too spoke of the Thirteenth Amendment as a means to pass national laws against unfair restrictions on family, property, and judicial autonomy.[22]

The proposal's opponents were well aware of the fundamental change it sought. The outspoken Kentucky Representative Robert Mallory warned that the amendment would make African Americans "American citizens" whose interests would be represented in Congress, and he upbraided Republicans for wanting freedom to lead to racial equality. Congressmen who supported the Union but considered abolition an infringement on property rights and state sovereignty argued that the proposal would antagonize the South and prolong the Civil War.[23]

By then, however, interest in civil rights was snowballing because many felt that the loyalty of black troops had to be rewarded. For example, the National Loyal Women's League gathered four hundred thousand signatures on a petition supporting a constitutional amendment freeing slaves.[24]

On January 31, 1865, an "uncontrollable outburst" greeted the passage of the joint congressional resolution to end slavery. Representatives in the House well and spectators in the galleries joined in the exuberance. Lincoln expressed his joy by—quite unnecessarily—signing the resolution. About ten months later, on December 6, the states ratified the Thirteenth Amendment. Shortly thereafter, on Dec. 18, Secretary of State William H. Seward proclaimed its addition to the Constitution.[25]

On the Heels of Abolition

On April 11, 1865, two days after General Robert E. Lee surrendered to General Ulysses S. Grant at Appomattox Court House, Virginia, Lincoln gave a speech that provided a snippet of his plan to reconstruct the South. He spoke about conferring voting rights "on the very intelligent, and on those who served our cause as soldiers." This so angered Booth, who was in the audience, along with coconspirators Lewis Paine (also known as Lewis Pow- ell) and David Herold, that on April 14, Booth fatally shot Lincoln at Ford's Theatre.

But the hope of equal freedom could not die with Lincoln; indeed, it had become part of the American ethos before the Continental Congress approved the Declaration of Independence. After the ratification of the Thirteenth Amendment, Congress began using its newly granted power over civil rights. The new president, Andrew Johnson, on the other hand, never tried to match his predecessor's vision.

Constitutional abolition offered newly freed persons unbounded hope. Finally freed of the shackles of forced servility, they often found the first tastes of freedom rapturous. Years later, Charlotte Brown recalled her first free Sunday: "We was all sittin' roun' restin' an' tryin' to think what freedom meant an' ev'ybody was quiet an' peaceful. All at once ole Sister Carrie who was near 'bout a hundred started in to talkin': 'Tain't no mo' sellin' today, / Tain't no mo' hirin' today, / Tain't no pullin' off shirts today, / Its stomp down freedom today. / Stomp it down!' An when she says, 'Stomp it down,' all de slaves commence to shoutin' wid her. . . . Wasn't no mo' peace dat Sunday. Ev'ybody started in to sing an' shout once mo'. . . . Chile, dat was one glorious time." Another ex-slave explained the drastic change in labor conditions: Her former master "never was mean to us after freedom. He was 'fraid the niggers might kill him." Black laborers refused to accept corporal punishment, asserting their sense of dignity by quitting and searching for work elsewhere or entering into sharecropping arrangements. Tens of thousands of African American families purchased land at depressed prices, earning an independent livelihood.[26]

Many freedpeople walked away from the homes of their captivity, hoping to find work elsewhere. Some took long deserved vacations. Freedom allowed them to enjoy the company of neighbors from other farms, whom they had been prohibited from visiting without a master's permission. Family members wandered the countryside searching for loved ones who had been sold away or leased to work at a great distance. Others simply wished to see places, like cities or plantation houses, that had previously been off limits to them. Those who were religious or politically active gathered in numbers that slave codes had prohibited.[27]

Schools and ministries taught children and adults whose potential had been stunted through legally enforced ignorance. All slave states except Tennessee, Maryland, and Kentucky had prohibited anyone from instructing slaves. Typical antebellum laws in the South fined anyone who educated blacks, regardless of whether they were enslaved or free. Georgia and North Carolina punished instructors with imprisonment, fines, and whippings. The public in these states equated literacy with an increased risk of slave insurrection or a higher incidence of fraudulent travel passes. While some owners violated these laws by giving their slaves private lessons, usually out of religious conviction, in 1860 more than 90 percent of all adult southern blacks were illiterate. Those who were literate typically had learned as children from young white playmates, siblings, and teachers. Some literate slaves went on to be renowned leaders, like the political activist Frederick Douglass and Lane College founder Isaac Lane.

After the Civil War, the Freedmen's Bureau and benevolence societies ran schools that helped ex-slaves compete in the job market. Education provided blacks with a chance at economic parity with whites. Ex-slaves and abolitionists built, taught, and funded schools, recognizing forced ignorance to be a surmountable incident of servitude. Hundreds of thousands of black children attended school in the postbellum South. In North Carolina alone, northern societies and religious organizations run by Quakers, Episcopalians, and Presbyterians enrolled 11,826 students. The Freedmen's Bureau, working in the same state, ran 431 schools with the help of 439 teachers who instructed about 20,000 pupils. In Alabama the Bureau provided protection and transportation for northern teachers, disbursed funds for school construction or facility rental, and sometimes paid salaries. This helped 5,325 students receive instruction in sixty-eight day schools and twenty-seven night schools from seventy-five white and twenty black teachers. More than half the teachers who served black schools in the South were women. Despite these tremendous advances, most schools that the Bureau subsidized remained segregated.[28]

Roving gangs set fire to schoolhouses and attacked students and educators. Nor was vigilantism the only reason many black children found schools beyond their reach. Several states enacted child apprenticeship laws that bound children to service for a term of years, effectively making it impossible for them to get a formal education. White judges' assessments of the children's best interests supplanted parents' concerns for their education. Obtaining a court order for indenture was not difficult in a culture that downplayed black familial ties. One judge, for instance, was amazed that freedwomen had "a great antipathy to their children being apprenticed." Masters received parental authority over their apprenticed servants; they could even inflict corporal punishment and pursue runaways. In return for their services, masters were required to provide children with room and board and to teach them reading, writing, and a trade. Alabama legislators provided a one-dollar financial incentive to Alabama judges who issued indenture orders. Mississippi boys were apprenticed until their twenty-first birthday and girls until their eighteenth, with preference given to placing them with former masters. Blacks turned to local provost marshals and Freedmen's Bureau officials for help against child abductions. Jack Prince asked for help when a woman took his orphaned niece into bondage. Sally Hunter requested aid in gaining the release of her two nieces. A white friend wrote the Freedmen's Bureau on behalf of an illiterate woman seeking her indentured granddaughter's release. In 1867 Bureau officials began ordering the revocation of indenture contracts.[29]

Child indenture was just one of the many ways the South tried to exploit forced labor to circumvent the Thirteenth Amendment's prohibition against slavery. Efforts to maintain the status antebellum relied on state control over civil rights. Southern states enacted a series of laws, collectively known as black codes, that excluded blacks from the privileges of national citizenship. These laws curtailed movement, ownership, and labor rights. Some states confined blacks to manual labor by prohibiting them from purchasing land. Keeping farms out of black hands, in a society where land ownership meant political power, reduced their occupational options and limited their ability to influence public policy. Mississippi, for instance, prohibited African Americans from buying or leasing lands outside cities. A Louisiana law forbade selling or leasing land to freedpeople but required them to find homes within a certain number of days.[30]

The central purpose of the black codes was to maintain a subjugated labor class. Determined to force agricultural laborers to stay on plantations, particularly during harvesting seasons, and to keep them from seeking alternative opportunities, southerners passed laws enabling white employers to corner blacks into adhesion contracts. The disparity in bargaining power between employers and employees nullified the contract rights blacks had gained after abolition. Georgia required any black "servant" who worked more than a month for a "master" to sign a binding agreement. Any worker who quit before the expiration of his contract forfeited all his past wages and was subject to imprisonment and a five hundred–dollar fine. The Georgia statute treated employers altogether differently. They could fire laborers without pay because of "disobedience . . . immorality, and want of respect." This provided laborers no job security and bound them to indentured peonage. In Mississippi anyone who left an employer before the termination of a labor contract was subject to arrest and forfeiture of up to a year's worth of wages. A Major General Hatch told the Congressional Joint Committee of Fifteen, investigating southern postbellum behavior, that whites in Mississippi "wish to control the negro and his labor in such a way that he will be compelled to remain with them for never less than a year, and upon their own terms."[31]

Legal barriers to freedom were by no means the only hurdles blacks encountered after the Thirteenth Amendment's ratification. White supremacists relied on whippings and lynchings to keep blacks from leaving plantations and seeking work elsewhere. Southern whites had long defined their sense of self-worth partly in relation to a degraded view of blacks. White supremacists were intolerant toward blacks who refused to comply with antebellum etiquette: failing to call whites "masters," resistance to corporal punishment, and protection of family members could be met with merciless reprisal. The congressional record in 1865 also contains complaints detailing violence against abolitionists and other antislavery advocates. Many southern state officials either participated in the mayhem, encouraged it, or did nothing to prevent it. Between 1865 and 1866, lily-white juries in Texas acquitted all five hundred whites who were tried for murdering blacks.

Confederate soldiers turned their military experience to terrorizing, stealing, and coercing blacks and Republicans. Confederate General Nathan Bedford Forrest's Ku Klux Klan changed the course of southern politics by intimidating and murdering Republican voters; in 1869 and 1870 the Klan "redeemed" states like North Carolina, Virginia, and Georgia to the Democratic Party. The Freedmen's Bureau provided some measure of protection against Klan injustices but could not prevent all the assaults. The efforts of such Republican politicians as Tennessee Governor William G. Brownlow and Arkansas Governor Powell Clayton, both of whom were committed to stamping out the Klan, were not enough to counter the racism that had entrenched itself through generations of indoctrination and practice. Militant support reestablished old social and racial stratification.[32]

Congress tried to use its newly acquired power to address the domestic turmoil. During December 1865, as states were ratifying the Thirteenth Amendment, Congress began relying on its enforcement authority. Moderates and radicals in Congress agreed that the amendment granted them unprecedented power to act against slavery and its effects anywhere in the United States. States could no longer assert exclusive sovereignty over the liberty of their citizens. Dual sovereignty meant that Americans enjoyed privileges of federal citizenship that no state could trump. Radicals thought that the amendment empowered Congress to end any form of discrimination impinging on the general welfare, while moderates thought that it guaranteed only labor and property rights.

During the first stages of Reconstruction, radical politicians were able to push through several laws that began to address the centuries of countenanced prejudice. A series of bills were introduced, which, while they did not become law, showed a willingness on the part of some congressmen to punish employment discrimination, protect freedom of movement, recognize a right to education, and prohibit arbitrary arrest. Over the next couple of years, four statutes emerged to enforce the Thirteenth Amendment: the Civil Rights Act of 1866, the Slave Kidnaping Act of 1866, the Peonage Act of 1867, and the Judiciary Act of 1867.[33] These laws evinced a radical departure from antebellum legal thought. They granted legislative, judicial, and executive authority on matters that before the Civil War had been left to the discretion of state governments.

Of these four, the Civil Rights Act of 1866 had the most long-lasting impact on the nation, serving even today as an effective tool against discrimination in employment and real estate transactions. Congress passed the act in response to black code restrictions on contractual and property rights. Unlike the Freeman's Bureau Act, which was a temporary wartime measure with no application outside the rebel states, the Civil Rights Act's reach was national. In its initial form, the bill proposed to confer citizenship on all persons, except untaxed Native Americans, who inhabited the states or territories. The initial bill further guaranteed equal enjoyment of the privileges and immunities of citizenship. Republican leaders regarded national citizenship as a trump to southern interests in governing interracial relations between state citizens. The bill rejected the antebellum constitutional view that protections on individual rights were solely at the discretion of states. Freedom meant the equal enjoyment of national rights, and Congress could legislate against their abridgement. President Andrew Johnson's unexpected opposition to the bill required Republicans to moderate their demands, but they could never do so enough to satisfy Johnson's proclivity to pardon Confederates and his ambivalence to blacks.

Radicals hailed the Civil Rights Act as only the beginning of their plan to secure long-denied rights. They did not realize the extent to which moderates would thwart their efforts by the 1870s. But from the vantage of 1866, they seemed on the verge of transforming the government into what political abolitionists had envisioned.

The act of 1866 secured the right to "make and enforce contracts, to sue, be parties, and give evidence, to inherit, purchase, lease, sell, hold, and convey real and personal property." The statute further provided citizens with the "full and equal benefit of all laws and proceedings for the security of person and property . . . any law, statute, ordinance, regulation, or custom, to the contrary notwithstanding." It prohibited public and private acts of discrimination. Federal courts were authorized to exercise original jurisdiction over cases, but state courts could also hear causes of action arising under it. Litigants could remove cases from state to federal courts, if state laws infringed on federal rights. State officials who violated the act could be criminally prosecuted. All violators could be imprisoned for up to a year and fined no more than one thousand dollars. States retained concurrent authority to pass civil rights laws.[34]

The act's criminal provisions evidenced a radical notion of civil rights federalism. States retained exclusive jurisdiction over private conduct, involving civil, criminal, and transactional matters, but the federal government now asserted its jurisdiction to regulate matters affecting nationally recognized fundamental rights. States could enact varying tort, penal, and contract laws, but they could not exclude an entire class of persons from their protections.

The Thirteenth Amendment effectively gave Congress plenary power to decide which rights were intrinsic to American citizens. President Andrew Johnson tried to thwart congressional efforts by vetoing several proposed laws, including the Civil Rights Act of 1866. The supporters of Reconstruction were able to summon the necessary two-thirds majority to override only some of those vetoes. Congress's successful effort against Johnson's veto of the Civil Rights Act ended on April 9, 1866.[35]

Republicans shortly decided that the ambiguities inherent in the enormous power under the Thirteenth Amendment to end all incidents and badges of involuntary servitude made further constitutional clarification necessary. The year Congress enacted the Civil Rights Act, it began debating the merits of an additional amendment.

The Fourteenth Amendment

Congressional leaders expected the Thirteenth Amendment to provide the power needed to make states conform to the national standard of fundamental rights and general welfare. Only a year after its ratification, however, questions arose about whether the Thirteenth Amendment protected equal rights and guaranteed the privileges and immunities of national citizenship.

Debates on the Fourteenth Amendment often referred to the intent to place the Civil Rights Act of 1866 on more certain constitutional grounds against potential court challenges. More than a month before Congress overrode President Johnson's veto of the 1866 act, it began debating the wording for a more comprehensive amendment. Key language of the first section of the Fourteenth Amendment, which now secures equal protection, privileges and immunities, and due process of law, had not been included in the 1866 statute. Members of the Joint Committee of Fifteen on Reconstruction, like Thaddeus Stevens, John A. Bingham, William P. Fessenden, and Jacob M. Howard, wanted to extend national power over civil rights beyond the protections that were enumerated by the act. Their aim was to clarify and expand the grant of congressional enforcement authority in the Thirteenth Amendment.

The committee incorporated into its drafts phrases with unmistakably abolitionist overtones. Like the Declaration of Independence, the Fourteenth Amendment forced the nation to examine its practices against an ideal government that protected individual rights to increase overall welfare. The terms of the amendment were broad enough to provide for the federal protection of natural rights in the abolitionist tradition. The amendment's future reach went well beyond the contemporary sensibilities of the framers. Through the process of appellate reevaluation, judges of the twentieth and twentieth-first centuries would interpret the "due process" and "equal protection" clauses to cover the rights of women, racial minorities, disabled persons, and gays.[36]

The 1866 debates on the Fourteenth Amendment were not as expository about fundamental rights as had been those on the Thirteenth Amendment. Radicals had already been weakened. The compromise measure harnessed enough moderate votes to move the amendment to the states for ratification. The primary focus of the debates was on representation and voting rights, in the second section, and the disenfranchisement of Confederate participants, in the third section.[37]

As for the first section, it received noticeably less attention than others, even though in the twentieth and twenty-first centuries it would become the most important part of the amendment. The Joint Committee of Fifteen's initial proposal, submitted to Congress on February 26, 1866, provided that "Congress shall have power to make all laws which shall be necessary and proper to secure to the citizens of each State all privileges and immunities of citizens in the several States, and to all persons in the several States equal protection in the rights of life, liberty, and property." It placed power in Congress to decide what laws were necessary for prohibiting unequal treatment of U.S. citizens. Had it passed, this proposal would have ended the persistent debate about whether federal or state governments would have the ultimate responsibility to safeguard equal rights against local prejudices.[38]

This proposed break from antebellum federalism ruffled the political feathers of many congressmen, especially those who had voted against the Civil Rights Act of 1866. John A. Nicholson, for one, thought this initial proposal, of January 12, 1866, would entail a "great change" in the "entire structure of our Government." He argued that the balance between state and federal government would be undone; it was the state that was properly entrusted with powers over life, liberty, and property, not the federal government. Nicholson especially decried the equal protection part of the proposal: "They are not [the negro's] friends who are striving to thrust him up to the same level with the whites, when the inevitable result must be a war of races; nor are they true lovers of their country's weal, who for such an object are willing to strike down the power of the States and consolidate the Government into a centralized despotism." For Congressman Andrew Rogers, "no resolution proposing an amendment to the Constitution of the United States had been offered to this Congress more dangerous to the liberties of the people and the foundations of this government than the pending resolution."[39]

More indicative of the initially proposed Fourteenth Amendment's unlikelihood for passage was its rejection by some of the congressmen who supported the Civil Rights Act.[40] Representative Thomas T. Davis, for example, believed that the proposal violated constitutional principles of limited government. He complained that it was counterproductive to unity "to inflict needless and wanton injury upon the people of the South because they are not ready in a moment to surrender the pride or the prejudice of generations." On the other hand, Frederick E. Woodbridge, a radical from Vermont, would have no more to do with old-time complacency with inequality. He found the proposal structurally republican:

> What is the object of the proposed amendment? It merely gives the power to Congress to enact those laws which will give to a citizen of the United States the natural rights which necessarily pertain to citizenship. It is intended to enable Congress by its enactments when necessary to give to a citizen of the United States, in whatever State he may be, those privileges and immunities which are guarantied to him under the Constitution of the United States. It is intended to enable Congress to give all citizens the inalienable rights of life and liberty, and to every citizen in whatever State he may be that protection to his property which is extended to the other citizens of the State.

Another radical, however, did "not regard it as permanently securing" rights but thought that it left them to the uncertainties of the biannual changes in congressional composition and legislative priorities.

Representative Robert S. Hale, who abstained from voting for the Civil Rights Act in the first place but later voted to override Johnson's veto, regarded the originally proposed Fourteenth Amendment as a "provision under which all State legislation, in its codes of civil and criminal jurisprudence and procedure, affecting the individual citizen, may be overridden . . . and the law of Congress established instead." Stevens replied that Hale's statement was exaggerated. The proposal aimed only "to provide that, where any State makes a distinction in the same law between different classes of individuals, Congress shall have power to correct such discrimination and inequality."

It became evident to the Committee of Fifteen that even though a congressional majority probably could have been found to vote for the Joint Committee's initial proposal, it was unlikely to get the necessary two-thirds vote of both houses of Congress needed to pass it onto the states for ratification. Further consideration of Bingham's initial proposal was postponed and never revived.[41]

The Committee of Fifteen's next draft of section one of the proposed Fourteenth Amendment sought to preserve the original aim of providing federal authority to protect civil rights, but it was expressed by a negative formulation that was less likely to be construed, by congressmen in Hale's camp, as intrusive on states' right to regulate their citizens' conduct. Selecting acceptable wording was critical for increasing congressional support. The first section made "all persons born or naturalized in the United States" citizens both of the country and of their respective states. The next sentence provided that "no state shall make or enforce any law which shall abridge the privileges or immunities of citizens of the United States; nor shall any State deprive any person of life, liberty, or property, without due process of law; nor deny to any person within its jurisdiction the equal protection of the laws." The elimination of the original preface, "Congress shall have the power to make all laws which shall be necessary and proper to secure to the citizens of each State all privileges and immunities of citizens in the several States," allayed the concerns, which Woodbridge and Representative Giles W. Hotchkiss had expressed, that future Congresses might try to set a low threshold for the rights of citizenship. Opponents of the proposed amendment saw even the toned-down second proposal as dangerous to the existing order. "The first section proposes to make an equality in every respect between the two races, notwithstanding the policy of discrimination which has hitherto been exclusively exercised by the States," warned Democrat Samuel J. Randall.[42]

In hindsight, the committee's negative formulation—"no state shall make or enforce any law which shall abridge the privileges or immunities of citizens . . . "—allows the judiciary to constrain the amendment's scope and undermine the purposes of Reconstruction. The committee had heard testimony concerning the hurdles freedpeople were encountering in the South following abolition. Most of that testimony indicated that black codes, which were specific state actions, were not the only sources of continued discrimination. To the contrary, the committee understood from extensive testimony that private acts of terror and fraud made it impossible for blacks to obtain equal civil and political treatment.

State and local actors often refused to prevent discrimination and racial violence. A Freedmen's Bureau agent observed that "of the thousand cases of murder, robbery, and maltreatment of freedmen that have come before me, and of the very many cases of similar treatment of Union citizens in North Carolina, I have never yet known a single case in which the local authorities or police or citizens made any attempt or exhibited any inclination to redress any of these wrongs or to protect such persons." The problem was not a lack of generally applicable laws against violent and property crimes but the southern states' unwillingness to enforce the laws against bigoted perpetrators.[43]

The federal government was hence to protect U.S. citizens against indifference and abuse of state power. "Privileges and immunities of citizens," as Senator Jacob M. Howard of Michigan pointed out at the opening of the Senate debate, was a legal term of art that Justice Bushrod Washington had parsed in an 1823 civil rights case. Washington's formulation of fundamental principles went far beyond the explicit protections of the Bill of Rights, the first ten amendments to the Constitution, to the core of individual rights and the general welfare:

> Protection by the government; the enjoyment of life and liberty, with the right to acquire and possess property of every kind, and to pursue and obtain happiness and safety; subject nevertheless to such restraints as the government may justly prescribe for the general good of the whole. The right of a citizen of one state to pass through, or to reside in any other state, for purposes of trade, agriculture, professional pursuits, or otherwise; to claim the benefit of the writ of habeas corpus; to institute and maintain actions of any kind in the courts of the state; to take, hold and dispose of property, either real or personal; and an exemption from

higher taxes or impositions than are paid by the other citizens of the state . . . to which may be added, the elective franchise, as regulated and established by the laws or constitution of the state in which it is to be exercised.

The Fourteenth Amendment would make this nonexhaustive list of rights the inviolable birthright of Americans. Howard further pointed out that the privileges and immunities clause secured Congress's ability to enforce the Bill of Rights against the states, while the original Constitution made it applicable only to the federal government. This view of nationalized rights comported with Bingham's, who earlier had explained that the Bill of Rights would become applicable to the states under this proposed amendment.[44]

The Equal Protection Clause was part of this broader effort that was linked to emancipation and abolitionism before it. The wording of the clause is reminiscent of Sumner's losing argument in *Roberts v. City of Boston* (Supreme Judicial Court of Massachusetts, 1849), where he had argued that separate schools are intrinsically unequal.[45] Later, as we saw, Sumner had failed to convince his colleagues to add an equal protection clause into the Thirteenth Amendment. Only with the Fourteenth Amendment did equal protection of citizens become a constitutionally recognized value. The final version of the amendment was broad enough to give radicals hope of further desegregation and moderates comfort of continued property-oriented reforms.

Section five of the amendment gave Congress the power to enforce the first section's provisions. The national government received the power to provide standards and enact regulations against the unequal treatment of various classes of United States citizens. The Reconstruction Congress planned to pass national statutes prohibiting segregation and racial violence. The fifth section meant more than any immediate legislative proposals. It allowed Congress to act against infringements on those privileges and immunities that were necessary to the welfare of a populace composed of intrinsically equal individuals.

Even before the Fourteenth Amendment came into force, in July 1868, the Republicans began to split on what conditions to place on Confederate states for their readmission to good standing in the Union. The prevailing faction was conciliatory, determining to readmit southern states "if they adopt the constitutional amendment, and comply with the terms prescribed by the reconstruction Committee and adopted by Congress." A minority group of Republicans, which included Sumner and Stevens, considered ratification only an incremental step toward reconciliation. For radicals, no state could gain readmission unless it provided for real equality along with universal suffrage.[46]

To that end, Congress passed the Reconstruction Act of 1867, requiring that the then as-yet unadmitted rebel states adopt constitutions conforming to the United States Constitution. The act provided that the male citizens of states, without regard to their race, color, or previous condition of servitude, pick delegates to state constitutional conventions. Some white southerners were to be disqualified from participating because of their past ties to the Confederate government. Additional guarantees on interracial political participation were included in other statutes on admitting Arkansas, North Carolina, South Carolina, Louisiana, Georgia, Alabama, and Florida. The states were never to amend or change their constitutions to deprive any class of citizens, other than criminals, the right to vote.

These steps to suffrage were only partly successful and did nothing to cure women's political disempowerment. Furthermore, they applied only to states that had been in rebellion without doing away with northern disenfranchisement. Another two constitutional amendments, the Fifteenth and Nineteenth, would be needed to more effectively protect voting rights.[47]

The Fifteenth Amendment and Suffrage Rights

Many Republicans thought that securing blacks the right to vote would be the crowning achievement of Reconstruction. Congressional leaders expected voting to enable blacks to elect representatives willing to further fundamental rights. Politicians would not dare to offend an important constituency whose support they would need for reelection, so the argument went; therefore government officials would be dependent on black voters. From the vantage point of 1869, as Congress crafted the language of the future Fifteenth Amendment, it simply could not have know that the Herculean effort would fail to shatter centuries of prejudice and racial oppression.

Even before ratification of the Fourteenth Amendment, moderate and radical Republican congressmen understood President Johnson to be politically unreliable. He showed as little enthusiasm for helping blacks secure suffrage as he showed for protecting their rights to due process and equal protection. In 1865 black citizens from South Carolina had requested Johnson's help in securing the right to vote. They brought to his attention that where only the white class has the power to tax and legislate it "distroys the safeguard of the disenfranchised, and undermines the piller of civil liberty upon which rests . . . prosperity happiness and improvement." The petitioners demanded respect for having "been tested before the Eyes of the World on many a hard fought battle field for the Restoration of the Union." Another supporter of black suffrage implored Johnson to use his military power to grant blacks "the franchise for their protection" against rebels planning to "wreak revenge on loyal blacks." He also pointed out that enfranchising southern blacks would provide Republicans with "850,000 *loyal votes that are always sure.*"[48]

Johnson's lenient treatment of Confederate leaders stood in stark contrast to his unsympathetic treatment of blacks. He had placed "loyal people" at the "*absolute* control of Rebels," wrote a New Yorker, by putting the "ballot into the hands of Rebels" while denying "it to loyal men who have fought for the *right of Suferage.*" J. Rhodes Mayo accused Johnson of allowing former rebels and "states rights-men," who have "intense hatred, or at least prejudice" toward African Americans, to reconstruct southern governments. The only solution, wrote another, was "to give the *Loyal* inhabitants . . . the protection of the *ballot.*"[49]

With Johnson unwilling to help, Congress sprang into action. It first passed the Reconstruction Act of 1867, but that helped only southern blacks gain the vote, while most northern blacks remained disenfranchised. Blacks in many northern states also required federal support. By 1860 they had equal access to the ballot box only in Massachusetts, New Hampshire, Vermont, Rhode Island, and Maine. Only 6 percent of the northern black population lived in those states, leaving the rest disenfranchised. New York had a discriminatory property and residency requirement, while the vote was entirely denied to blacks living in New Jersey, Pennsylvania, and Connecticut. By 1869 Wisconsin, Iowa, Minnesota, and Nebraska also granted blacks voting rights. These achievements were too intermittent for persons committed to full, immediate citizenship rights. Only an amendment could achieve nationwide change.[50]

Republican Party leaders anticipated white resistance to black suffrage in both sections of the country, but they determined to seize on the Union's victory to proceed with political reform. After the 1868 election, however, the Republican Party reduced its voting power by dividing into Liberal and Radical branches. The Liberals supported reconciliation, while the Radicals continued to press for complete equality. Their split made it impossible to pass a proposed amendment guaranteeing the universal right to suffrage.

The motivations behind the Fifteenth Amendment were partly pragmatic. Republicans hoped that gaining black votes would help them retain control of Congress against a resurgent Democratic Party. But to attribute no more than self-interest to those who struggled to gain voting equality disparages their sincere desire to exclude race as a criterion for political participation.

The desire to expand the franchise sprang from the same impulse to equality that had moved revolutionaries to fight for their political rights, abolitionists to struggle to end racial injustice, and the Republicans to pass the two earlier amendments meant to secure liberal equality. Future president James Garfield gave voice to a commonly held conviction: "I believe that the right to vote, if it be not indeed one of the natural rights of all men, is so necessary to the protection of their natural rights as to be indispensable, and therefore equal to natural rights." Yet he and other party leaders like James Blaine understood they would face northern and southern opposition.[51]

By the late 1860s it had become clear that Republicans might alienate more voters than they could gain by forging ahead with the suffrage drive. The historian William Gillette's contention that the amendment's proponents were "primarily" intent on gaining black votes for the Republican Party is belied by the losses the party experienced. LaWanda and John H. Cox's research revealed that from 1865 to 1869 referenda to enfranchise blacks were unsuccessful in six of eight northern states, passing only in Iowa and Minnesota. That should have given Republican leaders pause if the campaign for suffrage were primarily pragmatical, since the results demonstrated a lack of northern consensus for ending political prejudice. Moreover, the Coxes revealed that gaining the vote for blacks in northern states where they composed a small segment of the population—3.4 percent in New Jersey and 2.4 percent in Ohio—would probably have decreased overall party support. For each black vote the party gained, it stood to lose many more white votes.[52] The Coxes' thesis is borne out by the Democrats' retaking control of the House in 1874, after the Fifteenth Amendment had been ratified; Democratic support in northern urban areas demonstrated that the decision to pursue political reform had not secured Republican dominance. From that election, Reconstruction began its decline, and any arguments on its behalf became less influential.

In this unpredictable climate, it took devotion to the cause of freedom to pursue a voting rights amendment. For radicals, especially, but for other supporters of suffrage as well, strengthening the party was not an empty concept. It meant being able to pass more laws on the basis of the Thirteenth and Fourteenth Amendments. Additional Republican voters could help elect politicians whose agenda included civil rights. Those who would win elective offices would be answerable to an electorate personally interested in equality. And even if the continued pursuit of reform would bring on Republican electoral loss, the amendment would prevent statutory repeal of voting rights.

Most prominent supporters of suffrage, like Congressman George S. Boutwell, aimed to "secure universal suffrage to all adult male citizens of this county." Several versions of the proposed amendment were floated in Congress. Some of them would have stripped states of the power to delimit voting qualifications. An Ohio representative suggested that the amendment prohibit states from abridging the right of "any male citizens . . . of the age of twenty-one years or over" to have "equal vote at all elections." Representative George W. Julian of Indiana was well ahead of his time, pressing for political gender equality. He proposed that all U.S. citizens twenty-one years of age or older and of sound mind enjoy the right of suffrage "equally, irrespective of sex." Senator Samuel C. Pomeroy suggested that "the right of citizens of the United States to vote and hold office shall not be denied or abridged by the United States or any State for any reasons not equally applicable to all citizens of the United States."[53]

These formulations did not get enough support, and compromises had to be made. The ratified amendment vastly increased the number of people eligible to vote. It put the supporters of political local autonomy on their heels. It prohibited the use of three commonly used exclusionary categories: race, color, and prior condition of servitude. For all that, it was a valiantly flawed effort; it lacked any prohibition against the use of property and literacy voting qualifications.

Several congressmen, like Senators Willard Warner of Alabama, Oliver P. Morton of Indiana, and Henry Wilson of Massachusetts, warned that including only three criteria in the amendment would make it possible for the South to hide behind facially neutral laws that would be applied to keep blacks from voting and holding elective offices.[54] These fears were not idle, as the Fifteenth Amendment would be easy to thwart. Its shortcomings wound up severely undercutting its very purpose.

Had Congress enacted a more inclusive version of the amendment, states might have been unable to use arbitrary characteristics to deny adult citizens the right to vote. As it stood, states could disqualify persons for any characteristics except the three specified. The concerns of women, illiterates, and unpropertied persons were entirely disregarded, and they were left outside the national tent.[55]

Since the Jacksonian era feminist abolitionists, like the Grimké sisters and Lucretia Mott, had relied on equal rights ideology. Feminists looked upon suffrage as a critical means of lobbying on issues like domestic violence, temperance, and unequal economic conditions. Having lost the battle over adding "gender" to the Fifteenth Amendment, in 1871 Julian referred Victoria Woodhull's petition to the House Judiciary Committee. Woodhull requested that Congress enact a declaratory law to "secure to citizens . . . in the several States the right to vote 'without regard of sex'" pursuant to "the fourteenth amendment of the Constitution." The committee majority, with Bingham reporting its conclusion, resolved that it was powerless to require states to grant women the vote. Except in matters of race, color, or previous condition of servitude, voter qualification was a matter of state law. The minority report, on the other hand, was not so cavalier. It found that denying women the vote was an injustice that violated their equal right under the Fourteenth Amendment to the privileges of citizenship. Denying female citizens the right to vote, said the minority, was just as arbitrary as denying all redheads or six-foot-tall men that privilege. Voting was essential for citizens to select rulers; otherwise, despots would be given free rein. Excluding women from suffrage, according to the minority report, does not "'secure the blessings of liberty to ourselves and our posterity,'" which the Preamble sets as a purpose of government, instead depriving "one-half the citizens of adult age of this right and privilege." One year later, Elizabeth Cady Stanton, Susan B. Anthony, and others convinced the Senate Judiciary Committee to consider passing a law protecting women's right to elective franchise. After deliberation, the committee refused to act on the request, finding that denying women the right to vote did not violate the Fourteenth Amendment. It would take forty-eight more years, until 1920, for women to finally secure voting privileges.[56]

Quelling Racial Violence by Federal Enforcement

After passing the Reconstruction Amendments, Congress did not rest. To the contrary, it enacted additional laws meant to prohibit private acts of discrimination. These were critical because of the rampant violence perpetrated by terrorist groups like the Ku Klux Klan. The Klan was a white supremacist organization whose members dressed in white sheets to portray the ghosts of Confederate soldiers. The organization often enjoyed the support of local politicians, who ignored or participated in its violence.

Reports informed Congress of the Klan's atrocities. In Texas a black laborer named Jenkins filled out a criminal complaint after his employer had him severely whipped. When Jenkins walked out from the grand jury hearing, four men followed and murdered him. The story does not end there, and its sequel shows how difficult it was to obtain justice against vigilantes in the South. When brought before a court, the four men accused of committing the murder tried to intimidate the judge and district attorney, neither of whom abandoned his duty. After their conviction, just as the men were to be taken to jail, their friends fired off forty to fifty shots in the courtroom, enabling the convicts to escape. The gunfire caused many casualties. Throughout the South, Republican politicians, particularly African American ones, were at grave risk. In one case, an assailant killed Abe Turner, a "Negro Legislator."[57]

Many other reports of the crime wave came from high-ranking generals, who supplied names, dates, times, and circumstances of murders. General Joseph B. Kiddoo provided a report about happenings in Texas. On May 30, 1866, he reported the "willful murder of a freedman, Martin Cromwell," at the hands of his former master's son. Other descriptions are even more detailed: "Killed because he did not take off his hat to Murphy," and "Shot him as he was passing in the street to 'see him kick.'" In a case reported by Major General Joseph A. Mower, who was stationed in Louisiana, Martin Day answered a white boy "quickly." White men then dragged Day through town, stripped him, and choked him with a rope, but state authorities "took no notice of the affair." Atrocities were not, however, ubiquitous throughout the South; a colonel in Florida reported that violence against freedmen was a "rare occurrence." Some of the Klan activity was politically motivated. Klansmen in Laurens County, South Carolina, rode the countryside threatening blacks not to vote. On election day in 1868, armed whites in South Carolina drove blacks from polls, making a deep gouge in the votes cast for the Republican Party. That state's 1870 election was likewise wracked by violence.[58]

With President Ulysses S. Grant's support, Congress adopted three laws in response to the violence. The first Enforcement Act, passed in May 1870, relied on the Fifteenth Amendment's grant of authority. It prohibited state elections officials and private parties from interfering with voters because of their race. Of even more significance, the act prohibited private conspiracies such as the Klan's, "upon the public highways, or upon the premises of another," to interfere with federally protected rights. Congress further reconfirmed the Civil Rights Act of 1866, this time under the Fourteenth Amendment. To police the Enforcement Act, Congress authorized the Department of Justice to file cases in federal courts.[59]

The Second Enforcement Act, of February 1871, provided for federal election supervisors to be stationed where voting irregularities were likely. When it did little to arrest the spread of terror, Republicans relied on the Fourteenth Amendment to pass the Third Enforcement Act, better known as the Ku Klux Klan Act of 1871. That statute made it unlawful to enter into conspiracies for depriving persons of their equal protection under the law. The law covered both safeguards of statutory and constitutional rights, which meant that in passing it Congress understood the Fourteenth Amendment to include all rights covered under the Bill of Rights and any positive laws. Of critical importance to the victims of conspiracies, the third statute created a private cause of action that could be litigated in federal courts. Federal prosecutors could also pursue criminal remedies. To prevent local groups from colluding to acquit terrorists, no one who had taken part in a conspiracy against the enjoyment of rights could later sit on a jury. The act also granted power to the chief executive to suspend habeas corpus for the sake of public safety.[60]

Debates over the Ku Klux Klan Act focused on federal criminal authority. Several congressmen sought to dispel the notion that conspiratorial violations of individual rights fell outside the federal government's realm of responsibility. Representative Bingham remembered choosing language for the Fourteenth Amendment that enabled Congress to criminalize the abridgement of rights like those secured by the First Amendment. Senator Frederick T. Frelinghuysen explained that without the possibility of federal criminal prosecution, states could circumvent the Constitution by refusing to bring charges for "systematic violations of citizens' privileges and immunities." States were responsible for individual crimes, as Frelinghuysen saw it, while Congress's obligation was to make laws against the unfair infringement of citizenship rights.[61]

The protection of civil rights was a departure from the deference that the national government had traditionally shown to state police authority. Opponents of the Ku Klux Klan Act played up the novelty of a national role in "endeavoring to protect personal rights." In an attempt to ground the act on traditional federal powers, Senator George F. Edmunds of Vermont maintained that the Constitution had always dealt "directly with the people" by "guarantying rights, regulating affairs, prohibiting action to States, and so it has . . . been applied to the people directly to effect its purposes and to defend its powers." On the other hand, Congressman James A. Garfield maintained, in defense of the law, that the Reconstruction Amendments had so "modified the Constitution as to change the relation of Congress to the citizens of the

States." The Fourteenth Amendment granted Congress the authority to end arbitrary subordination through racial violence.[62]

Once the Ku Klux Klan Act went into force, the army or Justice Department officials accompanied by the army began making arrests. The U.S. attorney general, Amos T. Akerman, was personally committed to bringing Klan members to justice. Seven hundred fifty people were indicted in a Klan raid on Rutherford, North Carolina. In all, 559 cases were filed under the Enforcement Acts. Randolph Shotwell, leader of the Rutherford County Klan, spent two years in an Albany, New York, penitentiary. In South Carolina, where President Grant suspended habeas corpus rights in nine counties found to be in a "condition of lawlessness," prosecutors achieved resounding success against terrorists. The Klan there used murder, numerous whippings, and much political intimidation. In November 1871, five defendants were tried and convicted and another forty-nine pleaded guilty. Akerman urged vigorous prosecution. Black participation on juries and an unexpected willingness of whites to testify against the Klan helped prosecutors succeed. Because of the large volume of cases and the overall restoration of order, Grant's next attorney general, George H. Williams, decided to discontinue the trials in the spring of 1873. The numerous convictions and the threat of imprisonment crushed the Klan and drastically reduced violence throughout the South.[63]

Civil Rights Act of 1875

Senator Charles Sumner weathered the storms of abolitionism to find himself in the seat of power during the heyday of hope. Few had his sustained energy for achieving equal rights. After the Civil War he was among a group of white abolitionists who continued the struggle to end the continued inferior treatment of blacks. In the midst of the Enforcement Act period, Sumner asked to refer a civil rights bill to the judiciary committee. His proposal was designed to "secure equal rights in railroads, steamboats, public conveyances, hotels, licensed theaters, houses of public entertainment, common schools and institutions of learning authorized by law, church institutions, and cemetery associations." Initial failure led him to redouble his efforts, and he again offered the bill in much the same form.

Segregation was becoming common. The practice was not nearly as widespread during the 1870s as it became in the early twentieth century, making its collapse feasible. In the postbellum world, segregation was most common in schools. Since literacy had so long been denied to southern blacks, developments in black education were met with a fierce demand for separate schools. The 1870 Tennessee Constitution provided for separation of races in education. Kentucky opted for statutory restrictions on student racial mixing. All African Americans, Sumner said, "resent the imputation" that they are "seeking to intrude . . . socially anywhere." Separate but equal public facilities, Sumner said, "are the artificial substitutes for equality." To argue that there was "no denial of Equal Rights when this separation is enforced" was "vain."[64]

To bolster his advocacy for desegregation law, Sumner read petitions from ordinary folk, such as black delegates representing five southern states. Petitioners who dealt daily with discrimination laid bare the unfairness of segregation. J. F. Quarles of Georgia, who was a delegate to a Columbia, South Carolina, convention, understood that "legislative enactments alone cannot remedy these social evils" but demanded that "odious discriminations . . . cease." Even emancipation had disparagingly been labeled a form of social equality, and the same label was attached to school desegregation. Douglass C. Griffing of Oberlin, Ohio, also mocked use of the "bugbear" of "social equality" to "frighten" whites and deny colored people "many public privileges accorded to other American citizens." A member of the North Carolina House of Representatives, F. A. Sykes, gave examples of discrimination he had suffered after buying a first-class ticket on a steamship. Sykes had not been permitted to use the first-class accommodations, instead, being told to remove himself "below into the dirty department set aside for my race." He also recounted the similar experiences of his wife and of another married couple. Such practices managed to exclude thousands of citizens from equal privileges and immunities.[65]

The provisions to desegregate schools and cemeteries became the greatest hurdles to passing Sumner's bill into law. Out of principle, he refused to remove either to gain additional support. Sounding out the same concerns that the Supreme Court of the United States would voice in 1954 in *Brown v. Board of Education,* Sumner worried that separate schools "cannot fail to have a depressing effect on the mind of colored children, fostering the idea in them and others that they are not as good as other children." States with separate school systems maintained an unequal system, as Edmunds of Vermont demonstrated statistically. In Virginia 40.2 percent of all students were black but only 24.6 percent of schools were set aside for them. Of North Carolina's roughly 350,000 students, 33 percent were black, but they could attend only 22.5 percent of the schools. The educational system in Georgia similarly favored white over black students. As for southerners, Virginia Senator John W. Johnston insisted that the racial separation of students aimed to aid their development.[66]

While Sumner did not live to see the passage of his heroic effort into law, even on his deathbed he maintained the commitment to the equality principle that had been the central force of his political career. In March 1874, near death, he urged a friend, Massachusetts Representative Ebenezer R. Hoar, "You must take care of the civil-rights bill, . . . don't let it fail." The matter was not so easy, however, with Republicans reeling from the loss of an astonishing 96 seats in the House during the 1874 election. Democrats won 182 seats to the Republicans' 103, with 8 other seats in the hands of various independents. Republicans realized that if Sumner's brainchild were to become law, it would have to pass before the Democratically controlled Congress took office.[67]

The lame-duck Congress enacted the Civil Rights Act in 1875 in a modified form that ended segregation in public accommodations but excluded mention of cemeteries and schools. Prejudice could apparently be taken to the grave. Failure to include schools amounted to tacit approval of overt discrimination, and soon thereafter North Carolina (1876) and Georgia (1877) adopted constitutional provisions mandating the racial separation of students.[68]

Despite the act's shortcomings, it was a giant leap forward. The first section of the act declared "all persons within the jurisdiction of the United States" entitled to "the full and equal enjoyment of the accommodations, advantages, facilities, and privileges of inns, public conveyances on land or water, theaters, and other places of public amusement." Its second section set out the applicable criminal and civil penalties for denying these rights. Violators were subject both to private causes of action and to criminal prosecution. The third section gave federal courts exclusive jurisdiction over cases arising under the act, while the fourth section prohibited state and federal jury selection to be predicated on racial grounds. The Supreme Court later found the first two sections of the law to be unconstitutional, undermining its core purpose.[69]

The Civil Rights Act of 1875 provides a window into how Congress, acting shortly after the Fourteenth Amendment had come into effect, viewed the range of its power to protect the equal privileges and immunities of citizenship. Equality meant acting affirmatively to prevent discrimination in the public sphere. The act was not a procedural device for the administration of government but a substantive vehicle for securing nationally recognized rights. It was the last hurrah for radical abolitionism, as the nation turned its concerns elsewhere.

Limited Reconstruction

Constitutional guarantees against the infringement of freedom and equality seemingly provided the federal government with enough power to protect the rights of all Americans, regardless of race. Freedom from slavery, the privileges and immunities of national citizenship, and voting rights were a far cry from the *Dred Scott* decision, which had relegated blacks to noncitizen status. The Civil War might have ended with the Union forcing the Confederate states back into the Union but making no progress in civil rights. The decision to proceed was part of the American people's tendency to reflect on their shortcomings and then act against egregious forms of discrimination.

After Reconstruction, however, the nation retained many of the prejudices it had inherited from the colonies. Those prejudices tended to diminish the impetus of constitutional Reconstruction. Politicians began to focus on liberty to the exclusion of equality. This meant that traditionally excluded groups had few avenues of redress against private and state circumventions of Thirteenth, Fourteenth, and Fifteenth Amendment principles. Voters and a new generation of party leaders soon forced radicals out of politics, and moderates preferred national reconciliation to acrimony over civil rights.

The tragic mistake of congressmen who were genuinely committed to the revolutionary principle of liberal equality was the belief that local prejudices would abate without continued federal intervention. It was much like the error of revolutionary antislavery optimists who thought that the institution would rapidly wither without definitive federal provisions against it. In both eras prejudices merely became further entrenched when they were not snuffed out during opportune times. Discrimination remained the norm and often regained lost ground.

During the short span when radicals held sway in Congress, they were hampered by President Johnson's regressive policies, by other Republicans unwilling to force states to follow national standards of multiracial decency, and by Democrats resisting intrusion on southern interracial institutions. Little was done to allow freedpeople to enjoy the privileges and immunities of citizenship. The failures of Representatives Stevens's and Julian's land confiscation acts demonstrate how little support there was for proposals to help people just emerging from the handicaps of slavery attain the economic means for success. Legislators and some abolitionists of no less standing than Frederick Douglass thought, "If the negro cannot stand on his own legs, let him fall also. All I ask is, give him a chance to stand on his own legs! Let him alone!"[70] In a society where the vast majority of blacks not only had been relegated to begin life on a lower economic rung but also faced organized interference at every step, federal, state, and local help would have been critical.

Looking backward in time makes it much easier to judge the actions of contemporaries who thought that their constitutional achievements would change the dynamics of political and civil relations. The Thirteenth Amendment provided a dynamic means of protecting substantive freedoms. It enabled Congress to pass laws against individual, group, and state actions. The Civil Rights Act of 1866, enacted under Thirteenth Amendment authority a year after the amendment had come into force, demonstrated the willingness of the Thirty-Ninth Congress to protect everything from contacting to jury rights.

The Fourteenth Amendment added layers of specificity—due process, equal protection, and privileges and immunities—to the developing notion of federal powers. Its many supporters had no indication that using the term "state action" would allow the Supreme Court later to narrowly channel federal law to protect only against discrimination by persons working for the state. It also precipitated a focus on process instead of natural rights.

The Fifteenth Amendment already evidenced a weakening of radicalism, securing suffrage only for a limited group of previously disenfranchised persons. Even during the congressional debates, its supporters and detractors realized that it left gaping holes for state measures, like literacy tests and grandfather clauses, designed to exclude groups like African Americans and women. The Civil Rights Act of 1875 was the last gasp of principled reconstruction, and eventually the Supreme Court would strike it down.

CHAPTER SIX

Unraveling Constitutional Reconstruction

Reconstruction created a new constitutional reality in the United States. It reaffirmed the principles of individual liberty and equality through three constitutional amendments. The grant of enforcement authority provided Congress with the means of providing for the general welfare. A lasting commitment to civil rights, an assumed recognition of minority equality to enjoy the privileges and immunities of citizenship, and a continued willingness to confront the country's past would have achieved lasting change.

During this period many blacks won elections to state and national offices. On the local level, blacks served in many influential posts in the South, as sheriffs, chancery and circuit clerks, superintendents of education, aldermen, and county treasurers. In Atlanta, Nashville, Richmond, Raleigh, and Montgomery, blacks held city council positions. African Americans were finally able to influence the outcome of the judicial process as grand and petit jurors. In 1873 blacks won 42 percent of Mississippi's legislative offices—55 of the 115 seats in the state house and 9 of 37 senate seats. The state's speaker of the house from 1874 to 1875 was black. And the Mississippi secretaries of states from 1870 to 1878 were also black men. In many cases, black legislators, like state senator Matthew Gaines of Texas, were former slaves. Another ex-slave, Blanche K. Bruce, was a United States senator from Mississippi. Even before Bruce, Hiram R. Revels had briefly held a seat in the United States Senate. And numerous United States representatives, including Richard H. Cain of South Carolina, John R. Lynch of Mississippi, and James T. Rapier and Benjamin S. Turner, both from Alabama, were blacks. What seemed like a tearing down of old barriers did not last long.[1]

Once the immediate crisis of war and its aftermath passed, Congress returned to the daily tasks of constructing budgets, making roads, jockeying for committee assignments, and gaining patronage. No presidents were willing to do as much for civil rights as congressional radicals. The Compromise of 1877 manifested the executive branch's unwillingness to lend military might against state and individual abridgements of national rights. The Supreme Court, too, showed itself capable of stunting efforts to successfully prosecute intrusions into the privileges of citizenship. Poll taxes, grandfather clauses, and Jim Crow provisions excluded blacks from U.S. politics and relegated them to second-class citizenship.

Compromise of 1877

A shift in the country's priorities became increasingly evident during the presidential election of 1876. One hundred eighty-five electoral college votes were needed for a candidate to secure the executive office. With the vote of four states remaining undecided, the Democratic candidate, Samuel J. Tilden, was ahead with 184 votes and the Republican Rutherford B. Hayes had 165. Disputes arose about ballot results in the undecided states. Congress tried but was unable to resolve the problem. It then appointed a fifteen-member electoral commission.

Of the commission members from the primarily Republican Senate, three were Republicans and two Democrats. From the Democratically controlled House, three were Democrats and two Republicans. The Supreme Court had two from each party and a fifth member, Justice David Davis, who was regarded as an independent. The Democrats then made a strategic blunder by appointing Davis to the Senate from Illinois. Davis resigned from the Supreme Court and accepted the Senate seat. In his stead Justice Joseph Bradley, a Republican, became the deciding eighth vote on the electoral commission.

The commission voted for Hayes 8–7, strictly along party lines. In exchange for the vote of confidence, Hayes, who was a northerner, tried to mend fences between the sections. He withdrew federal troops from the South, thereby effectively ending any military enforcement of national civil rights statutes and leaving protection of the fundamental rights of newly freed slaves in the hands of southern officials. Upon seeing the precipitous drop in black votes in the 1878 election, Hayes admitted that the "experiment" of entrusting reform to the South "was a failure." Of the nearly 300 southern counties with black majorities, Republicans won only 62. Predominantly white counties continued seeing Democrats as best able to represent their interests. Republicans won only 9 of the 155 counties with less than 5 percent black population, 3 fewer than they had carried in 1876.[2]

Even the Supreme Court, a body that is not dependent on elections, responded to the national climate that the Compromise of 1877 represented. The decision not to enforce constitutional rights by force received judicial acquiescence when the Court denied federal authority to prevent egregious acts of lynching and public-place discrimination.

Judicial Counterrevolution

Constitutional reconstruction was partly a response to the Justice Taney's finding in *Dred Scott* that blacks were not citizens. The Thirteenth Amendment implicitly and the Fourteenth Amendment explicitly made all persons born in the United States citizens. Both provided Congress with the authority to protect fundamental rights. Given the judiciary's role as the final interpreter of the Constitution, a function it established long before Reconstruction, conservative judges found ways of undermining the new grant of federal authority. This judicial countermovement began gradually, in the 1870s, and picked up momentum after the Compromise of 1877.

The Court began to dramatically alter the course of constitutional history in 1873 with the *Slaughter-House Cases*. Butchers challenged a Louisiana law that gave a company an exclusive license to operate a slaughterhouse in the New Orleans area. Other than persons who made up the corporation, all other butchers had to pay a fee to use the facility. Butchers who were not part of the company challenged Louisiana's action in a state court proceeding. Eventually the matter reached the Louisiana Supreme Court, which held that the exclusive license was a legitimate public health regulation, not an unlawful restraint on the butchers' trade. The butchers' association eventually challenged the statute in the United States District Court for Louisiana, where the case was heard by Supreme Court Justice Joseph P. Bradley and district Judge William B. Woods, a future Supreme Court justice. The opinion, issued under Bradley's name, found that Louisiana had misused its police power to "confer on the defendant corporation a monopoly of a very odious character." The post-Reconstruction Constitution demanded "that the privileges and immunities of all citizens . . . be absolutely unabridged [and] unimpaired" by local sensibilities. States were prohibited from using unreasonable regulations to infringe on the benefits of national citizenship. And "one of the privileges of every American citizen" was "to adopt and follow such lawful industrial pursuit—not injurious to the community—as he may see fit." That privilege was "nothing more nor less than the sacred right of labor."[3]

When the case reached the U.S. Supreme Court, John A. Campbell represented the dealers and butchers. During the Civil War, Campbell had resigned from the Supreme Court and served as the Confederate assistant secretary of war. Curiously, Republican Senator Matthew H. Carpenter represented the monopoly. That same Supreme Court term Carpenter argued for a broad reading of the Fourteenth Amendment in a case, *Bradwell v. Illinois*, challenging Illinois' ban against licensing women to be lawyers. Justice Samuel F. Miller wrote the majority opinion in that case, joined by four other justices, holding that women could not demand to enter occupations of their choice on the basis of a national privilege.[4]

Carpenter, plying the advocate's trade in the *Slaughter-House Cases*, took a conservative perspective on republican state sovereignty. His argument convinced the majority of the Court, which maintained antebellum notions of states' regulatory discretion. And beyond resolving the controversy between the butchers and Louisiana, the Court established a far-reaching interpretation of the Fourteenth and Thirteenth Amendments.

Justice Miller's decision is best known for its distinction between the privileges and immunities of state and United States citizenship. The only national privileges Miller listed were those that were already enumerated in the Constitution and identified by a Supreme Court precedent, such as the right to travel to Washington, D.C., the right of protection on the high seas, and habeas corpus protections. Miller implied that courts lacked the power to enforce unenumerated rights. The Fourteenth Amendment, the majority found, never meant "to transfer the security and protection of all the civil rights" from state to federal governments. The Court evidently conceived its role to be the prevention of federal action on individual rights but not the rectification of state violations of those rights. Miller also rejected the butchers' Thirteenth Amendment argument, finding its focus on the incidents of involuntary servitude inapplicable to a matter that was primarily about the exploitation of property rather than of persons. The Court thus upheld the Louisiana monopoly. Of more dire consequence, it imposed a weak interpretation of the Thirteenth and Fourteenth Amendments with long-term ramifications.[5]

The continuing racial violence, segregation, and employment and property discrimination in the South made blacks the greatest losers in *Slaughter-*

House, even though the case had nothing directly to do with them. The power to govern civil rights returned, in great part, to southern governments, which were increasingly being "redeemed" from Republican control. Even though at first glance the opinion seems to be of minor consequence to any issue other than government-created monopolies, it dealt the cause of equal citizenship a staggering blow.

Four out of nine justices dissented from Miller's opinion, three of them writing separately. Justice Swayne argued against rolling back jurisprudence to antebellum state federalism. The Reconstruction Amendments were "a new departure" because they reduced state power.[6]

Justice Bradley, in his dissent, focused on the Reconstruction Amendments' effect on individuals' relationships to their communities. The Fourteenth Amendment, Bradley argued, had made United States citizenship "primary," permitting the federal government to step in if a state or local power "denied full equality before the law" to any classes of persons. In setting up a monopoly, Bradley thought, Louisiana had infringed on the butchers' citizenship right to "be left free" to pursue the profession of their choice.[7]

The third dissent in *Slaughter-House,* by Justice Field, focused on the equality of United States citizens. Bradley, Swayne, and Chief Justice Salmon P. Chase concurred with his dissenting argument. Monopolies, Field argued, infringed on the privilege to pursue the trade of one's choice. He also regarded a prohibition on the pursuit of a calling to be "a condition of servitude" that resembled black codes.[8]

Despite these forceful dissents, the majority left few citizenship rights that the nation could protect against state indifference or outright infringement.

The 1876 *United States v. Cruikshank* decision further diminished any expectation that federal prosecution would find a favorable audience in the Court. The case relegated the prevention of violence, even when motivated by racial hatred, to state authorities. Apparently, in the criminal realm, just as in the civil one, state sensibilities could trump concerns for the welfare of American citizens.

Cruikshank began its way to the Supreme Court at a time when the Grant administration's Justice Department had begun to scale back civil rights enforcement. The case concerned terrorism perpetrated in 1873 against blacks who were holding a political rally. The event came to be known as the Colfax Massacre. A white mob converged on a courthouse that blacks had taken over. The mob then set the building ablaze and shot at anyone emerging from it. More than one hundred black men and two whites lost their lives during the mayhem.[9]

Federal prosecutors secured one hundred indictments under the First Enforcement Act but could get only three convictions. The Supreme Court, in *Cruikshank*, overturned even those. Chief Justice Morrison R. Waite, writing for the majority, found the indictments incomplete because they merely charged the defendants with violating victims' civil rights rather than enumerating those rights. His opinion recognized that the United States could guarantee the right to peaceful assembly but found nothing in the complaint alleging that the defendants had prevented victims from assembling. The defendants thereby eluded justice because of the prosecution's technical mistake.

Of greater implication to future cases, the Court confined congressional Fourteenth Amendment power to state actions. Federal law could no longer punish private parties for private terrorist acts. By resorting to narrow construction, Waite successfully effaced the Enforcement Act's primary purpose, protection of citizens' privileges and immunities against supremacist conspiracies. Procedural devices on drafting complaints and naming proper party defendants had more resonance in the Court than did the vindication of civil rights.[10]

Approving Segregation

State civil rights initiatives met the same fate in the Supreme Court as federal ones. In *Hall v. DeCuir* (1877), the justices prevented Louisiana from desegregating public conveyances. In 1869 Louisiana had passed a law prohibiting any common carriers that were operating in the state from discriminating based on the race or color of passengers. DeCuir sued under that law when he was denied passage in a "whites only" cabin of an interstate steamship. The Supreme Court found the Louisiana statute to be an unconstitutional infringement on interstate commerce even though the law was drafted for purely domestic purposes. Chief Justice Waite found it problematic that a carrier operating in multiple states would be forced to integrate passengers in Louisiana and then segregate them when it reached a state with contrary requirements. His economic priorities were clear: "Commerce cannot flourish in the midst of embarrassments." This holding subordinated concerns for integration to commercial interests. Just as the Commerce Clause had facilitated the interstate exchange of slaves, the judiciary could now rely on it to snuff out efforts to end racial discrimination. Economic opportunism could deny blacks the right to choose their mode of travel.[11]

DeCuir did keep one hope alive, the Court finding that if the public good required desegregation laws, "it must come from Congress and not from the States." The same year the Court decided *Cruikshank*, Congress passed the long-debated Civil Rights Act of 1875, which prohibited discrimination in public accommodations like inns and taverns. When the Court decided the *Civil Rights Cases*, in 1883, Reconstruction had ground to a standstill, but individual cases were still making their way through the appellate system.

The *Civil Rights Cases* concerned litigation about five different causes of action. The first four were reviews of criminal prosecutions. Two of the defendants were charged with denying blacks access to an inn or hotel, a third with prohibiting blacks from enjoying the Grand Opera House in New York, and a fourth with refusing to seat a black person in the dress circle of a San Francisco theater. The fifth case was a Tennessee civil action against a railroad company that had forbidden a black woman from riding in the ladies' car. The national consensus to withdraw from federalist civil rights principles had become so apparent that four of the five defendants' attorneys did not even bother showing up for the final argument before the Supreme Court, but won nevertheless.[12]

The Court considered whether discrimination in public places was an incident of servitude that Congress could regulate under its Thirteenth Amendment authority. In the alternative, the Civil Rights Act was arguably a necessary and proper law for establishing equal protection and due process under the Fourteenth Amendment.

Justice Bradley wrote for an eight-person majority, with Justice Harlan alone in dissent. Bradley held that national interest in protecting civil rights arose only when "some state law has been passed, or some state action through its officers or agents has been taken, adverse to the rights of citizens." That formulation rejected Congress's affirmative duty to enact laws needed to protect life, liberty, and property for the general welfare. Under the Supreme Court's test, the Civil Rights Act's failure to name state wrongs it aimed to correct and its reach to private acts of discrimination became its undoing. The Joint Committee of Fifteen on Reconstruction's decision to scrap the initial affirmative statement of congressional power for the negative final Fourteenth Amendment formulation had become the hook for the Court to hang its hat on.[13]

As for the Thirteenth Amendment, Bradley conceded that it did more than end slavery. It also decreed "civil and political freedom throughout the United States." Congress received the power to pass all necessary and proper laws abolishing the "badges and incidents of slavery in the United State." Despite these convictions, Bradley found that amendment was not germane to the Civil Rights Act of 1875. He held the statute to be unconstitutional because being refused admission to public accommodations was not a vestige of slavery or denial of a fundamental right of citizenship. Bradley distinguished "the social rights of men and races in the community," which he decided did not fall under the Thirteenth Amendment, from "fundamental rights which appertain to the essence of citizenship," to which it applied. Yet Bradley limited the amendment's scope to matters of slavery, not willing to recognize its relevance to discriminations based on race, color, and class. Laws against such arbitrary distinction were left to state and personal prejudices. The Court made no connection between persistent impediments on blacks and their centuries of involuntary servitude, just as it had denied in the *Slaughter-House Cases* that monopolistic abridgments on occupational choice were an impediment to American freedom.

Justice Harlan was so troubled by the majority's decision in the *Civil Rights Cases,* as his widow recalled, that he would wake in the "middle of the night, in order to jot down" thoughts in dissent. His "pen fairly flew" at the thought of how *Dred Scott* had tightened "the shackles of slavery upon the Negro race in the ante-bellum days" and Sumner had sought "to protect the recently emancipated slaves in the enjoyment of equal 'civil rights.'"[14]

Harlan's dissent rejected the Court's interpretation as out of keeping with the Fourteenth Amendment's fifth section. He understood it to be an affirmative provision, enabling Congress to enact "appropriate legislation" that "may be of a direct and primary character, operating upon states, their officers and agents, and also upon, at least, such individuals and corporations as exercise public functions and wield power and authority under the state." He also found the majority's understanding of the Thirteenth Amendment to be a "narrow and artificial" one that undermined the "substance and spirit" of constitutional abolition. He sternly rejected the majority's notion that blacks were favored by national laws despite the incessant "class tyrany" that excluded them from enjoying public places. Because slavery "rested wholly upon the inferiority, as a race, of those held in bondage, their freedom necessarily involved immunity from, and protection against, all discrimination against them, because of their race, in respect of such civil rights as belong to freemen of other races." Both amendments enabled Congress to pass appropriate legislation for carrying out the constitutional decree that "no authority shall be exercised in this country upon the basis of discrimination."

Harlan may have been the only acting judge to buck the majority, but he received supporting letters from retired justices. Justice Swayne told Harlan that "in my judgement" the dissent was "one of the great, indeed one of the greatest, opinions of the Court." It "does you infinite honor, is all that could be desired, and will make a profound and lasting impression upon the Country." Likewise, former Supreme Court Justice William Strong relayed to Harlan that after reading the dissent he too recognized that the majority opinion was "too narrow-sticks to the letter, while you aim to bring out the Spirit of the Constitution."[15]

Non–legally trained minds also understood the combustive implication of the *Civil Rights Cases*. Two days after the decision was issued, it was read in a segregated opera house in Atlanta. Men in the white section "stood on their feet and cheered and ladies gave approving smiles." In contrast, "the quietude of the colored gallery was noticeable." Former Georgia Governor Rufus B. Bullock, who had held the office between 1868 and 1871, warned, along the same lines as Justice Harlan, that the case would "raise as great an issue in this country as the Dred Scott decision did in its day." Richard T. Greener, Harvard University's first black graduate who went on to become the dean of Howard Law School, likewise thought the case as "infamous" as *Dred Scott*. From his perspective, the freedom to use rail on an equal footing "without fear of being put off a car or denied food and shelter" was even more important than suffrage. A small group of blacks meeting in Springfield, Illinois, praised the opinion for recognizing their equal citizenship under state laws, but their sentiments were unusual. Black citizens gathered in many cities, including Chicago, Indianapolis, and Greensburg, Pennsylvania, denouncing the Supreme Court for issuing an opinion so contrary to universal abolition. Frederick Douglass thought that it set black civil rights back twenty years to a status before the passage of the Reconstruction Amendments.[16]

As part of its continuing rollback of Reconstruction, the Court shucked Congress's power to provide for the general welfare through laws meant to protect fundamental rights. Contemporaries understood that what had been clandestine discrimination in inns and other public facilities could now be done in the open. With the days of civil rights legislation over, the Supreme Court was eliminating the few existing laws that could have helped citizens against arbitrary acts of discrimination. Some Republicans began speaking about embodying the provisions of the Civil Rights Act of 1875 into a constitutional amendment, while others hoped it would bring new political life to the party and "revive the spirit of the old antislavery movement.[17]

Nothing came of these ambitions. To the contrary, in the absence of federal protections, from the late 1880s into the late 1890s segregation was the law in Florida, Mississippi, Texas, Louisiana, Alabama, Arkansas, Georgia, Tennessee, Kentucky, the Carolinas, and Virginia. Not until the next century would Congress resort to an alternative approach to ending enforced racial separation. Private establishments created a pattern of segregation. A Nashville saloon hung a sign informing patrons that blacks would not be served there. In Atlanta in 1888, only two of sixty-eight saloons served both whites and blacks; five others served blacks only. In Montgomery the Ruby Saloon served black customers at "a small counter" away from the main bar.[18]

The Court soon found the opportunity to give even greater license for discrimination. *Plessy v. Ferguson* further effaced the federal government's role in civil rights, finding segregation constitutionally permissible even when it was not merely the policy of private establishments but sanctioned by law. Justice Harlan again bucked the majority, finding himself alone in dissent.[19]

Homer A. Plessey was born free on March 17, 1862. One of his great grandmothers was black; all his other immediate relatives were white. His African ancestry, one of his attorneys later related, was "not discernable." Plessy bought a first-class ticket and sat in the railcar reserved for whites. In what was probably a prearranged maneuver, Plessy informed the conductor that he was one-eighth black but refused to go to the colored car. The conductor then called a detective, who arrested Plessy under an 1890 Louisiana statute.

The Separate Car Law required railway companies to provide "equal but separate accommodations for the white and colored races" and to prohibit racial mixing on any coaches. After his arrest, Plessy was released on bond of five hundred dollars. A citizen's committee helped recruit a prominent attorney, Albion W. Tourgée, who took the case for free and fervently advocated Plessy's cause. Tourgée had a record of boldness. He had sustained a spinal injury while fighting for the Union during the Civil War. Afterward, although he resided in North Carolina, he employed and represented African Americans. He also wrote books, including *A Fool's Errand. By One of the Fools* (1879) and *The Invisible Empire* (1880), criticizing the Ku Klux Klan.[20]

Louisiana Criminal District Court Judge John H. Ferguson, a native of Massachusetts who had relocated in the South, presided at the trial. This seemed like a stroke of good fortune for Plessy, since Ferguson appeared to be amenable to striking down the Louisiana statute. He had dismissed an earlier case brought under the law against an interstate traveler. The earlier decision had been based on a Louisiana Supreme Court holding, *Abbott v. Hicks*, which found that the state's attempt to regulate interstate travel intruded into

Congress's Commerce Clause power.[21] Plessy's case differed, however, because he wanted to travel between two points within the same state.

Tourgée determined not to rely on the Interstate Commerce Clause. He wanted to obtain a judicial ruling on whether the Louisiana act violated the Thirteenth Amendment's prohibition against literal or figurative incidents of slavery and involuntary servitude. In the alternative, he decided to argue that the law was state-sponsored discrimination that violated the Equal Protection Clause of the Fourteenth Amendment. Before the court reached the merits of the criminal allegations against his client, Tourgée filed a motion to dismiss the case because the Louisiana law was unconstitutional.[22]

Judge Ferguson denied the motion, finding that the act was no more than a constitutional use of state authority in regulating railroad companies that operated exclusively within Louisiana. On the Thirteenth Amendment issue, Ferguson relied on the *Civil Rights Cases,* holding that the amendment applied only to slavery and not to segregation on public carriers. Plessy next appealed to the Louisiana Supreme Court, which affirmed but nevertheless issued a "writ of errors" that brought the case before the United States Supreme Court. The constitutional issues had to be decided before the criminal charges against Plessy could proceed.[23]

Chief Justice Melville W. Fuller, who was at the Court's helm when it heard *Plessy,* was a member of the Democratic Party from Illinois. Decades earlier he had gained some notoriety in opposing the Emancipation Proclamation for being "unconstitutional, contrary to the rules and usages of civilized warfare." That stand was consistent with his support for a bill forbidding blacks from immigrating into Illinois. During the Civil War he also came out against President Lincoln's suspension of habeas corpus.[24] During Reconstruction, that background would have made it impossible for him to be appointed to the Supreme Court, but the political winds had shifted. His lack of judicial background was of no consequence to President Grover Cleveland, who appointed him to the Court. Twenty-three years after the end of the Civil War, he managed to become the Chief Justice.

The task of writing the opinion fell to Justice Henry B. Brown, who rejected Plessy's Fourteenth Amendment argument, finding that the act "neither abridges the privileges or immunities of the colored man, deprives him of his property without due process of law, nor denies him the equal protection of the laws, within the meaning of the fourteenth amendment." The majority also devalued black concerns about segregation's inherently different treatment: "We consider the underlying fallacy of the plaintiff's argument to consist in the assumption that the enforced separation of the two races stamps the colored race with a badge of inferiority. If this be so, it is not by reason of anything found in the act, but solely because the colored race chooses to put that construction upon it." Brown made this statement without even attempting to support it by precedent or any secondary source. The majority reiterated the *Civil Rights Cases* assertion that segregation was an abridgement only of social equality, with which the Constitution was unconcerned.

In arriving at this result, Brown formulated a theory as porous as had been Taney's *Dred Scott* claim that blacks had never been citizens of the United States. For instance, Brown's claim that "usages, customs, and traditions" justified segregation was belied by the initial trend in the postbellum South, in states like South Carolina, Virginia, and, in 1869, even Louisiana toward desegregated rail travel. Furthermore, if the law at issue in *Plessy* were unconstitutional, supremacist custom and usage born of slavery would have to give way to the individual equal rights guaranteed in the country's Declaration of Independence. Instead, the Court adopted the local prejudices into constitutional interpretation.[25]

Rather than give a close analysis to the mores and practices that were tied to the racial prejudices of slavery, the Court also rejected Plessy's Thirteenth Amendment argument. The holding provided judicial cover for a Jim Crow statutory system to rely on the racialism that had justified slavery. The majority interpreted "slavery" literally as a system that controlled "the labor and services of one man for the benefit of another, and the absence of a legal right to the disposal of his own person, property and services." That minimalist definition reduced the effect of the Abolition Amendment to little more than ending a system of peonage, discounting Congress's power to end incidents of discrimination.

Justice Harlan, writing only for himself in dissent, emphasized fundamental rights he thought inhered in each U.S. citizen. He realized Plessy's case was about much more than one man's struggle, especially a man whose African ancestry was not outwardly obvious. As he had done in the *Civil Rights Cases,* Harlan drew from Sir William Blackstone's Commentaries in explaining the meaning of "personal liberty." Everyone had a right to "locomotion, of changing situation, or removing one's person to whatever places one's own inclination may direct. The Louisiana law infringed on "the personal freedom of citizens" to move about in "public conveyances on a public highways."

Harlan had the foresight to realize the long-term ramifications of the majority's opinion. He realized that the opinion would justify segregation throughout public life, not only on railcars: "If a state can prescribe, as a rule of civil conduct, that whites and blacks shall not travel as passengers in the same railroad coach, why may it not so regulate the use of the streets of its cities and towns as to compel white citizens to keep on one side of a street, and black citizens to keep on the other?" Harlan foresaw that legal differentiation would legitimate white supremacy at the expense of black citizenship. As Sumner had understood during the effort leading up to the Civil Rights Act of 1875, Harlan refused to believe that separate accommodations for blacks and whites would put both on an equal footing before the law. "The thin disguise of 'equal' accommodations for passengers in railroad coaches will not mislead any one, nor, atone for the wrong this day done." Separation of the races, to the contrary, was a continuing mark of slavery that denied blacks the full enjoyment of "civil freedom and equality before the law established by the constitution." Echoing many of the protests that followed the *Civil Rights Cases,* Harlan wrote that *Plessy* would "prove to be quite as pernicious as the decision made by the tribunal in the *Dred Scott Case.*"

A leading Progressive Era newspaper editor, Ray S. Baker, at the turn of the twentieth century explained the differing attitudes between whites and blacks concerning segregation. African Americans, naturally, found their exclusion from first-class accommodations unfair. Whites, on the other hand, according to Baker, believed that "the Negro is inferior" and "he must be made to keep his place. Give him a chance and he assumes social equality, and that will lead to an effort at intermarriage and amalgamation of the races."[26]

Without close social contact between whites and blacks, Jim Crow simultaneously engendered and perpetuated prejudices. The Court's decision in *Plessy* eased the development of a racially based class system. Jim Crow became almost ubiquitous in the South. State and local laws perpetuated segregation, but where statutes and ordinances were silent, many businesses and individuals zealously enforced it themselves. During the 1890s blacks also increasingly found themselves barred from city and private parks. Beginning in 1900 numerous American cities responded to *Plessy* by segregating public streetcars. In Georgia alone, Atlanta, Rome, and Augusta enacted ordinances to that effect. Montgomery (1900), Jacksonville (1901), Mobile (1902), Houston, San Antonio, and Columbia, South Carolina (all in 1903) did the same, as did Virginia (1902), Louisiana (1902), Arkansas (1903), and Mississippi (1904). In 1906 Baker saw evidence of the "coloured line." States soon were separating the races "literally in every department of life." Blacks were separated in theaters, prohibited from using most white hotels and restaurants, having to find "their own eating and sleeping places," "many of them inexpressibly dilapidated and unclean." Residential segregation ordinances, which the Supreme Court eventually found to be unconstitutional, emerged in cities like Baltimore (1911) and Louisville (1914). These were used to separate white and black neighborhoods. Statutory segregation covered fishing holes, boating spots, racetracks, pool halls, and circuses. In some states, even hospitals were segregated. Oklahoma went so far as to require telephone companies to install separate telephone booths for whites and blacks.[27]

Education came in for special treatment because of its role in developing children's racialist sensibilities. In 1895 Florida made it a criminal offense to teach white and black students in the same grade school. Tennessee (1901), Kentucky (1904), Oklahoma (1908), and other southern states enacted similar laws in the wake of *Plessy*. In the North, Minnesota and Michigan prohibited discrimination in public schools but were silent about private schools.[28]

These forms of exclusion led to an increase in black activism. Black women's clubs and churches provided an alternative when blacks were shut out of most southern libraries. Unwilling to be degraded in Jim Crow cars in Nashville, blacks organized their own carriages. When the doors of unions and fraternal orders were shut to them, black clubs allowed the disenfranchised to vote on issues important to their communities. These substitutes by no means compensated for being relegated to worse facilities and diminished citizenship status. Nor was there any justification for the government to shirk its responsibility for the general welfare to private organizations.[29]

The Thirteenth and Fourteenth Amendments were designed to nationalize civil rights and grant Congress the power to safeguard fundamental rights for the common good. But the Supreme Court, as we have seen, shifted that power back to the states. Of course, southern states could have acted responsibly in matters of race relations; instead, they delimited equality and liberty in a way that was beneficial to white elites but deprived blacks of newly won rights. Racists' liberty right to freely enjoy public accommodations without having to share them with blacks trumped the Radical Republicans' determination to make the principles of the Preamble and the Declaration enforceable under the Constitution. When faced with the prospect of a new country committed to the welfare of the entire populace, the Court provided legal cover for the nation to backslide into its local prejudices. The justices discounted multiple sources—Harlan's reasoning, congressional debates, and abolitionist and revolutionary writings being just a few—that might have helped them chart a more inclusive course for the country. The Court failed to rise to the occasion, deciding instead to use narrow construction of the Constitution to undermine its civil rights clauses.

CHAPTER SEVEN

Political Restrictions and Developments

A democratically run political process might have arrested the proliferation of segregation laws. Had blacks been part of the electorate, they could have chosen reliable representatives to protect their interests. In post-Reconstruction America, however, southern states increasingly circumvented the Fifteenth Amendment's prohibition against racial discrimination. They chose the very methods for disenfranchisement that some Republican congressmen at the time of ratification had warned were outside the scope of the amendment. When given the opportunity, the Supreme Court put its stamp of approval on most state franchise laws and provided constitutional cover for the deprivation of political rights.

Racial and Class Provisions

Racial political exclusion did not come about immediately after the federal troops left the South in 1877. The process was gradual, taking almost a quarter-century to reach its apex. In 1869 the South Carolinian Joseph H. Rainey was the first African American to become a member of the U.S. House of Representatives. He served in that capacity until 1879, went on to be a South Carolina internal revenue agent, then worked in the banking industry. Between 1869 and 1875 sixteen blacks represented seven southern states in Congress. But only six served in the period following Reconstruction, two from North Carolina, three from South Carolina, and one from Virginia, the last being George H. White of North Carolina, who held a seat in the House until 1901. No black person would again be elected to that body until in 1929, when Oscar S. DePriest represented Illinois.[1]

The lack of federal enforcement of the Fifteenth Amendment allowed states to reassert their own visions of political participation. For a time, especially during the 1880s, blacks continued to hold various state offices. But the Supreme Court's increasingly constricted interpretation of federal powers, coupled with growing apathy in Congress toward civil rights and emphasis in the executive branch on reconciling the North and South, allowed states to circumvent equal political participation. Nowhere was this more apparent than in Mississippi. One hundred fifteen black Mississippi state legislators served during the 1867 and 1869 legislative sessions. By 1876 in that state only sixteen were serving. After 1896 no black served in the Mississippi legislature until passage of the Voting Rights Act of 1965. Almost 50 percent of Alabama's citizens were black, but after 1876 no African American won election to the legislature.

Tennessee was a curious case. Throughout Radical Reconstruction not a single black person was part of the Tennessee legislature; one was voted into office in the 1870s, twelve in the 1880s, and none after that until the 1960s. Blacks were driven out of Tennessee politics in predominantly black counties like Haywood and Fayette by a poll tax and by armed thugs brandishing shotguns, Winchesters, and carbines in cities that had voted for black candidates. During Reconstruction in Louisiana, which had a large black population, more blacks than whites voted, but by the 1890s Democrats came to power through bribery, white primaries, intimidation, and vote-stealing. In the Louisiana gubernatorial election of 1888, fraud was so overt that each of three Black Belt parishes gave the Democratic gubernatorial candidate more than 100 percent of the vote. Without federal enforcement, between 1880 and 1888 conspiracies, violence, and fraud caused a reduction of black voting in Florida by 27 percent, in Georgia by 50 percent, and in South Carolina by a startling 63 percent. Black political power was at a low ebb throughout the South by the 1890s.[2]

Misdeeds were so widespread that on more than thirty occasions between 1880 and 1901 the House of Representatives seated southern Republicans and Populists who had lost elections because of fraud. On occasion, the House also overturned election results based on the use of violence, terrorism, and intimidation.[3]

Law soon became a more systematic method than vigilantism or private deception for locking blacks out of politics. The Fifteenth Amendment made it impossible for states to place explicitly racial limitations on voting; hence outwardly race-neutral state constitutional sections and statutes were central to southern black disenfranchisement. Contrary to the statements of historians like Vladimer O. Key and Michael Klarman, state statutes and constitutions were important factors in systematizing the popular prejudices against black political participation. Beginning in 1882 South Carolina used eight boxes for voting: one for governor, another for lieutenant governor, a third for circuit collector, and so on. Florida and North Carolina later adopted similar multiple–ballot box systems. The boxes were shuffled often to keep illiterate persons, white and black, from exercising their political power freely. Later, the Australian ballot method, in states like Florida, which did not identify the candidates' parties, likewise favored literate voters. Elections officials could help voters but were unlikely to help blacks or white Republicans. Governors appointed the elections officials, all of whom, for decades after the multiple–ballot box system took effect, were Democrats. Furthermore, the high rate of black illiteracy in those states meant that they would be worse affected than whites. Florida's experience with the multiple–ballot box system is indicative. About 45 percent of black males in Florida were illiterate in 1890, one year after the multiple–ballot box law took effect. Absent the new system, one historian found that a straight prediction of voters for that year indicated that about 39,100 Democrats and 26,100 Republicans would have voted. Instead, 29,090 Democrats and 15,045 Republicans voted. That means that Democrats lost 26 percent of their projected vote and Republicans lost 43 percent. In South Carolina, following the Eight Box Law of 1882, Republican presidential returns of 1884 were 37.42 percent of their 1880 returns.[4]

States experimented with a variety of other methods—including grandfather clauses, literacy tests, and poll taxes—to curtail black voting rights. Constitutional disenfranchisement was a more formal development that proved even more durable than legislation. The symbolic value of restrictions that were set in the states' organic laws gave them a greater weight than statutes resting on the popular will of current legislative majorities. The primary aim of constitutional provisions was to eliminate black political participation and to establish white governments. Proponents of these measures were typically wealthy Democrats who wanted to prevent Republicans, uneducated whites, and Populists from becoming powerful forces in state governments.[5]

Constitutional disenfranchisement began with the Mississippi constitutional convention of 1890. Advocates of the plan explained their desire to move away from the fraud and violence that, since 1875, had been the principal means of preventing black voting. They had become concerned with the intrinsic lawlessness that had been common. As one Mississippian explained, contemporaries could not "afford to die and leave their children with shot guns in their hands, a lie in their mouths and perjury on their souls in order to defeat the Negroes."[6]

One of Mississippi's devices to achieve disenfranchisement was the requirement that voters live at least one year in the state before casting a ballot. This provision mainly targeted migrant farmers and sharecroppers, most of whom were black, as well as carpetbaggers. Another provision, which was both racially and economically motivated, required voters to pay a $2 poll tax and present the receipt at the time of voting. Another required that a voter "be able to read any section of the Constitution of this state" or "be able to understand the same when read to him, or give a reasonable interpretation thereof." This provision allowed voter registration officials to ask questions to evaluate the literacy and understanding of potential voters. The officials had it within their discretion to refuse to register anyone they deemed unable to read, understand, or interpret sections of the constitution. This amounted to a facially neutral means of preventing blacks and politically disfavored persons from registering to vote. As one author put it, registrars "practice[d] blatant discrimination against Negroes who [sought] to register by asking spurious and improper questions and requiring higher standards of Negroes than whites." The Jackson *Clarion-Ledger* remarked that a black man could vote in Mississippi "provided he has sense enough to 'read or understand the Constitution,' translate Hebrew, parse a little Greek or Latin, square a circle and solve a few other mathematical problems."[7]

Before adoption of the 1890 Mississippi Constitution, the state had roughly 190,000 black and 69,000 white voters. Following its passage, for the 1892 election, only 9,000 blacks remained on the voter rolls, and 50,000 white voters had also been excluded. From then on, white oligarchs dominated politics in Mississippi. In 1899 blacks made up only 13 percent of registered voters, even though they constituted 57 percent of the eligible voting population. Mississippi was able to skew the numbers so drastically from the pre-1890 figures because its constitution went into effect without approval by state voters. Only delegates to the 1890 convention, 133 of whom were white, with a single black colleague, had a say in passing the state's organic law.[8]

The Supreme Court of the United States reviewed the Mississippi literacy provision in *Williams v. Mississippi* (1898). Henry Williams claimed that a literacy requirement of the state constitution deprived him of equal legal protections and that it was administered in a discriminatory manner. His challenge was part of an appeal from a murder conviction. Williams claimed that the original grand jury indictment and petit jury finding of guilt should have been quashed because both were picked from voter rolls that systematically excluded blacks. Mississippi courts were unwilling to grant him relief, and the Supreme Court upheld their decision.[9]

The Court showed great reluctance to strike down election provisions, like the poll tax, that kept blacks off juries. The Court declared that "whatever is sinister in" those provisions' "intention, if anything," could "be prevented by both races" exerting "that duty which voluntarily pays taxes and refrains from crime." That perspective ignored evidence that while Mississippi voting laws were neutral, they were administered to have the harshest effect on black political and civil participation. The Court set such a high bar for proving voting roll abuses that *Williams* established a line of precedent as detrimental to African American political participation as *Plessy* had proved to be to their equal enjoyment of public places.

Even before the Court decided *Williams,* many states followed Mississippi's model. During South Carolina's constitutional convention, Senator Benjamin R. "Pitchfork Ben" Tillman, who had earlier been the state's governor, was the chairman of the South Carolina committee on suffrage during the 1895 constitutional convention. His views on black voters were, therefore, telling of its primary aims. At one point during the convention, Tillman shouted at a black delegate, "You dirty black rascal, I'll swallow you alive," to which that delegate replied, "If you do, you'll have more brains in your belly than you have in your head." In 1900, speaking on the floor of the United States Senate, he explained South Carolina's stratagem in eliminating black rule: "We had a hundred and twenty-five thousand negroes of voting age and we had a hundred thousand whites"; in response, "we took the government away. We stuffed ballot boxes. We shot them. We are not ashamed. . . . With . . . force, tissue ballots, and so forth we got tired ourselves. So we called a constitutional convention, and we eliminated . . . all the colored people whom we could under the fourteenth and fifteenth amendments."[10]

The 1895 convention walked the fine line of excluding blacks without diminishing the vote of 13,924 illiterate and landless whites. A simple literacy test and poll tax would have been counterproductive to the Tillman movement. The grandfather clause, which would have waived voting requirements for anyone who voted before the Civil War, seemed too crude a circumvention of the Fifteenth Amendment to be a viable alternative. Instead, as Tillman explained to the United States Senate, the 1895 convention adopted the "educational qualification" to "disfranchise as many [Negroes] as we could." The provision allowed persons to receive lifetime voting privileges as long as, by

January 1, 1898, they could read and write any section of the constitution or demonstrate an understanding of it. This provision was designed to provide officers with the discretion to enter white, illiterate South Carolinians into the voting rolls while arbitrarily excluding all black persons. It was also a means for whites who registered by the set time to avoid poll taxes and residency requirements.[11]

Following ratification of its constitution, the South Carolina legislature found a second effective means of disenfranchisement, authorizing political parties to orchestrate primaries for choosing candidates. The Democratic Party, which held the reins of state government, simply excluded all African Americans from its primary elections. Being unable to participate in the Democratic Party's "white primaries," they were ousted from any meaningful say in state politics. Impressed by South Carolina's success, Arkansas developed white primaries in 1897 and Georgia did so in 1898. The train of events kept rolling so that by 1903 direct primaries were the norm in the South. The scholars Thomas D. Clark and Albert D. Kirwan considered them to be "the great obstacle to Negro voting, more effective than all others combined."[12]

The direct-primary system worked hand in hand with state constitutional disenfranchisement. The president of the Louisiana constitutional convention, meeting in New Orleans on February 8, 1898, explained that "this convention has been called together by the people of the State to eliminate from the electorate the mass of corrupt and illiterate voters who have degraded our politics." To achieve that end, the 1898 Louisiana Constitution required voters to pay a poll tax, meet property requirements, and demonstrate an understanding of the constitution. The state did allow anyone unable to fulfill those criteria to vote so long as he, his father, or grandfathers had been eligible voters on or before January 1, 1867. Even Ben Tillman's minions had thought such a provision unconstitutional, being a transparent effort to keep illiterate, indigent, and unpropertied blacks from voting while rendering equally illiterate whites eligible. Prior to passage of the constitution, in 1896, Louisiana had 130,344 black and 164,088 white registered voters. Of those who were eligible, more blacks voted than whites. In 1900, the first voter registration year after the constitution's passage, only 5,320 blacks were eligible voters, compared with 125,437 whites. By 1904 1,342 black and 92,000 white voters were registered. In 1906 Louisiana placed party nominations at the exclusive discretion of direct primaries. There, as in South Carolina, the Democratic central committee allowed only whites to vote in its primaries. A 1912 update to the grandfather clause provided white voters a permanent exemption from educational and property requirements. The new version of the clause exempted anyone eligible to vote as of August 31, 1913. By then, white primaries had rendered any black voters who might have qualified under the new grand-father clause virtually invisible in Louisiana politics.[13]

The strategy of constitutional disenfranchisement was spreading like wildfire. North Carolina's 1900 constitution included a grandfather clause and reading and writing tests designed to bolster the number of white voters. The state instituted direct primaries in 1915.

Looking around at sister states, Alabama realized that it could simulta-neously deprive blacks of the vote and put down the state's Populist move-ment. The president of the state's 1901 convention, John B. Knox, provided direction for the participants. "If we would have white supremacy," he urged, "we must establish it by law—not by force or fraud." As had participants of the 1890 Mississippi convention, Knox gave voice to the desirability for for-mal, instead of mob- and county-run, racial disenfranchisement. To him, blacks were to be kept out of power because they "descended from a race lowest in intelligence and moral perceptions of all the races of men." Not a single delegate to the Alabama constitutional convention was black, even though the population of the state was made up of 1,001,152 white and 827,545 "colored" persons.[14]

While blacks were the most reviled group in the state, illiterate whites also fared poorly. An elite group of politicians decided to wrest political power from uneducated whites whose vote they thought to be easily manipulable.[15]

Alabama submitted its constitution to the state electorate. The signs of corruption and manipulation by supporters appear plainly in the final count. The 1901 constitution came into force though most white voters, 67,307 to 57,625, voted against it. Victory came because the final tally showed that the "Black Belt" favored the constitution, by a vote of 51,088 to 14,427. The results can only be read to have been manipulated; otherwise, we are left with the conclusion that blacks voted with white supremacists to deny blacks the right to vote. Numerous counties actually tallied more votes than the number of males over twenty-one living there.[16]

The Alabama Constitution of 1901 included so many voting requirements that it was effective at diminishing the total registered voters in the state. After 1903 residency, literacy, property, employment, and poll tax require-ments served to drastically alter the voting pattern in the state. Before 1903, however, exceptions to the requirements were made for anyone who had honorably served in one of several wars, including the Civil and Spanish-

American Wars; for those veterans' lawful descendants; and for persons deemed to be of good character and to have an understanding of the duties and obligations of citizenship. In 1900 about 181,315 black men were eligible to vote; by the January 1, 1903, deadline only 2,980 blacks had registered. By design, whites retained the majority of the franchise, but the provisions hurt that population as well. In 1900 about 232,000 white males were registered to vote, but by 1903 their number was down to about 40,000. Alabama had put universal suffrage to flight.[17]

The only available redress against Alabama's connivances was through the federal courts. Congress might have acted through its Fourteenth and Fifteenth Amendments' enforcement authority, but legislative will to do so was lacking; in any event, the Supreme Court would probably have found such an enactment unconstitutional. Therefore the African American educator and author Booker T. Washington secretly financed a legal challenge in two suffrage cases, *Giles v. Harris* (1903) and *Giles v. Teasley* (1904).[18]

Jackson W. Giles, who brought the challenge on behalf of himself and about five thousand other disenfranchised blacks, was a courthouse janitor from Montgomery, Alabama. He alleged that throughout the state, blacks were systematically denied the right to participate in elections in violation of their Fourteenth and Fifteenth Amendment rights. The evidentiary record contained examples of the absurd obstacles blacks faced to voting. In one case, Elbert Thornton, from Barbour County, swore that a registrar asked him to explain the "differences between Jeffersonian Democracy and the Calhoun principles as compared to the Monroe Doctrine." Thornton's inability to answer this complex question enabled the election registrar to exclude him from the voting roll without overtly violating the Fifteenth Amendment.[19]

Giles's lawsuit asked the court to grant equitable relief for him and other blacks, requiring registrars to put them on the list of voters. The Court, with Justice Oliver W. Holmes drafting the opinion, denied Giles relief. Holmes explained that the Court lacked equitable power to resolve a state political conflict. The opinion is indicative of the continuing abandonment of federal oversight that the Court had perpetuated since its holdings in the *Slaughter-House Cases* and the *Civil Rights Cases*. The jurisprudence used technical readings of Reconstruction Amendments to find no state-sponsored equal protection or voting rights infringement.

Justice Holmes callously mocked Giles's claim. If the Alabama suffrage provisions were illegal, he wrote, then the Court would become a party to an "unlawful scheme" by ordering the inclusion of additional persons under it.

"If the sections of the Constitution concerning registration were illegal in their inception, it would be a new doctrine in constitutional law that the original invalidity could be cured by an administration which defeated their intent. We express no opinion as to the alleged fact of their unconstitutionality beyond saying that we are not willing to assume that they are valid, in the face of the allegations." Furthermore, if the Court were to grant relief only to five thousand voters, the result would be selective where the claim was that thousands of others had also been denied the right to vote. The Court, in effect, stuck its head in the sand rather than evaluating whether Alabama's voting provisions were fraudulent.

The second reason for avoiding judgment on the merits was more frank. Even if the Court were to render judgment for Giles, judges were simply unprepared to "supervise the voting in that state." Judgment in equity would be no more than an unenforceable "empty form." The only glimmer of hope Holmes's decision offered derived from his conjecture that the plaintiff might have fared better had the cause of action been for monetary damages, rather than for equitable relief.

Justice Harlan's dissent argued that the Court lacked jurisdiction to dispose of the case on its merits. To be clear about his predilections, he nevertheless added that "my conviction is that upon the facts alleged in the bill (if the record showed a sufficient value of the matter in dispute), the plaintiff is entitled to relief in respect of his right to be registered as a voter." Justice David J. Brewer, in a separate dissent, also faulted the Court for making substantive findings in the case when only a jurisdictional issue was on appeal. But Brewer, unlike Harlan, thought that Giles could bring the case in federal court since it was centered on a constitutional issue.

Acting on the sliver of hope that he could get relief under a damages theory Holmes had left unresolved, Giles filed *Giles v. Teasley,* seeking five thousand dollars from the Alabama Board of Registrar for Montgomery County for refusing to register him. Giles alleged that county registrars had denied him and others—he maintained that more than seventy-five thousand people were in a position similar to his—the right to vote on account of their race, color, or prior condition of servitude. The Alabama Supreme Court got a crack at the case, holding first that if Giles was correct that the registrars lacked the federal constitutional authority to register anyone, they were therefore powerless to register Giles. On the other hand, if they were clothed with the authority to register persons, then they were immune from being sued for damages.[20]

Had the United States Supreme Court found Alabama's 1901 suffrage provisions to violate the U.S. Constitution, it could have ordered registrars to issue voting certificates to all qualified black voters. Whether such a mandate would have been effective and whether federal marshals could have enforced it is a matter of speculation. At a minimum, judgment on behalf of Giles would have subjected uncooperative registrars liable for contempt of court. The tragic flaw of Justice William R. Day's majority opinion in *Teasley* was that it was every bit as obscurantist as Holmes's had been. The Court proved itself unwilling to pursue the ideals of Reconstruction in the face of local prejudices. The majority refused even to review the decision of the Alabama Supreme Court, and Day pathetically claimed to be "not unmindful of the gravity of the statements of the complainant charging violation of a constitutional amendment." Thus reliance on the state's rights was a technicality that enabled the Court to avoid political controversy by not rendering any decision on the substance of the case. This time Justice Harlan was alone in dissent.

The two *Giles* cases, along with *Williams v. Mississippi*, which had approved, respectively, Alabama's and Mississippi's constitutional disenfranchisement schemes, along with *Cruikshank*, which denied federal power to prosecute private interference with voting, left the Fifteenth Amendment inoperative except to remedy the most overt forms of electoral discrimination. The vast majority of southern blacks remained disenfranchised until the early 1960s, when the Supreme Court, through the one-person, one-vote cases, came to terms with its responsibility to protect the right to vote, and the United States Congress enacted the Voting Rights Act of 1965.[21]

At the dawn of the twentieth century, however, the state-based trend to legally disenfranchise blacks was unremitting. The Alabama provision in *Giles* was only part of the continuing story. In 1885 the Anderson-McCormick election law in Virginia led to the fraudulent disenfranchisement of blacks and helped Democrats sweep the Virginia state elections. The backbreaking event in Virginia was enactment of its 1902 constitution, which disenfranchised all eligible blacks and a bit more than half of all white voters.[22]

A similar pattern took place in Texas. At first, legislative gerrymandering effectively disenfranchised black voters. The 1902 constitution excluded them even more effectively. Neither was Texas satisfied with these antidemocratic successes, passing the Terrell laws in 1903 and 1905 to regulate party primaries and keep blacks from joining the Democratic Party, which dominated state politics. Georgia found property, poll tax, and literacy requirements, as well as a 1908 constitutional amendment, to be effective means of disenfranchisement.[23]

With state restrictions on democracy multiplying, the solicitor general of the United States, in *Guinn v. United States,* convinced the Supreme Court that Oklahoma's 1910 grandfather clause was overtly unconstitutional. That provision exempted persons who could vote in January 1866 and their lineal descendants from having to submit to a literacy test. The loophole was a blatant attempt to circumvent the Fifteenth Amendment. The Court's decision that Oklahoma officials had conspired to deprive persons of their constitutional rights did not, however, enfranchise blacks. Less transparently racist tools remained available to states. The white primary system, for instance, made it virtually impossible for blacks to participate in southern politics. That system was eliminated only through a series of Supreme Court decisions rendered between 1927 and 1953.[24]

Most of the blame for black disenfranchisement is attributable to states that viewed electorate law in elitist terms. The Supreme Court was secondarily to blame for its lame attempt to act on the ideals of political equality that animated the Fifteenth Amendment. But neither were the framers of that amendment blameless: limiting the amendment to race, color, and previous condition of servitude was its undoing. Political concessions left lingering problems. Warnings of several Republicans during the congressional debates—that state literacy and property qualifications could be used to circumvent the Fifteenth Amendment—were ignored. Neither could Representative George W. Julian buttress enough support to prohibit voting discrimination based on gender. Blacks could at least claim partial victory; women's voting rights, on the other hand, were decades from constitutional recognition.

Women's Suffrage

As we have seen, during Reconstruction, before the spread of disenfranchisement, black men participated in local, state, and national politics; women, however, remained as politically powerless as they had been during the revolutionary period. Women had agitated for political participation since the nation's founding. Abigail Adams implored her husband, John Adams, who was then a member of the Continental Congress, to "remember the ladies" in working out the details of political representation. John's response—"I cannot but laugh" at the suggestion—typified his generation's attitude toward gender parity. Revolutionaries spoke about natural rights without acknowledging their significance to mothers, wives, and daughters.[25]

The abolitionist movement later transformed revolutionary rhetoric about natural equality into a doctrine that was as opposed to slavery as it was to sex discrimination. The sisters Angelina and Sarah Grimké, who played an essential role in researching documents for the groundbreaking book *American Slavery as It Is*, were willing to "bear the brunt of the storm," if only to "be the means of making a breach in the wall of public opinion which lies in the way of woman's true dignity, honor and usefulness." Sarah Grimké's *Letters on the Equality of the Sexes and the Condition of Woman* draws a parallel between the legal status of blacks and that of married women, an analogy later suffragists embellished. Some similarities between the groups' subordinate status made a female and black alliance natural. Black and white women worked together in the Philadelphia Female Anti-Slavery Society, refusing to kowtow to social stricture, and helped fugitives who were escaping through the Underground Railroad.[26]

Several feminists, including Lucretia Mott, Sarah Pugh, and a newly married Elizabeth Cady Stanton, hoped to unite the efforts for women's and men's equality in 1840, when they traveled to the World Anti-Slavery Convention in London. To their consternation, only men were permitted to formally participate in the convention. Organizers permitted women only to be observers. Wendell Phillips and other American abolitionist leaders futilely argued for admitting women to the convention as equal participants. Their efforts came up short, and women were forced to sit in a gallery behind a curtain for the remainder of the proceedings. To show his solidarity, William Lloyd Garrison sat with the women in the gallery and refused to take part in the debates.[27]

The unexpected barriers they faced at the World Anti-Slavery Convention led the established Mott and the young Stanton to redouble their efforts. The two organized the first U.S. women's conference on July 19 and 20, 1848, at Wesleyan Chapel in Seneca Falls, New York. The participants gathered to discuss broad changes needed to secure women social, civil, and religious rights. At the end, the meeting adopted a Declaration of Sentiments, which relied on core national concepts of liberty and equality. Participants drew inspiration from the Declaration of Independence, making the provisions of their own declaration even more remarkable: "We hold these truths to be self-evident: that all men and women are created equal." The convention participants willingly entered a tempest of controversy, accusing man of "never permitt[ing]" woman "to exercise her inalienable right to the elective franchise. He has compelled her to submit to laws, in the formation of which she had no voice." Sixty-eight women and thirty-two men signed the Seneca

Falls Declaration and eleven resolutions on women's rights, but only one man, Frederick Douglass, voted to adopt Stanton's resolution that women should be granted the right to vote.[28]

After the Seneca Falls Convention, many abolitionists and feminists merged their efforts, relying on a mutually beneficial philosophy about natural human equality. Their efforts were not limited to securing the vote. Slavery, of course, was central, but property rights, education, and family matters often appeared in speeches and publications. Voting, it was evident, was crucial for empowering groups limited by multiple legal handicaps.

Acrimony over "The Negro's Hour"

The Union's Civil War victory raised expectations that women and blacks would benefit from a reborn commitment to the nation's founding values. Supporters of the suffrage movement were surprised to find, however, that Republicans wanted to enfranchise black males before addressing gender inequalities or rewarding women's wartime efforts. At the thirty-second anniversary of the American Anti-Slavery Society, Phillips told an assembly that one question would need to be tackled at a time: "This hour belongs to the Negro." Phillips hoped "in time to be as bold as Stuart Mill and add to that last clause 'sex.'" Stanton curtly replied to Phillips by letter, "May I ask . . . just one question based on the apparent opposition in which you place the negro and woman. My question is this: Do you believe the African race is composed entirely of males?"[29]

For Stanton, women's rights were essential to abolitionist efforts to protect human rights. Equality was as much a birthright of female citizens as it was of male citizens. Full victory over slavery remained elusive so long as women's grievances went unredressed. Sojourner Truth warned that if only black men gained the right to vote, they would become "masters over the women, and it will be just as bad as it was before." Without the vote, half the nation remained in the despotic grip of a class system that was based not on wealth but on gender: "Universal manhood suffrage, by establishing an aristocracy of sex," as one declaration put it, "imposes upon the women of this nation a more absolute and cruel despotism than monarchy; in that, woman finds a political master in her father, husband, brother, son." Only a groundswell of effort could end that aristocracy. A vehement struggle would continue, in the words of an 1879 petitioner to the California Congress for a state suffrage amendment, until "we feel the shackles loosen and give way. . . . We are weary of sitting in the cellar of the temple of Liberty and listening to the distressing noise of the feet of our brothers overhead."[30]

Susan B. Anthony and Stanton unsuccessfully petitioned Congress to add a provision to the Fourteenth Amendment guaranteeing women's suffrage rights. Feminists were also offended that the amendment's second section, for the first time, introduced the word "male" into the Constitution. It provided that a states' congressional representation would be diminished proportionately to the number of males older than twenty-one who were arbitrarily excluded from voting. The provision was meant to prevent local prejudices from denying black males' voting rights, but its use of "male" extended the long-standing federal policy of noninterference with state disenfranchisement of women. Knowing how difficult it was to change the Constitution, Stanton warned her cousin and ally Gerrit Smith that the second section could "take us a century at least" to expunge. An unsuccessful petition drive gathered about ten thousand signatures to keep "male" out of the Constitution. Anthony demanded that the decision be reconsidered because enfranchising only black men meant that women were "left outside with lunatics, idiots and criminals."[31]

The Reconstruction Congresses and most abolitionists refused to battle sex-based political discrimination while blacks remained disenfranchised. In essence, women were told that they would have to quietly tolerate unequal treatment. Just as American revolutionaries had been told to trust the British Parliament to look out for their interests, so too women were told that male congressmen would look out for theirs. The argument against suppressed political participation was equally untenable in both cases. "The noble cannot make laws for the peasant," Stanton explained to the New York State legislature, "the slaveholder for the slave; neither can man make and execute just laws for woman, because in each case, the one in power fails to apply the immutable principles of right to any grade but his own." Women's suffragists extrapolated the revolutionary notion that citizens were free only when their right to individual franchise was secure. For these activists, the right to vote was essential for women's enjoyment of "equal personal rights and equal political privileges with all other citizens." Failing to achieve these ends through the Fourteenth Amendment, in 1869 Stanton and Anthony began advocating for the passage of a sixteenth, which Indiana Representative George Julian drafted. It proposed to prohibit discrimination against women voters.[32]

Testing Existing Constitutional Provisions

Julian's proposed amendment never gained much congressional support. Meanwhile, women's rights activists began to rely on already existing legal provisions rather than pursue new ones. Shortly after the Fourteenth Amendment was ratified, the Missouri husband-and-wife suffragists Francis and Virginia L. Minor alighted on the idea that the amendment's guarantee of equal citizenship implied that women had an equal right to vote. The Minors' was no abstract constitutional theory. It called for a "New Departure under the Fourteenth Amendment." They counseled women to go vote and file a lawsuit against any election registrar who prevented them from doing so.[33]

Victoria Woodhull, who was part of this New Departure movement, testified before the United States House Judiciary Committee that the Fourteenth Amendment had already enfranchised women. Unlike the Minors, Woodhull sought not to lodge a legal complaint nor to get judicial interpretation on the matter but to spur congressional action clarifying that all citizens, regardless of their gender, could vote. As we have seen, Woodhull's advocacy did not persuade the House Judicial Committee to support her proposed declaratory law. Neither could Stanton and Anthony convince the Senate Judicial Committee to interpret the Fourteenth Amendment to guarantee women's suffrage.[34]

Scores of women were unwilling to surrender to congressional inaction. In 1872 Susan B. Anthony and several other women persuaded election officials in upstate New York to allow them to vote. When Anthony was arrested, she used her trial as a public forum, publishing part of the procedures. The trial court, with Justice Ward Hunt presiding as a designated circuit court judge, found that no right to vote could be inferred from the Fourteenth Amendment. At the sentencing hearing, Anthony turned the tables on her judge, telling him that by the guilty verdict, "you have trampled underfoot . . . my natural rights, my civil rights, [and] my political rights. . . . Your denial of my citizen's right to vote is the denial of my right to consent as one of the governed, the denial of my right of representation as one of the taxed, the denial of my right to a trial by a jury of my peers as an offender against law." Manmade laws against voting, Anthony continued, were as flawed as the fugitive slave law had been. The court fined Anthony $100, but out of principle, she never paid.[35]

Virginia Minor initiated a lawsuit to test her interpretation of the Fourteenth Amendment. After a voting registrar had denied her the right to vote in St. Louis because the Missouri registration law allowed only "male citizens" to vote, she brought suit in a local court. When her case reached the Supreme Court of the United States, in *Minor v. Happerset,* her husband, Francis Minor, who was a St. Louis attorney, represented her. He argued that Missouri law infringed on Mrs. Minor's elective franchise, which was a constitutionally protected privilege of national citizenship, as well as the Due Process Clause of the Fifth Amendment and the Rights Retained by the People Clause of the Ninth Amendment.[36]

Chief Justice Morrison R. Waite wrote the unanimous opinion. Not one justice, not even Justices Swayne or Bradley, both of whom at the time had an expansive view of the Fourteenth Amendment, was willing to interpret the Constitution in a way that might have helped women overcome the political impotence of contemporary chauvinism.[37]

The Court did recognize that women were U.S. citizens; that is, they were members of a political community whose association aimed to promote the general welfare. Rather than regarding Reconstruction as engendering a new meaning for citizenry, Waite asserted that the Fourteenth Amendment "did not add to the privileges and immunities of a citizen. It simply furnished an additional guaranty for the protection of such as he already had." States were solely responsible for regulating elections, and if they chose to exclude some of their citizens from politics, the federal government had no power to impose voting standards on them. Thus only state law, not the Fourteenth Amendment, could provide the right to vote.

Suffragists' earlier concerns about section two were realized when the *Minor* Court relied on the explicit mention of "male citizens" to infer that states enjoyed the discretion to exclude any other class of voters, including women. In addition, the Court determined that voting was not a privilege of citizenship under the Fourteenth Amendment, since the Fifteenth Amendment had been needed to protect the franchise against the exclusionary use of race, color, or previous condition of servitude.

Differences and Racial Dynamics

As Anthony and Minor were litigating their cases on Fourteenth Amendment grounds, the women's suffrage movement began to fracture into two factions, the National Woman Suffrage Association (NWSA) and the American Woman Suffrage Association (AWSA), over whether to continue supporting the Republican Party. Stanton and Anthony headed the first faction.

They decided to pursue women's suffrage despite the party's decision to concentrate solely on black suffrage. Parker Pillsbury, who had formerly edited the *National Anti-Slavery Standard,* and Stanton became the principal editors of *The Revolution,* Anthony's radical newspaper. The first edition appeared on January 6, 1868. Their motto was "Principle, not Policy; Justice, not Favors.—Men, their Rights and Nothing More; Women, their Rights and Nothing Less." *The Revolution* was controversial from its inception because it often berated the Republican decision to pursue black suffrage at the expense of women's rights.[38]

One of the greatest sources of controversy was Anthony's acceptance of funding from a mercantile financier, George F. Train. Despite Train's well-known racist statements about black intelligence, *The Revolution* welcomed his contributions to the women's suffrage movement. Anthony sat silently during joint public appearances with Train while he mocked black suffrage. Sometimes Train resorted to verse: "Woman votes the black to save / The black he votes to make the woman slave." Anthony and Stanton were willing to tolerate Train's racism to retain his financing. Anthony considered Train "*a man terribly in earnest*—one who never fails." The alliance was unacceptable to most lifelong abolitionists. In a letter sent to Anthony, William Lloyd Garrison's criticism was pointed: "The colored people and their advocates have not a more abusive assailant" than Train.[39]

To better disseminate their message, Stanton and Anthony founded the NWSA in May 1869. At the head of the second faction was Lucy Stone and her husband, Henry Blackwell. They organized the AWSA in November 1869. On January 8, 1870, Stone and Blackwell began publishing *The Woman's Journal* as their organization's official voice. The *Journal*'s original editors boasted impressive credentials: Mary Ashton Livermore, the editor in chief, had edited several newspapers, including the *Agitator* on women's rights; Garrison had for thirty-five years edited the most important abolitionist newspaper in the United States, *The Liberator;* Julia Ward Howe was a well-known poet; and Thomas Wentworth Higginson wrote books on subjects from the equal rights of women to the autobiography of his experiences as the Civil War colonel of a regiment composed of former slaves. *The Woman's Journal* tended to be more narrowly focused on women's suffrage than *The Revolution.* In later years, Stone became the editor in chief and Blackwell and their daughter became associate editors.[40]

The NWSA and AWSA appear to have remained on relatively cordial terms until their dispute over the Fifteenth Amendment led to a decades-long rupture. During the 1869 meeting of the Equal Rights Association, held in New York City, the delegates became acrimonious over the proposed Fifteenth Amendment. Several of the delegates, including Stephen Foster, took offense at *The Revolution*'s opposition to the amendment and its connection with Train. Anthony's unwillingness to offer her support for an amendment that parted from the abolitionist cause of women's suffrage is no surprise. Her refusal to renounce Train, however, even when offered the opportunity to do so, rendered her views unsavory to those at the meeting who were willing to forfeit universal suffrage to gain the support needed to ratify the Fifteenth Amendment.[41]

Racist overtones also crept into speeches opposed to putting women's suffrage on hold. Anthony stuck to her hyperbolic rhetoric in the face of criticism: "The old anti-slavery school says women must stand back and wait until the negroes shall be recognized. But we say . . . if intelligence, justice, and morality are to have precedence in the Government, let the question of woman be brought up first and that of the negro last." A young law student from St. Louis, Phoebe Couzins, then spoke of the "degradation" women would be subject to if ignorant men, who "all regard[ed] woman as an inferior being," were given the vote. Her speech had much less suasion than it otherwise might have because she accused black men "as a class" of tyranny within their families. Couzins was echoing Stanton's earlier claim that "American women of wealth, education, virtue and refinement" should not be ruled by "the lower orders of Chinese, Africans, Germans and Irish, with their low ideas of womanhood to make laws for you and your daughters." Foster, Stone, and Blackwell spoke out against the suggestion that women should gain suffrage to the exclusion of uneducated persons. Stone told the Equal Rights Association that when she was a teacher, an old freedman student had studied to read and write after years of forced subjugation. Her point was that illiterate people should not be denied the right to vote.[42]

Anthony's and Stanton's longtime friends, like Blackwell, tried to moderate their views, reminding those "who know the real opinions of Miss Anthony and Mrs. Stanton on the question of negro suffrage, do not believe that they mean to create antagonism between the negro and woman question." Frederick Douglass remembered that before the Civil War, "when there were few houses in which the black man could have put his head, this wooly head of mine found a refuge in the house of Mrs. Elizabeth Cady Stanton."[43]

For obvious reasons, Douglass nevertheless found intolerable Stanton's uses of "Sambo" and "bootblack" to refer to members of his race. Stanton also "did not believe in allowing ignorant negroes and foreigners to make laws for her to obey." Douglass explained his support for enfranchising blacks before women:

> I do not see how any one can pretend that there is the same urgency in giving the ballot to woman as to negro. With us, the matter is a question of life and death. . . . When women, because they are women, are hunted down . . . when they are dragged from their houses and hung upon lamp-posts; when their children are torn from their arms . . . when they are the object of insult and outrage at every turn; when they are in danger of having their homes burned down over their heads; when their children are not allowed to enter schools; then they will have an urgency to obtain the ballot equal to our own.[44]

In response, Stone told the audience that while Douglass had accurately described the action of the Ku Klux Klan in the South, he failed to understand that women suffered from "Ku-Kluxes . . . in the North in the shape of men, [who] take away the children from the mother, and separate them as completely as if done on the block of the auctioneer."[45] Her statement apparently referred to the feminist efforts to equalize women's child custody rights. In the nineteenth century, typical state laws gave a fit father exclusive custody and allowed him to assign a guardian in case of death. Women were provided no recourse to challenge custody.[46]

Feminist use of the term "slavery" drew attention to wives' subservience to their husbands in the realms of domestic, civil, financial, and physical relations. The renowned philosopher John Stuart Mill's *Subjugation of Women* profoundly influenced American feminism. Mill regarded the institution of marriage to be analogous to slavery because the power dynamic so favored husbands that it denied wives the opportunity for advancement or contentment, and rendered them powerless against marital rape and other brutalities. Mill wrote that only a marriage between equals could be based on true consent. The marital laws of England and the United States facilitated the suppression of women's talents. Influenced by Mill and others, Stanton concluded that "men abuse wives," having been "taught by law and gospel that they own them as property." Some black women, such as Sarah Parker Remond, found the metaphor overblown, since one of the benefits of abolition was the right to marry, which all southern states had denied to slaves.[47]

While Stanton, Anthony, Stone, and Blackwell all wanted to liberate women from the "slavery of sex," they differed in their approaches. The majority in the 1869 American Equal Rights Association chose Stone's and

Blackwell's position. The association adopted a series of resolutions that endorsed the Fifteenth Amendment but scolded Republicans for the "short-sighted" policy of setting aside women's political aspirations. Stanton and Anthony opposed the decision to wait indefinitely to pass an amendment securing women the right to vote. Through the auspices of the NWSA, they continued to advocate for immediate women's suffrage; meanwhile, the AWSA committed itself to initially ending female disenfranchisement in the District of Columbia and the United States territories.

The NWSA nursed a legitimate grievance against their colleagues, including Garrison and Phillips, for deviating from the Garrisonian principle of acting on moral suasion without giving in to political compromise. They were deeply disappointed that after women had played so important a role in ending slavery, especially through their lobbying efforts and public lectures, their grievances took second place to black suffrage.

The most troubling aspect of Anthony's and Stanton's efforts would remain their decision to court women by pandering to accepted racial prejudices. They increasingly focused their efforts on gaining white women their rights while disregarding black women's political futures. This remained the case even after the NWSA and AWSA merged in 1890, into the National American Woman Suffrage Association (NAWSA), and Lucy Stone died in 1893. Anthony asked Douglass not to attend the 1895 equal suffrage convention in Atlanta. In a conversation with black suffragist and journalist Ida B. Wells, Anthony later rationalized her request as a maternalistic decision not to subject Douglass to the "humiliation" of southern attitudes, but the main impetus behind this seems to have been that Anthony "did not want anything to get in the way of bringing the southern white women into our suffrage association."[48]

This was a far cry from the 1848 Seneca Falls Convention, when Douglass showed no fear of humiliation, being the only man in attendance to vote in favor of a women's suffrage resolution. Stanton, one of the five organizers of that convention, also determined to build up the NAWSA by expressing solidarity with southern women. Yet in 1894 she continued expressing the Radical Republican view that "our mistake in the South . . . was not in securing the blacks their natural rights, but in not holding those States as territories until the white understood the principles of republican government." She sustained her inner sense of human rights, writing in 1893, "How my blood boils over these persecutions of the Africans, the Jews, the Indians, and the Chinese."[49]

Anthony approached women's suffrage from the same sense of urgency but with more single-mindedness than her lifelong collaborator Stanton, who had become too controversial a figure for the NAWSA after the 1895 publication of her *Woman's Bible* and after she showed public support for the widowed Douglass's remarriage to a white suffragist. During the 1899 NAWSA meeting, Anthony, as president, squelched a resolution to condemn segregated rail travel, explaining that "while we are in this" pressing political "condition it is not for us to go passing resolutions against railroad corporations or anybody else." She opposed segregation privately and spoke against lynching but preferred to garner more support for women's suffrage than to openly oppose all forms of racial discrimination. That decision astounded Stanton: "What would the sainted Lucretia Mott, Ernestine L. Rose, Lucy Stone and Angelina Grimké" have said, Stanton asked rhetorically, "had they been present when one colored woman stood alone, pleading for the protection of her sex?" Anthony refused to budge, just as she had during her lectures with the overtly racist George F. Train. In 1903 she silently presided over a meeting at which Belle Kearney, a white Mississippi suffragist, told NAWSA participants that "the enfranchisement of women would insure immediate and durable white supremacy, honestly attained."[50]

In retrospect, the NWSA correctly called attention to the deficiencies of the Fifteenth Amendment. Its shortcomings, as we have seen, also hurt blacks, but the amendment ignored women's political rights altogether. The NWSA's unjustifiable step was to deem white women's interests superior to those of blacks. Stanton and Anthony shifted their efforts from achieving human rights to achieving women's rights. This single-mindedness gave short shrift to the persistent effects of racism. Neither did the NWSA's pursuit of southern support speed the codification of women's suffrage. As for the AWSA, it stayed true to abolitionist advocacy. The NWSA's mistake lay in choosing to compromise ideals for women's suffrage rather than persisting in the advocacy for universal suffrage. Both movements met the expedients necessary for them to thrive, but their decisions to enter politics, rather than to stay above it, tended to undermine their principles.

The groups' merger into the NAWSA, along with a change in leadership, further shifted attention from all women to white women. Even Henry Blackwell, two years after the death of his wife, expressed his support for the increasingly popular southern literacy tests and property qualifications aimed to disenfranchise black and illiterate voters. "Society . . . has a right to prescribe, in the admission of any new class of voters," Blackwell told the 1895

NAWSA Convention, "such a qualification as every one can attain and as will enable the voter to cast an intelligent and responsible vote." He even clarified that those he was referring to as illiterates were, in the North, "foreigners" and, in the South, "people of the African race." Kearney's 1903 advocacy of preserving white supremacy by granting white women a vote in the South indicated that the organization had veered drastically from its former ecumenical orientation. A movement to end one of the greatest injustices in U.S. history wound up currying favor by resorting to local prejudices.[51]

One State at a Time

Representative Julian's efforts to add a sixteenth amendment for the protection of women's voting rights failed, despite Stanton's and Anthony's indefatigable endorsement of it. The first major extension of voting rights to women came in the Wyoming Territory in 1869. In 1890, when Wyoming entered the Union as a state, it left no doubt that political gender inequality would not be tolerated there. The state's constitution provided that "the rights of citizens of the state of Wyoming to vote and hold office shall not be denied or abridged on account of sex. Both male and female citizens of this state shall equally enjoy all civil, political and religious privileges." This was the first unequivocal statewide enactment of franchise since 1807, when New Jersey had withdrawn voting privileges from women. Some progress had occurred on the municipal level in the intervening eighty-three years. Kansas allowed women to vote locally and to hold city and school offices. Other states, including Colorado, Wisconsin, New Hampshire, North and South Dakota, New York, Oregon, Washington, Arizona, Idaho, New Jersey, Michigan, Vermont, and Montana, allowed women to vote and hold offices on school matters.[52]

Wyoming set the trend of granting women more than a minimal role in municipal politics. Other western states blazed the trail for women's suffrage provisions even before a U.S. constitutional amendment provided national protection of that right. Colorado was the first state to grant women's suffrage by popular referendum, with 55 percent of the vote. Most men in the state demonstrated a clear sense that women should be entitled to a vote. Suffragists found Davis H. Waite, Colorado's governor, helpful in gaining enough votes for women to vote. National leaders like Anthony, Stone, Blackwell, and Carrie Chapman stumped for women's suffrage in Colorado during a failed campaign in 1877 and again during the successful drive of 1893.[53]

Utah followed suit in 1895, when more than 80 percent of the male electorate voted for a constitutional provision to enfranchise women. The provision took effect in 1896 in connection with the state's admission into the Union. That year Martha Hughes Cannon, a mother, physician, and polygamist, was the first woman to become a Utah state senator. Then, in 1898, Utah augmented women's new equal citizenship status by becoming the first state to allow them to serve on juries. Idaho, another western state, conducted a women's suffrage referendum of its own in 1896. The voters resoundingly supported the proposition by a vote of 12,126 to 6,282.[54]

Fourteen years elapsed before another state, Washington, enfranchised women in 1910. Years of work had gone into the result. Susan B. Anthony and Abigail Scott Duniway extensively traversed the Washington and Oregon Territories in 1871, driving home the importance of suffrage. In 1883 the Territory of Washington, following the example set by the Wyoming and Utah Territories, enfranchised women. During the winter of 1887 the Washington Territory Supreme Court found the suffrage law unconstitutional, but women were increasingly pooling their efforts. In 1888, on the fortieth anniversary of the Seneca Falls convention, feminists convened the first International Council of Women in Washington, D.C. The convention's statement of purpose gave voice to "women of all Nations, sincerely believing that the best good of humanity" could be "advanced by greater unity of thought" among various women's suffrage groups.[55]

In August 1889 advocates failed to convince the Washington State Constitutional Convention to adopt a suffrage provision. Delegates to the convention apparently feared that Congress would vote against admitting Washington as a state with the provision in its constitution. After years of work, the Washington electorate finally enfranchised women in 1910 by a resounding vote of 52,299 to 29,676. The victory was not altogether satisfactory, however, because the same provision that gave women the vote also provided that untaxed Indians "shall never be allowed elective franchise." But the victory on behalf of women showed that unremitting effort could inspire the electorate to vote in favor of equalizing citizenship rights.[56]

The momentum generated in Washington carried over to California, where women became enfranchised in 1911. The campaign began long before that year. In 1883 the Woman's Christian Suffrage Association, working from its San Francisco office, promoted voting for women to take more control of their own lives and to be better able to help their children. Labor organizations often worked side by side with suffragists.

The pace of the campaign sped up drastically in 1910 and 1911. California suffrage leaders relied on popular participation to the achieve victory. Katherine Philips Edson, a prominent figure in state health and labor reform matters, founded the Political Equality League to spread the message. Edson's husband, Charles Farwell, helped too, even singing at least once before a mass suffrage meeting. Another of the league's leaders, Clara Shortridge Foltz, was a well-known figure, having been the first female law student and lawyer in California history. Foltz became just as well known for suffrage as for her initiative to obtain public defenders for indigent clients. John H. Braly was a banker and onetime professor, who financed some of the league's activities. The league pointed out that the state as a whole would benefit from women's suffrage because women were more likely to push for their children's interests than would men: "Who is so interested in questions of public sanitation, clean milk, pure food, school administration, playgrounds and moral atmosphere as the mother and teacher?" California suffragists also argued that the "revival of interest in woman's suffrage is part of a great world movement for justice and democracy, it is part of the revolt against class legislation, class suppression." By 1910 Shortridge, Braly, and other members of the Political Equality League boasted bipartisan support for women's suffrage. State Republicans even included it in their party plank. Governor Hiram Johnson, who later became a United States senator for the state, made women's suffrage an essential part of his administration.[57]

Numerous clubs helped the league spread the message to all corners of the massive state. The National Council of Jewish Women invited a speaker to help drum up support. Rabbi Isidore Myers displayed his "enthusiasm for the cause of political equality" by jumping on stage between a clown and chorus girl act at an "operatic farce" to speak of women's suffrage. "In America," he told the audience, "we have only two sexes, the fair sex and the unfair sex. The unfair sex, of course, is that sex which refuses to grant to woman the right to take part in the affairs of government under which she lives and the laws of which she must obey." The audience listened raptly to the rabbi for ten minutes but eventually tired of the theatric interruption and hissed him off the stage. A member of the Votes for Women Club wrote a catchy song about her desire to stand with other voters. A law student from the University of Southern California led the Latino branch of the Votes for Women Club. Teas, such as an outdoors event that Dr. Louise M. Richter sponsored, with Edson among the speakers, boosted the cause. By July 1911 the president of the Political Equality League centralized the southern California suffrage campaign in Los Angeles.[58]

The campaign met vocal opposition. One group, the Southern California

Association Opposed to Woman Suffrage, claimed to represent the majority sentiment of California women. They disdained "suffrage leaders' . . . contempt of domestic women," asking to be left without the burden of political obligation. They also feared that the vote would degrade women's moral position in society, which placed them above politics. Others considered women's suffrage a Socialist plot.[59]

The agitation throughout California captured the attention of many and created an almost even split on the issue. The margin of victory for the suffrage amendment was small—3,537 of the total 246,847 votes cast. The electorate commissioners sped up the vote count to allow women to vote in a December 1911 Los Angeles election.[60]

The following year, Oregon, Kansas, and Arizona adopted constitutional amendments guaranteeing women the right to vote. But the many losses that year illustrated the problem with state-by-state efforts. Members of the Virginia House of Representatives overwhelmingly defeated a proposed suffrage amendment to the state constitution. In New York it was the Senate that killed a suffrage bill in 1912 by only two votes. Almost all cities in Ohio voted against women's suffrage in substantial majorities, and the effort overwhelmingly went down in defeat there. Women wept openly in the Connecticut House of Representatives gallery after that body of the state congress refused to strike out the word "male" from the franchise section of its constitution. That year, popular referenda for women's suffrage failed in Michigan and Wisconsin. In Cook County, Illinois, which includes Chicago, women's suffrage went down to defeat by about seventy-five thousand votes. Marion Drake, the campaign manager there, put the best face on the loss, explaining that "the movement was too young and too novel to appeal to the average voter."[61]

The Illinois Constitution provided that all male citizens could vote in any election so long as they were at least twenty-one years old and met state residency requirements. Without altering its constitution, the state legislature passed the Woman's Suffrage Act of 1913. It allowed women to vote for a variety of state and local officers and presidential electors; however, women still could not vote in U.S. Senate and House elections or for members of the state legislature. The battle over voting rights in Illinois evolved during a seventy-two-year period, beginning in the 1850s. Leaders like Jane Addams, a social worker and founder of Chicago's Hull House, gave speeches, wrote editorials, and lobbied politicians. In one 1912 column, Addams asserted that women could advance economically only if they shared political power.

"Working women," she wrote, "cannot hope to hold their own in industrial matters where their interests clash with those of their enfranchised fellow workers and employers, in whose hands lie [*sic*] the solution of the problems which are at present convulsing the industrial world. . . . They are bound to feel more and more the disadvantages of being shut out from the sphere where questions connected with their wages and hours of labor are being fought out." One young woman organizer, Katherine Riley, refused to marry until the law passed. Riley would not even announce her engagement to the speaker of the Illinois House of Representatives, William McKinley, until he helped secure its passage. The day after McKinley maneuvered the bill through the House, Riley announced their engagement. The act of 1913, while limited in scope, was a clear advance for Illinois women, who had previously been confined to voting in school elections and for university trustees.[62]

Soon after the beginning of the First World War in 1914, Nevada and Montana adopted constitutional amendments granting women suffrage. The next year was bleak for the cause, however, with Massachusetts, New York, New Jersey, and Pennsylvania rejecting suffrage in 1915. After the loss in New York, by more than 200,000 votes, a correspondent for the *New York Times* wrote somewhat jubilantly, "The men of the mighty industrial State voted it down for the good of the State and the good of the women. The essential American conservatism . . . prevailed," unlike in the "carelessness of sparse Western populations." Little could the journalist imagine how quickly the tide would turn. In 1917, when a sizable majority of 102,353 New Yorkers voted to grant women full suffrage, the *Times* was downright supplicatory, fearful of the unknown: "The *Times* will not pretend to rejoice at the result to which it made no effort to contribute. May the experiment, if it is to be made, disappoint the fears and predictions of its adversaries. May the women justify by their behavior their fitness for the ballot. And, all division removed, may the feminists give henceforth the full measure of their strength and energy to the cause of freedom and democracy." In the opinion of Harriot Stanton Blatch, daughter of Elizabeth Cady Stanton and one of the foremost women's suffrage leaders in New York: "Hundreds of thousands of men went into the voting booths and voluntarily divided with us their sovereignty. They did it in a spirit of generous fellowship. . . . We, in turn, should vouchsafe them just that sort of fellowship."[63]

Nineteen-seventeen was a watershed year for women's suffrage. President Woodrow Wilson congratulated the National American Woman Suffrage

Association after the North Dakota legislature granted women the right to vote for presidential electors and municipal officers. On April 21, 1917, Nebraska Governor Keith Neville signed a law giving women in his state the same right. January 1917 was also the first time an East Coast state, Rhode Island, adopted a women's suffrage law, but it was limited to presidential electors. Similar laws passed in Ohio and Indiana, but they later had to be reenacted. Arkansas first allowed women to vote in primary elections the same year, and Vermont granted women suffrage on the municipal level. Michigan passed a presidential suffrage statute in 1917, and a state constitutional amendment granted women full suffrage the next year. In 1918 South Dakota and Oklahoma also granted complete suffrage. And nine states provided presidential suffrage between 1919 and 1920.[64]

This wearisome state-by-state approach, with its dependence on the vicissitudes of the male electorate, made clear that a national victory, of the type Stanton and Anthony had advocated in the 1860s and 1870s, was needed. Carrie Chapman Catt, the president of the NAWSA, determined that while progress in the states was desirable, achieving women's suffrage also required lobbying Congress to amend the United States Constitution. Catt's so-called Winning Plan of 1916 required widely dispersed suffrage groups to centralize their operations. They would henceforth need to coordinate strategy through the NAWSA. Catt created a political organization with a clear hierarchy. National leaders made overall policies and transmitted them to state planners, who in turn filtered them down to district workers. The NAWSA organized parades, advertisements, and petitions. The single-minded effort gained women the vote, but it did not address many persistent gender inequities.[65]

Constitutional Amendment

Nationally, women's suffrage had become increasingly accepted even before Catt began her centralized effort for a constitutional amendment. In 1910 the Congressional Committee of the NAWSA polled Democratic and Republican candidates for Congress. The results were heartening. Of the 180 candidates who responded, 107 favored full suffrage, many others favored limited suffrage, and only nine were altogether opposed to it. The national planks of both political parties supported women's suffrage in 1916, although there was some ambiguity as to whether they stood for national or state suffrage.[66]

To pass a proposed constitutional amendment onto the states for ratification requires that two-thirds of both bodies of Congress approve it. In a representative democracy, congressmen respond to their constituents, in part to avoid losing reelection. By 1918 the popular trend in the West and Midwest was in favor of extending voting rights to women. Twenty of forty-eight states already had laws providing women with the right to full or at least presidential suffrage. The enormous changes at the state level brought new respect to the suffrage movement. On January 10, 1918, suffragists were able to test their strength when the House of Representatives put the proposed amendment to a vote.[67]

The House debate focused on explaining how America could benefit from allowing women to vote. It also exhibited a sense of obligation to women for their war efforts, as well as a persistent desire to placate male prejudices. Southern representatives like John A. Moon argued for state sovereignty over issues of voter competence, deriding the Fifteenth Amendment and defending the "wishes and the sentiments of the people of our sister States struggling to maintain law and order and white supremacy." In response, Jeannette Rankin of Montana, the first woman ever elected to Congress, tried to soothe southern concerns, much as the NAWSA and the NWSA had done. Southern women, Rankin said, had stood by their men during "every struggle," including the "adjustment in the South" after the Civil War. "Are you going to deny them the equipment with which to help you, effectively simply because the enfranchisement of a child-race 50 years ago brought you a problem you were powerless to handle?" Rankin tried to explain the advantages of added white women voters: "There are more white women of voting age in the South to-day than there are negro men and women together." John E. Raker of California, a member of the House Committee on Woman Suffrage, used statistics to break down southern opposition, "There are over 8,788,000 white women in the South and 4,000,000 colored. You will have over 4,000,000 more white women than you will have colored. The total negro population is 8,294,274, and white women outnumber both negro males and females by nearly half a million." While Raker expressed concern about the use of property qualification for voters, he assured southerners that the proposed amendment would not alter that state qualification. While catering to southern prejudices, Raker somewhat contradictorily called on his colleagues not to fall behind other countries, since "woman suffrage has made amazing progress in foreign lands." Raker and Rankin were willing to achieve progress for white women while leaving black women behind. By implication, they encouraged the South to resort to trickery to retain the status quo for black men—the various means, as we have seen, used to disenfranchise black men without running afoul of the Fifteenth Amendment.[68]

Other supporters in the House concentrated solely on voting as a right rather than expressing sympathy for southern discrimination. Kansas Representative Philip P. Campbell spoke of the need to requite women for "doing every kind of work to-day that men are doing behind the lines—manufacturing arms, munition, clothing, and so forth." The American Congress should "catch the spirit of the times," urged Kentucky Representative James C. Cantrill. Melville C. Kelly of Pennsylvania was even more direct about the "fundamental principle of government by the people." Without granting women the vote, America would be a "laggard instead of a leader in this great movement for the democracy for which liberty-loving nations are battling around the world." Kelly pointed out that even the German Reichstag had committed itself to women's suffrage. "Let the oldest and greatest democracy in the world lead this movement. . . . Already more than one-fourth of the membership of this House and of the Senate come from States where women vote." Following the debate, the victory in the House was slim; it passed the proposed amendment on to the Senate by only two votes.[69]

Attention then turned to the Senate. It became evident that support there was weaker; consequently, President Woodrow Wilson and members of his cabinet, the retired Theodore Roosevelt, and members of the Democratic and Republican Parties made personal appeals for passage. Wilson, in his September 30, 1918, Senate address, described support for women's suffrage as "vitally essential to the successful prosecution of the great war of humanity in which we are engaged." The president asked senators to requite women for the "partnership of sacrifice and suffering" they continued to provide throughout the First World War. "This war could not have been fought . . . if it had not been for the services of women." Women's participation had become conspicuous through their steadily increasing contributions to emerging technologies, medical developments, and community policing. In the aftermath of the war, as Wilson put it, their "sympathy and insight and clear moral instinct" would clarify the American "vision of affairs." The president's backing was indicative of the extent to which suffrage had made its way into the forefront of American politics. On October 1, 1918, the proposed amendment nevertheless fell two votes short, and on February 10, 1919, one vote short of the necessary two-thirds in the Senate.[70]

Suffragists refused to quit. Sensing that victory was imminent after so many years of toil, they redoubled their efforts. The next Congress, the sixty-sixth, again took up the proposed amendment. It handily received the needed two-thirds in the House vote but only narrowly passed the Senate, on June 4, 1919. The proposal then went to the states for ratification.

The Illinois legislature acted overwhelmingly and speedily, within a week becoming the first state to adopt the resolution of ratification. Hours later, Michigan and Wisconsin did the same. The last and deciding vote for ratification came, more than fourteen months later, from Tennessee. In the early morning of August 26, 1920, United States Secretary of State Bainbridge Colby signed a proclamation at his home announcing the ratification to the Constitution of the Nineteenth Amendment.[71]

After 1923, when Delaware ratified the amendment, only nine holdout states remained, all from the South: Alabama, Florida, Georgia, Louisiana, Maryland, Mississippi, North Carolina, South Carolina, and Virginia. With these holdouts the process was slow. Maryland passed a resolution to ratify on March 29, 1941, but did not certify the ratification until 1958. Mississippi was the last state to ratify the amendment, on March 22, 1984.[72]

Women were first able to exercise their national franchise on November 2, 1920. Women in their nineties walked to the polls in West Harlem, New York, refusing rides in order to show their new sense of vigor. President Wilson and First Lady Edith Bolling Galt, who had become intrinsic to the day-to-day operation of the cabinet since 1919, when her husband had become bedridden as a result of a stroke, voted in Princeton, New Jersey. Carrie Chapman Catt, president of the NAWSA, and Mary Garrett Hay, president of the League of Women Voters, voted in New York City. Alice Paul, the chairwoman of the National Woman's Party, however, minimized the change, pointing out that women "had practically no voice in the selection of any candidates or in the drafting of the political platforms."[73]

Black women in the South continued to be disenfranchised because of their race. Savannah, Georgia, for example, denied many registered black women voters the right to vote in 1920, citing a technicality in the state law. The National League of Women Voters established the Committee on Negro Problems in 1924 to try to prevent similar restrictions in the future. Black women remained subject to the same discriminatory voting disqualifications long employed against black men, including literacy tests and poll taxes.[74]

CHAPTER EIGHT

Progressive Transitions

Racial issues continued to polarize Americans into the Progressive Era, which lasted roughly between 1890 and 1920. The systemic inequality that had plagued the country from its inception still afflicted it into the twentieth century. Racial tensions increased between 1910 and 1920, when about five hundred thousand blacks moved from the South to escape lynching, low-income jobs, and voting disqualification. Many northerners met black arrivals warily, concerned that their own property would depreciate and their jobs disappear. In response to an increasing black and immigrant urban population, some communities used intimidation, restrictive property covenants, and zoning laws to maintain racial hegemony.[1]

In *Plessy v. Ferguson* (1896), the United States Supreme Court determined that the federal government was powerless against segregation in social settings. Residential zoning, at least at first glance, seemed to represent the type of interpersonal contact that *Plessy* immunized from government safeguards. A number of cities, including Baltimore (1911), Richmond (1911), Winston-Salem (1912), Atlanta (1913), and Louisville (1914) enacted segregation ordinances. With the expansion of discrimination, creative legal assistance was crucial. Enter the National Association for the Advancement of Colored People (NAACP), which had already secured a victory in *Guinn v. United States* (1915), overturning the use of grandfather clauses to disenfranchise blacks and keep them out of politics. The NAACP went on to its second victory in *Buchanan v. Warley* (1917). In that case, the Court found that laws requiring neighborhoods to be racially segregated infringed on property rights without due process of law. In the years that followed, the NAACP brought successful lawsuits challenging residential segregation ordinances in Winston-Salem, Baltimore, Indianapolis, Norfolk, and Dallas.[2]

Some city governments simply ignored *Buchanan.* A New Orleans ordinance, for one, explicitly criminalized blacks and whites residing in certain districts "without the written consent of a majority of the persons of the opposite race inhabiting the 'community, or portion of the city to be affected.'" New Orleans enacted the ordinance pursuant to a 1924 Louisiana statute enabling "a negro or white community" to consent "to the establishment of a home-residence by a member of the other race." In 1925 the Supreme Court of Louisiana found that the law did not violate the United States Constitution. In order to get around *Buchanan,* Louisiana's highest court differentiated the police power to enact consent laws from the automatic deprivation of private property that the U.S. Supreme Court had found to be constitutionally unwarranted. In the spirit of *Plessy,* the Louisiana court found racial restrictions to be constitutional so long as they left it to whites and blacks, who were acting for "the promotion of their comfort, and the preservation of the public peace and good order," to choose whether they wanted to be neighbors. The Supreme Court of the United States, in *Corrigan v. Buckley* (1926), refused to review Louisiana's decision, finding that only private contractual rights were at stake, so the Fourteenth Amendment did not apply. Emboldened by *Corrigan,* New Orleans retained its segregation ordinance until 1972.[3]

While black voters were nearly powerless when it came to altering the dynamics of the Supreme Court, whose members are appointed rather than elected, their ability to participate politically had important consequences. Many African Americans broke with the Republican Party in 1912 to help the Democratic candidate, Woodrow Wilson, win the presidency. At first, this constituency had some reason to rejoice. President Wilson and Attorney General James C. McReynolds determined in 1914 to renominate the first black judge in Washington, D.C., Robert H. Terrell, to the municipal court. Mississippi Senator James K. Vardaman, at a meeting with the president to discuss Terrell's appointment, said that while he was "not against the negro as an individual," he would work against allowing "the negro and the white man" to "live together on terms of political equality." Wilson refused to budge, and later he sent the name of another black man to be appointed recorder of deeds for the District of Columbia.[4]

Even as it acted beneficently toward a handful of individuals, in 1913 the Wilson administration maintained racial segregation of civil service employees in government offices, restrooms, and lunch areas. William Monroe Trotter, the secretary and leader of the National Equal Rights League, wrote

Wilson to ask for an audience on the issue. In his letter Trotter reproved the president for the segregation of bathrooms and dining rooms at the Department of the Treasury, whereby the "Government deliberately denies equality of citizenship, in violation of the Constitution, and makes an inferior and a superior class of citizens." By segregating citizens the federal government tolerated prejudice and declared "blacks to be unclean, diseased or indecent as to their persons, or inferior beings of a lower order." The Post Office Department, the Department of the Navy, and the Bureau of Printing and Engraving were also segregated. Trotter and other delegates finally received an audience from Wilson in November 1914. During the forty-five-minute meeting, Trotter blasted segregation: "Have you a 'new freedom' for white Americans and a new slavery for your African-American fellow citizens?" he asked Wilson. Even though his administration was not ardent about enforcing segregation standards, the president's exchange with Trotter was heated. At one point, Wilson gave vent to his ire, telling Trotter that "segregation is not humiliating but a benefit." That assertion was not a mere slip of the tongue but an expression of the president's conviction. In August 1913 Wilson wrote Oswald Garrison Villard, William Lloyd Garrison's grandson, defending segregation as being in the "interest of the colored people."[5]

When Republican Warren G. Harding became president, he maintained Wilson's policy of separating blacks and whites, and President Calvin Coolidge extended that policy to other federal departments. Segregation had become a bipartisan and executive practice.[6]

Anti-Immigrant Sentiments

An increasingly hostile environment toward immigrants also had ardently racist overtones. The use of restrictive covenants on the West Coast was symptomatic of the increasingly widespread antagonism. In 1892, years before the Court decided *Buchanan*, Federal District Court Judge Ross voided a restrictive covenant on renting buildings or grounds to persons of Chinese origin.

The trend in immigration law tended to be xenophobic, fueled by virulently anti-Chinese sentiments. When Chinese laborers began arriving in the United States, they encountered a provision in the Nationality Act that permitted only "free white persons" to become naturalized citizens. Senator Charles Sumner tried to remove that clause from the statute, arguing that it violated the anticolor and antirace principles of the Declaration of Independence, but he received little support for the initiative. To make matters worse, the Chinese Exclusion Act of 1882 placed a ten-year bar against the immigration of Chinese laborers into the United States. Even Justice John Marshall Harlan's famous dissent to *Plessy v. Ferguson* (1896), opposing Jim Crow laws, claimed that the Chinese race is "so different from our own that we do not permit those belonging to it to become citizens of the United States."[7] Backed by popular sentiment, Congress renewed Chinese exclusionary measures in 1892, 1902, and 1904. Race-based exclusions placed the civil rights of Chinese American residents in a precarious state of political uncertainty.

The 1888 Scott Act prohibited Chinese laborers who left the United States from reentering. In one case, a Chinese laborer received a certificate to travel to China and returned to the United States just seven days after the Scott Act went into force. Upon his arrival in the port of San Francisco, he learned that the new law had nullified his certificate for reentry. The Supreme Court, his last hope for rectifying the situation, found that the bar to reentry was a legitimate use of congressional authority to exclude foreigners. Only in 1943 did Congress get around to repealing the Chinese exclusion laws.[8]

Fortunately, anti-Chinese sentiments were unable to supplant the Fourteenth Amendment. In 1886 the Supreme Court found that a San Francisco ordinance violated the Equal Protection and Due Process Clauses by preventing Chinese business owners from engaging in a trade. The case continues to represent the principle that those two constitutional clauses are "universal in their application," protecting the rights of "all persons within" the country's "territorial jurisdiction, without regard to any differences of race, of color, or of nationality." In an 1896 case the Supreme Court began recognizing that parts of the Bill of Rights apply to all persons in the United States, including alien residents of Chinese origin. Despite these holdings, race prejudice continued to influence immigration policy.[9]

A bulky forty-one-volume 1911 congressional report gathered by Senator William P. Dillingham's United States Immigration Commission reported that new immigrants, particularly eastern and southern Europeans, were economically and intellectually inferior to old-stock immigrants, who were primarily northwestern Europeans from England, Ireland, Germany, and Scandinavia. Even though this eugenic conclusion was widely condemned, it had a lasting effect on decisionmaking. In an attempt to arrest the flow of new arrivals, the Immigration Act of 1917 prohibited immigration from the "Asiatic barred zone," which included virtually all of south Asia except Japan and the Philippines. In an attempt to slow immigration from eastern and southern Europe, the 1917 statute also instituted a literacy test, requiring reading comprehension in any language. It did exempt religious refugees from the literacy requirement. Admissible aliens could also enter with their otherwise illiterate families. Ultimately, the literacy test made little difference. The last year it was in effect (July 1920–June 1921), 800,000 persons immigrated to the United States. During that period, the test kept only 1,450 persons from entering the country. All other excluded persons were deported on other grounds. Searching for a more effective measure to maintain the nation's traditional northern European majority, Congress adopted a quota-based system.[10]

The Dillingham Commission's influence was evident throughout the 1920 nativist immigration campaign. The chairman of the House Committee on Immigration and Naturalization, Republican Albert Johnson, considered Jews to be "unassimilable" and "filthy, un-American and often dangerous in their habits." The charge that anti-Semitism was central to the proposed immigration restrictions troubled Representative George Huddleston of Alabama. On the floor of the House, he questioned curtailing immigration of eastern European Jews who were fleeing vicious anti-Semitic persecution. A State Department report indicated that the overwhelming majority of Jews in Poland, the Ukraine, and Romania sought asylum from widespread carnage.[11]

Meanwhile, an anti-Asian movement on the West Coast received political and popular backing. United States Senator James D. Phelan of California was the chief supporter of the Oriental Exclusion League and sponsored the Anti-Asiatic League. The league's president in 1920, State Senator J. M. Inman, pressed to prohibit Japanese from owning property. At a 1920 hearing before the Committee on Immigration and Naturalization, Phelan described the Japanese as "immoral people" and warned that they would lead California into "mongrelization and degeneracy." The American Legion released a film claiming that the Japanese drove up prices, and the *Saturday Evening Post* and *Cosmopolitan* nationally syndicated anti-Japanese novels. One protagonist portrayed the Japanese as being "ruthless, greedy, selfish, calculating" and advocated "Jim Crow cars for these cock-sure sons of Nippon."[12]

Supporters of exclusion continued to shape national agenda. The 1921 Immigration Act, which Congress passed with President Harding's support, set an immigration cap at about 350,000 and limited each nationality to 3 percent of its number residing in the United States at the time of the 1910 census. That provision was to prevent changes to the country's demography.[13]

Along the same lines, the 1924 National Origins Act set a 2 percent entrance quota from countries based on "the number of foreign-born individuals of such nationality" resident in the United States as of 1890. By setting the cutoff point at 1890, Congress reduced the inflow of Jews, Italians, Slavs, and Greeks, since at that point few southern and eastern Europeans had made their homes in America. Just to get a sense of how limiting the law was, the Italian quota was set at 5,802 a year, compared with an annual average of 158,000 immigrants during the early twentieth century. The Greek quota was 307.[14]

The 1924 law also targeted Far East Asians. It barred persons ineligible for citizenship from immigrating, which was a clear reference to the continuing vitality of the Chinese Exclusion Acts. It further placed a complete bar on Japanese immigration, even though the 1907 "gentlemen's agreement" between the United States and Japan seemed to preclude such a proscription. Filipinos were the only Asians to remain relatively unaffected by immigration regulation until 1934, as the United States, entering the New Deal era, enacted a federal statute that set a fifty-person annual quota on Philippine nationals. Only in 1943 were Chinese allowed to become naturalized citizens, and a 1946 amendment also allowed Filipinos and Indians to be citizens.[15]

Anti-Semitic Developments

In a letter to the editor of the *New York Times*, the Japanese American Junzo Hishi wrote against immigration policies based on a privileged racial or nationalistic ideology. He counseled against following automobile industrialist Henry Ford's suggestion to get "rid of the undesirable element from the community."

Ford's favorite targets were Jews, whom he collectively considered to be "International Financiers" working against American interests. For years, his *Dearborn Independent*, with a circulation of at least three hundred thousand, disseminated anti-Semitic sentiments against Jewish immigration. Ford's conspiracy theory was so ardent that he declared Benedict Arnold's treason the work of the "Jewish front." Besides believing that Jews had tried to subvert the American Revolution, he echoed a widely disseminated anti-Semitic charge that Jewish bankers dominated the U.S. economy. In response, 119 well-known Americans, including former presidents Woodrow Wilson and William Howard Taft, denounced Ford's anti-Jewish propaganda. Ford apologized for his bombast only after two million-dollar defamation lawsuits were filed against him in 1927. In keeping with the times, the novelist Kenneth L. Roberts's widely read articles appearing in the *Saturday*

Evening Post in 1920–21 asserted that Polish Jews were "human parasites" whose presence in the country would create "a hybrid race of people as worthless and futile as the good-for-nothing mongrels of Central America and Southeastern Europe." Popular works like William Z. Ripley's *Races of Europe* (1899) and Madison Grant's *The Passing of the Great Race* (1916) denigrated eastern European immigrants based on a nativist racial theory. Elite universities like Harvard, Yale, Princeton, and Columbia restricted Jewish enrollment by quotas that favored Anglo-Saxons.[16]

During this period, a local prosecutor charged Leo Frank, the manager of a pencil factory in Atlanta and president of the B'nai B'rith organization, with sexually assaulting and murdering a thirteen-year-old factory girl, Mary Phagan. Even before the grand jury returned an indictment, ten state militia companies stationed themselves in Atlanta to be on guard because of rumors that Frank was to be lynched. The defense had a difficulty even securing the safety of its trial witnesses. Detective William J. Burns, who testified on Frank's behalf, was attacked by a large mob and fled to a hotel for shelter. During Frank's trial, a mob could be heard outside shouting "Hang the Jew!" The trial judge and jurors received threats, and some spectators in the packed courtroom were armed. Amid this intimidating atmosphere, the jury found Frank guilty of first-degree murder. After Frank's conviction, affidavit witnesses testified that a juror had exclaimed, "I am glad they indicted the God damn Jew. They ought to take him out and lynch him." The prosecutor likened Frank to Judas Iscariot.

Frank appealed to the Georgia Supreme Court, charging that the mob had influenced the conviction. After losing there, he applied for a writ of habeas corpus from a federal district court, which could have granted him freedom for the impairment of his constitutional rights. The district court denied Frank's motion, and the U.S. Supreme Court heard the appeal.[17]

For the majority, Justice Mahlon Pitney, a Taft appointee from New Jersey, rejected Frank's claim that a "hostile public sentiment and disorder in and about the court room, improperly influenced the trial court and the jury against him." Justices Holmes and Charles Evans Hughes dissented, writing that "mob law does not become due process of law by securing the assent of a terrorized jury." Federal courts should hear cases, Holmes asserted, even when a state supreme court affirms a decision of a jury that deliberated under the pressure of a "mob" that is "savagely and manifestly intent on a single result."[18]

Based on new evidence and aware of the mob pressures involved at the trial, Georgia Governor John M. Slaton commuted Frank's sentence to life imprisonment. In response, a crowd gathered outside Slaton's office threatened to lynch him. At that point, a group calling itself the Knights of Mary Phagan determined to act. They organized a mob that stormed the state jail, seized Frank, and lynched him. The ringleaders were men of high repute in Georgia. Photographs of the scene show his corpse dangling from a tree, noose around the neck, with handcuffs around the wrists and ankles, while a crowd mills about, wearing everything from overalls to business suits with ties.[19]

Anti-Semitism was not, however, able to capture the imagination of the country, as it did in Nazi Germany, the Ukraine, and Poland during the Second World War. To the contrary, many Jews living in the United States during the early twentieth century began to enjoy increased opportunities and equal legal protections. In 1906 President Theodore Roosevelt named Oscar S. Strauss secretary of commerce and labor, making him the first Jewish cabinet secretary. Louis D. Brandeis became the first Jewish justice on the United States Supreme Court after President Wilson nominated him in 1916. Moses Alexander of Idaho became the first Jewish governor in U.S. history in 1915. And in 1925, Florence Prag Kahn, a former high school English and history teacher, became the first Jewish woman to serve in Congress.

The Klan's Revival

The Knights of Mary Phagan, which instigated Frank's lynching, played a pivotal role in founding the modern Ku Klux Klan. Colonel William Simmons took the lead in organizing and inaugurating the movement. On the eve of Thanksgiving 1915, Simmons, along with sixteen other American-born Protestant men, several of them members of the Knights, ignited the movement with a cross-burning ceremony on Stone Mountain, Georgia. His father had been an officer in the Reconstruction era version of the terrorist organization, and he had long wanted to revive it. Besides the anti-Jewish hysteria that spread though Atlanta in 1915, Simmons saw other positive signs for the organization's success. A film that glorified the Klan, *The Birth of a Nation*, had been released that winter to rave reviews, anti-immigrant sentiments ran high, and the temperance movement was gaining support. These national issues helped buoy the KKK. Simmons fostered a sense of fraternity by designing a hooded uniform, establishing secret ceremonies, and maintaining a rigid hierarchy.[20]

The new Klan retained the vigilantism of its predecessor but adopted a broader agenda than just antiblack racism. In fact, its racism, anti-Semitism, anti-Catholicism, and xenophobia were primarily driven by what its swearing in ceremony described as "100 per cent Americanism, the sanctity of the American home, the chastity of American womanhood and the supremacy of the Caucasian race."[21] In its heyday, during the early to mid-1920s, the Klan appealed to persons of various economic strata throughout the country. Chapters operated in major cities far from the Deep South, like Indianapolis and Denver, and remote, small towns, like Canon City, Colorado. With chapters in all the states of the Union, the Klan was most powerful in Indiana. It is impossible to ascertain the precise size of the second KKK because its membership list was secret. In 1920 it was a small organization of five thousand members. By 1925, at its peak of popularity, the group boasted four to five million members.

Besides being a hate organization, the Klan administered a sense of communal morality. Abductors dressed from head to foot in white kidnapped a socialist, Herbert S. Bigelow, in Newport, Kentucky. They condemned him for pacifism during the First World War and whipped him in the woods. In the Atlanta district, which included the States of Georgia, Alabama, South Carolina and Florida, night-riders prohibited cotton ginneries from selling cotton until the prices per pound rose to their liking. Throughout Georgia, according to Governor Hugh M. Dorsey's official report, there were at least 130 cases of forced labor, cruelty, intimidation, and lynchings attributed to the Klan, which also used violence to force blacks out of white districts. It ordered others to get jobs, settle accounts, and stay home after dark. Learning of these events, Dorsey ordered a sheriff to investigate terror charges against the Klan. The sheriff's letter, which reassured the governor that the Klan was not responsible, was endorsed by the Ku Klux Klan and bore a seal reading "Cameron Klan No. 17, Realm of Georgia." To avenge a black man's quarrel with a white store owner in Putnam County, central Georgia, the Klan set fire to five black churches, two black schools, and a lodge hall. The Texas Klan forced blacks into virtual slave labor, requiring them to work and pick cotton at low wages; Beaumont, Texas, authorities reported numerous tar and feathering incidents; Klansmen flogged and tarred and feathered the editor of the *Florida Post,* J. H. Wendler, for writing a column which they disliked. Whites and blacks refused to be cowed, and offered a large reward for the offenders' arrest. In another part of the country, Rollin P. Jones, the principal of a Phoenix, Arizona, school, was acquitted of an alleged offense with a girl. The Klan disagreed with the outcome of the case and took matters into its own hands, whipping Jones and branding his forehead with carbonic acid. Three Chicago Klansmen tried to attack a chiropractor in Morris, Illinois, allegedly because he had "abused" a young girl. The chiropractor, for his part, claimed that the men were simply trying to drive him out of business.[22]

The Klan's lawless activities concerned lawmakers throughout the country. The situation in Texas became so tense that forty-nine state legislators asked the governor to "punish masked bands." A judge in Beaumont ordered Tom Garner, sheriff of Jefferson County, removed from office because of his membership in the Klan. Massachusetts mayors vowed to remove the Klan from their cities. By 1923 states began enacting legislation to prevent the Klan from functioning as a secret society whose members were difficult to trace to specific crimes. New York Governor Al Smith took a political risk by signing a law that required organizations operating in the state to disclose member rosters, officer lists, and headquarters addresses. His continued popularity in the state demonstrated wide backing for the initiative. Oklahoma Governor J. C. Walton issued an edict against masked assemblies. In Illinois, with the governor's approval, an anti-Klan statute prohibited appearing in public places for "evil or wicked purpose while hooded, robed or masked to conceal identity." Similar laws prohibiting masked meetings passed in Michigan, Minnesota, and Iowa.[23]

Even the Supreme Court, although still slow to overturn antimiscegenation, segregation, and disenfranchisement laws, stepped in to support the national effort to extinguish the second Klan. More was at stake than race; law and order were at risk. In a 1928 case the Court reviewed the constitutionality of a New York statutory requirement that every organization with more than twenty members file its membership list and detailed information of its purposes. Even though labor unions and several other secret lodges, such as the Masonic fraternity and the Knights of Columbus, were exempted from the registration requirements, the Court found that New York's use of police power to force the Klan's activities to become transparent did not deprive its members of the equal protection of law.

The Klan went into a decline after 1925 just as sharp as its rise to prominence had been. Laws requiring the Klan to reveal members' identities made many unwilling to join. For a time the organization seemed on the brink of political power, backing United States senators or governors in several states. Even when Klan-financed candidates for statewide or national offices won, they typically refused to follow its supremacist programs. Reeling from internal corruption and financial squabbles over membership dues, the Klan's influence quickly waned. Nevertheless, its rise to power was symptomatic of nativism that made its presence felt in areas as divergent as immigration policy, public segregation, and state politics.[24]

CHAPTER NINE

Rights in the Regulatory State

B y the 1920s the Supreme Court had severely diminished the Reconstruction Amendments' effectiveness. Literalist interpretations of the
amendments in *Plessy v. Ferguson*, the *Civil Rights Cases*, and *Williams v. Mississippi* hampered congressional ability to pass civil rights statutes.
With time, economic liberty, rather than equality, came to dominate national
affairs.

At the end of the nineteenth century and in the early twentieth, little
suggested that the Commerce Clause would become the important constitutional provision for furthering civil rights that it became during the New
Deal. To the contrary, laissez-faire, the leading economic philosophy, left it
up to individuals to bargain for fair transactions. Governmental protection of
individual rights was widely thought to be unnecessary and intrusive. An
influential Social Darwinist, Herbert Spencer, argued that poverty relief,
education reforms, sanitation provisions, and housing ordinances interfered
with economic natural selection.[1]

Overlooking the unequal bargaining power of laborers and employers,
courts repeatedly struck down legislation meant to protect workers from
exploitative practices. State courts issued more than eighteen hundred injunctions between 1880 and 1930 on behalf of employers against strikes and
boycotts organized by labor organizations. Each worker was thought capable
of securing favorable terms of employment for himself; organized labor was
treated like a conspiracy against commercial competition. Actual disparities
in bargaining positions were ignored because contracts, indicating agreements to work, were regarded as fair bargains among equals.[2]

Dominant jurisprudence regarded workers as free agents who could enter
into agreements about rates of pay and work hours without legal intervention.

State and federal courts found numerous minimum wage and maximum hour laws to be unwarranted interferences with occupational liberty. Employees' right to work long hours and earn modest pay was considered a freedom protected by the Due Process Clause and linked to the emergence from slavery. That judicial notion of liberty constrained legislators from interfering with employers who coerced laborers to work excessively long hours at slum wages.[3]

Only regulations of extremely dangerous industries were likely to survive judicial scrutiny. The United States Supreme Court ruled that Utah's law prohibiting miners from working more than eight hours a day was a legitimate use of state power. The state could limit mining for excessive hours because miners worked underground in such unhealthy conditions. This outcome was by no means representative of economic liberty cases.[4]

To the contrary, the pattern was set by *Lochner v. New York,* which found that a state law prohibiting bakers from working more than sixty hours a week violated the due process rights of employees and employers to contract freely. That decision established a judicial practice of immunizing social and economic practices that were traditionally the responsibility of legislators. Without any more explanation than a reference to the "common understanding," the Court determined that the state of New York was simply wrong in its finding that bakers' bargaining power was unequal to that of their employers. The decision went against the weight of evidence, which Justice Harlan's dissent relied on, indicating that bakers worked in some of the "hardest and most laborious . . . conditions injurious" to their health. The unusually low average age at which bakers died, Harlan wrote, provided the public health reason for the state to prevent bakeries from demanding long work hours that compromised bakers' health.[5]

After *Lochner,* between 1905 and 1937, judges regularly overturned state uses of police power on due process grounds, holding them to be paternalistic protections of "dependent" and "vulnerable" laborers. The problem with this uncertain method came through in the Court's wavering about minimum wage and maximum hour laws for women, first finding them to be constitutional and then quickly reversing itself with little more than a reassessment of legislative findings. The judiciary established itself as the final authority on the legitimacy of public choices about fairness and health. *Lochner* set substantive liberty on a collision course with policymaking aimed at preventing the unfair use of unequal economic means.[6]

The decision left wage and hour decisions in the hands of big businesses.

In many industries, like textile and steel, where men often worked twelve-hour days, seven days a week, this meant that government was virtually powerless to prevent the exploitation of workers despite the health risks they faced from overwork in dangerous conditions.

Initiatives to test the limits of *Lochner*'s vision of property ownership and self-regulating market mechanisms were typically limited to minimum wage laws for women and children. Between 1912 and 1925 fourteen states, Puerto Rico, and the District of Columbia enacted minimum wage legislation. Progressives who argued that workers deserved "fair" and "just" wages rested their case on the general principle of equality of rights. Their economic hypothesis was that improved worker welfare would increase productivity.[7]

Congress too began to recognize that initiatives for fair labor standards were linked to centuries of struggle against slavery. The second section of the Clayton Act of 1914 declared that "labor of a human being is not a commodity or article of commerce." It also forbade antitrust laws to be "construed to forbid the existence and operation of labor, agricultural, or horticultural organizations, instituted for the purposes of mutual help."[8] This implicitly meant that labor organizations were distinct from for-profit associations, like corporations or partnerships, whose core purpose was wealth maximization.

As it had done with Reconstruction legislation, the Supreme Court found ingenious ways to thwart Congress's attempt to diminish labor inequality. For instance, the Court held that the Clayton Act was limited to the union activities of employees against their own employers (*Duplex Printing Press Co. v. Deering*).[9] That decision enabled courts to grant employers injunctions against strikes until, in 1932, Congress superseded it with the Norris-LaGuardia Act.[10]

The Court also challenged Congress's ability to protect vulnerable groups against oppressive practices. In *Hammer v. Dagenhart* (1918), the Court found the Child Labor Act of 1916 an unconstitutional restraint on commerce that intruded on state powers. The act had sought to prohibit factories from employing children under fourteen years of age or from requiring children between the ages of fourteen and sixteen to work excessively long hours. When Congress responded with the Child Labor Tax Law of 1919, which imposed an excise tax on companies using child labor, the Court ruled that Congress was interfering in the interstate exchange of ordinary commodities. Then in 1923 the Court invalidated an act that set a minimum wage for women and children working in the District of Columbia.[11]

The Supreme Court's reliance on laissez-faire capitalism in due process cases meant that the Fourteenth Amendment's primary purpose became the protection of freedom to enter into contracts rather than the freedom to fair treatment. Decisionmaking about workers' rights was placed in the virtually exclusive province of state lawmakers. The civil rights efforts of progressives, unions, and laborers during the *Lochner* era shifted to obtaining workers' rights. In the words of one period journalist, "The crucial struggle for civil liberty today is among tenant farmers and industrial workers, fighting for economic emancipation and security."[12]

During the economic boom of the 1920s, relatively few complaints challenged the established hierarchy between the federal and state governments. The Great Depression changed this dynamic, converting the federal government into the administrator of agencies—dealing with topics as diverse as securities, banking, education, employment, and national parks management.

The change in Americans' willingness to submit to the national government came at a time of a precipitous decline in wages beginning with the 1929 depression. In response to their own losses and bank failures, businesses dipped into workers' pocketbooks. New York farm laborers earned $49.30 a month in 1929, $29.52 in January 1932, and $5 to $15 in 1933. Steelworkers earned 63 percent less in 1933 than in 1929, lumber and sawmill workers earned 45 percent less, shirt and collar workers 38 percent less. In the early 1930s automobile factories in Detroit were paying men about 35 cents and women 20 cents per hour, a 50 percent reduction from 1929.[13]

At a time when jobs were scarce, workers could be induced to take low wages for exhausting labor, especially without a national minimum wage and maximum hour law. In 1932 more than 24 percent of the workforce in the United States was unemployed, up from about 3 percent in 1929. During the Depression, the black community was the most adversely affected because of its concentration in unskilled and domestic services. While blacks made up only 10 percent of the population, they constituted 27 percent of the unemployed. In some urban communities, unemployment among them ran as high as 90 percent.[14]

Business interests felt so self-assured that in January 1933 *Fortune* magazine claimed that "wages disputes and hours disputes and safety demands are things of the past." Given the increasing human toll of the Great Depression, collective action was necessary. Soon the federal government, with President Franklin D. Roosevelt at the rudder, passed laws creating national retirement insurance (Social Security Act), a minimum wage and maximum hour law (Fair Labor Standards Act), and protection for unions and their organizers (Wagner Act).[15]

Presidential Policy

The federal government's role increased drastically during the New Deal. The executive branch developed a plethora of social welfare initiatives that enhanced the president's power. The Roosevelt administration often sent bills to Congress and lobbied for their passage, thereby injecting its agenda into the legislative process. That degree of executive participation in lawmaking altered the relationship between the branches of government.

Roosevelt promoted equal economic rights because he believed that political standing was partly a function of an individual's ability to earn a decent wage. He spoke of the New Deal as "fundamentally intended as a modern expression of ideals" that are located in the Preamble to the Constitution's guarantee of "a more perfect union, justice, domestic tranquillity, the common defense, the general welfare and blessings of liberty to ourselves and our posterity."[16]

Roosevelt's track record on racial issues was mixed. He was a pragmatist who understood the political import of recruiting African Americans into the Democratic Party. During his administration, the majority of blacks shifted to the Democratic Party from their traditional allegiance with the Republicans. Besides pragmatic influences, committed advocates of black causes found Roosevelt more receptive to their suggestions than his predecessors. He appointed blacks, like the college educator Mary Bethune, the judge William H. Hastie, and the economist Robert C. Weaver, to prominent posts in his administration. First Lady Eleanor Roosevelt was the most visible of prominent white liberals striving to codify antidiscrimination provisions. She was joined by many others inside the White House, including Secretary of the Interior Harold Ickes, who had been the president of the Chicago Chapter of the NAACP, and Will Alexander, a white southerner who was head of the Farm Securities Administration and the 1938 executive director of the Commission on Interracial Cooperation.[17]

The New Deal significantly improved the overall socioeconomic conditions of blacks, but Roosevelt's views on race were much in line with his congressional allies, many of whom were southern liberals. In 1911, as a New York legislator, he had noted in the margins of a speech that he was coming to "a story of a nigger." He thought of Georgia as his "second home" and visited there often for rest, recreation, and convalescence. He enjoyed the southern hospitality but disregarded his wife's prompting to speak against the state's segregation. The Warm Springs, Georgia, therapy resort for polio patients that Roosevelt founded in 1926 operated on a segregated basis. While in politics, he periodically told stories of "darkies." For eleven years, beginning in 1933, Roosevelt banned black journalists from presidential news conferences. Even with his immense power as commander in chief of the military during World War II, Roosevelt did not desegregate the armed forces. Arguably, the greatest disappointment in the president for black leaders was Roosevelt's unwillingness to openly endorse antilynching legislation.[18]

Antilynching

The number of lynchings around the country was on the decline by the 1930s, and there was a growing coalition to create federal jurisdiction for punishing vigilante violence. Before the Civil War, most lynchings were perpetrated against white men. During and after Reconstruction, it became an instrument of racist intimidation. Lynch mobs accused their victims of suing whites, scaring school children, "trying to act like a white man," refusing to pay a debt, inquiring about work at a restaurant, hog and horse stealing, killing cattle, refusing to complete the term of a labor contract, making "boastful remarks," raping white women, and murdering whites. In his classic study, Arthur F. Raper found that of the approximately 188 yearly lynchings from 1880 to 1899, about 68 percent were perpetrated against blacks. The peak of mob murder was 1892, when 231 persons were lynched. Of the 46.2 lynchings per year from 1920 to 1924, 90 percent of the victims were blacks. Many local police officers participated in the terror or did nothing to stop it. Between 1889 and 1899, 82 percent of lynchings were committed in fourteen southern states. In the first decade of the twentieth century, 91.9 percent of lynchings occurred there. Most of the remaining lynchings were perpetrated in states bordering the South. By the 1930s there was a sharp nationwide drop to about 10 a year, and by 1941 there were only 4. The method of intimidation became more subtle. Mobs time and again demanded that accused blacks be speedily tried and executed, else they would carry out their own sense of justice.[19]

Mob rule was increasingly condemned by mid-1920s, at the same time that support for the Ku Klux Klan waned. A number of organizations with large memberships, including chambers of commerce and the Rotary Club, decried lynching. During the 1930s, the Association of Southern Women for the Prevention of Lynching (ASWPL), organized by white women whose honor lynch mobs often claimed to be protecting, petitioned President Roosevelt to get involved because local and state officials often did nothing to bring participants to justice, even when their identities were known. The ASWPL enlisted the support of five national and sixteen state organizations, which endorsed its educational programs. The Commission on Interracial Cooperation, a related southern organization, promoted federal criminal charges against lynching. Nationally, the NAACP disseminated information and suggested legislative solutions against lynching.[20]

Many states, including Alabama, Georgia, Indiana, Kansas, Kentucky, North Carolina, and Virginia, enacted antilynching laws, but prosecutors regularly found it exceedingly difficult to persuade local jurors to indict or convict their neighbors under them. While trial judges could likewise be intimidated or sympathetic to attackers, several states' appellate courts were willing to act against mob-influenced convictions. Some states made progress even before the Supreme Court of the United States decided, in *Moore v. Dempsey* (1923), that it is a reversible error to rush a defendant to trial in order to stave off threats from a lynch mob.[21]

Mississippi, which led the South in ending Reconstruction and in disenfranchising blacks, unexpectedly established a persuasive precedent against mob-induced convictions. In 1903 the state's supreme court held that no fair trial could be obtained under circumstances in which a mob threatened to kill the defendant, the sheriff spirited him out of town to prevent a lynching, and six deputies had to guard him throughout the trial. Four years later, the Virginia supreme court similarly found that a court should have granted a "colored" defendant's motion to change the venue of his criminal trial. The trial followed on the heels of a mob's having burned his printing office. The situation was so dangerous that the defendant fled from the town and the governor of Virginia ordered troops to restore order there. The state supreme court found it implausible that the trial had been impartial and dispassionate.[22]

The Court of Appeals of Kentucky reversed the murder conviction of Rufus Browder, who claimed he acted in self-defense. The trial judge had denied Browder's motion for a change of venue even though the jailer had to hide him repeatedly, first at a graveyard and then in other cities, from men who were hunting for the him with shotguns. Not able to find Browder, the lynch mob gained access to a jail, took out four men who were unconnected with the crime, and "hung . . . them in the most cruel manner." Browder struggled to find any attorney who was willing to tolerate the inevitable popular ire that would come from taking his case. When the trial began, the governor sent troops to guard against disorder. The Court of Appeals found that under such circumstances, "when the public mind" was "excited by race hostility," the trial had been unfair. Appellate courts in Maryland and Texas similarly found that where there were threats of lynchings, courts had erred in rushing cases to trial rather than granting defendants' motions for continuances.[23]

These judicial precedents helped to prevent local prejudices from being determinative factors in cases. But they were no substitute for a federal lynch law since each had authority only within the state where it was rendered, and the appellate courts were precedential only in some parts of the states. Despite the increasing public outrage against lynching by the 1930s, the Roosevelt administration timidly chose not to push for a federal antilynching statute.

Roosevelt spoke out against lynching on several occasions, characterizing it, in a speech before the Council of Churches of Christ, as a "vile form of collective murder." In his 1934 annual address to Congress, the president reviled the "organized banditry, cold-blooded shooting, lynching and kidnapping have threatened our security" and called on the "strong arm of Government for their immediate suppression." In an attempt to placate both sides of the antilynching debate, at a news conference, Roosevelt said that he told congressional leaders to "try to get a vote on" an antilynching bill and, in the same breath, expressed his uncertainty about its constitutionality.[24]

Black leaders like Walter White, the NAACP executive secretary, urged the president to be more forthcoming. The official organ of the NAACP, *The Crisis*, opined that while the president said "a few words against lynching before the actual test of votes came . . . when that crucial hour arrived, he said nothing." At White's urging, Senators Robert F. Wagner of New York and Edward P. Costigan of Colorado cosponsored a bill that provided federal courts with jurisdiction to adjudicate lynching cases when states failed to apprehend and punish perpetrators. The bill provided penalties against officials who refused to protect prisoners. It further created a cause of action for a victim's heirs, allowing them to seek damages from the county where the lynching had been perpetrated. After meeting White at the White House, the president revealed his unwillingness to then support the antilynching bill for fear that alienated southern congressmen would try to thwart his economic programs.[25]

In 1937 the House passed the bill by a vote of 227 to 120; that was the closest it ever came to becoming law. Thereafter, southern senators filibustered against it for six weeks in 1938, their diatribe filled with all manner of irrelevancies, until the bill died, with no effort from Roosevelt to try to bring the filibuster to an end.[26]

Justice Department

Failure to pass a national antilynching statute left it up to the states to regulate and impose penalties for the crime. Indeed, the Roosevelt administration passed no law exclusively dealing with civil rights. Its efforts in the area were primarily limited to filing lawsuits under existing laws and adding antidiscrimination provisions to its class-based initiatives.

An alternative strategy to the antilynching bill relied on long-ignored nineteenth-century laws that were passed on the basis of the Thirteenth, Fourteenth, and Fifteenth Amendments. Just one month after Frank Murphy became the attorney general of the United States, in the winter of 1939, he created the Civil Liberties Unit (later renamed Civil Rights Section) of the Criminal Division. Murphy, who the next year was confirmed as an associate justice of the United States Supreme Court, established the unit's mission to prosecute individuals who have "jeopardized" individual rights "through beatings, violence, deprivation of freedom of speech or assembly, and . . . where workers have been denied certain rights under the Wagner Act, such as collective bargaining."[27]

The division primarily relied on two statutes derived from the Ku Klux Klan Enforcement Act of 1871, penalizing conspirators who planned to violate civil rights. This was the first serious attempt to revive Reconstruction era civil rights statutes, many of which the Court had decimated in the late nineteenth and early twentieth centuries.[28]

The Civil Rights Section secured an important victory in *United States v. Classic* that signaled a renewed willingness to craft civil rights relief. The case involved election officials' fraudulent deprivation of black voters' rights. The Court recognized that officials who were counting votes in a primary election could be prosecuted in a federal court because they were acting "under color of state law."[29]

The newfound power allowed the Justice Department to file lawsuits against civil rights violations when state authorities refused to pursue complaints. That was the circumstance in *Screws v. United States,* a case in which three drunken sheriffs severely beat and then dumped an African American in jail for filing a lawsuit against one of their colleagues. He subsequently died from the injuries. When Georgia refused to file a lawsuit against the sheriffs, the Civil Rights Section secured convictions against all of them. Justice William O. Douglas's majority opinion expressed shock and revulsion at the sheriff's actions. While the statutes under which the case was brought were constitutional, Douglas found the trial judge's jury instructions problematic and ordered a new trial. Justice Murphy, on the other hand, thought that Douglas's opinion emphasized legal minutiae rather than the applicability of constitutional statutes to a racially motivated murder. While they were almost on opposite ends of the spectrum about the outcome of the case, Douglas and Murphy agreed that federal prosecutors could vindicate civil rights violations committed by state officials.[30]

Public Programs

Outside the criminal realm, Roosevelt issued an executive order that prohibited defense contractors and government from discriminating based on race, creed, color, or national origin. The administration established the Fair Employment Practices Committee to monitor its implementation, but the president never adopted a systematic antidiscrimination policy, and certainly not an aggressive one.[31]

Roosevelt's preferred method of combating racism, sexism, and monopolism was to include provisions prohibiting them in various public programs. By the 1930s the nation was functioning more like a unified whole than at any point in its history. The federal government increasingly funded, inspected, and directed services for the general welfare. Preventing water pollution from mines, regulating sewage disposal, and inspecting food became executive department duties. Industry regulations affecting all citizens came under the auspices of federal agencies that were typically less insular than their local counterparts. State policies came into play through the workings of local committees that functioned under the auspices of relief programs like the Civilian Conservation Corps (CCC) and the Tennessee Valley Authority (TVA). Allowing these committees to retain so much power over the day-to-day workings of federal programs inadvertently enabled regional racial prejudice to influence decisionmaking. As for women, while they entered the workforce in larger numbers than ever before, they were paid lower wages and still excluded from some fields of employment.[32]

Just ten days after assuming the office of president, Roosevelt got input from his cabinet on a forestry work project that in April 1933 became the CCC. The Tree Army, as it came to be known, was interdepartmental, with the War Department running the camps and their services, the Labor Department and Veterans Administration selecting the men, and Agriculture's Forest Service and the Interior Department's National Parks Service developing the conservation projects. The CCC provided eighteen- to twenty-five-year-old unmarried men with an opportunity to work while enriching themselves through shared experiences in the woods. Between 1933 and 1942 the CCC employed approximately three hundred thousand men a year. Each received thirty dollars per month, room, board, clothing, and medical care. One author has estimated that between 1933 and 1940 one-quarter to one-third of the nation's indigent youths joined the CCC. Many of them had never before spent significant time outdoors. They were typically enrolled in the program for six months to a year. In terms of forestry, the CCC was a tremendous success. It reforested areas, fought forest fires, blazed trails, built wildlife shelters, fortified areas against floods, built dams, and laid roads. By 1939 the CCC had planted 1.7 billion trees, built 104,000 miles of truck trails or minor roads, set up 71,700 miles of telephone lines, and erected 4.7 million check dams.[33]

The CCC's enabling statute required that "no discrimination shall be made on account of race, color, or creed." This directive applied to both American citizens and immigrant workers. Some Native Americans, like the Chippewas of Wisconsin, derived an important part of their earnings through CCC.[34]

The program was beneficial to individuals and to the nation as a whole, putting otherwise idle youths to work and making them a part of the economy. A glaring deficiency in the statute was its exclusion of women. Two apparent reasons for their original exclusion were that they composed a smaller segment of the unemployed workforce and that they were less likely to commit crimes out of sheer economic desperation. Both of these rationales were modeled on stereotypes that in practice reduced opportunities for women.[35]

The most conspicuous racial inequality of the CCC lay in its director's decision to conform to local segregation practices. Roosevelt did nothing to intervene or change this indirectly approved discrimination. Blacks, whites, and Native Americans were separated by camps throughout the South. Writing for the *Crisis*, the correspondent Luther C. Wandall discovered that once in Camp Dix, New Jersey, black CCC recruits were separated from whites. Despite this overt discrimination, Wandall praised the "excellent recreation hall, playground, and other facilities" available to blacks at a permanent campsite. A surprisingly high living standard, with good food, bedding, clothing, library, canteen, and sanitary conditions—which seem to have been the same in white and black camps—made the CCC popular.[36]

One hundred fifty-two segregated camps dotted the country, more than half of them in the South. Seventy-one CCC camps were integrated, with fifty-nine of those located in New England. Out of the 2.5 million or so men who served in the CCC, about 200,000 (8 percent) were blacks, and of them only 30,000 served in integrated camps. In some southern states, like Georgia and Arkansas, it took appeals by such organizations as the Committee for Interracial Cooperation and the NAACP to high-ranking cabinet officials, like the director of the Labor Department's CCC section, to get even a token number of blacks enrolled in camps. When the South relented, under pressure, blacks were typically assigned to manual jobs, holding far fewer supervisory positions than their white counterparts. Some improvement was made on that score by the mid-1930s. After groups like the National Urban League complained of the disparity in advancement, some blacks became educational advisers in black camps. The first black camp commander was commissioned to that most important CCC position at a facility in 1936, and a 1940 report indicated that there were only two black camp commanders.[37]

The Julius Rosenwald Fund concluded in 1935 that blacks were not "placed in CCC jobs at anything like their proportion of the population, to say nothing of their greater need of employment as indicated by relief statistics." On the one hand, the CCC's value to the black community was borne out by the larger number of its members choosing to do longer stints of service than those of their white colleagues; on the other, the CCC failed to make national standards of liberal equality the litmus test for state participation.

The Tennessee Valley Authority, which Congress created in May 1933 at the advice of the president, was another agency that gave in to local sensitivities on race. Unlike the CCC, its focus was regional. The TVA was created to reduce flooding from the Tennessee River by building dams. The Norris Dam, named after the author of the TVA statute, Nebraska Senator George Norris, was its first major project, helping to deliver up to 131,400 kilowatts of electricity. The agency was also critical for improving the socioeconomic conditions of the Tennessee Valley, which extended over seven states. The TVA provided immediate work relief to a strikingly depressed part of the country. Its greatest successes, however, lay in regional economical development from inexpensive electrical power to households and businesses, improved agricultural irrigation, and diminished flooding of the Tennessee River.[38]

Blacks did not reap the same benefits as whites from the region's rejuvenation. Officials prohibited blacks from living in Norris, the federally owned and controlled town with 450 model homes built around the dam. Housing that was provided for black TVA workers was notoriously below the quality of housing for whites. At the Wilson Dam project, black children did not have access to recreational areas that served white children, and hovels for blacks were built without closets. Blacks had less access to training programs, such as those designed to prepare foremen. Lack of training, in turn, made them ineligible for skilled positions. Even where they could work as skilled artisans, as they did in Pickwick Landing Dam, they were limited to a Jim Crow village and prohibited from doing specialized work at a whites' village. Their pay was notoriously lower than that of white workers. When the TVA estimated that black participation was proportionate to the 11 percent of their population in the Tennessee Valley, as it did between May 1 and May 31, 1935, blacks received a lower rate of pay, accounting for only 9.5 percent of the budget. The *Crisis* called the TVA a "raw deal," playing on Roosevelt's "New Deal."[39]

Other federal policies also gave segregated housing an official stamp of approval. The Fair Housing Administration required that all government-insured home mortgages have racially restrictive covenants. In West Virginia, the Resettlement Administration's director in the homestead project at Arthurdale announced that the project was open only to "native white stock."[40]

Economic aid on a grand scale included a program "to relieve the existing national economic emergency by increasing agricultural purchasing power" through the Agricultural Adjustments Administration. The agency was first established by a May 1933 Agricultural Adjustment Act (AAA) of Congress, which the Supreme Court later found to be unconstitutional. Congress then passed a new AAA in 1938. Under the leadership of Secretary Henry A. Wallace, the Department of Agriculture sought to end the economic disparity between industry and agriculture. To stabilize decreasing farm revenues, the AAA tried to reduce the production of staples, including cotton, tobacco, sugar, rice, and wheat; take surplus products off the market; and develop conservation methods. In return for agreeing to comply with the requirements, farmers received monetary subsidies, which were derived from taxes.[41]

The day-to-day administration of the programs fell on local committees. These were composed of individuals who controlled land and capital, like businessmen, bankers, and large-scale landowners. In the South, whites administered these committees without black participation in any positions of authority. The AAA enlisted local support for the program but did not supervise the activities of county and local committees.[42]

In many cases, the committees refused to provide sharecroppers, almost all of whom were black, with their fair share of benefits. Landlords discovered means of maximizing their government payments and reducing or entirely depriving croppers, white and black, of subsidies. By 1935 there were many accounts of landlords receiving a disproportionate share of the subsidy payments while croppers saw little of it. Local committees typically discounted reports of irregularities allegedly committed by their fellow landowners. In the early years of the AAA, government checks were made out to the landlords, who then decided what to give tenants, sometimes keeping as much as 70 percent. In Arkansas black and white sharecroppers and cotton field hands organized the Southern Tenant Farmers' Union against the inequities, only to be stopped by a "reign of terror." Even when Roosevelt and senators, including Wagner, learned of the croppers' plight, they declined to intervene.[43]

The central administration of the AAA expected local conditions to work themselves out without federal intervention. The administration refused to act against planters who forced croppers into guardian contracts, allowing them to sell the croppers' staple without a full accounting to the cropper. Landlords continued to charge croppers to live on land that the government subsidized to lie fallow, thereby deriving double rent for the same tract of land. The NAACP documented cases in which croppers who were paid by commissary coupons, rather than in dollars, saw none of their share. The coupons allowed them only to purchase goods at landlords' commissaries for inflated prices. The plantation owners could then keep croppers in constant debt. This arrangement created a system of unpaid labor that was comparable to slavery. One U.S. Labor Department study concluded that the sharecropping community of Concordia Parish, Louisiana, presented a "picture of the evolution of the old plantation with its slave labor emerging as a unit operated with cropper or wage labor. The position of its laboring class has not changed materially from that of earlier times."[44]

National coverage of these abuses forced changes. AAA payments began flowing directly to tenants, and the amount they received became more nearly commensurate to their share of crops. To deal with the new barrier against self-enrichment, landlords simply began evicting tenants in order to keep the whole check. The eviction process actually accelerated an agricultural change away from cropping that had already been initiated by increased mechanization, especially through the greater availability of tractors. This development, coupled by the AAA decision not to interfere in local politics, reduced the number of nonwhite owners, managers, tenants, and croppers in the South from 885,000 in 1930 to 70,000 in 1935. Section 7 of AAA contracts required landlords to maintain their normal number of tenants and laborers, but the law proved impossible to enforce. By switching to day labor, the landlord got both a subsidy for the crop he produced and the share that croppers might have reaped. While a AAA stipulation prohibited an increase in landlords' payments, that condition did not apply as long as it could be shown that the labor reduction was part of a sound management strategy. Out-of-work croppers and tenants increased the glut in the job market.[45]

The demographic shift of so many eventually freed blacks and many poor whites from the cropping and peonage to which generations had been bound since the mid-1860s. That unexpected liberation did not ease the croppers' immediate losses. Minuscule effort was made to include landless farmers in deciding policies that affected them most. Political power remained in the hands of property owners. Sharecroppers also fared so poorly because they were mostly blacks who were barred from decisionmaking. In 1939, out of 52,000 Department of Agriculture employees, only 1,100 were blacks, three-quarters of whom were custodians.[46]

For persons living in cities, where blacks had increasingly migrated since the 1920s, the Federal Emergency Relief Administration (FERA), under the leadership of one of Roosevelt's most trusted advisers, the social worker Harry L. Hopkins, provided two years of emergency relief. In the same whirlwind month of May 1933 when Congress created the TVA and AAA, FERA began providing economic relief to millions of Americans through road, bridge, railroad, waterway, sewer, painting, and school maintenance and construction projects. FERA distributed aid directly to state and local agencies. During the course of its operation, FERA spent about $3 billion; meanwhile, state and local governments spent about $1 billion. The relief projects provided families with an income and increased consumer power to put dollars back into the economy. The federal government set standards against injustice, inefficiency, and dishonesty, but the actual administration was left up to state and local officials. Roosevelt issued an executive order prohibiting racial discrimination. Hopkins directed that "women are [to be] employed wherever possible." Officials were required to meet minimum wage and maximum hour requirements, but city and state officials retained control over hiring, firing, and supervising.[47]

Black economic conditions had become so precarious that in 1933 FERA provided relief for about 17.8 percent of the entire black population, and in 1935 about 29 percent of black families were on relief. In 1934, 65 percent of those on relief were unskilled laborers. FERA also provided educational funding, granting $281,000 in scholarships to black schools and colleges through its student aid program.[48]

State and community administrations, meanwhile, denied blacks an equitable subsidy. Blacks were commonly shut out of skilled jobs. In the South, preconceived notions of black living standards kept their wages lower than those of whites. Along the Mississippi River and in Georgia, there were reports of blacks being passed up for skilled jobs and paid below the minimum wage. In Atlanta the average 1935 relief check for whites was $32.66 and for blacks $19.29. Houston also violated Roosevelt's antidiscrimination directive, paying whites, on average, $16.86 and blacks $12.67.[49]

FERA made its final grant in 1935; thereafter the Works Progress Administration (WPA), later renamed the Work Projects Administration, changed into a more centralized organization, with local and state leaders still suggesting works projects. At its inception, Roosevelt issued Executive Order 7046 banning discrimination in administering work projects. The WPA continued to operate until 1942. The Emergency Relief Appropriation Act established guidelines for WPA wage policy. The act made it a criminal penalty for anyone "knowingly by means of any fraud, force, threat, intimidation . . . or discrimination on account of race . . . [to] deprive any person of any of the benefits to which he may be entitled." Another section of the act made it "unlawful for any person to deprive, attempt to deprive, or threaten to deprive, by any means any person of any employment, position, work compensation, or other benefit . . . on account of race, creed, color, or any political party." Unlike FERA, the WPA paid a standardized rate that was based on workers' skills and geographic location. Only differences in cost of living were to be used in setting regional differentials on monthly earnings. The agency supported up to 30 percent of the unemployed workforce. Its projects were not to interfere with private industry. It was authorized to carry out public projects like constructing roads, highways, streets, hospitals, airports, and government buildings. Besides manual laborers, the agency also hired artists, poets, writers, and actors. Humanities projects included transcriptions of slave narratives. The WPA also did an enormous national service for American memory by starting a file on medicinal plants used by Native Americans. In Texas, WPA workers interviewed Native Americans from Comanche, Kiowa, Wichita, Caddos, Lipan Apache, and Tonkawa tribes to get their oral histories. The agency also wrote on the successful pattern of Mexican migratory farming in Texas. The WPA Theater and Artist Projects provided for the dissemination of Latino cultural institutions. Similarly, Foster Lois studied the Chinese theaters in San Francisco for the WPA.[50]

The WPA significantly decreased black unemployment. While blacks often got no more than a subsistence wage from the WPA, for many even that ·was more than their pre-Depression earnings. An African American explained that the evenhanded distribution of a living wage by the WPA meant that "Negroes don't have to work for anything people want to give them." The program was so popular that it even made its way into a blues song:

> Please, Mr. President, listen to what I've got to say:
> You can take away all of the alphabet, but please leave that WPA
> Now I went to the polls and voted, I know I voted the right way—
> So I'm asking you, Mr. President, don't take away that WPA.

In Cleveland approximately 30 percent of the WPA workforce was black, with many working below their skill level in order to make ends meet. Job displacement hit Chicago so severely that even in 1940, 19 percent of employed black males were still on emergency work projects.[51]

When analyzed with more detail, however, the picture of the WPA is not so rosy. Blacks were consistently underrepresented at skilled levels, and local administrators regularly excluded them from supervisory positions. State officials retained much control over work assignments, often classifying workers according to local customs instead of actual ability. While blacks in the South made up more than one-fourth of persons on WPA relief, only 14 blacks served as supervisors in southern states, compared with 10,333 white supervisors. Noncitizens were rejected from the WPA in the late-1930s. Quotas were set on black and Latino employment. Consequently, 45,000 aliens were dismissed from relief roles. As with FERA, the inability or unwillingness to make concrete rules against discrimination crippled the official policy against it. In some cities WPA projects, such as park development in Gary, Indiana, were segregated after their completion.[52]

One of the WPA's greatest successes was the achievement of its educational division, the National Youth Administration (NYA). It was the brainchild of Aubrey Williams, who had previously been a high-ranking official in FERA. The NYA funded classroom and vocational instruction. It had a Division of Negro Affairs, under the directorship of the black educator Mary Bethune, president of Bethune-Cookman College and a close associate of Eleanor Roosevelt. Opponents of Williams's decision to improve black educational and economic competitiveness branded him a "nigger lover," because he forbade discrimination. The agency relied on the input of blacks and whites who worked together on advisory panels. It also employed white agents, like the youthful Texas director of the NYA, Lyndon B. Johnson. The future president set up black and white advisory committees and disbursed educational money by need, without regard to race.[53]

Black youths who enrolled in the college work program received professional and semiprofessional experiences, which were better than the maintenance work to which blacks had been relegated. They were paid exactly the same amount as white students. Some worked in classrooms, laboratories, museums, libraries, and think tanks. Others gained experience at office work and honed their clerical skills in university departments.[54]

In 1935 the program allocated $600,000 for black college students. While blacks accounted for 15.3 percent of the youth population on relief, this funding represented just 5.4 percent of the college aid in 1936–37. But blacks constituted only 3 percent of students enrolled in higher education, so from that standpoint the funding was more than equitable. About one out of a hundred whites attended colleges, but lack of adequate college facilities and segregation meant that only one in every five hundred blacks enrolled in higher education.[55]

The more than five hundred thousand blacks who learned to read and write through NYA, FERA, and WPA testified to the programs' success. Black illiteracy was cut by one-sixth of the level reported by the 1930 census. Reduced illiteracy, in turn, made blacks better equipped to join the job market and to engage in political activism. The rate of improvement was astonishing. From 1870 to 1930, black illiteracy among people sixteen years of age and older had decreased by an average of seventeen thousand per year, while under the emergency relief programs the annual decrease was nearly one hundred thousand. Blacks continued to lag behind, however, especially in the South, where segregation confined them to inferior schools with fewer government resources. In 1940 the median school education for blacks in the United States was 5.7 years, compared with whites' 8.8 years.[56]

To criticize the New Deal's inability to live up to the standards of American decency that Roosevelt set at the beginning of his first term as president is not to underplay significant strides. New Deal programs involved the federal government in the lives of its citizens to a greater extent than ever before. The Roosevelt administration demonstrated a concerted effort to flesh out the Preamble's general welfare mandate. Within a capitalistic framework of private ownership, agencies established services for the elderly, strengthened collective bargaining by unions, aided the handicapped, set minimum wages and maximum hours for work, prevented the exploitation of child labor, and maintained a variety of labor standards. Public works projects helped assure that individual talents would not be wasted from indigence. They provided out-of-work persons with income and gainful employment. In return for its emergency programs, the nation's capacity for commerce, travel, and medical treatment—through new and improved roads, hospitals, and airfields—grew enormously. The WPA alone built about 651,000 miles of roads, 124,000 bridges and viaducts, 8,000 parks, more than 850 airfields, and thousands of playgrounds.[57]

Public works and educational programs tended to explicitly prohibit discrimination. Even the leadership of the Public Works Administration, which lacked a statutory directive against discrimination, assumed that "Congress intended the program to be carried out without discrimination as to race, color, or creed of the unemployed to be relieved."[58] The New Deal gave the biggest boost to racial equality since Radical Republicans had held sway in Congress after the Civil War.

Roosevelt's reliance on black advisers, his so-called Black Cabinet, provided him with insight into the barriers that blacks faced and into the approaches that were needed to tear them down. The black community's decision to switch its allegiance from the Republican to the Democratic Party indicated its support for public works. The NAACP and National Urban League, along with white liberals like Eleanor Roosevelt, Harry Hopkins, and Aubrey Williams, helped shape the civil rights agenda. Unfortunately, the president himself rarely decried the illegitimacy of discrimination. Faced with the risk of losing the support of southern Democrats for his social programs, he decided not to criticize discriminatory state implementation. Roosevelt's placating strategy prevented the Justice Department from aggressively prosecuting local and state officials who refused to follow federal guidelines.

While blacks could increasingly expect the federal government to treat them as any other citizen, civil rights leaders criticized the failure to pass antilynching legislation or even to confront discriminatory hiring, wage, and segregation practices in the execution of federal programs. Work projects' antidiscrimination requirements were hardly effective so long as they could be circumvented by state and local agencies with little or no disciplinary response from Washington. Using local boards to aid in administration made the daily operations of programs more efficient, but it also allowed regional prejudices to intrude into relief efforts.

Women in the New Deal

Roosevelt appointed more women to prominent Washington posts than any president before him. The best known of them was Secretary of Labor Frances Perkins, the first woman to hold a cabinet position. Within the Labor Department, Clara B. Beyer was the assistant director of the Division of Labor Standards. Beyer and Director Verne Zimmer played a central role in developing health and safety regulations for industries. Roosevelt retained Mary Anderson as the director of the Labor Department's Women's Bureau, a post she had held since 1919. Women also served in other areas of government. Shortly after taking office in 1933, Roosevelt picked Nellie Tayloe Ross to be the director of the United States Mint. Ross had been the first female governor in the United States, serving in Wyoming from 1925 to 1927. She held the position at the mint until 1953. Also in Roosevelt's first term as president, he appointed the first woman to a federal court of appeals. At the age of fifty, Florence E. Allen took her place on the bench of the Sixth Circuit, drawing from her previous experience as a member of the Ohio Supreme Court.

Most employed women, of course, were not involved in policymaking. But they increasingly played a role in the workforce, comprising 15 percent of it in 1870 and 25 percent in 1930. By 1937 women were nearly one-third of the "gainfully occupied," which was partly a function of the increasing need for two-income households during the Depression.[59]

Many women found work through New Deal programs. WPA nursery schools helped to alleviate day care issues that kept many mothers out of the job market. The WPA paid them higher wages than many businesses; however, on average, women fared worse than men of their racial groups. Women encountered cultural employment barriers based on the widespread belief that their proper role was taking care of the hearth. Eighty-two percent of Americans, according to a 1936 Gallup poll, believed that married women should not work if their husbands held jobs. In line with this sentiment, the WPA disqualified wives whose husbands were physically able to work. Generally, married women were treated differently from unmarried women because of the unredressable prejudice against two-earner households. With a depression that was spiraling out of control, in 1931, the New England Telephone and Telegraph Company and Northern Pacific Railway Company dismissed all their married women employees. In a survey of fifteen hundred schools conducted between 1930 and 1931, the National Education Association discovered that 77 percent of them refused to hire wives and 63 percent of them fired teachers who married after being hired.[60]

Local operators of the WPA and NYA typically assigned women to unskilled jobs. Fifty-six percent of women were assigned to sewing rooms. In 1938, 56 percent of all employed white women but only 5 percent of all employed black women were involved in "white-collar services," such as transportation, communication, trade, professional and public work, and clerical service.[61]

Black women remained on the lowest rung of the economic ladder, barely eking out enough to purchase the most basic of necessities. The choices of available employment severely constrained their opportunities. Ninety percent of black women worked in agriculture or in domestic and personal services. They typically worked long hours for minuscule wages. In Lynchburg, Virginia, during the spring of 1937, black household employees received $5 or $6 a week for seventy-two hours of work. A 1934 study of twenty-six local associations reported that on average black household workers earned $6.17 for sixty-six hours a week.

Some wage and hour studies compared male to female workers. For both genders, wages in the North were higher than those in the South. For all male employees, the weekly average varied from $27.63 in Boston to $16.44 in Savannah, Georgia. Among all women, weekly wages averaged from $13.38 in Boston to $5.79 in Charleston, South Carolina. These differences often broke down further along color lines. In Atlantic City, New Jersey, white women's weekly earnings, $7.99, were on a par with black women's, $7.64; on the other hand, in Chicago, where black women earned $9.83 in weekly wages, the highest earnings for black women in the studies, white women earned $11.14. In the South, the disparities were significantly greater and the wages for both races less: In Memphis, Tennessee, white women averaged $9.21 a week, while black women received an average paycheck of $5.57 for that period; in Jacksonville, Florida, white women got $8.43 and black women $5.01; in Charlotte, North Carolina, white women earned $8.47 and black women $5.25; in Savannah, Georgia, white women earned only $7.62 a week, but they still did better than black women, who earned $5.32.

Among sharecroppers, conditions were grim for both genders, making it difficult to escape abject poverty, but black women's predicament was especially pronounced. A Department of Agriculture survey of labor conditions among croppers in October 1937 found that the average yearly salary for men was $177.53 and for women $62.36. Most black women could find work in the fields only ninety days a year.

Women were barely beginning to emerge from economic impotence. Even though they became more visible in the workforce, employers continued to deny them equal access to jobs and paid them subsistence wages. Husbands continued to be regarded as breadwinners and wives as relief workers who would gladly give their jobs up as soon as the threat of depression had passed. While this attitude suppressed women's options as a whole, it was black women who continued to be stuck with the dregs of progress.

Judicial Shift

The Roosevelt administration's class-based programs radically emphasized the federal government's central role in protecting individual rights. Without the judiciary's support, however, those programs could not have withstood constitutional challenges against the use of federal agencies to provide for citizens' general welfare.

The primary challenge lay in convincing the Supreme Court of the United States to qualify its precedents, which functioned to maintain control over race and labor relations in the hands of the states. As never before, the Great Depression required national solutions. At first, the Court tried to short-circuit New Deal initiatives, but it eventually gave its stamp of approval to key legislation. It further established a decisive standard for the judicial protection of insular minorities.

During Roosevelt's first term in office, the Supreme Court of the United States responded unfavorably to many regulatory programs. The Court's majority was disposed to strike down social welfare programs meant to provide for the general welfare.

A series of Supreme Court decisions were part of a resounding rebuke of federal policymakers. In 1935 the Court found the National Industrial Recovery Act (NIRA) to be unconstitutional (*Schechter Poultry Corp. v. United States*). The following year, during the course of a national election, it struck down the Agricultural Adjustment Act (*United States v. Butler*) and Bituminous Coal Act (*Carter v. Carter Coal Co.*), which set maximum hours and minimum wages for coal workers. Congress had found that the latter two laws were required for the general welfare, but the Court rejected that policy assessment. Also in 1936 the Court decided that a New York State minimum wage law was unconstitutional, signaling that states might be as powerless to improve workers' living standards as was the federal government (*Morehead v. New York*).[62]

Those decisions did not sit well with Roosevelt, and on February 5, 1937, he proposed a plan that threatened to expand the Supreme Court. The president proposed to add one new judge for each judge who had served for ten or more years and did not retire six months after his seventieth birthday. Roosevelt sought to allay criticism of his plan by explaining in a speech that he was acting to reduce inefficiency that was preventing the Court from attending to all but a fraction of cases seeking its review. His real intent, which offended the Court's supporters in Congress, was to add members to the Court who would prevent any further erosion of the New Deal. Of the nine Supreme Court justices, six met the criteria of Roosevelt's proposal. Had the law succeeded, the president could have immediately named six new associate justices.[63]

Roosevelt's plan went down to stunning defeat in the Senate, providing ammunition to the opponents of the administration along the way. By an odd twist, however, at Roosevelt's coaxing, the Court itself became more supportive of commerce and equal justice claims.

For three decades, the Court sided with *Lochner*-era notions of contractual freedom; meanwhile, Congress and the executive branch had begun acting to limit industry's ability to freely subordinate workers through unconscionable terms of employment. The political pressure Roosevelt exerted probably influenced a change in the Court's interpretation of government efforts at reform, but even without that change it was improbable that many in Congress would have voted for his proposal to overhaul the judiciary.

The Court's shift from its earlier reliance on substantive due process to strike regulations began with *West Coast Hotel Co. v. Parrish*, a minimum wage case. The case that Elsie Parrish filed against her employer, the Cascadian Hotel of Wenatchee, Washington, exemplifies how one person's lawsuit can affect contemporaries in distant states as well as future generations whose fortunes become interlinked by constitutional jurisprudence. The West Coast Hotel Company owned the Cascadian Hotel. After being fired from her chambermaid job, Parrish demanded back pay from the hotel because it had refused to comply with Washington's minimum wage laws during her employment. The Washington Supreme Court had twice found the statute to be valid, but United States Supreme Court's jurisprudence made the likelihood of Parrish's success seem, at best, improbable.[64]

Minimum wage and maximum hours for women emerged from a campaign in the late nineteenth and early twentieth centuries to enact protective labor laws. In *Muller v. Oregon* (1908), the Supreme Court had found that state statutes prescribing maximum work hours for women were constitutional. As an attorney, Louis D. Brandeis, an associate justice by the time the Court heard Parrish's case, had written the pivotal amicus curiae brief in *Muller* on behalf of the National Consumers' League. In support of the Oregon statute, most of his brief marshaled social science and empirical evidence about the ill effects of long work hours. The courtroom victory was of limited value since Justice David J. Brewer's opinion relied on the stereotype that "woman's physical structure and the performance of maternal functions place her at a disadvantage in the struggle for subsistence"; hence states could pass laws in response to women's special needs. This rationale built on a historical differentiation between men's and women's domestic and marketplace roles. On the one hand, special labor laws benefited women; on the other, legal distinction between the genders provided employers with a justification for paying women less than men and not hiring them in traditionally male professions.[65]

After *Muller* upheld laws on maximum hours, sixteen states enacted compulsory minimum wage laws. The Court ended that experiment with *Adkins v. Children's Hospital of the District of Columbia*, in a decision that seemed to loom before Parrish as she pondered the likelihood of her success. *Adkins* (1923) found the District of Columbia minimum wage law for women and children unconstitutional, explaining that since the ratification of the Nineteen Amendment in 1920, "differences [between the sexes, other than physical] have now come almost, if not quite, to the vanishing point." The Court could not "accept the doctrine that women of mature age, sui juris, require or may be subjected to restrictions upon their liberty of contract which could not lawfully be imposed in the case of men under similar circumstances." Justice Sandra Day O'Connor wrote decades later that *Adkins* "rested on fundamentally false factual assumptions about the capacity of a relatively unregulated market to satisfy minimal levels of human welfare." *Adkins* rejected stereotype but retained *Lochner*'s faith in individuals' having the same bargaining powers as businesses.[66]

The conditions of women's employment did not meet the theoretical equality that *Adkins* declared women to have achieved along with the right to vote. Women's wages lagged far behind men's. A United States Bureau of Labor Statistics study of nine industries from 1922 to 1932 found that women's wages were 45 percent to 84 percent below men's. Three-fourths of women's wages were at least 70 percent below men's. The Women's Bureau of the Labor Department explained what the exploitation of women's labor meant in cost-of-living terms. The average woman's weekly salary in New York in 1934 was $13.75, while the average needed for room and board was $11.63, leaving a meager $2.12 for essentials like laundry, transportation, clothing, and entertainment. Frances Perkins, then the industrial commissioner of New York State, reported that some "girls" were paid 5.5 cents and even 3.5 cents per hour. The Massachusetts commissioner of labor and industries, Edwin S. Smith, reported that more than half the female employees at a Fall River, Massachusetts, garment factory were earning 15 cents per hour or less. The Pennsylvania Department of Labor and Industry reported that half the women working in the textile and clothing industries earned "less than $6.58 a week and 20 percent of them less than $5." Since industry could hire women for a pittance, men's wages dropped, and many of them were laid off.[67]

While Parrish wanted no more than what West Coast Hotel Company owed her in unpaid minimum wages, she took on Supreme Court precedents and won on behalf of herself and others. Roosevelt's threat to enlarge the judiciary may have had its desired effect, since it was on February 6, 1937, one day after Roosevelt went public with his court-packing plan, that Justice Stone cast a deciding vote upholding Washington's minimum wage law and overturning *Adkins*. The Associated Press had reported on February 5 that Stone had "apparently read through the document" informing the Court of the president's proposal to increase its membership. However, it was Justice Owen J. Roberts's vote, along with that of Chief Justice Charles Evans Hughes, that gave rise to the phrase "a switch in time that saved nine." Roberts had joined in striking a minimum wage law in *Morehead*, while Stone had been in the dissent in that case. In *Parrish*, on the other hand, Roberts voted to uphold the constitutionality of a minimum wage law. *Morehead* had refused to evaluate whether *Adkins* should be overruled, while *Parrish* addressed the point head on and overturned it. Roosevelt's court-packing threat probably had no effect on Roberts's vote. Roberts and Hughes had recorded their vote in *Parrish* about a month and a half before the president's announcement, and there is no indication that news of the plan had been leaked to them so long before its public dissemination. Furthermore, both had drafted opinions before 1937 that upheld key New Deal legislation.[68]

Hughes decided to write the majority opinion in *Parrish*, and he was joined by four other justices. His opinion acknowledged the continuing due process significance of liberty to contact. This was only a prelude to the momentous change Hughes announced in the perspective of government's role in correcting social imbalance. The "Constitution does not speak of freedom of contract," he wrote. "It speaks of liberty and prohibits the deprivation of liberty without due process of law." In a constitutional state, "the liberty safeguarded is liberty in a social organization which requires the protection of law against the evils which menace the health, safety, morals, and welfare of the people." The Due Process Clause allows for restraints on liberty so long as the regulation is "reasonable in relation to its subject and is adopted in the interests of the community." The establishment of a minimum wage was reasonable where the legislature had found "exploiting of workers at wages so low as to be insufficient to meet the bare cost of living." Hughes also noted that minimum wage laws were concerned not only with individual rights but also with the public interest. Exploiting workers not only harmed their health but also burdened the community. "What these workers lose in wages the taxpayers are called upon to pay. The bare cost of living must be met." Minimum wage laws prevented economic recovery programs from becoming "a subsidy for unconscionable employers." The Court's decision meant that laws protecting workers against exploitation were reasonable limitations on individuals' freedom to contract so long as they were passed in the public interest.[69]

Parrish recognized that constitutional liberty encompasses not only personal interests but social ones as well. The state could rely on legislation that was reasonably expected to prevent one person from exploiting another for personal gain. Workers who are in desperate straits are not equally positioned when they accept jobs that pay below subsistence wages for excessively long hours of labor. Without the regulation of business, taxpayers are burdened with the increased assessments necessary to meet welfare payments.

The line of cases that followed *Parrish* made clear the extent of the Court's changed mindset about the use of federal power.[70] For a time the justices who were in favor of New Deal laws remained a slim majority. In another 5–4 decision, the Court upheld the National Labor Relations Act (*NLRB v. Jones & Laughlin*). That statute recognized Congress's power under the Commerce Clause to protect workers' right to collectively bargain about matters of wages, hours, or other working conditions as a means of achieving parity in negotiations with employers. Reasonable economic legislation designed to better the lives of citizens trumped a challenge based on the substantive due process of yesteryear. In *Helvering v. Davis*, the Court upheld the constitutionality of the Social Security Act's old-age pension provisions. The Court determined that Congress could help older workers because "among industrial workers the younger men and women are preferred over the older." The economic collapse of 1929 had taught the nation that Congress had to provide for the "general welfare" and "well-being of the nation" where there was a "solidarity of interests that may once have seemed to be divided."[71]

These decisions emboldened Roosevelt, who made clear his support for progressive social legislation to provide redress for laborers. He outlined his vision of every person's rights to "a comfortable living." It was the government's "formal and informal, political and economic" duty to provide an avenue for everyone "to possess himself of a portion of that plenty sufficient for his needs through his own work." This required the development of nothing short of "an economic declaration of rights, an economic constitutional order." Americans would need to come together with "faith in our tradition of personal responsibility, faith in our institutions" to establish "the new terms of the old social contract." He and other reformers, like Senator Wagner, emerged politically from the Progressive Era's advocacy for more rigorous governmental regulation of economic and social affairs. They saw the Constitution as a source of national growth and development, especially in an age when giant corporations tended to devalue individual workers. They conceived of national fair standards for workers as a safety net that would benefit individuals and the country as a whole. Those aims could not be accomplished with a recalcitrant Supreme Court.[72]

Operating with a narrow majority on the Court favoring progressive initiatives was not a problem for long. On June 2, 1937, Justice Willis Van Devanter, who had consistently resisted New Deal programs, retired. Then, on August 12, 1937, shortly before Roosevelt's court-packing bill went down to congressional defeat, he nominated a southern Democrat, Senator Hugo L. Black, to the Court. Despite the revelation during Senate hearings that Black had once been a member of the Ku Klux Klan, he got more than enough votes to win confirmation. During his thirty-four years on the Court, despite his previous involvement with the hate group, Black often played a central role in civil rights decisions. In the next two and a half years, Roosevelt was able to place four more supporters of the New Deal on the Supreme Court: Stanley F. Reed, Felix Frankfurter, William O. Douglas, and Frank Murphy. This core group of justices changed the role of judicial review. Instead of relying the Due Process and Commerce Clauses to strike down economic policy, the

Court devoted itself to statutory construction that granted Congress leeway
to make reasonable decisions.[73]

Criminal Procedure

The Supreme Court's determination to stop relying on freedom of contract to
trump civil rights protections was just one positive sign during this period.
On a case-by-case basis, the Court began establishing precedents to prohibit
the use of state authority to further discriminatory purposes. The gains from
these cases were monumental because they balanced liberty with equality
considerations. Their immediate impact, however, was limited by the Court's
institutional inability to enforce its own orders.

Long before the New Deal, the Court had found that excluding persons
from juries on racial grounds violates the Equal Protection Clause of the
Fourteenth Amendment. In *Strauder v. West Virginia* (1880), the Court overturned a black man's conviction for murder, finding a state law barring blacks
from serving on juries to be unconstitutional. Other states kept blacks out of
jury pools, even without an explicit law to that effect. Delaware had no overt
color barrier, but no black had ever served on a jury in the state before *Neal v.
Delaware* (1880) overturned an African American's rape conviction there. The
Court gave no credence to Delaware's claim that "the great body of black men
residing in [the] State are utterly unqualified by want of intelligence, experience, or moral integrity to sit on juries." After a series of other cases, the
justices provided more specific guidelines to lower court judges in *Carter v.
Texas* (1900). Equal protection of the law is denied to defendants, the Court
ruled, whenever a legislature, executive, or court excludes all blacks because of
their race. On several occasions, the Court also prohibited the use of mob
intimidation on due process grounds. It took a definitive stand against convictions obtained under threat of lynch mobs in *Moore v. Dempsey* (1923).[74]

The right to an impartial jury trial in criminal cases is located in the Sixth
Amendment, which also guarantees the assistance of counsel in criminal
proceedings. In 1932, a year before the start of Roosevelt's first term, the
Supreme Court provided a standard for obtaining meaningful legal advice
even before a jury heard opposing arguments. The first time the Court decided that there exists a constitutional right to attorney assistance at the
pretrial stage was in *Powell v. Alabama*. That case later served as a foundation
for Warren Court decisions on fair criminal procedures. It involved the highly
publicized Scottsboro incident.[75]

Nine transient black youths were charged with raping two white women aboard a freight train. Their trouble began when some of them fought with white youths and then threw all but one of them off the train. During the course of the fracas, Ruby Bates and Victoria Price, the two alleged victims, were also riding the train. When the black youths arrived in Scottsboro, Alabama, a sheriff's posse arrested them. The sheriff then called a militia to protect them against a visibly hostile community. At trial, Bates and Price, who had first been jailed with the threat of vagrancy and prostitution charges looming over them, testified for the prosecution, alleging that the black youths had raped them.[76]

All the defendants were from out of state, and none could afford an attorney. Instead of providing them with any particular counselor, the trial judge appointed the entire county bar, consisting of seven attorneys. None of the youths got any assistance from the bar before the day of trial. Some black citizens had taken it upon themselves to raise enough money to retain an attorney, Stephen Roddy, whose practice primarily involved real estate transactions. The proceedings began with Roddy stating that he was appearing on behalf of those who supported the defendants but would not represent the defendants themselves because neither was he familiar with Alabama procedures nor had he been "given an opportunity to prepare the case." A member of the local bar, Milo Moody, then volunteered to appear as the counsel of record. The attorneys met with the defendants for only twenty-five minutes before the trial got under way.

Just fifteen days after the initial altercation, eight of the black youths had been sentenced to death. The Alabama Supreme Court eventually affirmed seven of those convictions.[77] But the United State Supreme Court reversed, finding that the trial court's failure to provide the defendants with "an effective" and substantial "appointment of counsel was . . . a denial of due process within the meaning of the Fourteenth Amendment." The case was remanded for a new trial.

Following the Supreme Court's decision, four of the youths were released without being retried.[78] This time around, with national news coverage, exceptional trial attorneys represented the remaining defendants. Bates, one of the alleged rape victims, testified on behalf of the defense that neither she nor Price had been raped and that they had made the story up to avoid being charged with vagrancy. Besides direct evidence that cast doubt on the defendants' guilt, there was the additional question of racism in their treatment. The indictments had been issued in Jackson County, where for at least a generation there had been no black jurors, even though as of 1930 blacks made up about 7 percent of the eligible jurors living there. The preliminary jury roll contained the annotation "col." near the names of all eligible blacks. A writing expert concluded that the only six names of black men that appeared on the final grand jury roll had been forged.

Despite the weight of the evidence at Patterson's trial, an all-white jury returned a guilty verdict and recommended the death sentence. But the trial judge, James E. Horton, set that verdict aside, finding that the evidence was inadequate to justify it, and ordered a new trial. At the next election, Horton was voted out of office while the prosecuting attorney won the lieutenant governor's race. When the cases were transferred out of Horton's court room, Patterson and another defendant, Clarence Norris, were tried on the basis of almost the same faulty evidence, and both were again sentenced to death. The Alabama Supreme Court affirmed both convictions.[79]

The cases were then appealed to the U.S. Supreme Court, the main question being whether Alabama's longtime practice of excluding eligible blacks from juries was evidence of discrimination. Writing for the majority, Hughes held that evidence of blacks' long exclusion from grand and petit juries was prima facie evidence of discrimination in violation of the Equal Protection Clause. The prosecution had failed to rebut that evidence.[80]

After the second Supreme Court ruling, finding jury discrimination, Norris was retried, but there was still not a single black juror on the panel. Norris was once more sentenced to death; however, the Alabama governor commuted his sentence to life imprisonment because of the abundance of evidence that no rape had occurred at all. This was hardly the vindication of his innocence that Norris deserved. He was paroled in 1944. Patterson was sentenced to seventy-five years. He escaped from jail in 1948. Two more defendants, Charlie Weems and Andrew Wright, got seventy-five years and ninety-nine years, respectively. Weems was paroled in 1943 and Wright in 1944. In the years that followed *Powell, Norris,* and *Patterson,* the Supreme Court continued to issue opinions against the rejection of jurors based on race, with continuing interference in parts of the South.[81]

Higher Education

In a different area of law, the Hughes Court took initial steps toward undercutting educational segregation. The Hughes Court emphasized equality but did not entirely abandon the legacy of *Plessy v. Ferguson*'s "separate but equal" doctrine.

As the South increasingly separated its residents by race, three cases from the early twentieth century had given the Court's stamp of approval for school segregation.[82] In one of them, *Berea College v. Kentucky* (1908), Justice Harlan, writing in dissent, rhetorically expressed his frustration at the increasing use of segregation: "Have we become so inoculated with prejudice of race than [*sic*] an American government, professedly based on the principles of freedom, and charged with the protection of all citizens alike, can make distinctions between such citizens in the matter of their voluntary meeting for innocent purposes, simply because of their respective races?" Nine years before, Harlan had proved unwilling to speak out against segregation at the high school level. He wrote the majority opinion for *Cumming v. Board of Education* (1899), finding that Georgia had not denied equal legal protection to black taxpayers when, for fiscal reasons, it closed a black public high school while retaining a white public high school system.

The NAACP began to strategically assault educational segregation, first achieving a victory in *Missouri ex rel. Gaines v. Canada* (1938). After receiving an undergraduate degree from Lincoln University, a segregated black institution in Jefferson City, Missouri, Lloyd Gaines applied for admission to the School of Law of the University of Missouri. Gaines filed a lawsuit after he was denied admission because the state had a public policy against blacks and whites being taught together. He claimed that the school's curators had denied him an equal opportunity to get a legal education solely because of his race. There were no black law schools in Missouri for him to attend, but the state planned to open a law school for blacks in the near future.[83]

Curators of the University of Missouri took the position that rather than desegregation, equality required only that it subsidize Gaines's tuition to attend an out-of-state law school. Hughes, who wrote the *Gaines* opinion, did not buy into that argument. Even temporary discrimination, practiced until the new law school could be built in Missouri, ran against constitutional principles. The state had violated constitutional norms because it did not offer equal opportunities for whites and blacks to pursue legal education.

Following the Supreme Court's pronouncement, Missouri allocated $200,000 to establish Lincoln University Law School. The school opened its doors to black law students in 1939 and operated until 1955. As for Gaines, whose personal rights the Court found the curators had violated, he spent a year getting a graduate degree at the University of Michigan. But he never did attend law school; in fact, the NAACP lost track of him, leaving only speculations about his fate.[84]

Though the *Gaines* decision was well intentioned, its holding was too narrow to end discrimination in higher education. Congress might have stepped up with initiatives to end inequality based on legislative powers to enforce the Fourteenth Amendment or latitude under the Commerce Clause. Southern Democrats held too much sway for Roosevelt to push the issue, and there seems to be no indication that he ever tried to do so. Much credit for the integration of American universities must be given to the Court because after *Gaines* it continued to gradually review and overturn overt and subtle forms of educational subordination. The problem with relying on the Court to do the arduous work was that change came at a snail's pace. The requirements to get a case into court—that a plaintiff have standing and suffer an individual wrong for which a legal remedy exists—made it impossible to use the judicial system to address the group harm that segregation posed to all blacks and for which there were no federal remedies.

The higher education cases that advanced integration affected few people relative to the number of those whose opportunities racial segregation compromised. Southern universities did not suddenly change their practices following *Gaines,* so the Court again relied on equal protection reasoning in *Sipuel v. Board of Regents of University of Oklahoma* (1948). The Court held that Ada Sipuel, an otherwise qualified applicant to whom the University of Oklahoma Law School had denied access because of her race, was entitled to a legal education from a state institution. Oklahoma was ordered to enroll her "as soon as it does . . . applicants of any other group." The brief per curiam decision, not attributing authorship to any particular justice, implied that states could live up to the Court's requirement so long as they simultaneously operated segregated law schools.[85]

In the continuing chess game over education segregation, the Court moved against the disparate qualities of segregated schools. Herman Sweatt filed an equal protection claim against the University of Texas Law School for rejecting his application because he was black. At the time there were no segregated black law schools in Texas. Before the state trial court could adjudicate the case on its merits, Texas opened a separate law school for blacks.

Chief Justice Fred M. Vinson chose to write the opinion in *Sweatt v. Painter* (1950) to resolve a novel Fourteenth Amendment issue. There was no "substantial equality in the educational opportunities offered white and Negro law students by the State" when the established professional school was compared with an upstart. The University of Texas Law School was superior in terms of faculty quality and reputation, student body size, library holdings, student organizations like the law review, alumni network, and community reputation. By comparing the quality of the segregated school, Vinson provided important guidelines to lower courts for determining whether separate schools were qualitatively equal. The case did little to change the Jim Crow system. It dealt with only a narrow circumstance that could have little effect on the deep roots of segregation. Vinson noted that there was a "traditional reluctance to extend constitutional interpretations to situations or facts which are not before the Court"; hence the Court refused to extrapolate its decision to analogous disparate treatment based on race outside higher education.[86]

The same year that it decided *Sweatt,* the Court issued an opinion in *McLaurin v. Oklahoma State Regents* from a race-based admission denial to a graduate school. Vinson also wrote that opinion. Unlike *Gaines* and *Sweatt, McLaurin* presented the Court with a university that enrolled an African American student but then separated him from classmates. For a time, he was forced to sit in a railed-off anteroom to the classroom, somewhat like a cage; thereafter, he was confined to a row of chairs labeled "colored only." He was not allowed to sit with white students in the library or in the dining area. Vinson found that this sort of degradation violated the individual right to equal protection, but the harm was not solely personal. Discrimination was also detrimental to others. After the student's graduation, Vinson reasoned, "those who will come under his guidance and influence must be directly affected by the education he receives. Their own education and development will necessarily suffer to the extent that his training is unequal to that of his classmates." The Court did not naively expect its decision to end personal acts of discrimination, but at the very least, the state would no longer be permitted to deprive McLaurin of the ability "to secure acceptance by his fellow students on his own merits."[87]

Left intact by all these decisions was segregation in public elementary and high schools. There would be no change there until the Warren Court and the Civil Rights Act of 1964 altered race dynamics in the United States.

In the meantime, the higher education cases jump-started the Court to reduce state sponsored inequalities outside the realm of education. Beginning with *Shelley v. Kraemer* (1948), the Court maintained that any government support for racially restrictive covenants, even in the form of favorable court dispositions, was a violation of legal equal protection.[88] During the same active period, the Court also refused to tolerate unequal treatment of blacks by interstate carriers.[89]

The Penetrating Footnote

The Court's new direction on civil rights owed some of its intellectual foundation to footnote four of *United States v. Carolene Products*, written by Justice Harlan F. Stone. The key issues in the case had nothing to do with individual liberties, but a gem of pluralism lay within.[90]

Carolene Products concerned the constitutionality of the Filled Milk Act of 1923, which prohibited the use of interstate commerce to fraudulently ship any adulterated milk product that replaced milk or cream with fat or oil. The Carolene Products Company, which sold a version of this skimmed milk known as Milnut, was prosecuted under the statute. In its defense, it claimed that the statute was an unconstitutional use of commerce power and that it deprived the company of property without due process of law.

The Supreme Court had no difficulty deciding that the act was a constitutional use of Congress's commerce power to provide for public health. The Court also found that lawmakers had not violated the company's due process since they had a rational basis for deciding to prevent a fraud that could negatively affect the public's well-being. The decision was part of a broader break from *Lochner* jurisprudence, on which the Court had been relying before 1937 to overturn social welfare legislation. *Carolene Products* recognized that commercial interests sometimes had to give way to reasonable regulations.

Curiously, at a time when the Court found it difficult to make broad enough pronouncements in educational discrimination, the Court's fourth footnote provided essential constitutional direction beyond the immediate controversy. Louis Lusky, who was then Stone's law clerk, later reflected, "The Footnote was being offered not as a settled theorem of government or Court-approved standard of judicial review, but as a starting point for debate —in the spirit of inquiry, the spirit of the Enlightenment." Lusky's assessment, while no doubt accurate, only begins to get at the importance of the analytical method Stone framed.[91]

Footnote four pointed out that while the economic law involved in *Carolene Products* could be presumed to be constitutional so long as it was rationally related to a legitimate public purpose, no such presumption could be made when a statute intruded the rights of national, religious, or racial minorities. At the core of Stone's footnote lay the American tradition, often breached by self-interest though it was, of protecting minorities against the whims of powerful majorities. "Prejudice against discrete and insular minorities may be a special condition, which tends seriously to curtail the operation of those political processes ordinarily to be relied upon to protect minorities, and which may call for a correspondingly more searching judicial inquiry." That statement was the fulcrum for future elevated scrutiny cases that probed whether individuals were unfairly treated for being members of an identifiable group.

Stone's formulation needed further elaboration. On its face, it required the Court to critically review all regulations predicated on religious, national, or racial characteristics. One question the footnote left unanswered is whether any other groups require increased Court concern about the invidious nature of government action. Surely not all discrete and insular minorities would qualify; a group of traveling musicians might, for instance, be discrete and insular, but a general law regulating the volume, time, and location of musical performances would not "seriously . . . curtail the operation of . . . political processes." Furthermore, some groups, like women, are diffuse throughout the population but suffer from discriminatory treatment, and Stone did not even mention them in the footnote despite the many legal handicaps they faced.[92]

To better evaluate whether heightened judicial scrutiny was required, the Court still needed to establish what rights are fundamental to political participation. In a 1939 case that found leafleting ordinances targeting Jehovah's Witnesses to be unconstitutional, Justice Roberts held that freedom of speech and press are fundamental to "the maintenance of democratic institutions." Four years later the Court held that Jehovah's Witness children could not be forced to salute the flag at a public school. The Court made clear that "freedom of worship and assembly, and other fundamental rights may not be submitted to vote; they depend on the outcome of no elections." In a democracy "no official, high or petty, can prescribe what shall be orthodox in politics, nationalism, religion, or other matters of opinion." The government cannot infringe on the freedoms of speech, assembly, or worship unless there is a "grave and immediate danger to interests which the State may lawfully protect."[93]

Not even fair procedure can justify the exploitation of government authority to undermine liberal equality. Courts also have to determine whether the government has any narrowly tailored reasons for passing laws that impinge on individuals' fundamental rights. The Court relied on a value-laden rationale in *Skinner v. Oklahoma* (1942). A convicted petitioner questioned the constitutionality of a sterilization statute for habitual criminals. The law included provisions to protect procedural rights to notice, opportunity to be heard, and right to a jury trial. Justice William O. Douglas wrote that the presumption of statutory constitutionality must be laid aside in evaluating a law that can irreparably diminish "one of the basic civil rights of man," in this case the right to procreate. Douglas found it an equal protection violation amounting to a "clear, pointed, unmistakable discrimination" to presume that some recidivist criminal activities, but not others, could be transmitted from parent to child. The degree of legislative arbitrariness involved in Oklahoma's policy, which Douglas connected to the insular minorities in Stone's footnote, could have "subtle, farreaching and devastating effects. In evil or reckless hands it can cause races or types which are inimical to the dominant group to wither and disappear." To avoid that danger, "strict scrutiny of the classification which a State makes in a sterilization law is essential, lest unwittingly or otherwise invidious discriminations are made against groups or types of individuals in violation of the constitutional guaranty of just and equal laws." *Skinner* established that strict scrutiny was the appropriate standard, even when the statute under consideration contained procedural safeguards and the democratic values at stake are not explicitly articulated by the Constitution.[94]

During the 1930s and 1940s the Court increasingly provided protections for minority rights. It created important precedents for preventing discrimination in higher education, jury selection, attorney selection, property and labor contracts, and political primaries. These cases provided a basis for holding states accountable for inequalities based on arbitrary policymaking. More than ever before, the Court supported blacks' entitlement to equal treatment. Reflecting on the Roosevelt Court's successes, the historian Harvard Sitkoff concluded that if it "did not cripple the underpinnings of the Jim Crow system, it did make them wobble."[95]

While the Court was dismantling the vestiges of discrimination, its case law had little immediate relevance to average blacks. They were subjected to segregated schools, differential treatment in courtrooms, lower wages in government and private jobs, and exclusion from the political process through poll taxes. Without civil rights legislation, vehement presidential involvement, and judicial standing requirements, the Court had virtually no power to enforce its decisions.

Insofar as the New Deal economic and social programs uplifted Americans as a whole—through the Social Security Act, the Wagner Act, Fair Labor Standards Act, work relief programs, minimum wages, school lunches, and other initiatives—public policy included minorities as full citizens. The purposes of the New Deal were to provide tangible means to achieve the aims of the Declaration of Independence, as decisionmakers understood them. This was what Roosevelt promised from his first inaugural address. The country arrived at an understanding of liberty that differed from the rugged individualism that had dominated from roughly 1880 to 1933.[96] The market collapse of 1929 quickened the demise of government noninterference. In an increasingly industrial society with large corporations, liberty became a value that government had the obligation to protect.

As never before, the federal government became the primary source of economic and social programs. The new beginning for the nation stressed the importance of providing for the general welfare through government planning. The fiscal and administrative role of government altered the meaning of dual federalism as it had been understood at the turn of the twentieth century and throughout the *Lochner* era. Civil rights activism became more broadly spread throughout the population with the realization that government quiescence allowed local customs and business interests to supersede fundamental rights. Progress to become a liberal polity of equals was far from complete; indeed, achievements were only incremental, with compromises made all along the way to gain enough votes for passing legislative initiatives. In many parts of the country, blacks still got a disproportionately small piece of the total economic pie; discrimination against Asians, especially on the West Coast, persisted; children still lacked essential rights in the courtroom; and women continued to be treated as subordinates. These groups' participation in programs that helped workers organize, the elderly receive medical care, students receive support for education, and those out of work find gainful employment included them in the political process through which they could influence further progress. After long abandonment during the Reconstruction era, the view that opportunities should be made available on an equal basis gained influential support among policymakers in Washington. Their achievements provided a framework for additional gains.

CHAPTER TEN

The War against Tyranny

The cataclysmic events of World War II unified the country against common enemies. President Roosevelt referred to the need for cooperation of the citizenry in his 1944 state of the union address: "In this war, we have been compelled to learn how interdependent upon each other are all groups and sections of the population of America." Langston Hughes, an activist black poet, had a different view of how minority groups were interlinked in a country that continued to tolerate Jim Crow attitudes: "It is not the Negro who is going to wreck our Democracy, (What we want is more of it, not less). But Democracy is going to wreck itself if it continues to approach closer and closer to fascist methods in its dealings with Negro citizens—for such methods of oppression spread, affecting other whites, Jews, the foreign born, labor, Mexicans, Catholics, citizens of Oriental ancestry— and, in due time, they boomerang right back at the oppressor." Hughes's frustration with the United States' continued failure to address its racial past expressed blacks' increasing unwillingness to wait patiently for their piece of the American pie.[1]

On the brink of war, blacks remained in precarious circumstances. Segregation was widely considered a legitimate regional practice that only states could regulate. Separation of races remained the norm in many parts of the country. Blacks encountered systematically worse treatment throughout the South. Asians and Native Americans remained segregated in schools in California. Many states refused to grant Asians citizenship. Native Americans had been relegated to reservations, with few job opportunities and much-diminished property. Mexicans and Chicanos were excluded from public facilities that were designated for whites in Colorado and Texas. The nation's creed, "all men are created equal," had been qualified by status, race, gender, and economic group from the nation's founding. Whites maintained a hold on government, by disenfranchisement and judicial appointment, which allowed them to provide less money to minority facilities than to accommodations set aside for whites.[2]

Operating in a military theater against the Axis powers sped up legal efforts to remedy American shortcomings. Black servicemen, who had fought against European anti-Semitism and the multinational effort, instigated by Nazi Germany, to commit genocide against Jews, were indignant at the continuing oppressions they experienced at home. Paul Parks was among the black soldiers who liberated the Dachau concentration camp and saw the genocidal murder firsthand, an experience that changed his life. He went on to be the secretary of education in Massachusetts. He recounted, "Emotionally and psychologically, seeing the camps and being involved in Dachau said to me that unless we do something about seeing that more people have their rights and freedoms, this can occur again. . . . So when I came back to the States I had one thing in mind—that I had a legitimate right to fight for my freedom and rights." His sentiment was shared by many who never had so gruesome an experience. An economist told a University of Richmond audience that "we fight Hitler because of the way he treats Jews and Catholics, but we continue to assign a large percentage of our population to a disagreeable role." The war could "be fought more vigorously and wholeheartedly," wrote the NAACP, if "discrimination has been banished from the armed forces" and "the full rights of citizenship" granted to "the largest minority group in our nation." The emergency that sparked military mobilization galvanized the American public to reflect on its own shortcomings, and it allowed groups like the Congress for Racial Equality (CORE) and NAACP to make progress in attacking the remaining vestiges of white supremacism. White liberals like Attorney General Frank Murphy and Senator Robert Wagner compared white supremacism to German racism.[3]

The distinction made between democracy, on the one hand, and Nazism and Communism, on the other, led to a more vocal, politically savvy, and litigiously capable attack against racial, ethnic, religious, and gender discrimination. The universalistic rhetoric on human rights during the war years implied that class and status would play no role in decisionmaking. As Americans looked about their country, they found many shortcomings that needed to be addressed. Following the new federalism that had emerged after the 1930s, they increasingly regarded prejudice, bigotry, and chauvinism as national evils.

Some southern newspaper editors pointed to Nazi anti-Semitic extremism to highlight the immorality of homegrown racism. Soon after the Nazi Party came to power in Germany in 1933, the *Birmingham News* found a "striking parallel between the Nazi principles and those of the Ku Klux Klan" of the 1920s. Both political parties, the editorial went on, relied on brutal and lawless persecution, both racial and religious. Both were "willing to go to any extreme in order to insure the dominance of certain racial and religious classes." The editorial did concede that the Klan had never gone "quite as far as the Nazi organization"; nevertheless the parallels were important because they indicated the "ferocity and irresponsibility" that might have resulted if the Klan "had actually gained control of the United States government." The same year, a Tennessee newspaper reported that one of the Nazi Party's most influential members, Hermann Goering, putting a perverse spin on racial violence in America, had admitted that individual acts of violence had been perpetrated against Jews, but only "for reasons which in the United States would lead to lynching." The newspapers warned of what extreme racist elements in America would do if they gained power, but editors recognized that the centralized support for Jewish persecution in Germany was incomparable with opposition by southern states—de jure, if not always enthusiastically de facto—to lynch mobs. Meanwhile, the world stood idly by, with Britain unwilling even to expand immigration into Palestine, as Jews continued to be increasingly at risk until the Final Solution began in 1941.

Americans decried racism even before support of minority groups was needed for the war effort. Newspapers printed columns calling on America to overcome its own shortcomings lest it slip into an increasingly destructive vortex of racism. Editors compared the United States' continued failure to treat its citizens on an equal footing with Nazi depravities against German Jews. "Decent white men in the South no more approve these lynchings than they do the official persecution of Jews in Germany," wrote a Raleigh *News and Observer* editorialist. "There is a difference in the brutality undoubtedly. In Germany the hoodlum attacks are incited by the State. In the South lynching is a crime against the State." While that statement underplayed the role of unequal customs and segregation laws in legitimizing white supremacism, it sounded the alarm that the same sort of popular prejudice that helped elect a tyrannical party in Germany could support racist leadership in the United States.[4]

The challenge civil rights activists faced was how to permanently change disparaging social, political, and civil attitudes. Gallup polls conducted in the South during the 1930s and 1940s showed overwhelming white support for segregated schools. Without explicit federal commitment to individual rights, more national compromises at the expense of black rights were inevitable.[5]

Even before the attack on Pearl Harbor fully drew the United States into the war, Roosevelt called for the establishment of a "moral order" in which "freedom means the supremacy of human rights everywhere." The terms he used were universal and not limited by race, color, gender, religion, or national origin. Addressing Congress on January 6, 1941, after Germany had demonstrated its destructiveness by attacking and invading neighboring countries, Roosevelt spoke of "four essential human freedoms": freedom of speech and expression, freedom of religion, "freedom from want" during peacetime, and the freedom from fear of armed conflict. The Indian activist Mohandas Gandhi later pointed out that the president's appeal to individual freedom and democracy rang hollow so long as "America has the Negro problem of her own." Pearl S. Buck, a literary critic of racism and an expert on Asia, warned that "every lynching, every race riot, gives joy to Japan."[6]

After the United States declared war on Japan and then on Germany and Italy in December 1941, its priorities shifted to establishing a war economy. So much so that Congress began reallocating resources to the military and disbanding many of Roosevelt's New Deal programs. In 1943 Congress abolished the National Youth Administration, the Civilian Conservation Corps, and the Work Projects Administration. All three agencies had antidiscrimination requirements, but none of them had ever been entirely integrated.[7]

The National Resources Planning Board (NRPB) was another agency that fell into disfavor that year, and Congress refused to appropriate funds for it. From 1933 to 1943 the Planning Board had reported to the president about employment trends, made recommendations to him about developing national resources, and initiated the framework for future public works programs. It functioned as a think tank for social and economic policies. Before its termination, the Planning Board developed a program of postwar projects to employ workers who struggled to find work in private industry. The NRPB's 1942 report used inclusive terms about "A New Bill of Rights" for achieving Roosevelt's four freedoms. To lead the world away from dictatorial enslavement, the report proposed, democracies needed to "offer their people opportunity, employment, and a rising standard of living." In similar terms, Roosevelt spoke of the sense among "our young men and women" that "they have the right to work." The NRPB's plan was meant both to achieve the highest ideals of liberal equality and to discredit Axis propaganda about establishing an improved world order.[8]

In his 1944 state of the union address, Roosevelt adopted the NRPB's suggestions into his "second Bill of Rights" for security and prosperity that would apply "regardless of station, race, or creed." His vision of basic rights was grand. He thought not only that a useful and remunerative job was a right, but that laborers should receive a decent living to have enough for food, clothing, and recreation. Businesspeople also stood to gain from a guarantee against "unfair competition and domination by monopolies at home and abroad." All Americans, Roosevelt went on, were entitled to adequate medical care to enjoy good health. Education, too, was a right, as were protections against "the economic fears of old age, sickness, accident, and unemployment."[9]

Roosevelt's ideas set an agenda for protecting essential freedoms. It provided Americans fighting overseas and those who remained stateside with an inkling of the civil society they could expect after peace was achieved. Roosevelt indicated a willingness to direct the country to the recognition of rights predicated on American mores but neither explicitly provided for by the Constitution nor defined by Supreme Court precedents. His death before the end of the war makes it just as impossible to predict the extent to which he could have moved Congress to act in accordance with his plans as it is to know how much Lincoln could have directed Reconstruction if not for his untimely death. President Harry S. Truman was unable to harness enough political support to give the economic bill of rights much legal force. What remained was an influential suggestion of how the federal government could meet its obligation to provide for individuals and the general welfare. President Dwight D. Eisenhower did not share Roosevelt's view of federal involvement, but President Lyndon Johnson would return to New Deal ideals in his War on Poverty.

Racism at a Time of War

Racism remained a national, not merely a regional, problem. An American novelist, James Baldwin, succinctly explained changes in black attitudes at the time of the Second World War: "The treatment accorded the Negro during the Second World War marks, for me, a turning point in the Negro's relation to America. . . . You must put yourself in the skin of a man who is wearing the uniform of his country, is a candidate for death in its defense, and who is called a 'nigger' by his comrades-in-arms and his officers; who is almost always given the hardest, ugliest, most menial work to do, who knows that the white G.I. has informed the Europeans that he is subhuman."[10] Although most conspicuous in the South, as throughout United States history, bigots in the North as well treated blacks as second-class citizens.

Arguably the most egregious discriminatory practices excluded large seg-ments of the population from participating in representative democracy. Eight southern states continued to use poll taxes to prevent blacks and im-poverished whites from voting. A more direct form of discrimination was the assumption underlying Democratic primaries that political parties were pri-vate clubs which could, without violating the Fifteenth Amendment, keep blacks from joining and having a voice in selecting party candidates. Whites-only primaries were used in all parts of the South except Kentucky, Ten-nessee, and some counties in Virginia and North Carolina. The language of the Louisiana Democratic Party is illustrative: "That no one shall be permit-ted to vote at said primary except electors of the white race." Democratic control of the South meant that maintaining white monopoly over primaries would shut black, Latino, and Asian Americans out of political offices. As Rayford W. Logan, the NAACP's chief adviser on international affairs, put it, these political restrictions "violate the dictum of the Declaration of Inde-pendence that governments derive 'their just powers from the consent of the governed.'"[11]

A 1944 decision in *Smith v. Allwright* was a promising portent of the increasing role the Supreme Court would play after World War II in ending the undemocratic treatment of insular minorities. Just nine years earlier the Court had held in *Grovey v. Townsend* that Democratic Party officials could exclude blacks from participating in party primaries. Justice Reed's opinion in *Smith* overturned the holding in *Grovey*. The Fifteenth Amendment, the later case determined, prohibited discrimination on the basis of race in the primaries just as it prohibited it in general elections. Political parties could no longer hide behind the mantle of private organizations since they were crea-tures of the state that were governed by its authority. Despite *Smith*'s enor-mous impact on southern voting, the Court could have done even more. In this regard, it mentioned but failed to denounce the use of a facially neutral poll tax.[12]

The Court could issue constitutional analyses, but violence, intimidation, or outright fraud continued to keep blacks, more than any other minority group, from recording their political preferences. So long as local registration remained unregulated, there was little hope for a permanent solution. Only in 1965, with the passage of the Voting Rights Act, did the federal government undertake an intensive effort to arrest local prejudices.

Educational opportunities, which provided a means to equal political participation, were also much impeded in the South. State funding for black education trailed behind the funding of white institutions. In 1940 Kentucky allocated 3 percent of its higher education budget to its two black institutions. That was enough for only 40 percent of the state's black population. During the 1946–47 academic year, Florida spent $390 per black undergraduate student and $1,220 per white student at separate state institutions. The supposed equal system of segregated education was just as much a farce at the lower educational levels. During the 1944–45 academic year, South Carolina spent $25 on each black student enrolled in elementary school and $75 for each white student. That year, South Carolina expended $37 on each black high school student and $113 on each white pupil. Less interest in black education translated into less success. In Tennessee there were 1,598 black high school graduates and 12,788 white graduates in 1945. That was about 500 black graduates fewer than their ratio in the general population would predict. The lack of adequate resources for education and training sorely limited the number of black professionals.[13]

As might have been expected, the educational segregation of any group, Latino children for instance, tended to cause similar adverse consequences: higher dropout and lower literacy rates, discouragement of social interaction, and continued stereotyping. Soon after World War II, the Ninth Circuit Court of Appeals, in *Westminster v. Mendez* (1947), found that the segregation of Mexicans violated California law. While the decision prohibited school officials from independently segregating students, it did not restrict the legislature from passing a measure to the same effect. Furthermore, the court of appeals tolerated school segregation of "Indians under certain conditions and children of Chinese, Japanese or Mongolian parentage." *Westminster* thus provided an incomplete but auspicious achievement of school integration.[14]

The Armed Services

While educational segregation originated at the state and local levels, racial separation in the armed forces was a national policy. Roosevelt went along with military exclusionism that had "been proved satisfactory over a long period of years," as he put it, fearing that to do otherwise "would risk upsetting white soldiers and would lower their morale, thereby jeopardizing the war effort." In 1937 he scribbled his "OK" on the War Department's policy "not to intermingle colored and white personnel in the same regimental organizations."[15]

Henry L. Stimson, the secretary of war during World War II, resolutely carried out the president's policies out of both a sense of professional duty and personal conviction. Stimson struggled with his own demons, knowing that racism was related to "the persistent legacy of the original crime of slavery." He refused to abide by the exclusionary enlistment practices of World War I, but instead of integrating the military he insisted on establishing segregated units. He excused the army's complicity with unreconstructed southern attitudes by rationalizing that the "original crime of our forefathers . . . was almost incapable of solution." Stimson's own prejudices played a role in his willingness to commit resources to perpetuating military segregation. He deprecated black leaders' advocacy of integrated units as part of a plan to achieve "social equality" that he further linked to "the basic impossibility of race mixture by marriage." He further maintained that black troops were incompetent unless they were lead by white officers.[16]

With military leadership like that, it was no wonder that disparaging attitudes percolated through many in the officer ranks. The author of a 1925 Army War College report on "Negro Manpower" adopted a racist version of social Darwinism, claiming that "the American negro has not progressed as far as other sub-species of the human family." The report revealed an influential stereotype that kept blacks out of combat units: "The negro . . . cannot control himself in fear of danger. . . . He is a rank coward in the dark." With a disproportionate number of officers from the South and with many training camps located there, blacks faced adversarial circumstances. Northern soldiers who were not used to unabashed southern discrimination found the circumstances to be almost intolerable. "The treatment of Negro soldiers," remarked a black sociologist shortly after the war, "especially by southern whites who resented a Negro in uniform, tended more than any other factor to stir up resentment among Negroes against their traditional status in American life." An officer during World War I, Charles H. Houston, who went on to many legal victories in the NAACP, warned that "the Negro population . . . will not again silently endure the insults and discriminations imposed on its soldiers and sailors in the course of the last war." A study of Coahoma County, Mississippi, found that blacks expected "an important change" and had "a feeling of discontent and a growing consciousness of exclusion from social, economic, and political participation."[17]

During the Second World War, the lack of legal progress created a powder keg that exploded with six civilian race riots, at least forty lynchings, and twenty military riots. In the case of the military, harassed soldiers in places like Fort Jackson, South Carolina; Fort Bliss, Texas; and Camp Steward, Georgia, found that their complaints fell on deaf ears and took matters into their own hands, sometimes fighting pitched battles with white soldiers and police. The black press ran numerous stories of blacks who wrecked military base facilities or off-base restaurants that refused to serve them.[18]

Judge William H. Hastie, the civilian aid to the secretary of war, received many letters from black soldiers describing the degradations they faced in the South. Soldiers in Mississippi found whole towns that forbade them entry, despite their sacrifices for the country. White police in some communities shot and killed black soldiers who were on leave. More commonly, black soldiers who did enter southern cities had to conform to local segregation practices that forced them to sit at the back of buses, dine away from whites, and watch movies in separate sections. In some locations like Moore Field, Texas, whites protested having any black soldiers at all stationed near their communities. Several black soldiers at Jackson Air Base, in Jackson, Mississippi, reported that "civilian police have threatened to kill several soldiers here." At Fort Benning, Georgia, a black army private was hanged. The army refused to rule out suicide, despite a finding that the victim's hands and feet had been bound. At Hastie's prompting, Stimson issued an official statement on September 25, 1941, decrying the disturbances, but black soldiers continued to report incidents of racism.[19]

In addition to privately and locally sponsored discrimination against soldiers, the federal government maintained a policy meant to placate supremacist sensitivities. At the beginning of the Second World War, blacks were entirely shut out of the Air and Signal Corps, the Marine Corps, and the Coast Guard. The only job available for them in the navy was as messman. Black aviators were prohibited from entering combat squadrons. Neither were black women permitted to enter the navy's Women Accepted for Volunteer Emergency Service (WAVES), the marines, or the Coast Guard's Semper Paratus—Always Ready (SPARs). Blacks who were in the service received better food, clothing, and pay than many of them had ever had in civilian life. But those amenities did not dull the sting of discrimination they experienced from being relegated to boring jobs like guard duty or to the most arduous manual labor like road building, without the opportunity to show their bravery as soldiers.[20]

For some, like Charlie Jones of Chicago, the continuing irony of discrimination that loomed as they "headed overseas for duty" made them think that they were "fighting without a cause." Others turned to the federal government for help. An army corporal asked for assistance from the Civil Rights Section of the Justice Department. He had served oversees and received a good-conduct medal. In his letter he expressed shock to hear that "colored people" in his home of New Iberia, Louisiana, including his brother-in-law, had been forced out of their homes simply for setting up "a welding school for the colored, so they could build the tanks and ships we need so badly." He "thought we were fighting to make this world a better place to live" and wanted justice to be done in his city. In 1943 the Information and Education Division of the War Department conducted a telling survey of soldiers. While both whites and blacks felt that they were being treated like dogs and complained about the army's undemocratic nature, what came through uniquely from black soldiers was the number of racial affronts they perceived. Blacks tended to relate their own difficulties to being a member of a reviled group. The survey also allowed soldiers to offer a question to the president. Some illustrative ones from black soldiers were: "Will I as a Negro share this so-called democracy after the war?" "Why don't they make the people in the south treat the Negro right and then try to make the people in other countries do right?" "If the white and colored soldiers are fighting and dying for the same thing, why can't they train together?" and "What are the chances of moving Negro troops from the South?" When Otis Pinkard, a native of Macon County, Alabama, returned from serving "oversees fighting for democracy, I thought that . . . when we got back here we should enjoy a little of it." Many white veterans joined the call for tolerance through the American Veterans Committee, an integrated organization that addressed concerns over housing and employment. The Atlanta chapter of the organization protested police violence against black veterans.[21]

Hastie resigned in January 1943 to protest inaction, but his work ultimately resulted in important changes to the status of black soldiers. Even before he began agitating for change, the army had begun to make some advances. Benjamin O. Davis, Sr., became the first black to be promoted to the rank of general officer, in October 1940. His promotion helped ensure black support for the Democratic Party that year. Major Campbell C. Johnson held another prestigious post as the special assistant to the director of the Selective Service Administration. This was an important precedent because there was no record of any blacks in the Selective Service during World War I, but by 1943 about eighteen hundred blacks served on draft boards.

These leaders, along with the black press, helped initiate important changes in military policy. In 1941 the army air force started training black pilots, and in 1942 the navy and marines began enlisting them to various specialties. Secretary of the Navy William F. (Frank) Knox, who ardently supported segregation, died in 1944, and his successor, James Forrestal, declared segregation impractical; by February 27, 1946, the navy ended all limitations on assigning blacks to naval posts. Receiving many complaints about verbal affronts, the War Department issued a policy against commanding officers' using racial epithets. The number of black officers also increased, indicting a growing respect for individual ability and the decline of the degrading stereotype of cowardice. By 1943 there were about 3,000 black officers and 500,000 black soldiers. The number of black officers was more than twice the number who had served in World War I but still only 0.6 percent of the whole. Eventually 7,768 blacks received army commissions (1 percent of all officers) and 701,678 blacks were enlisted. Success was by no means the norm. To the contrary, most black officers found that barriers of white supervision prevented them from advancing based on merit. In total, blacks made up 10 percent of army personnel, up from 5.9 percent at the time of Pearl Harbor. Most served as quartermasters, engineers, and members of the transportation corps.[22]

The army did make some concerted effort to change military racial attitudes. Assistant Secretary of War John J. McCloy's Committee on Negro Troop Policies recommended that blacks be permitted into combat units. Black troops, who had long brought attention to the problems they faced while traveling in the South, were finally given access to more equitable on- and off-base transport services. To improve black morale and diminish prejudice, the army produced pamphlets and movies about blacks' role in the military.[23]

One of the most difficult barriers to break down was the prohibition against black troops serving in combat, which the military supported by claiming blacks to be innately timid. When combat units were finally opened to them, there were mixed reviews for the 92nd Infantry, which was exclusively led by white officers in Italy. The 2,500 black volunteers of the battle of Ardennes campaign, on the other hand, were commended on all sides for their performance in an integrated force. These troops were nevertheless returned to segregated units after the Battle of the Bulge. The fortitude of the Tuskegee Airmen was proven in Italian and Sicilian combat, and the 332nd Fighter group, made up of four black squadrons, was one of the most decorated in the air corps.[24]

Segregation of units, which had been the greatest cause of complaint by black leaders and soldiers, remained unaltered. Until 1944 there were separate black and white post exchanges, theaters, and transports, as if whites and blacks could not even recreate together on military bases. A directive issued in July of that year supposedly desegregated all base facilities, but in practice, segregated units were assigned to the same facilities they had used before the change in policy.

On July 26, 1948, President Truman courageously issued executive order 9981, which ended segregation in the armed forces, over objections from his military Joint Chiefs of Staff. The President's Civil Rights Commission noted the year before in its report *To Secure These Rights* that "the war experience brought to our attention a laboratory in which we may prove that the majority and minorities of our population can train and work and fight side by side in cooperation and harmony."[25] After years of claiming to fight for freedom of opportunity, the American forces finally set aside their harmful and inefficient policy of separation. The last all-black combat unit, the 24th Infantry, desegregated on July 30, 1951.[26]

Defense Industry

As with the military at the beginning of World War II, blacks did not enjoy equal opportunities in the civilian war industries. Robert Weaver, who was the head of the National Defense Advisory Commission's Labor Division, issued instructions that defense contractors "should not" discriminate against workers "because of age, sex, race, and color," but Weaver understood that management paid little attention to such guidelines. As the production of military equipment increased, so too did the need for laborers, but employers often preferred white workers. The president of North American Aviation decided that "under no circumstances" would blacks "be employed as aircraft workers or mechanics, regardless of their training." He was willing to consider taking them on only as janitors. That formula inevitability harmed the war effort, since experienced black mechanics were unable to lend their talents to arming pilots. Employment statistics reflect the racist standards. Between April and October 1940, when American munition production began its steady increase, white unemployment dropped from 17.7 percent to 13 percent nationally; meanwhile, among blacks, unemployment remained at 22 percent. A similar pattern was visible in the ranks of the unemployed. Whereas in 1940 blacks made up 24.8 percent of Philadelphia's unemployed, the next year they were 29.8 percent of that population, even as munition production had reached one-fifth of its later peak. The United States Employment Service failed to step in with clear policies against discrimination, and, as had been the case with New Deal programs, regional offices were thus free to follow local racial standards. Congress took a stand by prohibiting gender, race, or color discrimination in its October 1940 defense training proviso, but it allowed states to rely on segregated education so long as "equitable provision shall be made for facilities for training of like quality." Blacks' ability to be hired, retained, and promoted was also hampered by educational Balkanization. In southern states, where blacks made up 22.3 percent of the population, only 6.6 percent of the defense training budget went to equipping black schools; as of 1942 only 4 percent of those who benefited from the training program were black.[27]

Few employers hired blacks at equal wages in skilled positions. Some refused to hire them at all, and those who did typically placed them in unskilled, manual jobs, regardless of their training. A winter 1941 study of 227 defense plants that were located in industrial centers where defense orders were concentrated, including New York City, northern New Jersey, Pittsburgh, and Philadelphia, found that 39 employed no blacks, who made up only 4.8 percent of the employees at the defense plants in those areas. The airline industry also retained an "almost universal prejudice against blacks," though there was incremental improvement from 1940, when the industry employed approximately one hundred black employees, to 1941, when more than two thousand blacks were working for the airlines, including hundreds in production. Labor unions, especially those affiliated with the American Federation of Labor, were sometimes indirectly complicit with management, because many unions excluded blacks from their membership and refused to address discrimination against nonmembers.[28]

Inadequate or nonexistent enforcement of federal policy inflamed blacks, who believed that discrimination violated the principles Roosevelt had laid down in his Four Freedoms speech. A *Chicago Defender* editorialist expressed the increasing boldness in the black community by demanding the long-expected rewards of equal citizenship: "Democracy is never given. It must be taken."[29]

A. Philip Randolph, head of the Brotherhood of Sleeping Car Porters, organized the most successful effort to force the administration to honor its policy statements. The issues of black exclusion from defense jobs and army segregation came to a head in September 1940 after Randolph, Walter White, and T. Arnold Hill, director of the National Urban League, met Roosevelt at the White House. Secretary of the Navy Knox and Undersecretary of War Robert P. Patterson were also present. The meeting took place shortly after the Selective Service Act had become law, with a clause prohibiting discrimination and another making men between eighteen and thirty-six years of age eligible for the draft.[30]

The meeting came to nothing more than an agreement from Roosevelt, in his ever-affable manner, to take the matter under advice and a categorical refusal by Knox to desegregate the navy. Tired of being put off and having the black vote taken for granted, Randolph, White, and Hill issued a joint statement of shock that the president, "at a time of national peril, should surrender so completely to enemies of democracy." By March 1941 Randolph took matters a step further, calling for a massive black rally in Washington, D.C. Concerned about the spectacle of tens of thousands of protesters in the nation's segregated capital and unable to persuade Randolph to call the rally off, Roosevelt implemented executive order 8802, prohibiting defense industries and the government from discriminating on the basis of race, creed, color, or national origin. The order established the Fair Employment Practices Committee (FEPC) to investigate and redress valid grievances. In response, Randolph called off the march. The president strengthened the FEPC in 1943, providing it with authority to "conduct hearings, make findings of fact, and take appropriate steps to obtain elimination of such discrimination." The new act also enabled federal officials to cooperate with state and local ones.[31]

Some black leaders pointed out that the order lacked a specific penalty provision, rendering the punishment for discrimination uncertain. Roy Wilkins, then editor of the NAACP's *Crisis,* credited the president for speaking "on Negroes in defense" but cautioned that it remained "to be seen how much compliance will be secured." Wilkins found that "the sure justification for the FEPC thesis lies not alone in the war of the present, but in the basic conception of the American democratic ideal." Many black organizations expressed optimism. The *Negro Handbook* considered it the "most significant move on the part of Government since the Emancipation Proclamation." The *Amsterdam News,* which was devoted to black politics, saw it as part of the continuing struggle with inequality: "If President Lincoln's proclamation was designed to end physical slavery," an editorial there read, Roosevelt's order "is designed to end, or at least curb, economic slavery."[32]

Just as with Lincoln's Emancipation Proclamation, order 8802 was a war measure that, while limited in its scope, catalyzed further civil rights initiatives. The FEPC showed the power of black civil protest, which was critical for the future leadership strategy of Dr. Martin Luther King, Jr. Other executive orders would follow. President Truman created the Committee on Civil

Rights, which issued a detailed and influential report on racial injustice. Even more important was his 1948 executive order that integrated the armed services, something that Roosevelt had repeatedly refused to do. Then in 1953 President Eisenhower created the Fair Employment Board, which provided authority for the Government Contract Compliance Committee. President John F. Kennedy in 1961 issued an executive order that mandated affirmative action in every federal contract. Through these national commitments to end employment discrimination, the FEPC was crucially linked to the 1964 creation of the Equal Employment Opportunity Commission under the guidance of President Johnson.

The FEPC was just the beginning of a peaceful civil rights revolution. During its five-year life span, from June 1941 to June 1946, the agency handled nearly five thousand cases against employers, unions, and the government. About 80 percent of them were filed by blacks and another 10 percent by Jews, the other 10 percent primarily complaining of exclusion based on ancestry. Most complainants cited refusals to hire, discriminatory dismissals, and promotion denials. Yet an insufficient enforcement provision and the constraint of acting only in response to formal complaints limited the FEPC's efficacy. Many of its orders were disregarded, and the agency had to rely for the most part on voluntary compliance. Its successes were war related rather than global.

In one instance, the FEPC issued a directive to sixteen railroads and seven unions to desist from discriminatory employment practices. Southeastern rail carriers had entered into written agreements with unions, primarily with the Brotherhood of Firemen and Enginemen, that reserved a variety of skilled positions for white men. Black firemen were thereby prohibited from being promoted to engineers, irrespective of their skills and experience. The carriers also denied black employees seniority privileges. These and other limitations were perpetrated at a time when there was a national shortage of skilled employees needed for maximum war efficiency, pointing clearly to racial subordination irrespective of social harm. The carriers and three unions openly refused to comply with the FEPC order, and four unions simply ignored it. The agency then referred the case to Roosevelt, who set up an investigatory committee. The case was never resolved, showing the FEPC's impotence despite its good intentions. While it failed in this instance, there are a number of reasons to believe that the FEPC significantly contributed to changing attitudes and to decreasing employment discrimination.[33]

For black laborers, the FEPC hearings against southern railroads and railroad unions constituted a milestone in self-assertion. Hundreds of black men from southern states testified, disregarding the risk of reprisals, to bolster the government's case. The very existence of the FEPC was an affront to discriminatory social standards as they related to associational and labor rights. The committee's function was to prevent firms from denying employment opportunities based on stereotypes. The FEPC put government authority behind job equality. Relative to men working outside war-related industries, black men working in defense realized a significant improvement in their job status.

Although the FEPC lacked penalty provisions, in the North it played a positive role in advancing antidiscriminatory policy. The FEPC brought its limited authority to bear by providing guidance to firms, working with other federal agencies, and publicly chastising companies and unions that persisted in exclusionary practices. On one occasion, in the racially motivated Philadelphia Transit strike, Roosevelt even ordered the army to enforce the FEPC's nondiscrimination policies. These methods, however, did not work in the South, where, absent the fear of punishment, firms had no reason to fear the FEPC; after all, they were conducting themselves according to local custom, and public opinion was on their side. Still, by taking a stand against unfairness and investigating complaints, the federal government played an important role in securing blacks with increasing opportunities in industrial work. With the FEPC's backing, firms were more likely to take a stand against the instigators of racial incidents. Moreover, by the spring of 1943 most unions, like the United Steel Workers and Industrial Union of Marine and Shipbuilding Workers, actively cooperated and initiated antidiscriminatory policy. The FEPC seems to have provided important guidance for ending black economic disadvantages.[34]

Thanks in part to the FEPC, by 1944 blacks in manufacturing jobs doubled, to more than 1.2 million, including 300,000 women. By 1947 the Department of Labor reported that there were 450,000 more black women in the labor force than there had been in 1940. Between 1940 and 1944 a million blacks entered the civilian workforce. The number of skilled, semiskilled, or single-skilled black employees each doubled during that period. African Americans were able to break into industries, such as shipbuilding, car manufacturing, and aircraft construction, that had been closed to them. The improved industrial equality broke from the old pattern, enabling many blacks to work at their level of competence and provided the opportunity to develop relationships with white workers. Despite the significant improvements, the percentage of skilled jobs that blacks held was below their proportion of the population. The vast majority of blacks continued to be hired as domestics and laborers, jobs that paid less and were not as prestigious.[35]

The number of blacks in the federal government also rose significantly, from 9.8 percent of the total in 1938 to 11.9 percent in 1944. In headquarters offices, most of which were located in Washington, D.C., blacks were 19.2 percent of the total employees. The quality of black jobs improved drastically too. In 1938, 90 percent of all black federal workers were custodians, but that number was down to about 49 percent in 1944. These were remarkable changes that boded well for the country, with the government taking the lead.[36]

Two 1944 Supreme Court cases, decided under the Railway Labor Act, indicate the changed national climate on labor issues that emerged after Randolph had threatened to march on Washington and Roosevelt had countered by issuing executive order 8802. After years of inaction in the face of union exclusion of blacks, the Court established that a labor organization certified to be the exclusive bargaining agent for a specific craft was required to "represent all its members, the majority as well as the minority, and it is to act for and not against those whom it represents." Without representation, minorities would not be able to bargain equally for the same employment benefits as whites. Unions could no longer bargain on behalf of white workers at the expense of blacks. This created a union duty of fair representation. In turn, by the end of war black union enrollment had risen enormously.[37]

The stated purposes of U.S. involvement in World War II were to combat tyranny and spread democracy. These aims brought the incompatibility of homegrown racism into even sharper relief than during the American Revolution. Blacks and their leadership, most notably working through the NAACP and the Urban League, black journalists, and members of the cabinet and military, best understood the conflict between ideology and discrimination. Randolph, White, Wilkins, Weaver, and the editors of the *Chicago Defender* pressed the cause of racial equality, with growing success, by pointing out how racial subordination violated American principles of fairness. Popular novelists, like Richard Wright and Ralph Ellison, also brought the individual and social harms of racism into the public consciousness. They were pointing out how democracy had failed at home. A sense of common sacrifice increased the discontent with being left with no more than empty promises. The persistence of black voices and the support of whites, especially Eleanor Roosevelt, forced President Roosevelt to begin to tie national interests to reform. The changes in the war industry and in the army reflected a breakthrough in racial attitudes.

Women's Employment

The FEPC prevented defense industry discrimination based on race, creed, color, or national origin. Its limited regulatory jurisdiction, however, rendered the agency powerless to deal with gender discrimination. During the Second World War, many women entered military-related production fields. As more young men were drafted overseas, employers turned to women to fill work shortages. Women's salaries became increasingly important to their families. One survey of 155,000 women found that 60 percent contributed to the support of dependents. Another survey, this one of 370,000 women, found that 13 percent of them were the sole earners in their households.[38]

Advertisements in popular publications recognized that women "form our greatest potential pool of labor."[39] In multiple publications, such as *Business Week*, the *New York Times Book Review*, and *The Nation's Business*, women appeared in photographs working as telephone operators, nurses, and secretaries. These images—which depicted women driving forklifts, filling boxes with steel, drafting, using ninety-ton B. F. Goodrich machines, managing the nerve cell of electrical wire networks, tightening airplane screws, riveting, filling artillery shells, chopping wood, and picking engine sealants— challenged the stereotype of women as delicate homemakers. Some advertisements depicted women in their work overalls at home washing laundry, preparing meals, and sipping coffee. Liberal and conservative publications joined the promotion. The Office of War Information (OWI) released a recruitment film, *Women Wanted*, aimed at attracting women to join production. Josephine Von Miklos's *I Took a War Job*, Ann Pendleton's *Hit the Rivet, Sister*, and Susan B. Anthony II's *Out of the Kitchen—Into the War* provided spirited book-length accounts of women's experiences in the defense industry. They made the nation aware of opportunities that had been unavailable to women before the war.[40]

Efforts to attract more women into manufacturing were often presented as temporary expedients for the national emergency. As one advertisement put it, women were needed for "keeping the production lines moving while the boys are away." American mobilization propaganda, conducted through OWI, the War Advertising Council, and the War Manpower Commission, urged women to take unconventional employment outside the home to fill immediate labor shortages. The War Production Board suggested in 1942 that industries recruit "large numbers of women who do not normally consider themselves a part of the industrial labor supply." Females were needed in airplane and bomb manufacturing, metallurgy, electronic assembly lines, and shipping docks. The Department of Labor printed pamphlets explaining the complex manufacturing work women were doing and how their efforts provided the military with precision parts. Recruitment efforts did not rely on slogans of autonomous equality, as feminists might have done; instead, the heroines of factories were depicted as courageous, capable, and critical to wartime output. Many women found fulfillment helping their country and providing for their families. Positive characterization contrasted with prewar notions that working wives selfishly pursued vocations at the expense of their families.[41]

To recruit as many women as possible, government and private employers subsidized meals, convenient shopping centers, housing, and child care. These amenities were regarded as war expedients, but they were contiguous with New Deal services. In 1938 the WPA allocated $10.7 million for emergency nursery schools, up from $6 million for the same program in 1933. During any given year, the WPA enrolled 44,000 to 72,000 children of workers on relief. In 1940 Congress passed the Lanham Act, which provided federal grants or loans to both public and private agencies that were engaged in public works. That law's primary purpose was to house persons involved in the national defense, including workers of defense industries. A later administrative decree interpreted the act as covering child care centers in areas of war production. The enrollment fee was fifty cents a day. While estimates vary, during the four years the Lanham Act was operative, its funding served between 600,000 and 1.5 million children in 3,102 centers, leaving women greater liberty to work. With the elimination of the day care centers once the military crisis was past, many women had no choice but to quit working and return to full-time child rearing responsibilities. At President Truman's prompting, Congress then authorized a limited amount of funding for temporary child care, but it was not enough to provide women with long-term incentives to work.[42]

Even during the war, salary differentials between men and women endured. Lower rates of pay and the unequal treatment of women were accepted business practices. In 1940 the Department of Labor found that in all twenty-two surveyed industries men were paid more than women. In half of those industries, the average woman's pay was below the lowest man's wage. At that time, women made up 27 percent of the labor force. With the increasing demand for workers during World War II, 37 percent of women worked. In the gun-manufacturing industry, men earned from 60 to 74.6 cents per hour, while women earned from 43.4 to 45 cents. Among experienced men and women working the same machines, the lowest-paid man received 10 cents above the highest-paid woman. That disparity was not confined to manufacturing. Women teachers graduating from Mississippi colleges in 1945 earned an average beginning salary of $1,291, while starting male teachers got $1,600. Nonteachers experienced much the same thing, with average salaries of $1,800 for women and $2,400 for men.

After servicemen returned from military duty, many women were laid off or quit to make room for men. Some women left for personal reasons or lost jobs because they lacked the seniority of returning men. But layoffs had an overwhelmingly disproportional effect on women that can only be explained as part of a pattern of gender discrimination. They were laid off at a rate of 75 percent more than men were. The number of women working in industries in 1947 dropped from a wartime high to only 4 percentage points above that of 1939. Manufacturing plants, such as those in the automotive industry, reserved welding, riveting, and machine jobs for men. In 1945 one-third of five hundred plants in New York State laid off women and substituted men in the same jobs. In other instances, women were forced out by purportedly neutral employment practices. For instance, UAW grievance files from women who were employed by Ford indicate that they quit because they were demoted to janitors, given increased workloads, transferred to third and swing shifts, authorized shorter break times, provided with no child care options, and granted no guaranteed maternity leave. Consequently, by October 1945, 2.25 million women left work and another million were laid off.[43]

Congress was still far from enacting legal prohibitions against gender discrimination. A 1945 poll, conducted by the American Institute of Public Opinion, showed that 86 percent of the public still disapproved of any married woman holding a business or industrial job if she could rely on her husband for support. Similarly, a 1946 poll conducted for *Fortune* magazine found that only 22 percent of men and 29 percent of women agreed that "all women should have an equal chance with men for any job in business or industry regardless of whether they have to support themselves or not." A growing proportion of the population, however, agreed that equal work deserved equal pay, and that principle became part of the Democratic Party's 1944 campaign statement. In 1945 when Gallup asked, "Do you think women should or should not receive the same rate of pay as men for the same work?" 76 percent of respondents answered affirmatively. Those attitudes indicate that while married women continued to face widely accepted discriminatory hiring and retention practices, the public disapproved of arbitrary wage differentials. The failure of government and employers to confront the effects of maintaining traditional domestic and employment spheres in limiting women's opportunities undercut the women's war employment gains. Women who had worked in industry during the war were expected to make way for men. The country failed to provide women with legal safeguards for achieving economic independence, personal fulfillment, and professional achievement.[44]

Although state-of-emergency gains in the manufacturing sector turned out to be precarious, World War II was a watershed, as the historian William H. Chafe has pointed out, for changing the attitude that women are primarily keepers of the hearth. After the war, women's status in America changed. Major unions abandoned policies against hiring married women and firing women who married after being employed. Nine percent of mothers nationwide were in the workforce in 1940, and by 1972 their participation rate had risen to 42 percent. Although women's overall presence in the labor force fell from 36 percent to 29 percent in the year following the end of the war, that figure went up to 33 percent by 1950, and 47 percent by 1975. Between 1960 and 1990, there was a 200 percent increase in women working or searching for work. Not only had they been essential to the war effort, their skills had increasingly come to bear in lawmaking and diplomacy. There were 130 female state legislators in 1939 but 234 in 1945; the numbers fell immediately after the war, but by 1951 there were 249, and 296 two years later, indicating a slow trend of upward citizenship mobility.

On the international scene, President Truman appointed Eleanor Roosevelt to be a member of the U.S. delegation to the United Nations. Later Shirley Temple Black, whose first fame was as a child actress, served as a delegate to the United Nations and later became the U.S. ambassador to Ghana and Czechoslovakia. Another well-known diplomat, Jeane Kirkpatrick, served as a representative to the United Nations and the Council on Foreign Relations. And two former academics, Madeleine Albright and Condoleezza Rice, have now been secretaries of state.

In the first half of the twentieth century, women continued to have less political influence than men. They made few inroads in the federal legislature. There were only ten congresswomen in 1939, eleven in 1945, and eight in 1947. Six decades later Nancy Pelosi became the first female speaker of the House of Representatives. Truman's only female member of the cabinet was Frances Perkins, and she was a holdover from the Roosevelt administration. Presidents Eisenhower, Kennedy, Johnson, and Nixon had no women in their cabinets. Improvements in women's citizenship status remained incremental despite their steady contributions to the nation's political and economic life.[45]

Japanese Americans

The Second World War gave the nation an increased sense of common purpose. As Americans looked overseas at atrocities committed under Nazi and Japanese imperial regimes in Europe and Asia, they grew increasingly conscious of inequalities at home. Blacks and women benefited from this introspection. The Japanese American community living on the West Coast, on the other hand, saw a diminution of its rights. After the attack on Pearl Harbor, Japanese Americans endured displacement that was as disruptive as Indian removal had been, although far shorter in duration. In both cases, military might was used to infringe on individuals' liberty and property rights. The U.S. government deprived the communities of liberties and rights on the basis of arbitrary ancestral and racial prejudices.

Few persons of Japanese descent made their homes in the United States until the beginning of the twentieth century. In 1880 only 86 Japanese lived in California. Early Japanese immigrants found work on railroads, at logging and lumber camps, in mines and canneries, and in private homes. Their population rose to 10,151 in 1900 and 97,456 in 1930. By 1940 there were 97,717 Japanese living in California and 127,000 living in the continental United States. Japanese were major players in the California economy in 1941, accounting for 30–35 percent of all commercial truck crops grown in California, including 90 percent of the area's strawberries, 73 percent of the celery, 70 percent of the lettuce, and 50 percent of the tomatoes. Their achievements came despite land laws of 1913, 1920, 1923, restricting foreign-born Japanese from owning or leasing agricultural lands. With economic successes came antiforeign sentiments from businessmen and farmers who accused Japanese and Chinese of driving prices down and diminishing their returns, much as the same interests had attacked Jews, Irish, and Italians on the East Coast.[46]

When the United States declared war on Japan, decades-long animus against Japanese Americans was converted into discriminatory policies that far overstepped any compelling military expedient. In the early days of war, President Roosevelt established geographically defined military buffer zones around sensitive areas. The executive branch found this policy inadequate. A more aggressive measure targeted a minority based on alienage rather than compelling defense-based reasons. On February 19, 1942, the president acquiesced to the request of the army to relocate the Japanese population on the West Coast. The infamous executive order 9066 authorized the War Department to establish military areas from which it could exclude persons or set limits on their entry. The attorney general, Francis Biddle, the executive officer who was chiefly responsible for protecting civil rights in the nation, criticized military recommendations but went along with plans that affected Japanese of all ages, without charges being brought against them or any adjudicative process to challenge dislocation from homes, businesses, schools, and friends. At first Japanese Americans were asked to move voluntarily, but only about 8,000 responded to that plea. "Relocation centers" were then established to achieve the desired ethnic displacement, and by June 1, 1942, the mass relocation was achieved through civilian exclusion orders. In all, 112,000 persons of Japanese descent, including 70,000 U.S. citizens, were forced from their homes. Because many of the displaced had to sell homes, farms, and businesses with little notice, the community suffered a cumulative loss of approximately $400 million.[47]

Advocates of Japanese relocation branded the entire population as cunning, unfaithful, and self-interested. At the time, Earl Warren was the California attorney general. In the darkest point of his political career, his own attitudes represented local paranoia. While he disavowed the claim that all Japanese were traitors, he thought that it was more likely that native-born Japanese citizens would constitute the dreaded "fifth column." In his testimony to the House of Representatives hearing of the Select Committee Investigating National Defense Migration, Warren helped fuel the flames of distrust, suggesting that "the military . . . take every protective measure that it believes is necessary to protect this State and this Nation against the possible activities of these people." Cynically, he claimed that the Japanese had bought farms around air bases and strategic sections of highways that foreboded "untold danger to the United States." These allegations were not predicated on any fact. No attempt was made to understand the commercial, agronomic, and domestic reasons why Japanese Americans happened to live by locations that Warren considered to be vital installations.[48]

The western defense commander, Lieutenant General John L. DeWitt, announced that the West Coast was off limits to free Japanese, explaining the decision in racialist terms: "The Japanese race is an enemy race and while many second and third generation Japanese born on United States soil, possessed of United States citizenship, have become 'Americanized,' the racial strains are undiluted." In an appearance before the House Naval Affairs Committee, DeWitt curtly revealed his motivations: "A Jap's a Jap. It makes no difference whether he is an American citizen or not. I don't want any of them. We got them out. They were a dangerous element." These and similar statements led Congress, in 1988, to codify the finding that the "evacuation, relocation, and internment of civilians" were conducted despite the lack of any evidence of a real threat to security. The policy was "motivated largely by racial prejudice, wartime hysteria, and a failure of political leadership." Similarly, Congress determined, Alaskan Aleuts who had been relocated and inadequately provided for during World War II were entitled to compensation for their losses.[49]

Congress gave the president its approval with a statute that provided penalties for any Japanese Americans who dared to disobey executive order 9066. Despite the resulting negative propaganda abroad, the United States went forward with its policy of displacement. Elmer Davis, chief of the Office of War Information, informed Roosevelt that "Japanese propaganda to the Philippines, Burma, and elsewhere insists that this is a racial war." Roosevelt rejected Davis's urging that he speak out against anti-Japanese bills in Congress. Meanwhile tensions arose in detention centers from the monotony and lack of privacy and recreation.[50]

The country gave itself over to the West Coast hysteria. There are two indications that West Coast rather than national prejudices drove the internment effort. First, the Japanese population in Hawaii was treated entirely differently. Thirty-two percent, or about 160,000, of the 500,000 residents of Hawaii were ethnically Japanese. There, investigations were conducted on a case-by-case basis. About 750 Japanese aliens were arrested and interned. Fewer that 1,100 persons of Japanese descent were transferred to the mainland to relocation centers. No mass arrest occurred and none was needed to meet the military necessity of preventing espionage and sabotage. Second, contrary to DeWitt's stated desire, Secretary Stimson, Assistant Secretary of War John J. McCloy, and General George C. Marshall recruited loyal American-born Japanese for combat units operating overseas. Other internees were permitted to seek their release. Still, this later effort to put an end to the camps could not undo the harm of the initial presumption that Japanese were disloyal.

The military combat unit, the 442nd Regiment, showed a glimpse of how much Americans stood to gain from treating Japanese citizens with the respect they deserved. Members of the 442nd received a Congressional Medal of Honor, 52 Distinguished Service Crosses, one Distinguished Service Medal, 560 Silver Stars and 28 oak leaf clusters in lieu of second medals, 22 Legions of Merit, 15 Soldiers' Medals, some 4,000 Bronze Stars with 1,200 oak leaf clusters, 12 French Croix de Guerre with 2 palms to the Croix de Guerre, and 2 Italian Medals for Military Valor, plus nearly 9,500 Purple Hearts, including oak leaf clusters.[51]

Japanese, unlike other ethnic citizens, like Italians and Germans, were presumed to be a menace unless they could prove otherwise. The vast majority of West Coast Japanese remained interned until 1944.[52]

The president and Congress were not solely to blame for Japanese dislocation. The judiciary regarded exclusion to be a presidential wartime prerogative. At judges' disposal was the authority to carefully scrutinize laws adversely affecting insular minorities, which Justice Stone had famously drawn attention to in *Carolene Products*. In 1942 a district court heard a petition for a writ of habeas corpus from a Japanese American who had disobeyed a military order to leave his San Francisco home. The trial judge refused even to recognize that civil rights were involved, leaving the demarcation of military areas to the discretion of the executive branch. For a time, the Supreme Court also refused to assess the constitutionality of executive order 9066, leaving the military operation unchecked.[53]

Only in 1943 did the Court review a challenge to the displacement policy. Gordon Hirabayashi, a U.S. citizen and University of Washington senior, was convicted of refusing to report to a relocation center and of violating a curfew imposed on Japanese. The Court addressed only the curfew provision. Stone, by then the chief justice, wrote the majority, cautioning that "distinctions between citizens solely because of their ancestry are by their very nature odious to a free people whose institutions are founded upon the doctrine of equality." He nevertheless gave in to wholesale, ethnocentric innuendo. Japanese, Stone presumed, were given over to nationalistic propaganda: "There is support for the view that social, economic and political conditions which have prevailed since the close of the last century, when the Japanese began to come to this country in substantial numbers, have intensified their solidarity and have in large measure prevented their assimilation as an integral part of the white population." Under these circumstances, "Congress and the Executive could reasonably have concluded" that the Japanese as a whole could be rounded up since there may have been saboteurs among them. During a time of war, Stone further found, the country could rely on racially discriminatory classifications. Hence the misdemeanor curfew conviction did not infringe on Hirabayashi's Fifth or Fourteenth Amendment rights.[54]

A 1944 case appeared to signal a shift in the Court's thinking, although it still relied on legislative and executive authority. Mitsuye Endo, a United States citizen, brought a case contesting her detention under armed guard. The Justice Department did not even bother to contest that she was a "loyal and law-abiding citizen" against whom no charges had been brought. Justice

Douglas found that restraining a loyal citizen longer than was necessary to investigate whether she posed a national security risk was a greater restraint on her liberty than Congress and the president had ever intended.[55]

The Court's willingness to abrogate its duty to review governmental actions against a minority became clearer in *Korematsu v. United States* (1944). Fred Toyosaburo Korematsu was convicted and sent to a relocation center for his refusal to leave a designated military zone. Justice Black's majority opinion found the evacuation program to be a constitutional exercise of congressional and executive authority. Black did point out the dangers of discriminatory statutes, however: "All legal restrictions which curtail the civil rights of a single racial group are immediately suspect. That is not to say that all such restrictions are unconstitutional. It is to say that courts must subject them to the most rigid scrutiny." Despite the establishment of the seminal strict scrutiny test, which would come to play the essential role in much of modern day civil rights jurisprudence, Black went on to say that "pressing public necessity may sometimes justify the existence of such restrictions," though "racial antagonism never can." Striking as these words are, Black made no attempt to apply them to the case at hand.[56]

Justice Roberts wrote one of the dissents. From his perspective, Korematsu's detention was based "on his ancestry, and solely because of his ancestry, without evidence or inquiry concerning his loyalty." Justice Robert H. Jackson's dissent mocked the notion that the mere presence of a U.S. citizen in the state of his residency could be criminalized because his parents happened to be Japanese. The military order singled out Japanese like Korematsu because of their "different racial stock." This form of punishment assumed the absurdity that guilt was inherited at birth. The majority, Jackson continued, had trusted a military judgment without even reflecting on whether it was reasonable. The Court's upholding an emergency military order "is a far more subtle blow to liberty than the promulgation of the order itself." The judicial decision created a precedent that "has validated the principle of racial discrimination in criminal procedure and of transplanting American citizens."

Justice Murphy, in the third dissent, displayed the continued interest in rights that he had demonstrated as the attorney general of the United States. His perspective was analogous to Jackson's but even more caustic. Murphy was vehement that "no reasonable relation to an 'immediate, imminent, and impending' public danger is evident to support this racial restriction which is one of the most sweeping and complete deprivations of constitutional rights in the history of this nation in the absence of martial law." The expulsion of all persons of Japanese ancestry had no reasonable connection to the very real danger the country faced after Pearl Harbor. A "good measure" of "erroneous assumption of racial guilt" went into the forced exclusion order. The reasons for the initiative "appear . . . to be largely an accumulation of much of the misinformation, half-truths and insinuations that for years have been directed against Japanese Americans by people with racial and economic prejudices— the same people who have been among the foremost advocates of the evacuation." Without providing cases the individual review they deserved, the government left "open the door to discriminatory actions against other minority groups in the passions of tomorrow." Murphy concluded as vehemently as he began, dissenting "from this legalization of racism." All Americans, regardless of their ancestral background, are "heirs of the American experiment" and are "entitled to all the rights and freedoms guaranteed by the Constitution." Racial discrimination violates the Equal Protection Clause. It further deprives individuals of protections that are not explicitly enumerated by the Constitution, such as their "rights to live and work where they will, to establish a home where they choose and to move about freely." Rarely in the history of the Supreme Court has a dissenting justice so vigorously attacked a majority opinion for violating American values.

Murphy and Jackson faulted the majority for allowing the military to rely on untested assumptions about Japanese anti-American predisposition. The scholar Jacobus tenBroek pointed out that the majority's opinion overinclusively targeted all Japanese and that it underinclusively applied an emergency standard to them alone but to no other ethnic group. In 1944 a young law professor and future undersecretary for political affairs, Eugene V. Rostow, decried the "familiar West Coast attitudes of race prejudice" that fomented the policy of forced removal. Local prejudices and DeWitt's overtly racialist comments initiated the program. Rostow understood the "tragic and dangerous mistake" committed against Japanese Americans to be a "threat to society" as a whole because it undermined "every value of democracy."[57]

Japanese internment was so colossal a harm because all three branches of government colluded to deprive Americans of their rights. The government understood that it was overstepping its peacetime authority but claimed that discriminatory rules were permissible at a time of war. Yet no emergency could justify dislocating an entire ethnic group and forcing it to live under armed guard. Executive order 9066 infringed on constitutional principles of equality, and Congress furthered the injustice by making persons disobedient to military orders subject to criminal penalties. The Court, for its part, formulated and then shirked its responsibility to conduct a "rigid scrutiny" of a policy that infringed on a minority's liberty rights. The government did not and could not provide any evidence that the entire Japanese American population had to be imprisoned.

In the mid-1980s, district courts overturned the convictions of Gordon Hirabayashi and Fred Korematsu because the government's evidence against them had been misleading. Those decisions followed President Gerald Ford's presidential proclamation recognizing the "tragedy" of Japanese internment and resolving "that this kind of action shall never again be repeated." The Civil Liberties Act of 1988 went much further by acknowledging "the fundamental injustice of the evacuation, relocation, and internment of United States citizens and permanent resident aliens of Japanese ancestry during World War II." It apologized for the injustice and offered twenty thousand dollars in reparations to any surviving Japanese American internees.[58]

CHAPTER ELEVEN

Expanding Civil Rights

A fter the Second World War, the federal government became increasingly responsive to demands for greater economic freedom, equal rights, and procedural justice. The availability of information about Nazi and Communist atrocities led to more self-realization of American shortcomings on matters of race and ethnicity.

The NAACP, the Urban League, Robert Weaver, Eleanor Roosevelt, Gunnar Myrdal, A. Philip Randolph, and a host of others insisted that the military and civilian sectors afford African Americans the dignity and respect of equal citizens. Although only partially successful, President Roosevelt's Fair Employment Practices Committee created opportunities for blacks in the workforce, and women increasingly entered the job market. Even as the Supreme Court was sanctioning Japanese internment, it indicated the unacceptability of most race-based government decisions. The reasoning for reform was there, even as the application to specific cases still was bent to accommodate regional racism.

Post–World War II

Several 1948 Supreme Court decisions signaled the judiciary's halting willingness to function as a barrier against government intrusion on fundamental rights. *Sipuel v. Board of Regents of the University of Oklahoma* required states to provide persons of all races with an equal opportunity to obtain a legal education, but the Court still refused to assert that segregation was unconstitutional. The Court, in *Shelley v. Kraemer,* also found that the Equal Protection Clause prohibits judges from enforcing racial covenants. *Oyama v. California* invalidated a state scheme to prevent non-native-born Asian Americans from possessing land through their American-born children, and *Takahashi v. Fish and Game Commission* found that licensing regulations meant to discriminate against resident aliens violated the Equal Protection Clause.[1]

President Truman's Civil Rights Committee, which was appointed in December 1946, was a symbol of the changing times. The committee worked to bolster the Department of Justice's Civil Rights Section (CRS). Truman's executive order creating the committee acknowledged the federal government's "duty to act when state and local authorities abridge or fail to protect" the Constitution's "guarantees of individual liberties and of equal protection under the laws." Though no lawyer, Truman understood that "the Federal government is hampered by inadequate civil rights statutes." The CRS needed additional staffing and a greater variety of prosecutorial options.[2]

The committee issued its report on October 29, 1947. It found that segregation, which still existed both in the South and in the North, branded "the Negro with the mark of inferiority and asserts that he is not fit to associate with white people." The federal government should rely on the "idealism and prestige of our whole people" to "play a leading role" in improving "our civil rights record." The federal government's "direct dealings with millions of persons" require it to "assume leadership in our American civil rights program." The committee also quoted Dean Acheson, who was then undersecretary of state and whom Truman would soon appoint to be secretary of state. Acheson asserted that it was "next to impossible to formulate a satisfactory answer" about "the gap between the things we stand for in principle" and the "existence of discrimination against minority groups in this country."[3]

The resolution to the problem, according to the committee, was increased federal and state enforcement. Specifically, it recommended that the CRS be granted authority to impose civil penalties. Additional federal laws were also needed, including an antilynching statute, a statute punishing police brutality, a criminal statute against involuntary servitude, and a protection of voters during primaries and general elections. The report further proclaimed the need to eliminate "segregation, based on race, color, creed, or national origin from American life . . . [through] conditioning by Congress of all federal grants-in-aid and other forms of federal assistance to public and private agencies for any purpose on the absence of discrimination and segregation based on race, color, creed, or national origin." Coming from a federal agency, these findings emboldened and directed the president's strategy on civil rights.

Truman delivered a civil rights message to a joint session of Congress in

February 1948, requesting lawmakers to further protect voting rights, abolish poll taxes, provide federal criminal penalties for lynching, create a permanent commission against employment discrimination, and pass a measure against discrimination in interstate transportation. Southern segregationists immediately voiced their strong displeasure. Senator Henry F. Byrd of Virginia was indignant at what he sensed was a "devastating broadside at the dignity of Southern traditions and institutions." Representative John Bell Williams of Mississippi felt that the president had "seen fit to run a political dagger into our backs and now [was] trying to drink our blood." Truman also received many letters against his proposals. One man wrote, "I am Mr. Average Voter of the South, and expecially [*sic*] in Virginia. We voted the party straight, through thick and thin. . . . This time the exception will be—Mr. Harry Truman." Southern governors, meeting five days after the presidential message, adopted South Carolina Governor J. Strom Thurmond's resolution calling on the administration to reconsider the perceived insult to the South.[4]

In a recent article, Michael Klarman asserted that "Truman's landmark civil rights initiatives of the late 1940s" were variously motivated, but they were "principally inspired by the perceived necessity of 'bidding' for the black vote." According to Klarman, Truman thought that seeming to befriend blacks would help him gain victory in the 1948 election. Klarman's premise failed to take into account how much more political support Truman stood to lose by his decisiveness. A March 1948 Gallup poll revealed that 82 percent of the respondents opposed Truman's civil rights program. Many more white votes stood to be lost than black votes gained. Truman knew long before that November's election how much opposition he had stirred.[5]

The president was unwavering in his civil rights initiatives, despite the increased risk of losing the Democratic primary and never reaching the general election, where the black vote might help him. A southern faction of Democrats reacted to his decision to run on a civil rights platform by bolting from the party in favor of Thurmond as a so-called Dixiecrat presidential candidate. Truman's loss of southern support put the odds against his reelection. He further showed his commitment to reform on July 26, 1948, by issuing executive order 9981, prohibiting discrimination in the armed services. In the fall of 1948 popular preelection polls projected Thomas E. Dewey, the Republican candidate, to win the presidential election. On election day Truman was as surprised at his victory as some journalists. This is borne out by the famous photograph of him, grinning from ear-to-ear, holding up a *Chicago Daily Tribune* newspaper with the premature headline "Dewey Defeats

Truman." With the final popular vote tally being less than 2.2 million in Truman's favor, it is impossible to establish with certainty whether his civil rights policy decreased or added to his overall returns. His successful "whistlestop" campaign, during which he crisscrossed states by train, is the more likely cause of his unexpected victory. The Social Science Research Council established a Committee on Analysis of Preelection Polls and Forecasts to analyze why the predictions for the November 1948 presidential elections had been so inaccurate. So for Klarman to characterize Truman's civil rights policy as having been "largely" an attempt to gain the black vote is too cynical. The overwhelming black vote for Truman in cities like Chicago, Cleveland, and Los Angeles was a show of confidence rather than a sign of bamboozlement about his real intent. Truman was unwavering after the election, too. In his January 5, 1949, state of the union address, he demanded that Congress act on his whole civil rights program.[6]

Truman's legislative program had no chance in a Congress where southerners could effectively use the filibuster in the Senate and chaired some of the most powerful committees in both chambers. Pursuant to the president's recommendations, Senator James H. McGrath proposed four bills on April 28, 1949. The bills would have made lynching a federal crime, abolished the poll tax, and forbidden employment discrimination. All of these initiatives went down in defeat. That year Senator Harry P. Cain proposed an anti-segregation and antidiscrimination amendment to a housing bill, but it too was defeated. The House and Senate also voted down a proposed amendment of the Selective Services Act to end military segregation.[7]

Under that legislative predicament, the president turned to executive action. On October 15, 1949, he nominated Judge William H. Hastie, an African American, to the Third Circuit Court of Appeals. Then on December 12 the administration announced that the Federal Housing Administration would refuse to fund projects that discriminated against blacks. That decision reversed the segregated trend of public housing throughout the country. There was also progress elsewhere, with New York, New Jersey, Pennsylvania, and Wisconsin prohibiting segregation in publicly financed housing. Acting on Truman's policy, Secretary of the Interior Oscar L. Chapman succeeded in desegregating the six Washington, D.C., swimming pools under the department's control. Executive order 9980 created a Fair Employment Board to eliminate racial discrimination and segregation in federal employment. Later, executive order 10,308 created a committee to improve compliance with nondiscrimination provisions of federal contracts.[8]

That effort did little, however, to alter local prejudices. In 1949 segregation remained the norm in southern schools. Segregated public schools also
existed in Arizona, Kansas, and New Mexico. In some states, such as Arizona, California, and New Mexico, Latino children were segregated in public
schools. Blacks, Chinese, and whites were taught on a segregated basis in San
Francisco. About three-fourths of Native Americans continued to live on
reservations with few adequate educational opportunities and little means of
self-sufficiency; Mexican Americans, who labored under their own set of
stereotypes and typically received low wages, got little help from labor organizations; Jews, while not segregated or barred from exercising the franchise,
were still the victims of educational, housing, and employment discrimination. Local fair employment practice initiatives failed in San Francisco and
Tucson, Arizona, and a proposed Portland, Oregon, ordinance that would
have punished discrimination in public places met the same fate.[9]

Despite these setbacks, advances continued in states. New Jersey and
Connecticut strengthened statutes providing safeguards for racial and religious minorities to enjoy equal accommodations in hotels and restaurants.
New Jersey adopted a constitution in 1947 that prohibited segregation in both
public schools and its militia. The same year, Connecticut passed a fair employment practice act that categorized "segregation and separation" to be
forms of discrimination. Also in 1947, Illinois, Indiana, and Wisconsin enacted laws to end segregation in public schools. Massachusetts adopted a fair
education practices act and enlarged protection to cover public housing and
places of public accommodation. By 1950 there were even some feeble signs of
change in the South, with more than one thousand blacks enrolled in previously all-white schools. Kentucky amended its laws to allow black students
to attend colleges and universities with whites, but only when nothing of
comparable quality was available to blacks. Following Supreme Court rulings
in *McLaurin* and *Sweatt,* the University of Louisville closed its black liberal
arts college and began admitting blacks to the general institution. Just as with
northern abolition at the end of the eighteenth century and western women's
suffrage at the end of the nineteenth, these achievements were beneficial only
to persons in a limited geographic area.[10]

What was needed was national action based on universal principles of
liberal equality, and Congress would not budge on Truman's proposals. The
insufficiency of civil rights laws, together with the small size of the Civil
Rights Section, made many forms of discrimination beyond the reach of
federal prosecution. So few national civil rights statutes had been passed after

Reconstruction that the CRS had almost no alternative but to rely on two 1870 statutes: section 242, prohibiting public officials from willfully depriving individuals of constitutional rights, and section 241, punishing conspiracies to injure, oppress, or intimidate citizens from enjoying their constitutional rights and privileges. There were clear limits to this ancient approach. Section 242 applies only to persons acting under color of state law. The statute also has little deterrence power because it provides for no more than one year's imprisonment. Section 241 provides up to ten years' imprisonment, but it is useless if more than one person is involved in the constitutional deprivation.[11]

Only in 1957, during the Eisenhower administration, did the CRS expand into the Civil Rights Division (CRD). Pursuant to the Civil Rights Act of 1957, the CRD received power to investigate, conduct hearings, and subpoena witnesses. That was the first time since the Enforcement Act of 1871 that Congress had relied on its Fifteenth Amendment power to pass a statute. A 1957 statute addressed voting discrimination patterns that Truman's Committee on Civil Rights had identified in its 1947 report. The law's primary aim was to protect voting rights. The division persisted in criminal prosecution under sections 241 and 242; in addition, it received authority to bring civil cases to enjoin any voter fraud. The attorney general's power to institute cases was critical because the CRD no longer needed to rely on individual complainants, who could be intimidated, to file causes of actions. A further improvement was the elimination of the "under color of law" requirement. A person could be prosecuted for intimidating, threatening, or coercing persons from voting for primary, special, or general elections. In addition to its prosecuting function, the CRD was to "investigate allegations that certain citizens of the United States are being deprived of their right to vote and have that vote counted by reason of their color, race, religion, or national origin."[12]

To bolster the policy of the 1957 act, Congress passed the Civil Rights Act of 1960. It prohibited state registrars from destroying records. If individuals were deprived by a "pattern or practice" of racial discrimination, then persons of the same race living in the area could likewise petition the court to protect their voting privileges. On paper, both of these statutes appeared to be enormous steps forward, but in practice the Department of Justice instituted only forty-two suits between 1957 and 1963. This enfranchised a mere six thousand black voters.[13]

There was much left undone when President Kennedy succeeded to the White House in 1961. The nation continued on the path of incrementalism, which provided promise but only intermittent achievement. During his 1960 presidential campaign, Kennedy maintained a neutral stand on civil rights, instead, drawing attention to the "unsolved problems of peace and war, unconquered pockets of ignorance and prejudice, unanswered questions of poverty and surplus." The use of neutral terms helped Kennedy solidify enough black and southern Democratic support to win the 1960 election.[14]

The nation was agitating for change with the coordinated efforts of freedom riders, sit-ins at segregated public businesses, and demands for educational integration. In 1962 President Kennedy sent federal troops to force the integration of the University of Mississippi. Then in 1963 Kennedy federalized the Alabama National Guard to end Governor George Wallace's opposition to integration at the University of Alabama. As with President Eisenhower's 1957 enforcement of school desegregation in Little Rock, Arkansas, these were essential achievements, but they were only sporadic.

Yet Kennedy committed himself to civil rights law only after the march on Birmingham in April 1963, when Dr. Martin Luther King, Jr., was arrested. King's "Letter from Birmingham Jail," as well as the sight of other civil rights protesters being hosed with water cannons and mauled by dogs, shocked the nation out its complacency about the use of state power to further white supremacism. Encouraged by his vice president, Lyndon B. Johnson, by June 1963 President Kennedy had shifted his civil rights policy. Johnson, a Texan considered a traitor to his heritage by many southern Democrats, dramatically challenged Kennedy to "stick to the moral issue" of fair treatment. He recommended that Kennedy give a speech in the South to declare that "we are all Americans." As commander in chief, Johnson urged, the president ordered men "without regard to color. They carry our flag into the foxholes. The Negro can do that, the Mexican can do it, others can do it. We've got to do the same thing when we drive down the highway at places they eat." Kennedy should "ask the Congress to say that we'll all be treated without regard to our race." Without the president acting as a moral force, executive orders and legislative actions would be ineffective.[15]

Kennedy's June 11, 1963, speech followed Johnson's formula. The president spoke of civil rights as "primarily . . . a moral issue" predicated on a sort of golden rule: that "every American ought to have the right to be treated as he would wish to be treated." Mirroring Johnson's comment about multiracial composition of the army, Kennedy spoke of the worldwide struggle for freedom, which "we do not ask for whites only." Every American deserves "equal service in places of public accommodations," like hotels, restaurants, theaters, and stores. A nation "founded on the principle that all men are created equal" could expect nothing less of itself. Moving from this allusion to the Declaration of Independence, Kennedy evoked the Privileges and Immunities Clause of the Fourteenth Amendment. All Americans "should enjoy the privileges of being American." The injustices perpetrated in Birmingham indicated the importance of equality to public safety. "This is one country" with the same standards for all, the president declared. Eight days later Kennedy sent a comprehensive civil rights bill for congressional action. Dr. King's August 28, 1963, "I Have a Dream" speech, delivered to hundreds of thousands from the Lincoln Memorial, energized support for national guarantees of liberal equality.[16]

Kennedy's ability to work with Congress to safeguard Americans' equal rights was left in limbo after twenty-four-year-old Lee Harvey Oswald shot him during a parade in Dallas, Texas. Johnson, in his first presidential address to Congress, just five days after Kennedy's assassination, urged, "We have talked long enough in this country about equal rights. We have talked for one hundred years or more. It is time now to write the next chapter, and to write it in the books of law."[17]

Civil Rights Era: Legislative Initiatives

The civil rights movement reached its apex during the presidency of Lyndon Johnson. Johnson understood that nominal freedom and equality were not enough. "We seek not just freedom but opportunity, not just equality as a right and a theory but equality as a fact and as a result," he told the graduating class at Howard University in 1965. "You do not take a person who for years has been hobbled by chains and liberate him, bring him to the starting line and then say, 'You are free to compete with all the others.'"[18]

So many landmark laws were enacted during Johnson's presidency that a work of this scope can hope to capture only a panoramic sense of the achievements. Epochal social changes included desegregation, enfranchisement, immigration reform, protection against employment discrimination, and increased welfare entitlements to the poor. A well-organized, multiracial grassroots coalition pressured Washington to act. The federal government became involved in the interaction of U.S. citizens in a way that had previously been confined to emergency measures meant to end depression or war. Johnson imbued the political process with a moral voice. He led efforts on the Civil Rights Acts of 1964 and 1968, the Voting Rights Act of 1965, and the Immigration Act of 1965. He also used his power of appointment to bring black talent into the government, most notably by appointing Thurgood Marshall to the Supreme Court. While blacks remained underrepresented in the cabinet and administrative agencies, Robert C. Weaver was appointed secretary of housing and urban development, Andrew Brimmer governor of the Federal Reserve Board, and Carl T. Rowan director of the United States Information Agency.

Johnson was the fulcrum for supporters of the Civil Rights Act of 1964, the most comprehensive such law in the country's history.[19] Measured by the sheer number of his administration's legislative efforts and by his vision of equality, Johnson achieved more than any other president to further civil rights. He relied on hours of face-to-face conversations, telephone calls, and letters with activists and congressmen. Before hanging up the phone, he'd often say, "I love you!" to his interlocutors. Johnson cajoled, insisted, and convinced leaders of organizations—the NAACP, the AFL-CIO, and the Southern Christian Leadership Conference among them—who then rallied their members. By combining forces, a variety of laws codified the moral compunction to treat others equally.

The House of Representatives passed the Civil Rights Act of 1964 on February 10 and forwarded it to the Senate. There the bill encountered scathing opposition. It was debated for eighty-two days, including a 534-hour filibuster. Johnson worked painstakingly to force an end to the filibuster, relying on personal contacts he had made during his years as Senate majority leader. He enlisted the help of the Senate minority leader, Everett M. Dirksen of Illinois. The Senate floor manager of the bill, Hubert Humphrey of Minnesota, showed his enormous passion for the task: "I courted Dirksen almost as persistently as I did [my wife,] Muriel." The hours of pleading paid off; with Dirksen's decision to vote for cloture, enough votes were found to put an end to the southern diatribe. That accomplished, the Senate easily passed the bill by a vote of 73 to 27.[20]

The Civil Rights Act of 1964 was an omnibus law, whose significance would later become clearer through judicial interpretation. It remains the most comprehensive civil rights legislation in the United States. Title I prohibits state officials from discriminating against qualified voters in federal elections. Anyone who completes at least six grades in a school primarily taught in English is presumed to be literate enough to vote. That provision prevents the use of arbitrary literacy tests. The Twenty-Fourth Amendment to the Constitution, which was ratified the same year, imposes a ban on poll taxes and other taxes in federal elections, dealing a death blow to facially neutral laws disproportionately disadvantaging the indigent. To prevent registrar cover-ups, Title VIII requires the maintenance of registration and voting statistics.

Title II prohibits discrimination based on race, color, religion, and national origin in public places of accommodation, like hotels, restaurants, and entertainment places. As a result of a political compromise, Title II exempts private clubs.

The statute relies on Congress's power to regulate interstate commerce, which had been expanded during the New Deal. That approach avoids legislative collision with late-nineteenth-century cases under which Congress lacks the Fourteenth Amendment authority to promulgate laws against segregation in public places. Title II allows for injunctive relief, putting the onus on courts to hold violators of their orders in contempt, but it lacks a criminal provision like the one in the Civil Rights Act of 1875.[21] As a practical matter, this constitutional hairsplitting avoided a direct attack on eighty-year-old decisions that had probably been rendered wrongly in the first place. On a moral level, it was problematic because it placed civil rights in the realm of the federal government's economic regulation rather than under its obligation to safeguard liberal equality.

Until the 1960s discrimination in public facilities had been one of the most odious of social impositions. John Lewis, a civil rights activist–turned–Congressman, related that his family's trips in the 1950s had to be planned around the locations of "colored" restaurants and bathrooms. The family relied on an uncle's familiarity of the route to coordinate their rest stops. Title II meant to make life easier and more pleasant for Americans by prohibiting discrimination in facilities like restaurants, hotels, and places of entertainment. Title III similarly prohibited discrimination in public facilities, such as prisons and courts.[22]

As controversial in 1964 as Title II was the prohibition under Title VII against employers, labor organizations, and employment agencies engaging in discrimination based on race, sex, color, religion, or nation of origin. The measure was part of an effort to promote equal employment opportunities. Congress intended to make "victims of unlawful employment discrimination whole," as the Supreme Court explained in *Franks v. Bowman Transportation Company*. To this end federal courts could fashion a remedy, including restoration to a job or a mandate of back pay. Any employer intentionally discriminating, without bona fide reasons, against qualified persons of a protected group is liable for disparate treatment. In a 1971 decision the Court put additional bite into Title VII. Even facially neutral employment policies are actionable if they create "artificial, arbitrary, unnecessary barriers" that disproportionately affect protected groups of talented individuals. A business necessity could be a legitimate excuse for policies that incidentally affect one group more than others, but not if equally effective nondiscriminatory alternatives are available.[23]

To this day, the Equal Employment Opportunity Commission (EEOC) investigates whether "there is reasonable cause to believe that the charge" against an employer is valid. If its investigation reveals likely discrimination, Title VII authorizes the agency to reconcile the parties by informal "conference, conciliation, and persuasion." Should these fail, a provision allows the agency to issue a right-to-sue letter for the complainant to bring a federal lawsuit. The attorney general is also permitted to bring complaints for injunctions and other remedies. A 1972 amendment to the law, likewise, grants the EEOC enforcement authority. A further amendment, of 1991, provides compensatory and punitive damages for harm. These provisions have significantly increased investigative, prosecutorial, and remedial powers that the Fair Employment Practices Committee, which was the EEOC's predecessor, had at its disposal.

Another groundbreaking provision of Title IV of the act enables the Department of Health, Education, and Welfare to assist in desegregating schools. It further empowers the attorney general to sue schools when the injured parties cannot bring a complaint for lack of funds or fear for safety, employment, or property.

The 1964 act's voting provision was ineffective because it required a case-by-case review of state voting practices. A single case alleging a pattern of discrimination could take up to six thousand court hours to comb through voting records. Even then, when state provisions were found to violate federal law, state officials could rig other alternatives for keeping blacks from voting, biding their time until the next round of litigation. Nor did any court have the resources or staff to respond quickly to creative circumventions of the Fifteenth Amendment. After four years of litigation in Dallas County, Alabama, which contained Selma, the House Judiciary Committee found that only 383 of 15,000 blacks were registered to vote. Given the civic handicaps of disenfranchised voters, the Court later found that "Congress might well decide to shift the advantage of time and inertia from the perpetrators of the evil to its victims."[24]

To address ongoing problems, President Johnson signed the Voting Rights Act of 1965 into law. It immediately provided an administrative process to avoid the slowdown of judicial deliberation. Disenfranchisement devices like literacy tests were immediately suspended in Alabama, Mississippi, Louisiana, Georgia, South Carolina, Virginia, and parts of North Carolina. In other states, the U.S. attorney general was granted the authority to file lawsuits challenging the constitutionality of poll taxes in nonfederal elections. The original act prohibited interference with voting on account of race and color; a 1991 amendment was added to protect language minorities. States with substantial histories of discrimination were required to get "preclearance" from the Justice Department or the District Court for the District of Columbia before implementing new voting procedures.

The act quickly fostered a series of successes. Before its enactment 24.6 percent of blacks in the Deep South were registered to vote; by 1967 the number was 56.5 percent. The shift in the region was remarkable. Between 1964 and 1970 black voter registration in Mississippi rose from 6.7 percent to 68 percent; in Alabama from 19.3 percent to 51.6 percent; in Georgia from 27.4 percent to 52.6 percent; in Louisiana from 31.6 percent to 58.9 percent; and in South Carolina from 37.3 percent to 51.2 percent. These gains translated into increased black voting, candidate eligibility, and office holding.[25]

The Johnson administration promoted a series of landmark laws meant to provide hope and opportunity to ordinary Americans. In 1965 alone Congress adopted public health insurance measures under the Medicare and Medicaid programs. The president established an advisory panel whose findings led to congressional appropriations of funds earmarked for the victims of heart diseases, cancer, and strokes. The Higher Education Act of 1965 provided large student loans and grants to colleges. It worked in concert with the antidiscrimination provision of Title VI of the Civil Rights Act of 1964; however, neither act addressed discrimination against women in higher education. The Elementary and Secondary Education Act of 1965 provided literacy aid for indigent students; the act further gave schools financial incentive for following desegregation orders. The Vocational Rehabilitation Act of 1965 doubled the budget, expanded facilities, and established advisory boards that embellished an Eisenhower administration social assistance program.[26]

Among the most outstanding and long-lasting achievements in President Johnson's last two years in office were the Age Discrimination in Employment Act of 1967 (ADEA) and the Fair Housing Act of 1968 (FHA). ADEA prohibits employers from firing or intentionally avoiding hiring qualified older workers. The original statute applied to workers between the ages of forty and sixty-five. Subsequent amendments to the law increased the maximum age to seventy and then altogether eliminated the upper age limit. The FHA was a part of the Civil Rights Act of 1968. The act also contained other antidiscrimination measures that prohibited selling or renting housing because of race, national origin, color, and religion. Gender, handicap, and familial status were added to the list of covered categories through 1974 and 1988 amendments.[27]

Another congressional initiative directed specifically against gender inequality was the Equal Pay Act, passed on June 10, 1964. The act prohibiting discrimination "between employees on the basis of sex by paying wages to employees . . . at a rate less than the rate at which he pays wages to employees of the opposite sex . . . for equal work on jobs the performance of which requires equal skill, effort, and responsibility, and which are performed under similar working conditions." A woman doing the same job as a man and being paid less for it can bring a claim under the act, regardless of the employer's motivations.[28]

Never in the history of the United States has so much been done for civil rights within one presidential administration. A genuine commitment to end inequality appears to have been at the root of legislative initiatives that changed millions of lives, forcing local prejudices to give way to national sensibilities. Change was driven not by foreign policy or the Cold War with the Soviet Union. While the United States was concerned that continued inequality at home would cast the country in a negative image abroad, as Mary L. Dudziak has pointed out, the desire to maintain America's place as a world leader was only one of the moving forces behind civil rights progress in the 1950s and 1960s.[29] Dudziak's is an important part of the story, but it does not adequately take into account how national crises, including the Revolution, the Civil War, World War II, and the Cold War have always drawn the nation to reflect on its failures to live up to its ideals.

Lyndon Johnson was able to galvanize congressional and popular forces that, in turn, catalyzed a national will to follow through on centuries of effort to improve the equality of citizens' status. Johnson's interest in civil rights had been evident even during his New Deal days as the Texas director of the National Youth Administration. A landslide Democratic victory in the 1964 election and a knowledge of legislative leadership, born of years as the Senate majority leader, allowed him to seize the moment as has no other president. If anything, as Dudziak recognizes, the quagmire of the Vietnam War and the American urban riots of the 1960s drew attention away from his incredible start at putting principles into practical terms.

CHAPTER TWELVE

The Warren Court's Achievements

T he Johnson administration acted in concert with other branches of the federal government. As early as the New Deal, in the famous footnote to *Carolene Products,* the Supreme Court had established a foundation for conducting exacting scrutiny in cases involving (1) fundamental rights, "such as those of the first ten Amendments"; (2) "legislation which restricts those political processes which can ordinarily be expected to bring about repeal of undesirable legislation"; and (3) "statutes directed at particular religious, or national, or racial minorities." Only the second set of cases concerned process alone, and all three were about substantive constitutional rights.

That triumvirate of analyses enabled the Warren Court, which sat from October 1953 to June 1969, to change American civil, social, and political dynamics. Its many landmark decisions ranged from desegregation of schools and public places, to legislative redistricting, to family autonomy, to criminal justice.

The constitutional scholar John Hart Ely correctly pointed out that the *Carolene Products* criteria facilitate democratic participation; however, Ely mistakenly thought that the three "focus not on whether this or that substantive value is unusually important or fundamental." To the contrary, Warren Court decisions indicate that judges must determine whether a state action involves some underlying purpose of government—the protection of individual rights for the public interest. Retention and promotion of democracy is not the end-all; where members of a political majority trample on minority rights, a large segment of the population is dissatisfied with democratic outcomes. The principal civil rights issues of the 1950s and 1960s required the Court to determine whether a substantive right—be it privacy, autonomy, speech, or some other good—was involved and then to fashion a procedural remedy with a concern for a decision's effect on later regulations. The Warren Court's frequent references to rights were not "almost entirely rhetorical," as Ely suggested, but descriptions of nationally recognized constitutional entitlements.[1]

Educational Desegregation

The most important desegregation case in U.S. history was *Brown v. Board of Education.* It emerged from a line of higher education cases. In *Missouri ex rel. Gaines v. Canada* (1938), involving a black applicant to a white law school, the Court found that the state failed to provide substantially equal opportunity to get a legal education because Missouri had no alternative black law school. The Court did not, as it made clear in *Sipuel v. Board of Regents of University of Oklahoma* (1948), disturb the premise that a state could operate segregated professional schools of substantially equal quality. When Texas claimed in *Sweatt v. Painter* (1950) that a newly opened law school was qualitatively on a footing with a long-established University of Texas program, the Court found the state's argument unconvincing. Oklahoma's decision, in *McLaurin v. Oklahoma State Regents* (1950), to separate a black graduate student from his peers violated his right to equal treatment. As promising as these decisions were, they all continued to rely on the separate-but-equal mantra of *Plessey v. Ferguson* (1896).[2]

Despite these triumphs, the Court was reluctant to tackle the issue of elementary and high school segregation until 1954. *Brown v. Board of Education* was a consolidation of four cases originating in Kansas, Delaware, Virginia, and South Carolina. A companion case, *Bolling v. Sharpe,* arose in the District of Columbia. All involved black minors who sought admission to schools that state laws restricted to white children only. Their cases were significant to them individually, to other blacks, and to members of other groups, like Latinos, who continued to be relegated in the West and Southwest to so-called Mexican schools. Overt segregation of Chinese American and Japanese American students had ended, but national standards were needed to prevent its resurgence.[3]

The Supreme Court first heard oral arguments in *Brown* during the October 1952 term, when Fred M. Vinson was the chief justice. At that time, the Court might have upheld segregation, but Vinson died unexpectedly. The recess appointment and later Senate confirmation of Earl Warren altered the course of history. Chief Justice Warren, who had previously been the governor of California, wrote a unanimous opinion finding that school segregation violates the Fourteenth Amendment's Equal Protection Clause.

Warren found evidence "inconclusive" on whether the framers of the Fourteenth Amendment intended it to cover school desegregation. Justice Felix Frankfurter's judicial clerk Alexander Bickel, who went on to become one of the leading constitutional theorists in U.S. history, wrote a lengthy memorandum concluding that there was no definitive proof that the framers expected the amendment to end segregation. To the contrary, legislative history immediately following ratification, in 1868, indicated that the opposite might have been the case. Bickel was right that the actual debates on the amendment were scant in their mention of desegregation. Nevertheless, as Professor Michael W. McConnell, later a federal appellate judge, pointed out, the number of congressmen who between 1871 and 1874 favored a civil rights act containing a school desegregation provision—with votes in favor as high as 29–16 in the Senate—indicates that a significant proportion of the Reconstruction Congress believed that the amendment was applicable to desegregation in general and school desegregation in particular. Indeed, those who had voted for a school desegregation provision in the 1870s correlate almost exactly with those who voted for the Fourteenth Amendment. Only political disagreement on other issues kept that majority from passing the proposals on to the president for his signature.[4]

Turning from his historic analysis in *Brown*, Chief Justice Warren considered "the effect of segregation itself on public education." Education was important to a democratic society and "the very foundation of good citizenship." Children must be provided education on equal terms, he argued; otherwise, they are unlikely to succeed professionally. In the final analysis, the Court found that racial segregation, even where facilities were of equal quality, deprives children of an equal educational opportunity. Joint education is not merely important to the process of democratic enrollment; separate education is "inherently unequal." Later Supreme Court concurrences and dissents, contrary to some recent academic claims, recognized that *Brown* implicitly overturned *Plessy*'s "separate but equal" doctrine.[5]

Rather than viewing educational segregation as some abstract problem, the Court sided with black, Latino, and Asian students around the country. In an often cited article Herbert Wechsler objected to the Court's finding that segregation is in principle "a denial of equality to the minority against whom it is directed." According to Wechsler, the Court should have decided nothing other than the specific legal controversies in the five cases before it. He argued that judges must follow neutral procedural rules rather than coming to substantive determinants about equality, freedom, and fairness. To the contrary, the Warren Court had decided to step into a fracas of constitutional public policy: it did not have to wait for the other branches of government to tell it that the right to live in an integrated society was one of equal citizenship's emoluments. *Brown* stands for the principle that discrimination intrinsically violates the Equal Protection Clause. The process of making equality relevant to each American and providing an inclusive sense of the common good, necessarily involves value judgements.[6]

The Supreme Court announced national standards of equality for the guidance of all three branches of government, a curious fact given that the Reconstruction Congress had expected the Fourteenth Amendment to make civil rights reform congressionally driven. The Court might have made even more sweeping statements against the separate but equal regimen that *Plessy* had infamously legitimized. It could have, for instance, likewise explained the Congress's and the president's role in safeguarding equal treatment.

Despite these minor shortcomings, the Court's willingness in *Brown* to provide a constitutional footing for desegregation proved to be one of the most farsighted decisions in the nation's history for improving citizens' relations. Separation of the races in education had long been used to demean black students and to frustrate their aspirations. Despite the historic record of subjugation associated with keeping students segregated and the decades of struggles against it, Derrick Bell and several other prominent law professors have lately taken the position that *Brown* wrongly found segregated schools to be unconstitutional, wishing the Court had instead rigorously enforced *Plessy*'s "separate but equal" standard. This is either a suggestion that the country should administer a "fair" form of Jim Crow education or merely a provocative counterfactual argument; one hopes the latter to be the case.[7]

Bell relies on W. E. B. Du Bois's 1935 argument that black separate schools were preferable to mixed ones taught by unsympathetic white teachers; however, Du Bois's argument is only tangentially similar to Bell's. Unlike Bell, Du Bois observed that "other things being equal, the mixed school is the broader, more natural basis for the education of all youth. It gives wider contacts; it inspires greater self-confidence; and suppresses the inferiority complex." Other black intellectuals of that period shared the conviction of Horace Mann Bond that "the basis for the separate school is apparently an unwillingness of the white population to accept the Negro as a full participant in the life of our Democracy." A lesser-known black psychologist, Howard Hale Long, also writing in 1935, explained that "the segregated school literally forces a sense of limitation upon the child. He is reminded of it whether in home, school, or theatre, or on the streets." Separating black students from other American children heightened their sense of alienation, undermining the "fundamentals of democratic philosophy and practice."[8]

One of *Brown*'s most controversial sections relied on social science findings in accord with Long's. Warren weathered much criticism for his dicta citation to social science research in the eleventh footnote to the decision. In hindsight, the sources he relied on were weak, but that mistake did not undermine the Court's assertion that "modern authority" supported the finding that separating students by race "generates a feeling of inferiority as to their status in the community that may affect their hearts and minds in a way unlikely ever to be undone." The social science was merely peripheral. The core of the decision was the Supreme Court's conviction that individuals, be they members of the minority or of the majority, are an integral part of American democracy whose arbitrary exclusion from opportunity violates the Equal Protection Clause of the Fourteenth Amendment. Defining the problem in sociological terms explained the context within which the Court decided to set constitutional principles in line with the nation's long-standing image as a bastion of liberty and equality. *McLaurin* had already spoken to the negative educational effect of state-imposed racial ostracism at the graduate school level, without resort to empirical studies.[9]

Beyond the logical connection between inequality as it is perpetrated in graduate education and in primary education, social science had made its way into other civil rights decisions. Justice Louis D. Brandeis's brief in *Muller v. Oregon,* which relied on statistical analyses to explain the state's legitimate public health reasons to establish maximum working hour laws for women, set the stage for advocacy using secondary sources. The NAACP also found the use of statistics to be helpful in extending equal protection advocacy in one of the nation's most important restrictive covenant cases, *Shelley v. Kraemer.* During a Georgetown University lecture, Justice William J. Brennan explained the importance to judicial deliberation of interdisciplinary research. The "insights scholarship can furnish" help judges better understand "the totality of human experience." Lawyers, he counseled, should use "knowledge and experience of the other disciplines" because law "is not an end in itself. . . . It is pre-eminently a means to serve what we think is right." In *Brown* it is quite possible that the Court had already decided that segregation was unequal and unjust and turned to precedent, intuition, and social science to bolster its conclusion. The cumulative experience of the United States—including its principles, its history with slavery, its failed Reconstruction, its growing civil rights movement, and its foreign policy—went into the determined break from past deference to local segregation standards.[10]

Brown's most serious shortcoming was its failure to provide a specific remedy for educational segregation. In 1955, during the second phase of the case, the Court ordered federal trial courts to "enter such orders and decrees consistent with this opinion as are necessary and proper to admit to public schools on a racially nondiscriminatory basis with all deliberate speed." To be in compliance, school districts were to make a "prompt and reasonable start." But the Court refused to set specific deadlines, as Thurgood Marshall, the attorney for the NAACP, had requested. Rather than fashioning a single endpoint for the whole nation, the "primary responsibility for elucidating, assessing, and solving" how to desegregate was granted to school boards. Each community would be free to act within the constitutional parameters of the substantive decision.[11]

The phrase "all deliberate speed" signaled flexibility rather than requiring school districts to immediately alter their racial practices. The lack of a deadline allowed for divergent local interpretations. It also preempted claims of judicial impotency that might have been leveled if specific deadlines had been violated. During the justices' conference on the matter, Black pointed out that in light of inevitable southern resistance, the Court "should not issue what it cannot enforce."[12] These pragmatic, judicial considerations were practically meaningless to the litigants in *Brown*, who obtained no immediate relief: a very different result from the specific remedies granted to the plaintiffs of higher education cases, like *Sweatt* and *McLaurin*. On a national scale, many a segregated school district exploited this ambiguity to stall implementation.

Delayed segregation left the future uncertain. Success required other parts of the government to offer support. After President Eisenhower sent the 101st Airborne Division and federalized the Arkansas National Guard to assist in the desegregation of Central High School in Little Rock, Arkansas, the Court confirmed federal authority over constitutional interpretation. No state governor could gainsay the Supreme Court's decision that some school practices violated constitutionally protected rights. Children wishing to exercise their constitutional rights need not yield to violence and disorder. "Our constitutional ideal of equal justice under law is . . . a living truth" that must be respected.[13] That federalism traditionally assigned school administration to the states and that *Brown* allowed states some transitional period for implementation constituted no license for denying citizens' rights.

Arkansas' resistance showed no letup. The governor closed the entire Little Rock School District for a year. When this action was found to be unconstitutional, the Board of Education sought to transfer its responsibility to a private school system operated on a segregated basis. A circuit court forbade that transfer. Over the next decade litigants repeatedly returned to court to challenge Arkansas' innovative delay tactics.[14]

President Eisenhower's disinclination to get further involved after sending federal troops emboldened southern opposition. Eisenhower failed to show adequate executive leadership, just as he had during some other hot-button civil rights issues, especially during the Montgomery bus boycott and the Emmett Till lynching. Herbert Brownell, Eisenhower's attorney general, instructed the FBI not to involve itself in school desegregation and to leave matters to local authorities. As one contemporary commentator remarked, "Without the support of the Department of Justice, prompt and sweeping implementation of *Brown* was doomed." The NAACP lacked the resources of the federal government and persistently operated under the threat of violence.[15]

The one-case-at-a-time remedial method of enforcing *Brown*'s principles was lengthy, costly and unpredictable, and it yielded mixed results. The "all deliberate speed" formula galvanized opposition to disobey court orders by threats, violence, and simple recalcitrance. On the flip side, by providing the South enough time to adjust, the Court appeared to be neither radical nor dogmatic, winning the battle of public opinion against southern foot-dragging. Given the Court's limited power to adjudicate only actual legal controversies, putting an end to underlying inequality was to require legislation furthering Court-recognized constitutional interests.

Federal trial courts easily found student placement laws with racial criteria to be unconstitutional.[16] More obscurantist were placement laws with seemingly nonracial criteria that assigned students to attend the same schools they had been enrolled in before *Brown*. Assignment statutes often provided complicated administrative procedures designed to keep desegregation issues from reaching federal courts. Between 1954 and 1957 ten of eleven states that had previously used overt racial classifications turned to neutral-sounding pupil assignment laws.[17]

These statutes varied from state to state, but they typically required that anyone seeking to change schools first exhaust lengthy state proceedings. That process involved filing a transfer application for a school board's consideration. Any request that was denied had to be contested through school administrative processes. In the event that further proceedings were required, cases shuffled their way through the state court system. If after all this an unsatisfied student had not yet graduated, he could finally get to the less locally influenced federal court. This effectively defanged *Brown*'s remedial approach. Federal courts typically upheld state provisions requiring persons to exhaust administrative procedures; on the other hand, federal courts of appeal refused to classify state courts as part of the administrative process. This meant that federal trial courts could hear cases challenging segregation directly after individuals had exhausted all the administrative school channels of seeking redress rather than having to go through state court judges and juries who, like their legislative counterparts, were likely to think favorably of segregation.[18] To further thwart mass change, statutes in Mississippi, South Carolina, and Tennessee required that each enrollment alteration be considered individually, rather than allowing pupils to file joint lawsuits. Federal courts refused to permit this end-around of *Brown*, allowing courts to certify classes of litigants who challenged state placement laws.[19]

The Dallas School Board adopted a plan, which a district court upheld, allowing students' parents to voice their unwillingness to integrate and "thereby give all concerned what they prefer" in order to avoid an undesired result. This so-called freedom-of-choice plan was a wholly ineffective means of integrating because white students tended to want to stay in their schools, while black parents and students were often concerned that asking to be transferred would subject them to "violence, eviction, loss of jobs, and other forms of intimidation."[20]

The U.S. Commission on Civil Rights reported in 1962 that pupil placement laws, like the one in Dallas, were "the principal obstacle to desegregation in the South."[21] The ability of states to manipulate the Supreme Court's mandate of "all deliberate speed" as an excuse for evading meaningful change is another example of how inadequate federal supervision can encourage local mismanagement. The New Deal's antidiscrimination provisions had been similarly disregarded by local administrators.

Ultimately, the judiciary played a critical role in setting constitutional guidelines for the government, but the Court's institutional limitations made it impossible to effect the grand-scale change of executive and legislative decisionmaking. Private litigants had to initiate suits, which they often lacked time and resources to pursue. At the end of a grueling legal process, success often meant obtaining an equitable remedy that segregationists found ways around.

For a decade battles raged in state and lower federal courts without Supreme Court input. By 1964 the Court got back onto the playing field, declaring that the "time for mere 'deliberate speed' has run out." A 1968 case, *Green v. County School Board,* dealt a deathblow to freedom-of-choice plans, which were then used in nine southern and border states. The school board of New Kent County, Virginia, had only two schools, and white and black students continued to be taught and transported separately. Even extracurricular activities evinced a "pattern of segregation." A Virginia placement statute required each student to continue attending the same segregated school as before unless she applied to the state board and was reassigned. No white student had ever asked to be reassigned, and few black students had been allowed to attend the historically white school. A unanimous Supreme Court determined that school officials were not acting in good faith to further the public's interest. From *Green* on, the Court required that proposed plans demonstrate the likelihood of "meaningful and immediate progress." The decision empowered lower federal courts to require the defendant school boards to provide plans for a unitary system that did not "burden children and their parents with a responsibility" that *Brown*'s remedial measures "placed squarely on the School Board."[22]

A determined Court went further in 1969, after Warren E. Burger had taken over chief justiceship. Reluctant to reverse earlier decisions, the Court was nonetheless resolute that "'all deliberate speed' for desegregation is no longer constitutionally permissible." Desegregation was only part of the solution; where necessary, lower courts could facilitate integration to end racial discrimination. Only in 1971 did the Court come up with a uniform solution, redrawing school zones and busing students to integrate schools, a strategy that increased the length of some students' commute. Despite the "awkward, inconvenient, and even bizarre" situations that this might create, bus transportation was important for facilitating racially balanced school systems.[23]

These four cases, coupled with Title VI of the Civil Act of 1964 and the Elementary and Secondary Education Act of 1965, which tied federal funding to desegregation and allowed the Justice Department to join lawsuits, were far more effective than the unwieldy "all deliberate speed" standard. The political intransigence that reigned in 1954, when *Brown* was decided, rendered that standard ineffective in the South. In 1964 only 1.2 percent of southern black schoolchildren attended schools with whites. By 1967, 16.9 percent of southern black children attended integrated schools; five years later 91.3 percent of black students in the South were in schools with whites. The change was less

drastic but also noticeable in border states, where 54.8 percent of black elementary and secondary students attended schools with whites in 1964, 71.4
percent in 1967, and 77.3 percent in 1972.[24]

The Supreme Court was critical to the advancement of liberal equality; in
a tricameral system of government, however, without the other two branches'
participation, judges lacked mechanisms to quickly end segregation. Some
scholars have suggested that *Brown* achieved little beyond bolstering violent
opposition to desegregation; such misguided analysis resembles Southern
Revivalism's censure of Reconstruction for the emergence of the Ku Klux
Klan.[25] The Court led the way, with Congress and the president following the
moral tone it set for the country. In substance, *Brown* did much more than
end school segregation. In the mid-1950s to early 1960s, the Court issued
several cursory opinions citing no other case than *Brown* for the proposition
that segregated golf courses, lakes, buses, and restaurants were impermissible
under the Fourteenth Amendment of the Constitution.[26]

Although *Brown*'s remedial portion was completely inadequate for
achieving lasting change in the South, within another decade the Court demanded that school boards stop dragging their feet, compared with the almost
a century it took for the Fourteenth Amendment to play any significant role in
protecting minorities. Only when federal funding to schools was statutorily
tied to desegregation was it possible to enforce the Court-recognized standards of national conduct.

Brown applied only to state-sponsored dual education systems, particularly those found in segregated public schools. In *Runyon v. McCrary*
(1976) the Burger Court found that a Civil War era statute prohibits private
schools from denying admission to potential students because of their race.
The federal government's interest in prohibiting interpersonal discrimination
supersedes parents' and school boards' desire to disassociate themselves from
minority students.[27]

Public Accommodation Desegregation

The Supreme Court relied on the Equal Protection Clause in its school
desegregation cases. However, even before *Brown v. Board of Education*, it
began deciding lawsuits challenging private businesses operating segregated
facilities. For decades after the *Civil Rights Cases* (1883), when the Court
found key desegregation provisions in the Civil Rights Act of 1875 to be
unconstitutional, and the executive and legislative branches of government

looked for no alternatives. The justices entered the abandoned field with creative and steady holdings. However, until Congress followed with supporting legislation, each Supreme Court decision met new attempts by state and private actors to thwart the majority's central purpose, the equal protection of fundamental rights.

The desegregation movement had its rebirth at the end of the New Deal, after decades of quiescence. U.S. Representative Arthur W. Mitchell of Illinois took a trip in 1937 from Chicago to Arkansas, paying for first-class passage. Before the train entered Arkansas, a conductor threatened to arrest Mitchell if he did not move to a second-class "colored passenger" car in compliance with an Arkansas statute. Mitchell, who had been Booker T. Washington's student at the Tuskegee Institute before becoming an attorney, complied but later filed a complaint with the Interstate Commerce Commission. The case eventually reached the Supreme Court, which unanimously held that the railroad's actions had violated the Interstate Commerce Act. The case nevertheless conformed to *Plessy*'s separate-but-equal model, finding that the carrier's violation consisted of its failure to provide accommodations with equal comforts and conveniences for colored passengers, rather than requiring it to end segregation altogether.[28]

Irene Morgan's defiance provided the Court with an opportunity to further examine the issue in 1946. Nine years before Rosa Parks's refusal to comply with bus segregation in Alabama, Morgan refused to give up her Greyhound bus seat for a white passenger in Virginia. Morgan had been traveling at the front of the bus from Virginia to Maryland when the bus driver told her to move to the rear. In *Morgan v. Virginia*, the Supreme Court ruled that imposing state segregation restrictions on interstate travelers undermined the U.S. Congress's role in formulating nationally uniform commercial policy. But the Court did not prohibit Virginia from applying its statute to intrastate travelers. Similarly, in 1950 the Court found that racially segregated dining cars violated federal law on interstate commerce; however, restaurants operating only within a single state were not thereby forbidden from openly discriminating against minority patrons.[29]

The 381-day boycott of the Montgomery bus system in the wake of Parks's protest led to a 1956 case, *Gayle v. Browder*, prohibiting segregation in local bus travel. The Warren Court rejected the argument that private organizations can refuse to serve patrons on account of their race.[30]

Parks initiated one of the most effective grassroots movements in United States history. Sit-in protests likewise started with individual social action.

On January 31, 1960, Joseph McNeill, a seventeen-year-old black freshman at North Carolina Agricultural and Technical College in Greensboro, North Carolina, was denied service at a bus terminal lunch counter. The next day, he and three other freshmen spontaneously decide to start a boycott. McNeill, Ezell Blair, Jr., Franklin McCain, and David Richmond went to Woolworth's Five and Dime store, sat down at the lunch counter, and ordered coffee. Although the manager, in compliance with local practice, refused to serve them, the young men stayed put for the rest of the day. During their sit-down strike, other students were shopping at the store. When the freshmen returned to their college, more than twenty other students decided to join the four freshmen the next day. They established ground rules against raising voices, uttering complaints, or resorting to insults. They returned the third day with increasing numbers of supporters. Students from Bennett College and Woman's College of the University of North Carolina joined their protest. The freshmen had ignited a fire. By the next week, students were protesting in Winston-Salem, Durham, and Charlotte. Soon the NAACP, the Student Nonviolent Coordinating Committee (SNCC), the Congress of Racial Equality (CORE), and Martin Luther King, Jr. provided national leadership for the boycott movement. King was arrested on October 19, 1960, at Rich's Atlanta department store. John F. Kennedy, during a September 6, 1960, campaign speech, committed himself "to help bring about equal access to public facilities—from churches to lunch counters—and to support the right of every American to stand up for his rights—even if that means sitting down for them." The sit-ins inspired wade-ins at public pools and kneel-ins at churches. Thousands of blacks were arrested in their quest to end gross unfairness. By the end of 1960 the sit-ins led to 126 cities desegregating lunch counters, and by the end of 1961 that number rose to about 200.[31]

After *Morgan* and *Gayle* states could not enforce overtly racist segregation statutes, so they tried relying on laws against "disturbing the peace." During its 1961 term the Court made clear that peaceful sit-ins at "white lunch counters" did not qualify as criminal disturbances of the peace. Convictions of persons for sitting peacefully "in a place where custom decreed they should not sit" violated their Fourteenth Amendment right to due process.[32] The likelihood that racist attitudes were "likely to give rise to a breach of the peace" was no justification for preventing orderly people from using facilities that local customs had set apart for whites.[33]

Segregation of lunch counters did not cease. Officials turned to ostensibly neutral trespass laws instead of overtly race-based restrictions and antidisturbance provisions to achieve the same end. The manager of a Greenville, South Carolina, S. H. Kress store called the police when ten "Negro boys and girls" requested service at a white lunch counter. In the presence of the police, the manager told them to leave, not on racial grounds but because the lunch counter was closing. The protestors were arrested and later convicted of misdemeanor trespass for remaining seated. In maintaining a segregated business, the manager's decision not to serve black customers in the first place complied with a city ordinance. That law mandated that stores serve blacks apart from whites and use different utensils and dishes for each race. When the Supreme Court heard the protesters' case, it found that their Fourteenth Amendment rights had been violated by a discriminatory criminal process. The ordinance significantly involved the city in segregation and removed the matter from the private sphere of simple trespass into the public realm, within the purview of the U.S. Constitution.[34]

With explicit state and local segregation policies foreclosed, it remained uncertain whether the Court would countenance a store's own segregation policy. The key was to challenge the practices of a private business that was not relying on any legal authority. The opportunity presented itself in Maryland, which had no law either for or against segregation. Several black students went to Hooper's restaurant in Baltimore, planning to engage in a sit-in protest unless they were served. The hosts refused to take their orders for racial reasons and ordered them out of the restaurant. When they refused to leave, the police arrested members of the group, twelve of whom were subsequently convicted of trespass.

The Supreme Court accepted the case, *Bell v. Maryland,* but found consensus difficult to achieve. Justice Brennan, who wrote for the majority, decided the case on technical legal grounds. He thereby avoided the constitutional question of whether the Fourteenth Amendment applies to a private business's discrimination. The Court moved cautiously because as it was internally debating the merits of a decision Congress was considering a civil rights bill, specifically that part that would become Title II, that banned just the sort of private practices involved in the case. After the Maryland Court of Appeals affirmed the convictions, Baltimore and Maryland enacted laws abolishing racial segregation in places of public accommodations. On the basis of these supervening enactments, the majority reversed the convictions.[35]

Justice Douglas, who wrote one of the two concurrences, did address the competing constitutional claims. He traced the problem to slavery, which segregated blacks and kept them out of public accommodations except at their masters' sufferance. "Segregation of Negroes in the restaurants and lunch counters . . . is a relic of slavery. It is a badge of second-class citizenship." Any state whose courts rely on trespass laws to maintain that old status are violating the Reconstruction Amendment's principles. Hooper's restaurant was not the private sphere of a person's "home . . . or yard. Private property is involved, but it is property that is serving the public." Douglas's point was aimed at Justice Black's dissenting opinion that all the case involved was the right of a property owner to "choose his social or business associates." The constitutional right to enjoy personal property, Douglas argued, was not a trump for keeping blacks out of public places. The police and the judiciary may not further the discriminatory practices of businesses open to the public. Justice Arthur J. Goldberg, in his concurrence, found that the prohibition against segregation stemmed from the Declaration of Independence's American Creed. The ability of the public to use public accommodations on an equal basis, Goldberg believed, was intrinsic to the Fourteenth Amendment.

The Civil Rights Act of 1964, with its provision against public accommodation discrimination, became law ten days after the Court's decision in *Bell*. Title II of the act prohibited discrimination based on race, color, religion, and national origin in such public places of accommodation as restaurants, lunchrooms, motels, hotels, and entertainment venues. By covering various facilities in one statute, Congress could avoid the institutional limitation of courts, which must deal with one issue at a time. Congress passed a policy that covered a variety of locations based on its Commerce and Fourteenth Amendment Powers.[36]

Moreton Rolleston, the owner of the 216-room Heart of Atlanta Motel, filed a lawsuit challenging the law just two hours after President Johnson signed it. The motel was located near two multilane U.S. highways, making it an attractive layover for interstate travelers. It offered a restaurant, air conditioning, telephone services, and even a swimming pool. Rolleston, who was an attorney, claimed that the law exceeded Congress's Commerce Clause powers, deprived him of property without due process, and subjected him to involuntary servitude by requiring him to rent rooms to unwanted patrons.[37]

The Court upheld the constitutionality of Title II in *Heart of Atlanta Motel v. United States* (1964), but it relied on Congress's Commerce Clause power alone, remaining silent on its Fourteenth Amendment authority to pass statutes directed at businesses serving the public. This was a relevant distinction. It placed Congress's ability to act against discrimination within its purview over the interstate exchange of goods, products, and other property rather than in its power to punish individuals interfering with citizens' privileges and immunities. As a consequence, the *Slaughter House Cases* (1873), which had eviscerated Congress's ability to define the privileges and immunities of citizenship, remained unaffected. The majority in *Heart of Atlanta*, written by Justice Tom C. Clark, also missed the opportunity to overrule the *Civil Rights Cases* (1883).

In a concurrence, Justice Goldberg agreed that Congress had legitimately relied on Commerce Clause authority, but he wrote separately to emphasize that the "primary purpose of the Civil Rights Act of 1964 . . . is the vindication of human dignity and not mere economics." In his opinion, Congress's authority to pass the Civil Rights Act of 1964 derives both from section five of the Fourteenth Amendment and from the Commerce Clause. Justice Douglas, in a separate concurrence, was likewise reluctant to rest the opinion entirely on commerce authority since the "right of persons to move freely from State to State occupies a more protected position in our constitutional system than does the movement of cattle, fruit, steel and coal across state lines." The downside of resting the majority opinion on the Commerce Clause would become abundantly apparent thirty years later when the Rehnquist Court began diminishing Congress's ability to connect civil rights policy to the national economy.

The same day the Court decided *Heart of Atlanta Motel*, it released an opinion on *Katzenbach v. McClung*. The controversy in *McClung* involved a family-owned restaurant in Birmingham, Alabama. Ollie's Barbecue did $350,000 worth of yearly business primarily with in-state diners. The owner was not even aware of having served interstate customers, nor did he advertise. Yet Ollie's bought much of its meat from a facility outside the state, thereby affecting the national economy. White customers were served in house, while blacks could purchase only take-out orders.

Congress, wrote the majority of the Court, had a "rational basis for finding that racial discrimination in restaurants had a direct and adverse effect on the free flow of interstate commerce." The Court relied on Congress's assessment rather than requiring the U.S. attorney general to provide detailed proof of its findings. The Court's resort to the Commerce Clause is subject to the same criticism that Justices Goldberg and Douglas leveled in *Heart of Atlanta*.[38]

The Court had no tolerance for businesses using the label "private clubs" to evade Title II and gain exemption from integration. In one case, the Court even extended the statute's application to a business that charged twenty-five cents for a seasonal membership. The club's radio advertisement to tourists and use of food and boats from outside the state evinced its public character and put its discriminatory practices within the Civil Rights Act's reach.[39]

The closest the Court got to using the Reconstruction Amendments in the post-1964 desegregation cases was *Jones v. Alfred H. Mayer.* Mr. and Mrs. Jones wanted to purchase a new house from the Alfred H. Mayer Corporation, a private real estate developer. The company turned down their offer because Mr. Jones was black. The case offered a fresh interpretation of the Thirteenth Amendment and showed its applicability to contemporary injustices.[40]

Justice Potter Stewart's opinion relied on some Radical Republican principles on the scope of the Civil Rights Act of 1866. With Congress having done little with its Thirteenth Amendment enforcement power following Reconstruction, the Court had little law to choose from, so that ancient statute became pivotal. Justice Stewart found that the amendment's second section empowered Congress to pass legislation specifically designed to promote personal autonomy and to eliminate the "badges and incidents" of involuntary servitude. Stewart recognized that the framers of the amendment had anticipated the need for additional safeguards after abolition to prevent endemic discrimination. The second section was a legislative tool used for combating local prejudices and giving practical effect to abolitionist ideals. *Jones* concluded that Alfred H. Mayer had committed an offense against the Joneses' right to contract by trying to keep them out of the emoluments of liberty. Maintaining a segregated society, even by privately excluding blacks "from white communities," deprives them of constitutional liberty and functions as a "substitute for the slave system."

The Warren Court was instrumental to ending segregation in public places of accommodation. The Civil Rights Act of 1964 was the apex of American achievements in the area, but it was not enacted from scratch. The justices had established principles of liberty, equal citizenship, and dignity that Congress further broadened. Afterward, the judicial branch remained critical to constitutionally legitimizing the act.

Voting Rights

The Warren Court recognized the "one person, one vote" principle even before Congress adopted the Voting Rights Act of 1965. Until the 1960s deference to state political prejudices foreclosed voting for all but a fraction of southern blacks. *Williams v. Mississippi* (1898), *Giles v. Harris* (1903), and

Giles v. Teasley (1904) gave the Court's imprimatur to literacy tests and poll taxes. For decades afterward, the Court characterized facially neutral electoral qualifications as political matters that were beyond the reach of judicial authority.[41]

Legislative reapportionment cases broke from that tradition, finding that electoral discrimination harmed individuals, not merely the political process. In *Baker v. Carr* (1962), the Court dealt with a quiltwork of state apportionment schemes. When the case was decided, many states allocated votes to legislative districts based on decades-old census figures. Rural areas were overrepresented, enabling a small segment of the population to elect the majority of congressmen. A contemporary political scientist, Herman C. Nixon, determined that "the typical southern legislature . . . provides . . . inadequate representation for all urban people. . . . It is chiefly a body of Democratic, small town or rural, white men, a majority of whom represent a minority of the population of the state." The rural bias was so pronounced that in 1947 residents of urban areas elected about 25 percent of state legislators in the country, even though urban dwellers made up 59 percent of the U.S. population. Urban areas tended to have a higher incidence of poverty, but they had less representation to appropriate adequate funding for social services. In seventeen states, including Arkansas, Kentucky, and Virginia, 40 percent of the population could elect a legislative majority. The situation was worse in other states. In Georgia, Alabama, Tennessee, and Oklahoma about one-fourth of each state's population could elect a majority to the legislature. In eleven states, the majority of senators could be voted in by just 20 percent of the population. And one-eighth of the Florida electorate could select a majority.[42]

Many states were reluctant to redraw voting districts that would accurately reflect the decline in rural population and the ensuing migration into urban centers. As a result, the number of eligible voters whom members of the United States and state congresses represented varied significantly. Some voters thus had significantly less say in picking a representative than others. In Arizona, for instance, the disparity between the most populated and least populated congressional districts was 465,274; in Connecticut, the difference was 370,613; in Florida, 423,110; in Georgia, 551,526; in Michigan, 625,563; and in Texas, a whopping 735,156. These states' population differences reflected others in the country.[43]

The Court began transforming legislative apportionment with *Baker v. Carr*, which Earl Warren later characterized as "the most vital decision" of his

chief justiceship. The Court derived the constitutional mandate for reapportionment from the Equal Protection Clause of the Fourteenth Amendment.
The *Baker* Court refused to follow a 1946 plurality that had found a dispute
involving population discrepancies between Illinois' urban and rural congressional districts to be a nonjusticiable political matter.[44]

Baker arose from a challenge to Tennessee's continued apportionment of
legislative districts on the basis of a 1901 statute, despite the dramatic demographic shift from rural areas that had taken place over sixty years. The
disparity in some areas was enormous. The 2,340 voters of rural Moore
County, Tennessee, had a single representative, while urban Shelby County,
with a voting population of 312,345, had eight representatives. That meant
that some 39,000 voters in Shelby had as much representation as Moore's
2,340. The Supreme Court, with Justice Brennan articulating the majority's
opinion, resisted the trial court's finding that reapportionment was a purely
political issue outside judicial purview. To the contrary, the Court held that
federal courts can assert jurisdiction in malapportionment cases. While the
Court did not reach the merits of the case, it found that the Equal Protection
Clause provided plaintiffs with the right to file a claim challenging the repre-
sentational disparity arising from Tennessee's failure to redistrict congressional boundaries.[45]

In *Wesberry v. Sanders* (1964), the Court took another step toward requiring mathematical electoral equality. The majority determined that state congressional districts must contain roughly equal populations. A large population disparity among districts "grossly discriminates against voters." Article I,
section 2 of the Constitution decrees that each vote "be given as much weight
as any other vote." Accordingly, the Court struck down Georgia's scheme,
where nine districts, whose average population was 394,312, were represented
by one congressman each while the district around Atlanta, with its population of 823,680, was also entitled to one congressman.[46]

Rather than tolerating skewed results, *Reynolds v. Sims* (1964) required
equipopulous congressional districts. In an earlier case the Court had indicated this scheme's connection to U.S. history: "The conception of political
equality from the Declaration of Independence, to Lincoln's Gettysburg Address, to the Fifteenth, Seventeenth, and Nineteenth Amendments can mean
only one thing—one person, one vote." A series of equal protection cases
tailored this doctrine to the federal, state, and local legislative levels, demanding that all citizens be equally represented irrespective of their race or place of
residence. It requires that electoral districts be equiproportional on the basis

of the most recent census figures. Thus substantial population differences in voting districts are unconstitutional.[47] Malapportionment results when voters in one district have unequal influence in representative politics.

> How then can one person be given twice or 10 times the voting power of another person in a statewide election merely because he lives in a rural area or because he lives in the smallest rural county? Once the geographical unit for which a representative is to be chosen is designated, all who participate in the election are to have an equal vote—whatever their race, whatever their sex, whatever their occupation, whatever their income, and wherever their home may be in that geographical unit. This is required by the Equal Protection Clause of the Fourteenth Amendment. The concept of "we the people" under the Constitution visualizes no preferred class of voters but equality among those who meet the basic qualifications.[48]

The right to suffrage is too fundamental to a "government of the people, by the people, (and) for the people" to be satisfied with any rational justifications for large representative population differences. To comply with the "one person, one vote" requirement, state redistricting had to create "substantial equality of population." Each citizen's vote was to be afforded "approximately equal" weight as any other citizen's.[49]

In later years, the Court maintained that "equal representation for equal numbers of people [is] the fundamental goal for the House of Representatives." No state may deviate from absolute population equality unless it can show that it first made "a good-faith effort to achieve precise mathematical equality."[50] State district population deviations are typically not kept to the same stringent standard for federal congressional districts, where even a deviation of 1 percent might be found inappropriate under constitutional scrutiny.[51]

Warren Court decisions on election law were not the end-all. The Voting Rights Act of 1965 was essential for preempting the case-by-case challenge to years of abuse of the democratic process. Among its provisions, for example, the act ended the use of literacy tests, which the Court in 1959 had found to be constitutional. While the Court never reversed itself outright, the ruling was practically nullified in 1966 when it upheld congressional authority under the Voting Rights Act to prohibit the disqualification of any voters who had completed six grades in an American school. The effectiveness of the statute's provisions derived from Congress's Fifteenth Amendment authority to safeguard democratic voting.[52]

Legislative reform increased the significance of the voting rights revolution sparked by *Wesberry* and *Reynolds*. By 1968, thirty-seven states had redrawn their congressional districts. Out of the other thirteen, five were single-representative states, several were already found to be equitably districted, and two had representatives at large. There remained only nine states where district populations varied by more than 10 percent of the state average. One explanation for this success might be the significance to the populace of the legal victories. Once the Court recognized the constitutional duty to provide the electorate with a coequal share of political expression, the minority of voters could no longer rely on local rationales for denying parity. Nevertheless, incumbents sometimes retained enough latitude to remain in office by gerrymandering reapportioned districts.[53]

Reapportionment altered state fiscal policy, bringing a more proportional allotment of funds into urban areas. With an increased diversity of political input, especially from urban areas, states tended to spend more on education, welfare, health, and hospitals. That is not to say that urban, suburban, or rural representatives voted solely in the interests of their regions. Increased urban and suburban representation following reapportionment led to more fair representation for a variety of constituents. The system provided for more democratic means of representation. Differing political alliances often pitted urban politicians against one another as they did with rural politicians, much as before reapportionment. At least these differences reflected actual community opinion rather than the privileging of small segments of the population.[54]

Familial Rights

Just as the Warren Court promoted public rights with the public accommodations and reapportionment cases, it also deepened the constitutional foundation of private rights. Justice Douglas, writing for the Court in *Griswold v. Connecticut* (1965), explained the constitutional foundation of familial privacy.[55]

Douglas was a prolific author who elsewhere had explored the extent to which people retained rights against government intrusion. "The Constitution is a compendium," he wrote, not an exhaustive "compilation of laws" but a statement of principles.[56] The Bill of Rights is a sampling of protected rights rather than an exhaustive list; the Bill also implies unenumerated rights in several provisions, including the First, Third, Fourth, Fifth, and Ninth Amendments. Douglas understood the people to be sovereign, and the Constitution to be an instrument for the common good.

By the time Douglas wrote his seminal opinion in *Griswold*, the Supreme Court had already decided several cases on privacy. They covered people's ability to live unencumbered by unreasonable searches and seizures, to refuse providing self-incriminating testimony, to preserve "the sanctity of" their "home and the privacies of life," and to associate with others freely. Justice Douglas had written a majority opinion to *Skinner v. Oklahoma* (1942), which found unconstitutional, on equal protection grounds, a state law for the sterilization of certain convicts. Douglas did not mention "privacy," but he spoke in terms of a "basic liberty" involved in procreation. In a dissent to *Public Utilities Commission v. Pollak* (1952), he then connected the constitutional protection of liberties to "privacy" and the "right to be let alone." His 1958 book, *The Right of the People*, posited that the "penumbra of the Bill of Rights" protects natural rights that "have a broad base in morality and religion to protect man, his individuality, and his conscience against direct and indirect interference by government."[57]

Griswold arose from a constitutional challenge brought against a Connecticut law prohibiting the use of contraceptives or counseling about their use. Douglas located the right to make reproductive decisions and associate without unnecessary governmental intrusion in the "penumbras" of privacy "formed by emanations from those guarantees that help give them life and substance." This rights-based argument was a far cry from the solely procedural viewpoint of the Constitution that John Hart Ely and Herbert Wechsler had popularized among legal academics.[58] The Court could, according to Douglas, derive the unenumerated "zones of privacy" from the specific provisions of the Bill of Rights. Marital privacy is "a right of privacy older than the Bill of Rights—older than our political parties, older than our school system." If the state were given power to prevent spouses from using contraception, by extension it would be able to conduct a "repulsive" search of "the sacred precincts of marital bedrooms." The Due Process Clause protects marital couples using or seeking counseling about contraceptives. In 1972 the Burger Court extended the right to unmarried individuals' use of birth control.

Where Douglas, in *Griswold*, located penumbras in the first eight amendments to the Constitution, Justice Goldberg's concurring opinion found them not in the letter of the Constitution but in the "fundamental principles of liberty and justice which lie at the base of all our civil and political institutions." Chief Justice Warren and Justice Brennan joined Goldberg's argument. Instead of substantive due process, to which Harlan's concurrence alluded, Goldberg found more convincing the Ninth Amendment's assurance that the people retained rights other than just those enumerated by the Constitution. The marital right to privacy was one of those rights retained by the people even after they ratified the social contract.

Justice Black had become increasingly formalistic over the years. He dissented in *Griswold:* "I like my privacy as well as the next" person, he wrote, "but I am nevertheless compelled to admit that government has a right to invade it unless prohibited by some specific constitutional provision." He found nothing explicit about marital intimacy in the Constitution.

The majority's recognition of conjugal privacy rights raised the possibility of ending other marital discrimination. As we have discovered, laws against racial intermarriage date back to the colonial period. At the end of the nineteenth century, the Supreme Court upheld a discriminatory scheme for punishing interracial adultery and fornication. Sexual liaisons between white men and black women were not uncommon, but various colonies, and later states, refused to countenance the change in social status that intermarriage could initiate. As the sociologist Gunnar Myrdal has pointed out, antimiscegenation laws and customs were meant to prevent blacks' attainment of social equality. This racism went hand in hand with the centuries-old myth of uncontrollable urges in black men for white women.[59]

The Court turned down the opportunity to confront the festering problem in 1956. *Naim v. Naim* arose when a white woman, Ruby Elaine Naim, filed to get either a divorce or an annulment from her Chinese husband. The judge chose to annul their marriage, finding that it had violated the Virginia Act to Preserve Racial Integrity. That antimiscegenation statute prohibited whites from marrying persons of any other race. The annulment subjected Han Say Naim to deportation. On appeal, he argued that the statute was unconstitutional. The case reached the Virginia Supreme Court of Appeals, which upheld the trial court's annulment order. As for the statute, the Virginia court claimed that the creation of marital law, even when it overtly discriminated, was a state prerogative preserved by the Tenth Amendment of the United States Constitution. No federal provision could justify interfering with the state's policy to "preserve the racial integrity of its citizens" from "a mongrel breed of citizens."[60]

Instead of ruling on the constitutionality of the Virginia statute, which it might have overturned based on its recent antidiscrimination ruling in *Brown v. Board of Education*, the U.S. Supreme Court issued a perfunctory statement. It found Virginia's judicial decision to be "devoid of a properly presented federal question." That action effectively permitted states with antimiscegenation laws to continue to enforce them. Warren told his law clerks that the procedural decision was "total bullshit." Between 1955 and 1967 fourteen states repealed such laws. As of 1967, sixteen states continued to prevent and punish intermarriage.[61]

Virginia stuck by its Racial Integrity Act and actually invaded marital bed chambers much as, in *Griswold,* Justice Douglas had warned states might do if their power over marital privacy was not curtailed. On July 11, 1958, just five weeks after they were married in Washington, D.C., Richard and Mildred Loving awoke to the glare of a law officer's flashlight pointed at them in bed. Richard was white and Mildred part black and part Cherokee; they had dated from their youth. Caroline County Sheriff R. Garnett Brooks demanded of Richard, "What are you doing in bed with this lady?" Richard pointed to their marriage certificate on the wall, but the sheriff told him that the document was invalid in Virginia and jailed them. Subsequently, Judge Leon M. Bazile sentenced each of them to one year in jail but commuted the sentence on condition that they leave the state and not return together for the next twenty-five years. The judge allowed them to enter Virginia singly "to visit his or her people as often as they please." His reasoning relied on religious bigotry: "Almighty God created the races white, black, yellow, malay and red, and he placed them on separate continents. . . . The fact that he separated the races shows that he did not intend for the races to mix." To comply with the terms of their sentence, the couple moved to Washington, D.C., but later, in violation of their conditional release, returned to rural Virginia. The spouses eventually contacted two Alexandria, Virginia, lawyers, Philip J. Hirschkop and Bernard S. Cohen.[62]

The Supreme Court accepted the case, *Loving v. Virginia,* after the Supreme Court of Appeals of Virginia refused to vacate the Lovings' convictions. Chief Justice Warren, writing for the Court, rejected Virginia's argument that its statute did not violate the Equal Protection Clause since it disadvantaged whites and nonwhites alike. Warren did not mince words: Virginia's prohibition of intermarriage was a measure "designed to maintain White Supremacy." Critical race theory founder Richard Delgado has pointed out that the Court went far beyond merely announcing a color-blind norm. It pointed out that Virginia's intrinsic policy was eugenic, intended only to keep the white race pure, since it allowed other minorities to intermarry so long as none of them married whites. There was, as the Court understood, "no legitimate overriding purpose independent of invidious racial discrimination" for the state to intrude on the Lovings' basic liberty. Antimiscegenation statutes do not meet the most rigid scrutiny of Equal Protection. The right to marry is "one of the vital personal rights essential to the orderly pursuit of happiness by free men." That statement went beyond *Griswold*'s recognition of marital privacy in only individual terms. In *Loving*, the Court comprehended that the liberty to choose a spouse, unencumbered by racialist laws, is also critical to the general welfare. The Lovings' convictions violated their due process rights under the Fourteenth Amendment.[63]

After they won the case, Richard rejoiced that "for the first time, I could put my arm around her and publicly call her my wife." Richard Loving met a tragic end in 1975. A drunk driver broadsided a vehicle in which he, Mildred, and her sister Garnet were making their way back from a visit to friends. Garnet was not seriously injured, but Mildred lost an eye and Richard died, at the age of forty-two. Before this tragedy befell them, the couple had gained respect for themselves and other victims of racial intolerance.[64]

Criminal Procedure

The Warren Court's criminal jurisprudence is a component of its civil rights legacy. Opinions that emphasized the constitutionality of criminal adjudication incorporated many provisions of the Bill of Rights into the Fourteenth Amendment. They applied federal protections of individual rights against abuses committed by state police officers. Criminal procedures in county, municipal, and state courts around the country also became governed by constitutional standards rather than by local fiat.

Beginning with *Mapp v. Ohio*, the Court relied on the Due Process Clause to protect individuals against coercive law enforcement tactics. *Mapp* extended the Fourth Amendment's prohibition against unreasonable searches and seizures to the states. The following year, *Robinson v. California* incorporated the Eighth Amendment's prohibition against cruel and unusual punishment. In the years that followed, the Court found that additional clauses of the Bill of Rights also governed state criminal proceedings. Defendants now have rights against self-incrimination and double jeopardy under the Fifth Amendment; and the rights to confront witnesses, be provided a speedy trial, have compulsory process for calling witnesses in their favor, and demand a criminal jury trials under the Sixth Amendment.[65]

The ability to incarcerate individuals had often been abused on racial grounds, with the state failing to provide defendants with an adequate opportunity to present their defense. National coverage of the Scottsboro cases in the 1930s brought home just how difficult it might be to get a fair hearing relying solely on state criminal devices, especially where race and poverty are at play. Warren Court decisions provided state and federal criminal defendants nationally recognized protections against the abuse of local prejudices.

The Court also showed sensitivity to the unequal allocation of justice between rich and poor. In *Gideon v. Wainwright* (1963), it required states to provide indigent criminal defendants with a lawyer. That principle of adequate representation, irrespective of wealth, was expanded to first appeals in *Douglas v. California* (1963). The latter decision furthered fair and equal process requirements of *Griffin v. Illinois* (1956), which ruled that states must provide indigent defendants with free transcripts for appellate review. Justice Black's plurality opinion showed a genuine concern for the hardships of poverty: "There can be no equal justice where the kind of trial a man gets depends on the amount of money he has." Justice Brennan even regarded *Miranda v. Arizona* (1966), which required the police to inform suspects of their right to remain silent and to seek legal counsel, as a case equalizing criminal protections for the poor. Constitutional rights were more important than the extra fiscal burden required to treat suspects fairly.[66]

Critics of the Warren Court point out that added due process criminal procedures led to more guilty suspects going free, and there is undoubtedly some truth in that. But the recognition of procedural rights during investigation, incarceration, trial, and appeal also provides innocent people with recourse against false arrest, unjustifiable imprisonment, and prosecutorial abuse. The value of vindicating innocence requires the establishment of rigorous courtroom process. During the 1960s the criminal justice system also became more equitable for indigent defendants by providing them with the right to counsel and other essential components to a fair trial.

Changing Times

The Warren Court expanded American notions of justice, equality, due process, and individual liberty. It established a two-part framework of government for determining both its limited authority and its obligations to the people. After a deliberately slow-paced start in school desegregation, the Court required states to integrate without delay. Although the Court failed to provide adequate remedial guidelines in the sentencing stage of *Brown v.*

Board of Education, the substantive portion of that case heralded principles underlying the Civil Rights Act of 1964. *Brown,* further, turned out to be central to desegregating other areas, like lunch counters.

In the field of family privacy, *Griswold* was about the right to be let alone from government interference in matters of conjugal intimacy. *Loving* was about both negative and positive constitutional rights. States not only are barred from interfering with interracial marriages, they must also recognize the legality of those unions by providing mixed couples with marriage licenses. Beyond that, states must provide interracial couples with the same intestate, property, and parental rights as any other spouses.

A similar twofold government duty exists in the realm of elections. The government is barred from interfering with the right to vote and is responsible for drawing districts to guarantee that each eligible voter's ballot counts equally in choosing congressional representatives. In *Gray v. Sanders, Wesberry v. Sanders,* and *Reynolds v. Sims,* the Warren Court set a voter equality standard to end favoritism on the basis of economic status and place of residence. Including *Harper v. Virginia Board of Elections* (1966), as well, which invalidated the use of poll taxes as voting qualifications, the Court's equal protection findings enabled the poor to enter the political tent of democracy. In Justice Douglas's words in *Harper,* "Wealth, like race, creed, or color, is not germane to one's ability to participate intelligently in the electoral process."[67]

As for criminals, their rights can be limited, and their freedom of movement denied, but only when the procedures used for their convictions meet constitutional prerequisites. The ability of the police sometimes to solve crimes through illegal searches or interrogations of unrepresented suspects does not justify the risks that the wide net of authoritarian behavior casts on innocent citizens. The Court sought to provide proper assistance at trial and at first appeal, granting indigents the right to counsel in *Gideon* and *Douglas.* Those decisions placed the cost of indigent legal representation on states.

The Warren Court blazed a trail for the jurisprudence of individual rights. The Burger Court went on to expand Fourteenth Amendment protections against discrimination on the basis of gender, alienage, or illegitimacy. But as with any other judicial decision, Warren Court precedents were subject to later qualification. To that end, the Burger Court established the intent requirement in equal protection claims, refusing to countenance lawsuits based only on a government program's disparate impact on a protected class. That left a legal loophole for governments to adopt policies that were not overtly racist but tended to substantially disadvantage minorities or women. During that period, the Court also found unconstitutional race-conscious policies for helping historically disadvantaged groups achieve equality. Decreased concern was also shown for protecting indigents' right to counsel, as the Court refused to extend the requirement for states to provide them with counsel in cases accepted by state supreme courts for discretionary review.[68]

On the desegregation of schools, the Burger Court periodically tolerated de facto segregation. Initially, it seemed willing to provide school districts with guidelines, finding mandatory school busing to be legitimate. In subsequent years, the Court in *Milliken v. Bradley* (1974) rejected redrawing school districts beyond the areas directly affected by discrimination, countenancing suburban flight of white students and the increasingly black character of urban schools like those in Detroit. Rather than allowing school boards to provide overall integration in districts with "racially imbalanced schools," the Supreme Court rejected the extension of desegregation orders outside the boundaries of a school district that a court had determined to be segregated. *Milliken* initiated a pattern for rejecting lower court desegregation orders. Neither did the Court consider education to be a constitutional right, and hence, in *San Antonio Independent School District v. Rodriguez,* rejected the claim that school finances must be equalized.[69]

The Rehnquist Court refused to provide federal court oversight for desegregation as long as school boards were "unlikely [to] return to [their] former ways." Its emphasis was no longer on raising a unified citizenry or maintaining affirmative state obligations but on a formalistic dichotomy of federal and state functions. Burger and Rehnquist Court decisions legitimized the resegregation of public schools. The lack of judicial oversight enabled schools to rely on programs closely related to the freedom-of-choice plans the Warren Court had found to be smokescreens for retaining racial separation.[70]

In the area of criminal law, the Burger Court concerned itself more with getting accurate evidence than with establishing constitutional rules for criminal procedure.[71] The Rehnquist Court provided additional leeway to police officers, refusing to extend protections against abuse in cases of pretextual searches, upholding arrests for minor traffic violations, and countenancing some failures to give Miranda warnings that produced self-incriminating statements which were not later used at trial.[72]

By eliminating disproportionate voting districts, the Warren Court did much to end voting discrimination. Certain roadblocks remain, though, preventing the complete implementation of the "one person, one vote" maxim of *Reynolds* and *Wesberry*. Certain states continue to prohibit ex-felons from voting. Furthermore, as the 2004 presidential election showed, different voting devices, such as keypunch voting machines, make technological failures that result in discarded votes more likely in some districts than in others.

Felons and ex-felons are the most politically excluded of adult United States citizens. In 1970 the vast majority of states had laws disqualifying felons from their voting rolls. Some statutes denied voting rights for infamous crimes, others for any felony; still others enumerated specific crimes as making perpetrators ineligible to vote. There were restrictions that could logically be justified. For example, Massachusetts and New Hampshire disenfranchised anyone who engaged in treason or corrupt practices dealing with an election. Other state statutes, however, barred persons convicted of crimes completely unrelated to the franchise, like bigamy, fornication, sodomy, and miscegenation. A person could lose the right to vote in Alabama for crimes ranging from vagrancy to spouse beating; in North Dakota all that was needed was a conviction for breaking a water pipe; in Ohio, horse stealing was enough; not to be outdone, Texas included conviction for theft of "any wool, mohair, and edible meat."[73]

As early as 1890, in a case involving convicted polygamists, the Supreme Court established that states can withhold voting rights from felons. The Court returned to the issue in 1974. Justice William H. Rehnquist, before becoming the chief justice, wrote for the majority in *Richardson v. Ramirez*. He found that the Equal Protection Clause does not prevent states from disenfranchising felons. His reasoning was based on the section 2 of the Fourteenth Amendment, which contains an injunction against abridging male inhabitants' right to vote, except for those who participated in a "rebellion, or other crime." That section of the Constitution, according to Rehnquist, signifies that withholding the vote from any felon is not an equal protection violation.[74]

Rehnquist's conclusion allows states to prohibit felons from voting even for convictions entirely unrelated to the franchise. Such an understanding leaves the recovery of political equality to the discretion of state and local officials, rather than of the federal government. That level of elective control enabled the Redeemed South to disenfranchise eligible voters by arbitrary devices like the Black Codes, labor contracts, and vagrancy laws.

Given section 2's specific provision about rebellion and its initial purpose of disqualifying ex-Confederate officers, a compelling reason for disenfranchisement can extend to certain political crimes, such as treason or election fraud. But for a jury to determine whether such a disqualification is appropriate, a prosecutor should prove beyond a reasonable doubt the existence of politically aggravating factors to warrant the deprivation of this right. Without connecting disenfranchisement to any political issue the due process interests of citizens with unique representative interests remains precarious.

Since *Richardson* was decided, the Court has found one exception to its rule. In *Hunter v. Underwood,* another opinion Rehnquist drafted, disenfranchisement provisions that were adopted for discriminatory purposes did not withstand equal protection scrutiny. That holding, while positive in its own right, has limited impact since few state provisions were overtly adopted to exclude classes of citizens.[75]

Today, thirty-four states deny the vote to some felons who are no longer in jail, and fourteen deny the vote to ex-felons even if they were sentenced to parole or probation. Nationwide, in 2000, those laws disenfranchised roughly 4.7 million voters. The significance of this practice on the "one person, one vote" standard is dramatic. One study estimated that if Florida did not disenfranchise ex-felons, Albert A. Gore, Jr., would have gained between thirty-one thousand and sixty-two thousand votes, easily winning of the state's electoral votes and making him the president of the United States, rather than George W. Bush. At their core, these laws deny convicted persons the opportunity to exert their political will. In the terminology of the American revolutionaries, they are slaves even after serving their sentences. Not all states take so draconian an approach. Maine and Vermont lie at the other end of the spectrum, permitting even prisoners to cast votes. The current diversity in statutes governing felon franchise renders the "one person, one vote" partly dependent on state policy. With so essential a right as voting at stake, national uniformity of policy is necessary for establishing equal representation.[76]

CHAPTER THIRTEEN

Sketches of the Continuing Legal Effort

The Warren Court and the Johnson administration consummated reforms that tied the equal protection of liberty to the general welfare. Their groundbreaking achievements were tempered by later permutations of the Supreme Court and presidential administrations, but their grand achievements remain intact. Overt segregation in schools and public places of accommodation has ended, "one person, one vote" is the national standard, political dissent has become more acceptable, criminal defendants have nationally recognized procedural protections, and the right to privacy is embedded in constitutional theory. The American people have continued on their unending quest of living up to the ideals of the Declaration of Independence.

In this chapter I take a look at some of the most recent accomplishments in the realm of civil rights, but I by no means intend to provide an exhaustive review. I recognize the risks of confronting contemporary passions but think it necessary to reflect on a few areas where strides have been made while significant challenges remain. I touch upon several tangentially related areas, well aware that they are somewhat disparate. Unwilling to set myself up as a seer, I take in the main a descriptive rather than critical approach.

Women's Status

By the early 1970s women had made great strides. The most striking achievements were in political participation, gains in the labor force, inclusion on juries, property ownership, and independence in contracting. More women than ever before obtained college and advanced degrees, became professionals, and were elected to public offices. Domestic violence and sexual harassment in the workplace became legally actionable problems. Despite these gains, gender inequality remains a persistent problem. Even today women lack economic parity and are the predominant victims of domestic violence, and their reproductive choices are still subject to a political game of ping pong.

Feminists influenced President Nixon to appoint a Task Force on Women's Rights, and prevailed on Presidents Gerald R. Ford and Jimmy Carter to establish similar advisory councils. Nixon, like his predecessor, Johnson, also supported the Equal Rights Amendment. The amendment easily passed in the House of Representatives on June 15, 1970, but on its first round in the Senate it failed to garner the needed support. During the next Congress, however, the amendment passed in the Senate by a vote of 84-8. The proposed amendment had significant backing during the ratification process, but failed by three votes to get the needed thirty-eight-state approval.

The Supreme Court of the United States had long countenanced laws overtly limiting women's opportunities. States were given free rein to prohibit women from working as anything from attorneys to bartenders. State legislation treating women and men differently remained mostly unchecked until 1971, when the Court found that an Idaho statute treating male and female estate administrators differently violated the Equal Protection Clause of the Constitution. Chief Justice Burger held that preferring male administrators was an "arbitrary legislative choice" that was unjustifiable by any reasonable legislative purpose.[1]

At the time, feminists were pursuing a dual agenda of pushing for ratification of the ERA and demanding recognition of their existing constitutional rights. Ruth Bader Ginsburg argued the next major case before the Supreme Court, *Frontiero v. Richardson.* The lawsuit had been brought by a lieutenant in the United States Air Force who wanted to receive dependent benefits for her husband. Such benefits were automatically granted to the wives of male service members, but women in the air force were required to demonstrate their husbands' need for support. Justice Brennan wrote the Court's judgment on the merits, but he was unable to get majority consensus for his rationale. Brennan thought that like race and nationality, gender was an immutable characteristic. As with discrimination based on race or nationality, gender discrimination was invidious, "relegating the entire class of females to inferior legal status without regard to the actual capabilities of its individual members." Recent congressional passage of the ERA and the previous decade's enactment of statutes against gender discrimination—specifically the Equal Pay Act and Title VII—indicated to Brennan that Congress also considered arbitrary gender discrimination to be invidious and hence subject to strict judicial scrutiny. Three of the justices who concurred in the case did not, however, agree that gender was a "suspect classification."[2]

The Court settled on the current judicial level of scrutiny for gender-based classifications in 1976. Forced to lower his expectations, Justice Brennan proposed an intermediate scrutiny test to get a consensus in *Craig v. Boren*. Gender classifications can withstand constitutional challenges only if the government has important rationales for relying on them and the means it uses are "substantially related to achievement of those objectives." Applying that standard, the court found that a lower drinking age for females than males violated the Equal Protection Clause.[3]

The Court affirmed the intermediate scrutiny standard when Joe Hogan filed a lawsuit against the Mississippi University for Women. The institution provided instruction to women in several fields. Hogan applied and was rejected by the nursing program at MUW because of his sex. He was permitted to audit classes, however, in lieu of admission. The Court ultimately held that no such "mechanical application of traditional, often inaccurate, assumptions about the proper roles of men and women" could justify the university's policy.[4]

The same level of scrutiny applied to a 1996 case, with the now-Justice Ginsburg writing for majority in *United States v. Virginia*. The Virginia Military Institute sought to maintain an all-male student body. The Court found that VMI's rejection of any female applicant relied on an unwarranted stereotype about women. Differences between the sexes, the Court made clear, were a "cause for celebration" but "not for denigration." The automatic exclusion of women, without providing any of them the opportunity to demonstrate the ability to perform well in the VMI setting, was not substantially related to an "exceedingly persuasive justification." The government has an obligation to treat individuals equally, without impairing women's opportunities by confining them to professions that have traditionally been held by females. Neither had Virginia escaped liability when it opened the Virginia Women's Leadership Institute. Just as in the race segregation case *Sweatt v. Painter*, the newly built institution qualitatively lagged behind the long-established school in instruction, prestige, faculty quality, and course offerings. Ginsburg considered the VMI decision to be a culmination of decades of effort, telling an audience at the University of Virginia School of Law that "there is no practical difference between what has evolved and the ERA."[5]

The reliance on intermediate scrutiny for gender discrimination cases, rather than the more stringent burden of proof Justice Brennan proffered in *Frontiero*, permits different treatment of men and women based on their distinct biological characteristics. That exception to the overall bar against discrimination was the determining factor in *Nguyen v. INS* (2001). The Court in that case ruled that a father who petitions the Immigration and Naturalization Service to naturalize his noncitizen, illegitimate child must provide proof of paternity before the child's eighteenth birthday. On the other hand, a mother petitioning for the same noncitizen child need not provide any proof beyond a birth certificate. Justice Anthony M. Kennedy, a moderate conservative writing for the Court, found that the legal distinction between unmarried mothers and unmarried fathers was predicated on a biological reality, rather than simply on a stereotype. Women bear their children, while unmarried fathers have no automatic physical confirmation of paternity. Failure to provide that information to INS ended a father's bid to stop deportation proceedings instituted against his son.[6]

From an intermediate scrutiny standpoint, the Court might have remanded the case for the individualized evaluation it ordered in the VMI case. The father might then have provided a DNA sample to prove his paternity. Even more poignant criticism of the decision was offered in Justice O'Connor's dissent. According to her, the holding smacked of the "paradigmatic . . . historic regime that left women with responsibility, and freed men from responsibility." The gender-based immigration classification was premised on an impermissible administrative stereotype, O'Connor went on to say, "that mothers are significantly more likely than fathers . . . to develop caring relationships with their children." Rather than make a decision based on generalization, the dissent held that the Constitution requires greater reflection on particular circumstances. Indeed, Nguyen's father had raised the child, who "apparently . . . lacked a relationship with his mother."[7]

A 2003 decision gave hope that despite the holding in *Nguyen*, in O'Connor's words, precedents on gender discrimination might continue to have "depth and vitality." In *Nevada Department of Human Resources v. Hibbs*, the Court recognized Congress's authority to require state governments to abide by the Family Medical Leave Act's provision for family emergencies. The extent to which states still rely on gender discrimination, the Court recognized, extends to "stereotype-based beliefs about the allocation of family duties." The "gender stereotype" that "women's family duties trump those of the workplace" had a historically negative impact on "the hiring and promotion of women." The federal government can prohibit the use of that stereotype by codifying national standards of gender equality.[8]

Traditional female roles were also challenged in reproductive decisions. *Roe v. Wade* has withstood decades of withering attacks. The decision to recognize women's right to abort a fetus involved challenges to criminal abortion statutes from Texas and Georgia. Justice Harry A. Blackmun derived women's right to reproductive privacy from the "Fourteenth Amendment's concept of personal liberty." *Roe* was an extension of the argument about constitutional "penumbras" found in *Griswold.* A woman's right to abort her fetus was reserved to the people through the Ninth Amendment and cannot be taken away by state fiat, the Court found. That right is not unqualified and must be balanced against important governmental interests in a woman's health and, as the she nears delivery, the survival of the fetus.[9]

Instead of leaving the contours of change to the gradual operation of the states, as the Court had in *Brown v. Board of Education,* Justice Blackmun provided a verifiable framework. During the first trimester, "the abortion decision and its effectuation must be left to the medical judgment of the pregnant woman's attending physician." Throughout the second trimester, a state may "regulate the abortion procedure in ways that are reasonably related to maternal health." In the final stage of pregnancy, "the stage subsequent to viability," a state may promote its interest in "the potentiality of human life" by regulating or proscribing "abortion except where it is necessary, in appropriate medical judgment, for the preservation of the life or health of the mother."[10]

In a later decision, *Planned Parenthood v. Casey,* four justices argued that the trimester framework was not central to *Roe.* The key, for them, was the proper trigger for governmental interest, which they determined was when the fetus becomes viable. Thus the plurality linked technological advance—an increasing ability to keep premature babies alive—with the constitutional right to privacy. Most recently, in 2000, a majority of the Court reaffirmed *Casey*'s conclusion that the state may not place an undue burden on a "woman's decision before fetal viability."[11]

The Supreme Court has also found that parental consent laws are sometimes permissible but become unconstitutional when they lack an exception for girls seeking emergent abortions.[12] As for spousal consent requirements, the Court has determined that they are never permissible because of the risk some women would face at the hands of abusive domestic partners if they were required to disclose a decision to abort.[13] Irrespective of the right to personal liberty involved, the Court has found, the government is not required to subsidize low-income women who cannot afford to have elective abortions. That decision renders indigent women less able to exercise their recognized right than those who are affluent or in the middle-income brackets.[14]

Women also found allies in Congress during the period of Supreme Court equal protection initiatives. The original draft of Title VII lacked any mention of women in its provisions on employment discrimination. When congressional committees were debating the bill, no organization even submitted any testimony about the propriety of including women among the protected groups. Even the amendment that did add women to the bill was a fluke, opposed by the Johnson administration, whose attorney general, Nicholas Katzenbach, argued that including "sex" in Title VII was likely to torpedo the entire omnibus civil rights bill.[15]

Katzenbach enlisted the help of Oregon Representative Edith Green, who argued that including a provision against employer discrimination of women would lead to the bill's demise. She considered it more important to end racial discrimination, since "for every discrimination that has been made against a woman in this country there has been 10 times as much discrimination against the Negro of this country." The amendment's sponsor was Virginia Representative Howard Smith. His purpose was either to scuttle the entire civil rights bill or, in lieu of that, to make sure that white women were not forced into low-paying jobs by employment provisions on behalf of black men. Except for Green, all the women in Congress supported the amendment. The House and then the Senate passed it, and its inclusion by no means slowed civil rights momentum.[16]

As for the other groups designated by Title VII—those defined by race, color, religion, and national origin—discrimination because of gender can be proven by either disparate treatment or disparate impact. A complainant bringing a lawsuit must prove either that the employer intentionally discriminated based on gender or that the employer's seemingly neutral practices had an unequally negative effect on the protected group. The burden then shifts to the employer to prove the allegations false or to show that the different treatment was based on some business necessity rather than on illegal discrimination. The claimant may afterward seek to demonstrate that the employer's response is merely pretextual.

Another important law dealing with gender discrimination is Title IX of the Education Amendments of 1972, which relies on Congress's constitutional spending authority. The statute prohibits public and private primary, secondary, and postsecondary schools that receive federal funds from discriminating based on sex. As for colleges, they must provide opportunities that are "substantially proportionate" to their male and female enrollments or demonstrate a responsiveness that "fully and effectively" adapts to the "interest and abilities" of both sexes. Private claims predicated on Title IX must be based on intentional discrimination. A question that the Court has left unresolved is whether, as with Title VII, private causes of action can challenge facially neutral educational practices that operate to the disproportionate disadvantage of women. As in other areas of civil rights law, private schools not receiving federal funding are given a pass, not being covered by the law's provisions.[17]

Title IX's greatest accomplishment lies in its provision for equal opportunities for male and female athletes, allowing females to participate in amateur athletics as never before. Before the enactment of Title IX, 300,000 girls participated in high school sports, and fewer than 32,000 women were involved at the intercollegiate level. By 2002, 2.8 million girls were in high school athletic programs and 170,000 women were participating in college sports. In some cases, women who otherwise might have been unable to afford a higher education found an opportunity to obtain one through athletic scholarships. In addition to the host of professions higher education opened to these women, their experience in college athletics enabled some to enter professional sports in the Women's National Basketball Association, the Women's Professional Volleyball League, and the Women's United Soccer Association.[18]

Congress also demonstrated its commitment to women's rights through a variety of lesser-known provisions. Prohibitions against gender discrimination are included in laws as varied as the Federal Water Pollution Control Act, the Comprehensive Health Manpower Training Act, amendments to the Works and Economic Development Act and the Appalachian Regional Development Act, and the Nurses Training Act.[19]

In one instance, the Supreme Court gutted a 1994 statute that provided a federal civil remedy, including compensatory and punitive damages, for the victims of gender-motivated crimes.[20] Women are overwhelmingly, albeit not exclusively, the victims of sexual violence. The United States Department of Justice reported that in 1998, 72 percent of intimate murder victims and 85 percent of the victims of nonlethal intimate violence were women. In 2002 and 1993 women were the victims of 87 percent of all rapes, sexual assaults, robberies, aggravated assaults, and simple assaults at the hands of intimates. Despite women's increased opportunities in work and education, the threat of physical injury hindered hundreds of thousands of women from fully entering professional and social fields. Individuals who were unable to work because of injuries sustained at the hands of spouses or boyfriends benefited little from Title VII. To avert gender-based attacks, many women avoid taking jobs "in certain areas or at certain hours that pose a significant risk." Battered women sometimes absent themselves from work to recover from injuries or simply to prevent anyone from seeing the physical signs of brutality.[21]

Legislative committees investigated gender-motivated violence over the course of four years. The "mountain of data" compiled—which indicated that violence against women significantly affects interstate commerce—came from nine congressional hearings, more than one hundred witnesses, and reports from gender bias task forces in twenty-one states. After analyzing the information, authors of a Senate report concluded that "gender-based crimes and the fear of gender-based crimes restricts movement, reduces employment opportunities, increases health expenditures, and reduces consumer spending." The Violence Against Women's Act (VAWA) addressed crimes targeting women within the context of gender discrimination law. The statute allocated funding for battered women's shelters, education, and hotlines. More controversially, it provided victims with a civil remedy against abusers. Offenders were required to pay victims restitution, which might include medical services, physical and occupational therapy and rehabilitation, temporary housing, and child care. Congresspersons determined that ordinary tort and criminal law is insufficient to deter violence against women because it involves harm to a group rather than solely to an individual. As with other civil rights statutes, VAWA sought to protect an entire class of persons from harms that Congress regarded as limitations on their ability to compete equally in the national economy.[22]

A federal law against these national harms was essential because, as the congressional conference found, "existing bias and discrimination in the criminal justice system often deprives victims of crimes of violence motivated by gender of equal protection of the laws and the redress to which they are entitled." State procedures that require polygraph tests, prompt reporting, and explanation of previous relationship with an attacker subject the victims of intimate cruelty to shame that no other criminal complainants suffer. Criminal and civil laws against random acts of violence have proven to be inadequate for halting gender-motivated violations that diminish the welfare of millions of Americans. Congressional reliance on its Fourteenth Amendment section 5 authority to pass the law appeared to be foolproof. That provision, along with similar ones in the Thirteenth and Fifteenth Amendments, was meant to empower legislators and to inhibit judges bent on thwarting civil rights in a manner similar to the Court's obliteration of black citizenship in *Dred Scott*.[23]

In *United States v. Morrison*, the Rehnquist Court refused to defer to congressional findings. It decided that VAWA's civil remedy provision was an unconstitutional intrusion into state powers. Congress's power to protect civil rights was not triggered because the act dealt with private conduct rather than state action, a doctrine established more than a century earlier in the *Civil Rights Cases*. The Warren Court had decided not to overturn that doctrine, relying on the Commerce Clause instead to uphold civil rights legislation in *Heart of Atlanta Motel* and *Katzenbach v. McClung*. Rehnquist garnered the support of four other justices in *Morrison* for his long-standing belief that Congress may regulate only conduct having a substantial effect on the national economy. VAWA did not meet this standard according to the majority because it prohibited "noneconomic, violent criminal conduct based solely on that conduct's aggregate effect on interstate commerce." The opinion diminished Congress's ability to enact laws against civil rights violations. Congress reenacted VAWA in 2000 but without the civil remedy provision.[24]

Affirmative Action

While violence disrupts some women's careers, the overall place of women in the job market steadily improved, as we have seen, after World War II. Affirmative action has expanded recruitment, hiring, and retention opportunities for groups that have historically been subject to discrimination, such as women and racial, ethnic, or national origin minorities. Those programs are not meant to equalize social stations; instead, the underlying purpose of affirmative action is remedial: it seeks to equalize social opportunities for groups who are at greater risk of discrimination. In working to diversify work and educational settings, government entities rely on both disincentives against discrimination and incentives for integration.

During the New Deal, the executive and legislative branches of government worked to end the Great Depression through a range of public works projects, many of them including components for the diversification of the workforce. For instance, a caveat to the Unemployment Relief Act of 1933 banned discrimination on the basis of race, color, or creed. So did statutes authorizing the creation of the Civilian Conservation Corps, the Civilian Pilot Training program, and the Nurses Training program. A 1941 executive order banned discrimination on the basis of race, creed, color, or national origin in defense industries. The government, employers, and unions were responsible for carrying out the initiative.[25]

President Kennedy's executive order 10,925 was the first to mention the need for "affirmative action to ensure that applicants are employed . . . without regard to their race, creed, color, or national origin." That order also established a President's Committee on Equal Employment Opportunity. The committee was responsible for monitoring the United States' policy of promoting and ensuring "equal opportunity for all qualified persons." The Justice Department was responsible for bringing lawsuits against offenders. Any contractor who violated nondiscriminatory policies was subject to sanction and revocation of any agreement with the government.[26]

The Johnson administration followed this overall policy and eventually added "sex" among the protected categories. The Nixon Department of Labor demanded greater specificity of contractor compliance. The Revised Order no. 4 of 1971 required government contractors to establish "goals and timetables" indicating that a contractor's "good faith efforts" were being "directed to correct the deficiencies." While goals were not to take the form of "rigid and inflexible quotas," they were to be "reasonably attainable" targets. Minority groups covered by the order included "Negroes, American Indians, Orientals, and Spanish Surnamed Americans." After some Labor Department revision to the order, a contractor could be evaluated for "having fewer minorities or women in a particular job classification than would reasonably be expected by their availability." Those provisions were meant to equalize contracting opportunities. In 1978 President Carter's Department of Labor advanced the policy behind Revised Order no. 4 through the Uniform Guidelines on Employee Selection Procedures. Accordingly, the Equal Employment Opportunity Commission adopted an empirically verifiable standard for evaluating whether a protected group was being adversely impacted by public and private employers.[27]

During the 1970s the Supreme Court began defining the constitutionally permissible parameters of affirmative action. Some of its key decisions dealt with university programs aimed at increasing minority enrollment. In the 1968–69 academic year, Big Ten Conference schools began enrolling more minority students, sometimes by quotas and other times by careful scrutiny of socioeconomic hardships. The University of Illinois' Project 500 recruited 250 black students to a freshman class of 5,630. Group 19 was the name of Indiana University's program for "disadvantaged" students, most of whom were black. The University of Michigan's minority enrollment increased to 1,000. Professional schools established their own programs. Law schools recognized the importance of increasing the number of minority lawyers and began recruiting blacks, Latinos, Asians, and Native Americans. From 1969 to 1978 the combined number of students in these groups increased from 1,552 to 3,571. Medical schools also showed a willingness to provide additional minority opportunities, with one survey reporting that ninety medical schools in 1974 had special recruitment programs. Between 1968 and 1972 the black representation in mainly white medical schools rose from 1.1 percent to 5.4 percent, representing roughly a fivefold increase in the number of African American medical students.[28]

Beginning in 1964 the University of California established Educational Opportunity Programs to increase the enrollment of minority and low-income students. The state's admission goals included economic and racial diversification. The University of California at Davis Medical School then reserved sixteen of one hundred admissions seats for qualified minority applicants. The school was particularly keen to recruit blacks, Chicanos, Asians, and Native Americans. Both special-enrollment applicants and others were evaluated by grade point averages, personal interviews, Medical College Admissions Test (MCAT) scores, recommendation letters, and extracurricular activities. Between 1971 and 1974, twenty-one black students, thirty Mexican Americans, and twelve Asians were admitted under the affirmative action program. During that period, one black student, six Mexicans, and thirty-seven Asians were admitted through the regular admissions process.[29]

Allan Bakke applied to the U.C. Davis Medical School first in 1973 and again in 1974. He was rejected both times even though his grade point average, MCAT score, and other scores were well above those of students admitted to the special program. Bakke challenged the program under Title VI of the Civil Rights Act of 1964 and the Equal Protection Clause.[30]

In *Regents of the University of California v. Bakke* (1978), the Court found the special-admission program to be based on racial and ethnic criteria. Such classifications were permissible only to further compelling government interests. Justice Powell agreed with four other justices that the program was unconstitutional, but he alone argued that it offended rights afforded by the Equal Protection Clause. He thought to be illegitimate any racial quotas deliberately limiting the enrollment of whites or any other racial group. Accordingly, the Court ruled, university admission programs may use race as one relevant factor for assessing applicants but not as the determining factor. Powell's approach does not preclude recruiting applicants based on their race but takes diversification to be a legitimate goal as long as the school gives weight to other desirable qualities, such as work background, leadership ability, compassion, "history of overcoming disadvantage," and "ability to communicate with the poor." However, limiting seats based on group preference for members of the majority or minority was found to violate individual rights.[31]

Justice Brennan, whose reasoning Justices White, Marshall, and Blackmun shared, regarded affirmative action programs that were administered for an important governmental reason to be constitutionally unproblematic. This foursome saw no problem with U.C. Davis's decision to remedy the "effects of past societal discrimination" on the basis of a race-conscious policy. They simply did not buy the argument that whites have the same risk of being shut out of the "majoritarian political process" as do minorities.[32]

In a separate concurrence, Justice Marshall sardonically pointed out that blacks had for centuries suffered class-based discrimination, belying Powell's individualized perspective. Given the underrepresentation of blacks among professionals, including physicians, he wrote, the university could "remedy the cumulative effects of society's discrimination by giving consideration to race in an effort to increase the number and percentage of Negro doctors."[33]

For years after *Bakke,* the Court failed to provide clear guidelines for affirmative action programs. A 1989 case found no compelling state interest for a city to set aside a proportion of its building contracts to minority-owned businesses. National patterns of discrimination were inadequate to justify such a program. Only a showing that there was previous contract discrimination in that city might have sufficed. And a 1995 case similarly invalidated the use of federal and state programs providing financial incentives to general contractors who hired minority-controlled subcontractors.[34]

Given the Supreme Court's repeated opposition to affirmative action programs, two 2003 challenges to the University of Michigan's race-conscious admissions programs were unlikely to fare any better. The first case, *Gratz v. Bollinger,* was filed by two rejected applicants to the university's College of Literature, Science and the Arts (LSA). They claimed that the university's undergraduate admissions procedures violated their Fourteenth Amendment right to equal protection. Admissions officers made decisions on the basis of a variety of factors that included racial and ethnic status, grade point average, and standardized test scores. Points were assigned to each category to help the university compare applicants' qualifications. Any candidates who were members of an underrepresented racial or ethnic group were automatically entitled to twenty points. Blacks, Latinos, and Native Americans were automatically deemed to be underrepresented minorities.[35]

LSA's allocation of a set number of points to members of minority groups, the Court found, constituted a quota that was "not narrowly tailored to achieve the interest in educational diversity." To increase minority enrollment the college relied on racial generalizations rather than on individuated evaluations of applicants' likelihood to contribute to educational diversity. One dissenting opinion regarded membership in a racial minority to be like any other characteristic, be it writing style, running speed, or reasoning ability, for which the university might set a numerical value. Another dissent found "no constitutional infirmity" in an inclusive plan. According to the latter line of thought, the college could correct legal and social practices that historically relegated the designated minorities to an inferior status. Rather than seeking to exclude whites, the policy was calculated to rectify "class-based discrimination" that persists despite decades of efforts to end it.[36]

As with the holding in *Gratz,* a companion decision, *Grutter v. Bollinger,* took an individuated perspective on affirmative action, but with diametrically opposite results. Both looked to Justice Powell's plurality opinion in *Bakke* for defining the extent to which the Equal Protection Clause permits government to promote the advancement of a race or ethnic group.[37] *Grutter* dealt with the admission policy of another University of Michigan institution. The university's Law School required admissions officials to evaluate a variety of applicant information, including undergraduate grades, standardized test scores, and several indicators about how potential students could enrich others' educational experiences. Race and ethnicity were among the nonacademic factors that the Law School considered. Expert testimony indicated that race was "an extremely strong factor" in the admission process, but "not the predominant factor." The minority student representation in the entering class would have dropped dramatically, from about 14.5 percent to 4 percent in 2000, if the law school were to have discontinued its affirmative action program.

Grutter expressed concern that racially conscious plans not unfairly burden "members of the favored racial and ethnic groups." Unpersuaded by Marshall's dissent to *Bakke,* the *Grutter* majority prohibited institutions from maintaining affirmative action programs to punish innocent parties for the persistence of social ills. To the contrary, those programs must add to the general welfare of the whole by infusing the educational setting with diverse perspectives. As in so many realms, matters of academic diversity individual rights were found to be intrinsically connected to the common good. Much as did *Brown v. Board of Education*'s footnote 11, *Grutter* relied on sociological studies indicating the benefits of classroom diversity. The Court found that obtaining a higher education among diverse classmates helps to prepare graduates for the challenges of a global marketplace, exposing students to others with differing life experiences, thereby undermining stereotypes. When schools train highly qualified students who represent a cross-section of the population, the "dream of one Nation, indivisible" is more likely "to be realized." Yet affirmative action cannot be allowed to continue indefinitely, but "must be limited in time."

A number of scholars have found *Grutter*'s insistence on individual treatment and its express embrace of a race-conscious policy to be incongruous.[38] A closer look might reveal that there is no contradiction between the two. The Court rejected any criterion that relied on overgeneralization about an individual's race or ethnicity as the determinant of contribution to the diversity of the classroom. There are infinite variations among members of any identifiable race or ethnicity. A minority student who grew up in an affluent household and attended excellent private schools is likely to have a perspective less at odds with that of his peers at an elite law school than would a majority race student who came from an impoverished home and went to inner-city schools. The reality in contemporary American society is that minority students, particularly blacks, Latinos, and Native Americans, are more likely to come from disadvantaged backgrounds than are whites, but the generality does not hold for all members of each respective group.[39] "Our Nation's struggle with racial inequality," as the Court characterized it, requires positive steps to end prejudices that create added barriers to any upward socioeconomic mobility. Race bias, as Justice Ginsburg pointed out in a concurrence to *Grutter*, continues to impede the realization "of our highest values and ideals," rendering liberal equality a yet unachieved national aspiration. Law school diversification is a positive step in that direction, but not when it automatically elevates race or ethnicity above any other relevant trait.

Children and Fair Process

For diversity in education to alter stereotypes, it cannot start in college. It must begin at the elementary and high school levels. Arguably the important children's rights decision in United States history was *Brown v. Board of*

Education. It not only changed the face of public education but also provided the judicial precedent for ending segregation in a variety of social settings. Later Courts, however, found that education was not a constitutionally protected right and allowed for wide disparities in financial resources available to public schools.[40] This left children in neighborhoods with lower real estate taxes at a great disadvantage for self-advancement in an industrialized computer age that increasingly relies on technical knowledge.

The state has a well-established right to provide special care to secure the health and safety of children well beyond their schooling. Far more than placement in underfunded schools, violence against the young puts them at risk for civic alienation. Children are more liable than adults to become victims of such violent crimes as battery, molestation, rape, and kidnapping. Because children are among the nation's most at-risk citizens, many of them defenseless against abuse by adults resulting in suffocation, drowning, severe shaking, scalding, and spinal fractures, government protections are essential. In 1995 the United States Department of Health and Human Services (HHS) found that the murder of children can be better prevented through improved cooperation of police, schools, judges, and child welfare counselors. HHS's report concluded that "the system created in the United States to ensure that adult homicides are thoroughly identified, investigated, and prosecuted is failing to serve infants and children who die of maltreatment." According to current Court doctrine, unless a social service agency actively puts children in danger, it cannot be held liable for failing to remove them from abusive parents. Neither can the police be held responsible for failing to enforce a restraining order against a parent violating a judicial decree. Child victims thus have no federal recourse against state agencies that neglect to jail or otherwise restrain abusers.[41]

For children in foster care, inadequate supervision sometimes leaves no feasible legal recourse. The Adoption and Safe Families Act of 1997 (ASFA) requires that "reasonable effort" be taken in foster care and adoption placements, a mandate so ambiguous that it invites state and local inefficiency. Its terms are just as unclear as the "all deliberate speed" standard was for school desegregation. On the plus side, ASFA requires state performance reports to track outcomes of programs and does not list "long-term foster care" among the permanent options for children. As of 2004 no state had met all the act's factors, indicating an endemic problem in need of further federal involvement.[42]

The longer a child is in foster care, the more at risk he or she is for engaging in criminal activity in later childhood or as an adult.[43] Fair criminal procedure is as essential to innocent children as it is to adults. Some of the most significant advances in children's rights occurred during the 1960s, when the Supreme Court began realizing that children have many of the same constitutional rights to due process in criminal procedures as adults do.[44]

In re Gault, a 1967 case, was essential for securing juveniles the right to a meaningful defense against criminal charges. Before then it was commonly believed that no attorneys were needed in juvenile proceedings. Cook County, Illinois, was the first to establish a juvenile court system in 1899; all but two states had juvenile courts by 1925, and every state had them by the mid-1940s. The function of juvenile courts was to be rehabilitative instead of punitive. They were to improve youthful characters rather than punish offenders. A 1964 survey found that in the nation's seventy-five largest cites, 81 percent of judges reported that 10 percent or fewer of children involved in delinquency cases in their courts were represented by attorneys. Ultimately, the decision of whether to appoint counsel or even to inform a child that he has the right to an attorney was at the discretion of judges. The 1967 President's Commission on Law Enforcement concluded that the juvenile court system had not significantly succeeded in "bringing justice and compassion to the child offender."[45]

The case that changed this dynamic began when Gerald Gault, a fifteen-years-old in Arizona, was charged with making lewd phone calls. Gault was taken to Children's Detention Home without any notice provided to his parents. The juvenile judge did not require the boy's accuser, a Mrs. Cook, to appear at the proceedings, nor did the judge himself speak to her at any time. At the end of a proceeding, in which Gault was unrepresented by counsel, the judge sentenced him to six years in an industrial school—a euphemistically named juvenile penitentiary. Had an adult been charged with using vulgar language, the term of imprisonment could not have exceeded two months. That sentencing disparity raised an equal protection concern, as Justice Black pointed out in his concurrence to *Gault*.

As no appeal was available in Arizona from this perfunctory juvenile proceeding, Gault's one available option was a habeas corpus petition, permitting him to argue that the confinement violated his constitutional right to receive due process of law. The majority opinion, written by Justice Abe Fortas, sardonically suggested that "the condition of being a boy does not justify a kangaroo court." The Bill of Rights, although not all of its protections apply to children, is not the sole province of adulthood, the Court ruled.

Gault acknowledged that there were benefits to dual juvenile and criminal systems, but the Court refused to shut its eyes to the high rate of recidivism, the lack of confidentiality about the juveniles' records, the failures to rehabilitate, and the partiality of juvenile adjudications. Those who were interned in juvenile homes, no matter how minor or major their offenses, lived not among their family but among guards, rapists, and violent offenders. The protections then available to juvenile respondents were entirely inadequate for the risks they faced.

The Supreme Court required the state henceforth to provide juveniles and their parents or guardians written notice of any delinquency proceedings that might result in institutional confinement. Where children's liberty might be curtailed, the Court made clear, the Fourteenth Amendment protects their right to the effective assistance of counsel who can guide them through the nuances of law. Gault's inability to confront the complainant also had infringed upon his right to a fair trial. Juveniles have a right to cross-examine their accusers, the Court found, and thereby to test the veracity of the inculpatory evidence against them. Neither can the state rely on self-incriminating statements unless juvenile respondents have first waived their right to remain silent. With the ruling, protection against the introduction of false statements into evidence became just as critical to juveniles as to hardened criminals.

Fortas's decision indicated that the entire juvenile justice system was in need of overhaul. The notion that children would fare better than they would in criminal court wound up being no more than a progressive hope, and social experimentation cannot justify the abridgement of constitutional rights. Procedural rights are essential for credible, rehabilitative sentencing. Yet *Gault* too requires some bolstering. For instance, while indigent children are assured the right to appointed counsel, financial circumstances are evaluated according to their parents' or guardians' resources. Sometimes waivers of counsel of children by middle-class or affluent families are predicated on concerns extraneous to their best interest, including how their parents' or guardians' monetary interests might be harmed.[46]

Three years after *Gault*, *In re Winship* established a burden of proof of "beyond a reasonable doubt" for both delinquency and criminal cases.[47] In *McKeiver v. Pennsylvania* (1971), however, the Court refused to extend the right of a jury trial, to which criminal defendants are constitutionally entitled, to delinquency proceedings. The case was an appeal from the trial court's denial of Joseph McKeiver's request for a jury hearing. He and twenty or thirty other youths chased down three teenagers and then took twenty-five cents from them. For this foolish but relatively innocuous prank, McKeiver was found delinquent for committing larceny and robbery, and for receiving stolen goods—all felony offenses. Evidence at the hearing indicated that juvenile proceedings were "substantially similar to a criminal trial": attorneys filed comparable motions in both, juveniles were charged with state criminal code violations, and children adjudicated as delinquents were confined to facilities resembling jails. The Supreme Court, nevertheless, refused to recognize the need for a jury to decide delinquency charges. Juvenile judges, it found, could conduct similarly "accurate factfinding." That reasoning fell short of explaining why jury trials were any different from other constitutional privileges the Court had determined to apply to juveniles, including the right to cross-examination and proof beyond a reasonable doubt. Of these, only jury trial is explicitly mentioned in the Constitution. Relying on any procedural device, including jury deliberation, makes for more adversarial hearings, but, more important, it minimizes the risks of mistake, abuse of discretion, and unwarranted confinement.[48]

The notion that "the consequences of [delinquency] adjudication are less severe than those flowing from verdicts of criminal guilt," which Justice Byron White's concurrence to *McKeiver* flagged, is also suspect, since at least twenty states rely, in part, on delinquency findings to enhance adult criminal sentences. The U.S. Sentencing Guidelines Manual also allows for serious juvenile offenses to be used as aggravating circumstances in adult-level sentencing.[49]

Several recent Supreme Court decisions have divided appellate courts on the continued use of juryless juvenile adjudications for adult sentence enhancement. A 2004 case, *Blakely v. Washington*, established that only facts determined by a jury can be used for sentence enhancement. In fact, relying on a judge's findings of fact for increasing sentences violates the Sixth Amendment. That decision followed on the heels of *Apprendi v. New Jersey* (2000), which required that all sentence-increasing factors be submitted to a jury. *Apprendi* built on a holding from the year before, *Jones v. United States*, which found the guarantees of jury trial, notice, and proof beyond a reasonable doubt indispensable to criminal justice.[50]

It remains unsettled how that line of cases will affect the use of juryless juvenile findings to enhance later adult sentences. The Ninth Circuit Court of Appeals understood *Apprendi* to allow only the use of prior juvenile "proceedings that afforded the procedural necessities of a jury trial and proof beyond a reasonable doubt." That intermediate appellate court refused to increase a criminal sentence based on a prior adjudication that foreclosed a juvenile's right to a jury. Only decisions rendered pursuant to the "triumvirate of procedural protections" identified in *Jones,* the court ruled, can be calculated for purposes of sentencing. To the contrary, the Eighth Circuit found that prior juvenile adjudications were exempted from the jury requirement and could function as "prior convictions" for sentencing enhancement. However the Supreme Court resolves this matter, the use of juvenile records originally obtained without a jury trial raises troubling concerns about procedural fairness.[51]

As in the field of criminal law, lack of procedural safeguards in the area of juvenile mental health law can interfere with children's civil rights. The due process requirements of *Gault* and *Winship* do not apply to childhood institutionalization. A child can be committed into a mental health ward without the fundamental fairness protections of delinquency hearings, much less a jury trial.

In *Parham v. J.R.* (1979), the Supreme Court countenanced relying on mental health professionals, rather than judges or administrative officers, as neutral diagnosticians for commitment determinations. Despite the confinement intrinsic to mental treatment, the Court regarded the issue as "essentially medical in character" and ruled that it could be decided by an "independent medical decisionmaking process." In most circumstances, the Court believed, parents and guardians would work for the child's best interest. To prevent parents from dumping their children into institutions, psychiatrists were to rely on interviews. "It is unrealistic to believe that trained psychiatrists, skilled in eliciting responses, sorting medically relevant facts, and sensing motivational nuances, will often be deceived about the family situation surrounding a child's emotional disturbance." Nevertheless, the Court acknowledged, "on occasion, parents may initially mislead an admitting physician or a physician may erroneously diagnose the child as needing institutional care." Despite the peril of unnecessary deprivation of freedom, the Court was unwilling to overturn the statutory and administrative scheme of more than thirty states with minimal procedural protections for institutionalized children.[52]

Several studies indicate that the mental health industry is not as objective as the Court represented it. To the contrary, some private-practice psychiatrists and private hospitals have a financial interest in enrolling more children, even when the cases are borderline to uncertain. Mental health professionals are not neutral in the same sense as judges, juries, or administrative hearing officers, none of whom have any pecuniary interest in institutionalized treatment. According to the National Institute of Mental Health, between 1980 and 1988, immediately after *Parham* was decided, the number of freestanding psychiatric facilities doubled. Another study found that from 1980 and 1984 the number of adolescents in private mental hospitals increased more than fourfold (from 10,764 to 48,375). Fewer than a third of these youths were found to be psychotic or to have other serious mental disturbances.[53]

The likelihood of accurately diagnosing a child during a brief initial screening at a hospital is less than can be expected from a full and fair hearing. Even if a minor needs urgently to be committed for posing an immediate risk to self or others, there is little reason to believe that a judicial or administrative adjudication could not follow within seventy-two hours. Indeed, most institutionalized adolescents are committed for behavior problems rather than for mental illnesses. The characterization of juvenile patients in mental health facilities has changed drastically in the past two decades. Previously, most juvenile patients experienced "severe disabilities or psychotic behavior," but now most of the youths "have eating disorders, run away, have problems in school, or are generally in disagreement with their parents or other authorities." In order to receive insurance reimbursement, some clinical staffs label these children as having mental disorders with menacing names, such as "conduct disorder, personality disorder, or transitional disorder." Such labels, and the accompanying stigmatization and deprivation of liberty, can be given to children who have never had a fair hearing on the merits of the diagnoses.[54]

Institutionalization in mental hospitals or private treatment programs involves many of the same due process concerns as incarceration. Once confined, the child can be placed in a locked ward, medicated, and required to undergo psychological treatment.[55] Before children who exhibit signs of mental instability are placed in closed-door psychiatric facilities, they should enjoy the same constitutional due process protections that *Gault* and *Winship* established for delinquents. States or private hospitals can notify the youths and parents of their alleged illnesses and why treatment would be beneficial. When parents seek commitment, a guardian ad litem could represent the children's interest. Most of all, children whose right to play and study in ordinary settings might be curtailed need the assistance of counsel who can call opposing experts and help a child in need of treatment find the best alternative. These points can be brought out during probable cause hearings that would allow juveniles to contest their detention. After that, a standard of beyond a reasonable doubt is just as important for extended mental health internment cases as for juvenile delinquency proceedings.

Several states, including Utah, Michigan, and California, have enacted protections for children that go well beyond the minimal due process rights recognized in *Parham*.[56] However, the lack of national uniformity carries with it all the same threats to civil rights that the nation has experienced throughout its history by leaving it up to states to decide whether to safeguard individual liberties against arbitrary deprivation.

Intimate Privacy

Individual privacy has received some of the most defining national safeguards against governmental intrusion. From 1954, when it decided *Brown v. Board of Education,* the Supreme Court regularly relied on the Fourteenth Amendment in its civil rights jurisprudence. The Court adopted its generation's sensibilities, born of the nation's traumatic experience with discrimination, to better realize the framers' assertion: "We hold these truths to be self-evident, that all men are created equal, that they are endowed by their Creator with certain unalienable Rights, that among these are Life, Liberty and the pursuit of Happiness.—That to secure these rights, Governments are instituted among Men." The federal government had long delegated its responsibility to "secure these rights" to the states, and they had instituted a series of differing, and sometimes disparate, civil rights regimes.

As a corrective measure, the Supreme Court gradually created a unitary standard of rights secured for the people by the Constitution. *Griswold v. Connecticut* established what should have been a self-evident principle: that government lacks the authority to interfere with intimate marital decisions. *Eisenstadt v. Baird* then expanded the right of contraception to unmarried couples. Married and unmarried persons' right to make various procreative decisions was further buttressed against governmental intrusion through *Roe v. Wade, Planned Parenthood v. Casey,* and *Carey v. Population Services.* That line of cases raised the question of whether states could criminalize gay and lesbian behavior or whether it falls within the realm of sexual privacy.[57]

The first legal challenge to criminal sodomy laws to make it to the Supreme Court was *Bowers v. Hardwick* (1986). Around the country, the trend had been to revoke such laws. While in 1961 all states outlawed sodomy, by 1986 more than half the states had curbed or dropped such restrictions, but twenty-four states and the District of Columbia persisted in criminalizing such private sexual behavior between consenting adults. *Bowers* reviewed the constitutionality of a Georgia prohibition that did not distinguish between homosexual and heterosexual sodomy. The punishment for conviction was between one and twenty years' imprisonment. After Michael Hardwick was arrested under that statute, the district attorney decided not to press charges against him. Hardwick then determined to vindicate his rights by filing suit in a federal court. Once the case made its way to the Supreme Court, the majority of justices were unsympathetic to Hardwick's claim that the statute infringed on his rights of privacy and association. Justice Byron R. White, who wrote the opinion, rejected the challenge to the law, finding it ungrounded in history and notions of "ordered liberty."

While Georgia's statute was facially neutral, White confined his analysis to homosexual sodomy. In finding that a state had a legitimate, rational reason for prohibiting that behavior, *Bowers* criminalized the sexual lifestyles of gays and lesbians. Such a result was divisive. It left undisturbed heterosexuals' nonprocreative privacy but refused to recognize the same privacy for same-gender relations; seemingly predicating the scope of constitutional principles on sexual orientation, a stance that seemed to many observers as illogical as the targeting of racial, ethnic, nationality, or gender groups. Like any other arbitrary classification, laws targeting gays and lesbians created a second-class citizenship, one that barred a large group of individuals from enjoying fundamental liberties secured by the Fourteenth Amendment.[58]

Some communities understood the decision as a license for denying not only constitutional privileges but statutory ones as well. The voters in Colorado relied on the exclusionary holding of *Bowers* to add to the state constitution a provision known as Amendment 2. Once ratified, the measure prohibited municipal and local governments from granting homosexuals protected status against discrimination. The popular measure came as a response to the enactment of ordinances in Boulder, Aspen, and Denver banning discrimination in "housing, employment, education, public accommodations, and health and welfare services." Amendment 2 nullified those public accommodations laws. That, the Supreme Court found in *Romer v. Evans* (1996), excluded gays, lesbians, and bisexuals from "the safeguards that others enjoy." The statute violated the Equal Protection Clause by imposing "broad and undifferentiated disability on a single named group." Colorado's constitutional provision was based an illegitimate government action that was "born of animosity toward the class of persons affected."[59]

In 2003 the Court took the next step of addressing the insult *Bowers* had leveled at the gay community. The corrective case, *Lawrence v. Texas,* was set in motion by a neighbor's false report of a weapons disturbance. When the Harris County Police Department of Houston arrived at John G. Lawrence's apartment, they encountered him intimately involved with another man. The two were arrested, kept in jail overnight, and later convicted under Texas's criminal prohibition against homosexual conduct. At the time, thirteen states still had laws against sodomy, and of those, four specifically targeted gays. The nation's overreliance on states to protect the civil rights of its citizens preserved this anomaly even after *Griswold, Eisenstadt,* and *Roe* had recognized consensual adult intimacy to be a fundamental right.[60]

Justice Kennedy, writing for the Court in *Lawrence,* approached privacy from a Due Process Clause perspective. That is, rather than considering whether gays' equal rights were violated, as Justice O'Connor did in her concurrence, Kennedy reflected on whether the Texas law infringed on a uniform constitutional right. While he found the equal protection approach "tenable," Kennedy decided not to pursue it for fear that neutral sodomy laws, treating "same-sex and different-sex participants" alike, might remain intact. *Bowers*'s claim that gay intimacy is solely about sexual contact, Kennedy wrote, was as demeaning as it would be to claim that the private affections of married couples are entirely predicated on coitus. Physical intimacy, in both cases, may be part of a more sublime connection on which individuals impart meaningful significance. Laws against sodomy sought to degrade individuals and to belittle their sense of dignity in a way similar to that under which school segregation statutes had engendered a feeling of inferiority. Rather than countenance such an anomaly of injustice, the Court overturned *Bowers,* using broad parameters for defining the limits of government and the breadth of personal liberty: "The State cannot demean" gays' and lesbians' "existence or control their destiny by making their private sexual conduct a crime." The Texas statute was "an invitation to subject homosexual persons to discrimination both in the public and in the private spheres."

The Court adopted a progressive perspective on the Constitution. The majority recognized that the nation's founders had not foreseen all the implications of the Enlightenment principles they had embraced. So, too, the framers of the Fourteenth Amendment may not have had the same notions of liberty as does our generation, but that does not mean the country is limited by their understanding. "They knew times can blind us to certain truths," Justice Kennedy explained, "and later generations can see that laws once thought necessary and proper in fact serve only to oppress." Each generation can reexamine principles to remove the arbitrary impediments to liberty.

Increased tolerance for gays did not come overnight. As with other civil rights progress in U.S. law, including recognition of racial and gender equality, developments came about gradually. The slow-moving tempo of constitutional law can never excuse the commission of injustices against individuals waiting for regime change. Demands for justice are most poignant when they are absolute in their renunciation of inequality, but their advocates must be realistic in their expectations. As with other areas of law, self-evaluation has enabled the country to understand that the harmless exercise of individual rights cannot be trumped by subordinating dogmas. The people's common good is reduced by the arbitrary infringement of one group's rights for the sake of a supremacist theory of citizenship. We are one nation, and we stand, stumble, or fall together. Denying opportunities to some creates intergroup friction, and it reduces the available pool of talent and creativity. The Preamble to the Constitution makes the federal government primarily responsible for the general welfare.

Supreme Court opinions have not been the sole vehicles of civil rights progress in the United States, although by the end of the New Deal they had become critical to the protection of democratic process and minority rights. Often—as with the Bill of Rights, the Reconstruction Amendments, and the Women's Suffrage Amendment—the Constitution had to be amended to better achieve parity among citizens. At other times, statutory enactments have been sufficient. The Citizenship Act of 1924, the Civil Rights Act of 1964, the Americans with Disabilities Act, and the Age Discrimination and Employment Act have worked wonders in opening the doors of opportunities to people who had long been hindered from fully enjoying the American Dream. The New Deal relied on presidential initiatives for relief against classist favoritism. The civil rights era was likewise fueled by a presidential passion for equality. Popular champions of rights—including abolitionists, feminists, and sit-in strikers—have drawn from the American tradition and demonstrated to the country where it fell short of its ideals and self-image. In each generation, there are reformers who work through popular government or governmental bodies to advance the causes of liberal equality.

From a nation conceived in liberty but born into slavery, gender inequality, and assumptions of ethnic superiority, evolved a nation conscious both of its great purpose to protect rights for the general welfare and of its many shortcomings. In this work I have surveyed the meandering road of enormous accomplishments and tragic shortfalls. Many stops and starts have led us to antidiscrimination laws and protections of political rights. Backsliding has at times undermined the expectations of rapturous progress. The United States emerges as a country willing to be self-critical and to continue its unending quest for civil rights.

Notes

Introduction

1. By this, I do not mean that Wechsler and Ely were unconcerned with rights. My point is rather that their constitutional theories focus on the acceptable parameters of governmental decisions rather than the outcome of those decisions. Wechsler, for instance, thought *Brown v. Board of Education,* the landmark case on school desegregation, was wrongly decided because it was predicated on attaining equal rights rather than on the application of neutral principles. Herbert Wechsler, *Toward Neutral Principles of Constitutional Law,* 73 Harv. L. Rev. 1 (1959). Ely thought "participational values" are procedural, but he was unable to entirely shed normative judgments, saying at one point that "participational values [are] the values which our Constitution has preeminently and most successfully concerned itself." John Hart Ely, Democracy and Distrust: A Theory of Judicial Review 75 (1980). Elsewhere Ely wrote, "A neutral and durable principle may be a thing of beauty and a joy forever. But if it lacks connection with any value the Constitution marks as special, it is not a constitutional principle and the Court has no business imposing it." John H. Ely, *The Wages of Crying Wolf: A Comment on Roe v. Wade,* 82 Yale L.J. 920, 949 (1973). For criticism on the process-based school *see* Saikrishna B. Prakash and John C. Yoo, *The Puzzling Persistence of Process-Based Federalism Theories,* 79 Tex. L. Rev. 1459 (2001); Laurence H. Tribe, *The Puzzling Persistence of Process-Based Constitutional Theories,* 89 Yale L.J. 1063, 1067–72 (1980); Ronald Dworkin, Freedom's Law: The Moral Reading of the American Constitution 76–81 (1996). For other process school authors *see* Henry M. Hart, Jr., and Albert M. Sacks, The Legal Process (1958); Harry H. Wellington, *The Nature of Judicial Review,* 91 Yale L.J. 486 (1982); Harry H. Wellington, Interpreting the Constitution: The Supreme Court and the Process of Adjudication (1990).

2. I distinguish fundamental rights from basic rights. I take the former to be those rights everyone has by nature—say, the right to travel—and the latter to be state created, like the right to get a driver's license. *See* Alexander Tsesis, Destructive Messages: How Hate Speech Paves the Way for Harmful Social Movements ch. 10 (2002).

3. Mary L. Dudziak, Cold War Civil Rights: Race and the Image of American Democracy (2000); Derrick Bell, *Brown v. Board of Education and the Interest Convergence Dilemma,* 93 Harv. L. Rev. 518 (1980).

4. Gunnar Myrdal, An American Dilemma: The Negro Problem and Modern Democracy (1944).

5. Rogers M. Smith, Civic Ideals 6, 499–500 (1997).

6. Foner, The Story of American Freedom xx (1998).

7. Kammen, A Machine That Would Go of Itself: The Constitution in American Culture (1986).

CHAPTER ONE. Liberty through Revolution

1. Samuel Adams, The Rights of the Colonists (Report of the Committee of Correspondence to the Boston Town Meeting Nov. 20, 1772), *available at* http://www.consti tution.org/bcp/right_col.htm; Peter Laslett, *Introduction* to John Locke, Two Treatises of Government 125–26 (Peter Laslett ed., rev. ed. 1965); Alexander Hamilton, The Farmer Refuted 38 (1775).

2. *Result of the Convention of Delegates Holden at Ipswich . . ., in* Memoir of Theophilus Parsons 359, 365 (1778; rpt. 1861); John Adams, A Dissertation on the Canon and Feudal Law, *in* 3 The Works of John Adams 447, 449 (1782; Charles F. Adams ed., 1851); Hampden, The Alarm (no. III) (Oct. 15, 1773).

3. Alexander Hamilton, The Farmer Refuted, *supra,* at 6 ("the origin of all civil government, justly established, must be a voluntary compact, between the rulers and the ruled; and must be liable to such limitations, as are necessary for the security of the *absolute rights* of the latter"); Alexander Hamilton, The Full Vindication of the Measures of the Congress 5 (1774); *Result of the Convention of Delegates Holden at Ipswich . . ., supra,* at 367.

4. Spartanus, *The Interest of America,* New-Hampshire Gazette, June 15, 1776; John Locke, The Second Treatise 54, *in* Two Treatises of Government 346 (1690; Peter Laslett ed., rev. ed. 1965).

5. James MacGregor Burns, The Vineyard of Liberty 23–25 (1982); Forrest McDonald, Novus Ordo Seclorum: The Intellectual Origins of the Constitution 10 (1985); Eric Foner, *The Meaning of Freedom in the Age of Emancipation,* 81 J. Am. Hist. 435, 439 (1994).

6. William Patten, Discourse at Hallifax in the County of Plymouth, July 24th 1766 (1766); James Iredell, *To the Inhabitants of Great Britain, in* 1 Life and Correspondence of James Iredell 205, 217 (1774; 1857) (liberty "is the right of every human creature"); Silas Downer, A Discourse, Delivered in Providence . . . the 25th Day of July, 1768, at 4–5 (1768); Arthur Young, Political Essays Concerning the Present State of the British Empire 19 (1772).

7. Thomas Shippen, *Loose Thoughts on Government, in* 6 American Archives, 730, 730 (1776; Peter Force, ed., 4th ser. 1846); Thomas Paine, Dissertations on Government, *in* 2 The Complete Writings of Thomas Paine 367, 372 (Philip S. Foner ed., 1945); John Hurt, The Love of Our Country 10 (1777); John Dickinson, New York Journal, or The General Advertiser, Apr. 21, 1768, page 1, column 3.

8. The Federalist no. 45, at 309 (James Madison) (Jacob E. Cooke ed., 1961); *id.* no. 51, at 348, 352 (Madison); *id.* no. 10, at 61 (Madison) (government's role is to "secure the public good, and private rights"); Samuel West, *Sermon Preached before the Honorable Council . . . May 29th, 1776, in* The Pulpit of the American Revolution 259, 297 (1776; John W. Thornton ed., 1860); Jacob Duché, *The Duty of Standing Fast in Our Liberties, in* The Patriot Preachers of the American Revolution, 1766–1783, at 74, 81–82 (1775; 1862).

9. *Result of the Convention of Delegates Holden at Ipswich . . ., supra,* at 365; Samuel Adams, *supra.*

10. *In* 1 The Works of John Adams 193, 193 (1776; Charles F. Adams ed., 1851); John Dickinson, *An Address to the Committee of Correspondence in Barbados, in* 1 The Writings of

John Dickinson 251, 262 (1766; Paul L. Ford ed., 1895); Letter from Samuel Adams to John Adams (Nov. 25, 1790), *in* 4 The Writings of Samuel Adams 344, 344 (Harry A. Cushing ed., 1908); James Otis, The Rights of the British Colonies Asserted and Proved 10 (1764).

11. Virginia Declaration of Rights n.p. (June 12, 1776); 1 The Records of the Federal Convention of 1787, at 605 (July 13, 1787; Max Farrand ed., 1911).

12. James Madison, Speech June, 6, 1787, *reprinted in* 1 The Records of the Federal Convention on 1787, *supra*, at 134–36; Virginia Declaration of Rights (June 12, 1776); John Adams, Novanglus, *in* 4 The Works of John Adams, *supra*, at 79 (1774).

13. *Notes of Proceedings*, 1 The Papers of Thomas Jefferson 309, 309, 313–14 (1776; Julian P. Boyd ed., 1950); 1 Diary and Autobiography of John Adams 253, 336–37 (L. H. Butterfield ed., 1961, ser. 1, pt. 3); Letter from Thomas Jefferson to Richard Henry Lee (May 8, 1825), *in* 16 The Writings of Thomas Jefferson 117, 118–19 (Andrew A. Lipscomb and Albert E. Bergh eds., 1905).

14. Philip F. Detweiler, *The Changing Reputation of the Declaration of Independence: The First Fifty Years,* 19 Wm. and Mary Q. 557, 566–67 (3d ser., 1962).

15. The Constitution of Va. (1776), *in* 7 The Federal and State Constitutions, Colonial Charter, and Other Organic Laws 3812, 3813 (Francis N. Thorpe ed., 1909); 5, *id.* at 3082 (Pa.); 3 *id.* 1889 (Mass.); Const. Vt. Ch. 1, 1 (1777), *available at* http://www.yale.edu/lawweb/avalon/states/vt01.htm.

16. Strictures upon the Declaration of the Congress of Philadelphia 9–10 (1776).

17. *Quoted in* Tania Tetlow, *The Founders and Slavery: A Crisis of Conscience,* 3 Loy. J. Pub. Int. L. 1, 11 (2001); William W. Freehling, The Reintegration of American History: Slavery and the Civil War 26, 187 (1994); John Hope Franklin, From Slavery to Freedom 128 (2d ed. 1956).

18. Samuel Adams, To the Legislature of Massachusetts, *in* 4 The Writings of Samuel Adams, *supra*, at 357 (Jan. 17, 1794).

19. *Amendments to the Constitution* (June 8, 1789), *in* 12 The Papers of James Madison 203 (Robert A. Rutland *et al.* eds., 1983) (speech in the House of Representatives).

20. Judah Champion, Christian and Civil Liberty Considered and Recommended 7 (1776); A Full Vindication, *in* 1 The Works of Alexander Hamilton 6 (1774; Henry Cabot Lodge ed., 2d ed. 1904).

21. *Id.* at 5–6; *Result of the Convention of Delegates Holden at Ipswich in the County of Essex, supra* at 362.

22. Boston Gazette and Country Journal (Jan. 21, 1771) (signed "Vindex"); Virginia Gazette (Dixon and Hunter) (June 8, 1776) at 2 (signed at the next publication date, June 15, 1776, as "Philanthropos"); David Ramsay, An Oration on Advantages of American Independence 3, 7 (1778).

23. Samuel Webster, A Sermon Preached Before the Honorable Council . . . May 28, 1777, at 29 (1777).

24. N.C. Const. art. XLI (1776), *in* 5 The Federal and State Constitutions, *supra*, at 2794; Pa. Const. 44 (1776), *in id.* at 3091; Const. Vt., *supra*, at 40; N.H. Const. art. 83, *available at* http://www.state.nh.us/constitution/lit.html.

25. Anthony Benezet, A Short Account of That Part of Africa, Inhabited by the Negroes . . . 52, 66 (1762); John Wesley, Thoughts upon Slavery 46–47 (1774).

26. Benjamin Rush, Address to the Inhabitants of the British Colonies in America, upon Slave-Keeping 6–7 (1775); Letter from Thomas Jefferson to James Madison (Oct. 28, 1785), *in* 8 The Papers of Thomas Jefferson, *supra*, at 682.

27. Charles A. Beard, An Economic Interpretation of the Constitution of the United States (1913); John Adams letter to Mercy Otis Warren (Apr. 1776), *quoted in* Philip Greven, The Protestant Temperament: Patterns of Child-Rearing, Religious Experience, and the Self in Early America 346 (1977).

28. Second Treatise, *supra*, 123.

29. *Id.* 131, at 371.

30. 1 The Records of the Federal Convention of 1787, *supra*, at 147 (June 6, 1787) (Madison); *id.* at 302 (Rufus King of Massachusetts) (June 18, 1787); *id.* at 534 (John Rutledge) (July 5, 1787).

31. Benjamin Throop, Thanksgiving Sermon, Upon the Occasion, of the Glorious News of the Repeal of the Stamp Act 11 (1766).

32. Locke, Second Treatise, *supra*, at 142; Stephen Hopkins, The Rights of Colonies Examined 16 (1765).

33. Boston Gazette and Country Journal, Feb. 22, 1768.

34. *See, e.g.*, 1 The Records of the Federal Convention of 1787, *supra*, at 428 (George Mason); Noah Webster, An Examination into the Leading Principles of the Federal Constitution . . . 49 (1787).

35. Clinton Rossiter, Seedtime of the Republic 19 (1953).

36. Georgia Gazette, Sept. 19, 1765; Daniel Dulany, Considerations on the Propriety of Imposing Taxes in the British Colonies 9 (1766); Alexander Hamilton, The Farmer Refuted 22 (1775).

37. J. Franklin Jameson, The American Revolution Considered as a Social Movement 39–40 (1926); Census of the State of New York, 1825, *available at* http://nysl.nysed.gov/uhtbin/cgisirsi/uAoldxuDk7/NYSL/114310095/523/73358.

38. Albert E. McKinley, Suffrage Franchise in the Thirteen English Colonies in America 218 (1905); J. F. Jameson, *Did the Fathers Vote?*, 7 New Eng. Mag. 484, 485, 487–88 (1890); Lyon G. Tyler, *Virginians Voting in the Colonial Period*, 6 Wm. and Mary College Q. Hist. Magazine 7 (1897).

39. 2 The Debates in the Several State Conventions, on the Adoption of the Federal Constitution 29 (Jonathan Elliot, ed., 1854); *id.* at 167.

CHAPTER TWO. Constitutional Republic of Equals?

1. David B. Davis, Inhuman Bondage: The Rise and Fall of Slavery in the New World 124–40 (2006); Ira Berlin, *Time, Space, and the Evolution of the Afro-American Society on British Mainland North America*, 85 Am. Hist. Rev. 44, 69, 71 (1980); John E. Cairnes, The Slave Power: Its Character, Career, and Probable Designs 44–45 (1862). *See, e.g.*, Pennsylvania Gazette, Feb. 22, 1744, Mar. 1, 1744, Mar. 15, 1744; Virginia Gazette, June 18, 1752.

2. Aaron S. Fogleman, *From Slaves, Convicts, and Servants to Free Passengers*, 85 J. Am. Hist. 43, 48 (1998); 2 Bureau of the Census, Historical Statistics of the United States, Colonial Times to 1970, at 1168 (1975); Joyce Appleby, *Liberalism and the American Revolution*, 49 N. Eng. Q. 3, 12 (1976); Marc Egnal, *The Economic Development of the Thirteen Continental Colonies, 1720 to 1775*, 32 Wm. and Mary Q. 191, 197 (1975); Jason A. Gillmer, *Suing for Freedom*, 82 N.C. L. Rev. 535, 552 (2004); Alexander Tsesis, Destructive Messages: How Hate Speech Paves the Way for Harmful Social Movements 32–38 (2002).

3. *New-England Weekly Journal*, May 1, 1732, page 2, col. 2; *New Jersey Gazette*, Dec.

20, 1780, page 3, col. 3; Diary of William Dunlap, *in* 1 Collections of the New-York Historical Society 118 (1929) (July 29, 1797, diary entry). Letter from Lieutenant-Colonel Elijah Clark to his Son Lardner Clark (May 17, 1782), *in* 28 Pa. Mag. of Hist. 107–8 (1904); Letter from Vernon to Captain William Pinnegar (Feb. 18, 1756), African American Documents of the Eighteenth and Nineteenth Centuries, Series C1, Northwestern University, Special Collections, Folder F1; *Ebenezer Hazard's Travels through Maryland in 1777,* 46 Md. Hist. Mag. 44, 50 (Fred Shelley ed., 1951). The relatively less harmful slavery in New England is recounted in Charles W. Brewster, Rambles about Portsmouth 210, 212 (1st series, 2d ed. 1873); Marquis de Barbé-Marbois, Our Revolutionary Forefathers 156 (Eugene P. Chase trans., 1929); 1 François-Alexandre-Frédéric, duc de la Rochefoucauld-Liancourt, Travels through the United States of North America 543–44 (H. Neuman trans., 1799).

4. 7 The Statutes at Large of South Carolina 352, 352–53, 363 (David J. McCord ed., 1840).

5. 3 Statutes at Large: Being a Collection of All Laws of Virginia 86–87 (William W. Hening ed., 1823); 3 *id.* at 453–54; 1 Archives of Maryland 533–34 (William H. Browne ed., 1883); 33 *id.* at 112 (Clayton C. Hall ed., 1913); 4 The Statutes at Large of Pennsylvania 62–63 (1897); 1 Acts and Resolves, Public and Private, of the Province of the Massachusetts Bay 578–79 (1869).

6. Alexander Hamilton, A Full Vindication of the Measures of Congress 4 (N.Y. Rivington 1774); N.Y. Evening Post, Nov. 16, 1747 ("according to the . . . "); Hawley, *To the Inhabitants of the Massachusetts-Bay* (no. 5) (Mar. 9, 1775), *in* 2 American Archives 94, 96 (Peter Force ed., 4th ser. 1839); Richard Price, Observations on the Nature of Civil Liberty, *in* Two Tracts on Civil Liberty, the War with America 11 (1778); Moses Mather, America's Appeal to the Impartial World 48 (1775).

7. Josiah Quincy, Jr., Observations on the Act of Parliament . . . 69 (1774); Stephen Hopkins, The Rights of Colonies Examined 4 (1764); John Dickinson, Letters from a Farmer in Pennsylvania, to the Inhabitants of the British Colonies 38 (1768); Letter from Washington to Bryan Fairfax (Aug. 24, 1774), *in* 3 The Writings of George Washington 240, 241 (John C. Fitzpatrick ed., 1931).

8. John Allen, The Watchman's Alarm to Lord ---- H 27–28 (1774); Boston Evening-Post, Nov. 5, 1770, at 4, col. 1.

9. *Quoted in* Thomas J. Davis, *Emancipation Rhetoric, Natural Rights, and Revolutionary New England: A Note on Four Black Petitions in Massachusetts, 1773–1777,* 62 New Eng. Q. 248, 262 (1989); Philip S. Foner, From Africa to the Emergence of the Cotton Kingdom 303 (1975).

10. Winthrop D. Jordan, White over Black: American Attitudes toward the Negro, 1550–1812, at 291 (1968); 3 Collections of the Massachusetts Historical Society 432–33 (5th ser. 1877); Thomas J. Davis, *supra,* at 255, 261; William Lincoln, History of Worcester, Massachusetts, 99 (1862).

11. *Id.* at 68; Foner, *supra,* at 303–4 (Darien County petition).

12. The General Advertiser (Philadelphia), July 6, 1792, at 3, col. 1; *id.,* July 6, 1793, at 3, col. 1; Baltimore Patriot and Mercantile Advertiser, July 9, 1818, at 2, col. 1.

13. American revolutionists came from a British tradition that regarded freedom to be a natural birthright. Arthur Young, Political Essays Concerning the Present State of the British Empire 19 (1772); William Patten, Discourse at Hallifax in the County of Plymouth, July 24th 1766, at 12 (1766); 1 William W. Henry, Patrick Henry: Life, Correspon-

dence, and Speeches 266 (1891) (Mar. 23, 1775) ("Forbid it, Almighty God! I know not what course others may take; but as for me, give me liberty or give me death!"); Alexander Hamilton, The Full Vindication of the Measures of the Congress 5 (1774); Thomas Paine, *African Slavery in America, in* 1 The Writings of Thomas Paine 4, 7 (1775; Moncure D. Conway ed., 1894).

14. James Otis, Rights of the British Colonies Asserted and Proved 29 (1764); James Otis, Considerations on Behalf of the Colonists 30 (2d ed. 1765); Samuel Hopkins, A Dialogue Concerning the Slavery of the Africans 50 (1776); Abraham Booth, Commerce in the Human Species 22 (1792); James Dana, The African Slave Trade 28–29, 31–32 (1791).

15. Richard Wells, A Few Political Reflections . . . 79–81 (1774); J. Franklin Jameson, The American Revolution Considered as a Social Movement 23–24 (1926); Address of a Convention of Delegates from the Abolition Societies, to the Citizens of the United States 4 (1794).

16. Paine, *African Slavery in America, supra;* Anthony Benezet, A Short Account of That Part of Africa, Inhabited by the Negroes . . . 29 (1762).

17. Anthony Benezet, Some Historical Account of Guinea ch. 11 (1771); Benezet, A Short Account . . ., *supra,* at 71–72.

18. Jordan, *supra,* at 298; Letter from Rush to Granville Sharp (Oct. 29, 1773), *in Correspondence of Benjamin Rush and Granville Sharp,* 1 J. Am. Stud. 1, 5 (John A. Woods ed., 1965).

19. Letter from Patrick Henry to Robert Pleasants (Jan. 18, 1773), *reprinted in* George S. Brookes, Friend Anthony Benezet 443–44 (1937); Thomas Jefferson, Notes on the State of Virginia 162–63 (1787; 1955). On Jefferson's paltry condemnation of slavery see Jordan, *supra,* at 430–36; David B. Davis, The Problem of Slavery in the Age of Revolution, 1770–1823, at 164–84 (1975); Duncan J. MacLeod, Slavery, Race, and the American Revolution 126–29 (1974).

20. Thomas Jefferson, A Summary View of the Rights of British America 16 (1774); 1 The Papers of Thomas Jefferson353 (1776; Julian P. Boyd ed., 1950); 2 The Records of the Federal Convention of 1787, at 370 (Max Farrand ed., 1911) (Mason).

21. John Mein, Sagittarius's Letters and Political Speculations 38–39 (1775); Johnson *quoted in* Philip S. Foner, 1 History of Black Americans 303 (1975); *see also* A Letter from *****, in London . . . on the . . . Slave-Trade 15–16 (1784).

22. Letter from Thomas Jefferson to Edward Coles, Aug. 25, 1814, *in* 11 The Works of Thomas Jefferson 416–19 (Paul L. Ford ed., 1905). Coles, who had been a secretary to President James Madison and was a cousin of Dolley Madison, set his slaves free only after calling Madison out about his hypocritical conscience on slavery. *See* Ralph Ketcham, James Madison: A Biography 551–52 (1971).

23. Brewster, *supra,* at 154–56; David Brion Davis, Inhuman Bondage 144 (2006).

24. The Writings of George Washington, *supra,* 275, 275–77; Eugene E. Prussing, The Estate of George Washington, Deceased 158–59 (1927); Eli Ginzberg and Alfred S. Eichner, Troublesome Presence: American Democracy and Black Americans 45–46 (1964); Benjamin Quarles, The Negro in the American Revolution 187 (1961).

25. Elder Witt, Congressional Quarterly's Guide to the U.S. Supreme Court 809 (2d ed. 1990).

26. 2 Francois J. Chastellux, Travels in North America in the Years 1780, 1781, and 1782, at 199 (trans. 1787).

27. William P. Quigley, *Reluctant Charity: Poor Laws in the Original Thirteen States,*

31 U. Rich. L. Rev. 111, 172 n. 401 (1997); Michael D. Hawkins, *John Quincy Adams in the Antebellum Maritime Slave Trade: The Politics of Slavery and the Slavery of Politics,* 25 Okla. City U. L. Rev. 1, 5 (2000); W. E. B. Du Bois, The Suppression of the African Slave-Trade to the United States of America, 1638–1870, at 45–57 (1896); Peter Kolchin, American Slavery, 1619–1877, at 78–79 (1993); Northwest Ordinance art. 6, *available at* http://www .earlyamerica.com/earlyamerica/milestones/ordinance/text.html.

28. Quarles, *supra,* at 40–41.

29. A Declaration of the Rights of the Inhabitants of the State of Vermont, *available at* http://www.yale.edu/lawweb/avalon/states/vt01.htm; N.H. Bill of Rights art. 2, *available at* http://www.state.nh.us/constitution/billofrights.html; Commonwealth v. Jennison (1783), *quoted in* Philip S. Foner, 1 History of Black Americans 353 (1975).

30. *See, e.g.,* 10 Records of the State of Rhode Island and Providence Plantations in New England 132 (1865) ; Lois E. Horton, *From Class to Race in Early America: Northern Post-Emancipation Racial Reconstruction,* 19 J. Early Republic 629, 639 (1999); Jameson, *supra,* at 25. By 1830 fewer than 3,000 blacks remained enslaved in the northern and middle states, compared with those states' 125,000 free black inhabitants. Gordon S. Wood, Revolution and the Political Integration of the Enslaved and Disenfranchised 13 (1974); Arthur Zilversmit, The First Emancipation: The Abolition of Slavery in the North 180–82, 192–93 (1967).

31. Leon F. Litwack, North of Slavery: The Negro in the Free States, 1790–1860, at 103, 154, 157–59 (1979) (concerning the difficulties free blacks faced in finding decent employment opportunities); Ira Berlin, Slaves without Masters: The Free Negro in the Antebellum South 61–63, 96–97, 225–26, 229 (1974) (surveying state impediments on black ownership, trade, and labor).

32. 2 The Records of the Federal Convention on 1787, *supra,* at 371, 373.

33. Ellsworth, *"Landholder," VI,* Conn. Courant, Dec. 10, 1787; James Madison, Notes of Debates in the Federal Convention, Wednesday, August 21, at 503 (1987) (Ellsworth); 2 The Records of the Federal Convention on 1787, *supra,* at 364, 370; 3 The Debates in the Several State Conventions, on the Adoption of the Federal Constitution 452–53 (Jonathan Elliot ed., 2d ed. 1901).

34. *Conclusion of Mssrs. Arms's, Maynard's and Field's Reasons for Giving Their Dissent to the Federal Constitution, in* 4 The Complete Antifederalist 259, 261 (Herbert J. Storing ed., 1981); 2 The Debates in the Several State Conventions on the Adoption of the Federal Constitution, *supra,* 203–4; David B. Davis, *American Slavery and the American Revolution, in* Slavery and Freedom in the Age of the American Revolution 262, 266 (Ira Berlin and Ronald Hoffman eds., 1983).

35. 1 The Records of the Federal Convention on 1787, *supra,* at 580, 593, 594.

36. *Id.,* at 587–88; 2 *id.,* at 222.

37. *Id.,* at 220–21.

38. Michael Kent Curtis, *A Story for All Seasons: Akhil Reed Amar on the Bill of Rights,* 8 Wm. and Mary Bill Rts. J. 437, 453 (2000); Ruth Colker, *The Supreme Court's Historical Errors in City of Boerne v. Flores,* 43 B.C. L. Rev. 783, 795 (2002); Forrest McDonald, States' Rights and the Union 60 (2000).

39. Paul Finkelman, *The Color of Law,* 87 Nw.U. L. Rev. 937, 971 (1993) (reviewing Andrew Kull, The Color-Blind Constitution).

40. Frederick Douglass, *The Constitution and Slavery, in* 1 Frederick Douglass, The Life and Writings of Frederick Douglass (Philip S. Foner ed., 1950) (first published in The

North Star, Mar. 16, 1849); Prigg v. Pennsylvania, 41 U.S. (16 Pet.) 539 (1842); Robert R. Russel, *The General Effects of Slavery upon Southern Economic Progress*, 4 J. S. Hist. 34, 40 (1938).

41. The Observer, Conn. Courant (Nov. 27, 1786), at p. 3, col. 2; Lyle Koehler, A Search for Power: The "Weaker Sex" in Seventeenth-Century New England 38 (1980) (quoting "are yoak-fellows . . . ").

42. New-York Weekly Journal (Sept. 22, 1740); *An Answer. By a Gentleman*, 6 Am. Museum 418 (1789).

43. James Otis, The Rights of the British Colonies . . . 6 (1764); *The Propriety of Meliorating the Condition of Women . . .*, 9 Am. Museum 248, 248–49 (1791); *Woman's Hard Fate*, 6 Am. Museum 417, 417–18 (1789); Lyon G. Tyler, *Virginia Voting in the Colonial Period*, 6 Wm. and Mary College Q. Hist. Magazine, 7 (1897).

44. Marylynn Salmon, Women and the Law of Property in Early America 190 (1986); Richard B. Morris, Studies in the History of American Law: With Special Reference to the Seventeenth and Eighteenth Centuries 133 (1930).

45. Clinton Rossiter, Seedtime of the Republic: The Origin of the American Tradition of Political Liberty 99 (1953); Salmon, *supra*, at 7–10, 23–24, 32; Morris, *supra*, 130; Anastasia B. Crosswhite, Note, *Women and Land: Aristocratic Ownership of Property in Early Modern England*, 77 N.Y.U. L. Rev. 1119, 1125 (2002).

46. Serena Zabin, *Women's Trading Networks and Dangerous Economies in Eighteenth-Century New York City*, 4 Early Am. Stud. 291, 296–97, 300 (2006).

47. *See, e.g., An Act for Prevention of Undue Election of Burgeses* (April 1699), *in* 3 The Statutes at Large; Being a Collection of All of the Laws of Virginia from the First Session of the Legislature in the Year 1619, at 172 (William W. Hening ed., 1823).

48. Eliza Wilkinson *quoted in* Mary Beth Norton, Liberty's Daughters: The Revolutionary Experience of American Women, 1750–1800, at 171–72 (1980).

49. Letter from Lee to Corbin (Mar. 17, 1778), *in* 1 The Letters of Richard Henry Lee 392 (James Curtis Ballagh ed., 1911); Letters of Eliza Wilkinson during the Invasion and Possession of Charleston, S.C., by the British in the Revolutionary War 60–61 (Caroline Gilman ed., 1839).

50. Edward R. Turner, *Women's Suffrage in New Jersey, 1790–1807*, 1 Smith Col. Studs. 165 (1916); Mary Philbrook, *Woman's Suffrage in New Jersey Prior to 1807*, 57 Proc. N.J. Hist. Soc'y 87, 95–96 (1939); William Griffith, Eumenes 33 (1799).

51. Judith Sargent Murray, On the Equality . . . *available at* http://www.hurdsmith .com/judith/equality.htm.

52. Benjamin Rush, Thoughts upon Female Education . . . 5–12 (1787).

53. Norton, *supra*, at 259, 272–74; Janet Wilson James, Changing Ideas about Women in the United States, 1776–1825, at 75–76 (1981); Senex, *Female Education in the Last Century*, 1 Am. Annals of Ed. 524, 525–26 (1831); Sally Schwager, *Educating Women in America*, 12 Signs 333, 339 (1987).

54. Ellsworth, *supra;* The Federalist no. 84, at 578 (Alexander Hamilton) (Jacob E. Cooke ed., 1961); James Wilson, Nov. 28, 1787, *in* 2 The Documentary History of the Ratification of the Constitution 383–84 (Merril Jensen ed., 1976); Thomas Hartley, Nov. 30, 1787, *in id.* at 430; Mr. Maclaine (N.C.) *in* 4 The Debates in the Several State Conventions on the Adoption of the Federal Constitution, *supra*, at 161 (July 29, 1788).

55. Thomas McKean, 2 Documentary History of the Ratification of the Constitution, *supra*, 412; Rush, *in id.* at 440.

56. U.S. Const. art. III, 2, cl. 3; *id.* art. I, 9, cl. 3; *id.* art. IV, 2, cl. 1; *id.* art. VI, 3; *id.* art. I, 9, cl. 2.

57. Stanley Elkins and Eric McKitrick, The Age of Federalism: The Early American Republic, 1788–1800, at 60 (1993).

58. Letter from Thomas Jefferson to James Madison (Feb. 6, 1788), *in* 10 The Papers of James Madison 473, 474 (Robert A. Rutland *et al.* eds., 1977); Letter from James Madison to Thomas Jefferson (Oct. 17, 1788), *in* 11 The Papers of James Madison, *supra*, at 295, 297–99; *Amendments to the Constitution* (June 8, 1789), *in* 12 The Papers of James Madison 205.

CHAPTER THREE. The Controversy about Slavery

1. T. D. Clark, *The Slave Trade between Kentucky and the Cotton Kingdom,* 21 Miss. Valley Hist. Rev. 331, 331 (1934).

2. Daniel J. Flanigan, *Criminal Procedure in Slave Trials in the Antebellum South,* 40 J. S. Hist. 537, 540, 543–44 (1974); Peter W. Bardaglio, *Rape and the Law in the Old South: "Calculated to Excite Indignation in Every Heart,"* 60 J. S. Hist. 749, 761–62 (1994) (see notes accompanying text).

3. Theodore D. Weld, American Slavery as It Is 116 (1839); Thomas Jefferson, Notes on the State of Virginia 162–63 (William Peden ed., 1982) (1782); Frances A. Kemble, Journal of a Residence on a Georgian Plantation in 1838–1839, at 57–58 (1863); Letter from Charles Manigault to His Overseers (Mar. 1, 1847), *in* 2 Plantation and Frontier, 1649–1863, at 31–32 (Ulrich B. Phillips ed., 1910).

4. *See, e.g.,* E. A. Andrews, Slavery and the Domestic Slave Trade in the United States 147 (1836); 1 Frederick L. Olmsted, Cotton Kingdom: A Traveler's Observations of Cotton and Slavery in the American Slave States 51–52 (1861); Isaac Holmes, An Account of the United States of America 327–28 ([1823]).

5. For public statements of these fears see American Weekly Mercury (Philadelphia), Aug. 3–10, 1738, Va. Gazette, Apr. 10, 1752, S.C. Gazette, Oct. 17, 1754, May 1, 1756.

6. [Richard Hildreth], Despotism in America 113 (1840) ("With respect to the other laboring class at the south, to wit, the poor whites, their industry is paralyzed by a fatal prejudice which regards manual labor as the badge of a servile condition"); 4 The Debates in the Several State Conventions on the Adoption of the Federal Constitution 285–86 (Jonathan Elliot ed., 2d ed. 1907); Edwin C. Holland, A Refutation of the Calumnies . . . against . . . Slavery . . . 43–45 (1822).

7. N. Beverley Tucker, A Series of Lectures on the Science of Government 336 (1845).

8. Thomas R. R. Cobb, An Inquiry into the Law of Negro Slavery in the United States of America ccxiii (1858); Toombs, Lecture Delivered in the Tremont Temple, Jan. 24, 1856, *available at* http://www.constitution.org/cmt/ahs/consview19.htm; Henry A. Wise, Cong. Globe, 27th Cong., 2d Sess. at 173 (Jan. 26, 1842).

9. J. H. Steffy, *Slavery and the Poor White Men of Virginia,* Nat'l Era, Jan. 11, 1849, at 8.

10. University of Va. Library, Historical Census Browser, http://fisher.lib.virginia .edu/collections/stats/histcensus/.

11. Luther P. Jackson, *Manumission in Certain Virginia Cities,* J. Negro Hist. 278, 288–90, 298 (1930); Bruce E. Steiner, *A Planter's Troubled Conscience,* 28 J. S. Hist. 343, 346 n. 4 (1962); J. Merton England, *The Free Negro in Ante-Bellum Tennessee,* 9 J. S. Hist. 37, 41–42 (1943); David Skillen Bogen, *The Maryland Context of Dred Scott: The Decline in the Legal Status of Maryland Free Blacks, 1776–1810,* 34 Am. J. Legal Hist. 381, 406 (1990).

12. Elkison v. Deliesseline, 8 Fed. Cas. 493 (no. 4366) (C.C.S.C. 1823); H. Jefferson Powell, *Attorney General Taney and the South Carolina Police Bill*, 5 Green Bag 2d 75, 76 (2001).

13. 2 John C. Hurd, The Law of Freedom and Bondage in the United States 117, 118 (Ohio); 176, 177 (Iowa); 216, 217 (Oregon) (1862; 1968) (providing the text of state laws and constitutions); Frank U. Quillin, The Color Line in Ohio: A History of Race Prejudice in a Typical Northern State 20–24, 38–40, 88 (1913) (Ohio); Allan Nevins, Ordeal of the Union, Selected Chapters 38–40, 44 (1973) (Illinois, Iowa, and Indiana); Henry H. Simms, A Decade of Sectional Controversy, 1851–1861, at 127–29 (1942) (New England states, Ohio, Illinois, Iowa, and Oregon); N. Dwight Harris, The History of Negro Servitude in Illinois and of the Slavery Agitation in that State, 1719–1864, at 235–36, 239 (1904) (Illinois).

14. Louis Filler, The Crusade against Slavery 1830–1860, at 20–21 (1960); Giles B. Stebbins, Facts and Opinions Touching the Real Origin, Character, and Influence of the American Colonization Society 9–10 (1853); *Mr. Key's Address*, 4 Afr. Repository and Colonial J. 298, 299–330 (1828); Henry Clay, The First Annual Report of the American Society for Colonizing the Free People of Colour of the United States 9 (1818); Robert C. Harper's letter, *id.* at 14, 16; *Report of the Naval Committee*, 26 Afr. Repository 265, 268 (1850); Clay's Speech to the Colonization Society of Kentucky (Dec. 17, 1829), 6 Afr. Repository and Colonial J. 1, 23 (Mar. 1830).

15. Benjamin Quarles, Black Abolitionists 5–8 (1969) (Woodson and Cornish); John B. McMaster, 4 History of the People of the United States: From the Revolution to the Civil War 562–63, 566 (1895); Baltimore petition *in* William L. Garrison, Thoughts on African Colonization part 2, at 22 (1832); Hartford, *id.* at 28–29; Brooklyn, *id.* at 23–24.

16. W. B. Hesseltine, *Some New Aspects of the Pro-Slavery Argument*, 21 J. Negro Hist. 1, 1–2, 7 (1936).

17. George Best, *in* Richard Hakluyt, 7 Principal Navigations Voyages Traffiques and Discoveries of the English Nation 263–64 (1578; 1904). This dogma was irreconcilable with proscription in Ezekiel against holding descendants accountable for the sins of their ancestors. Ezekiel 18:20.

18. *Speech Known as "The Corner Stone" . . . , March 21, 1861, in* Alexander H. Stephens, In Public and Private, with Letters and Speeches 717, 723 (Henry Cleveland ed., 1866); William S. Jenkins, Pro-Slavery Thought in the Old South 73 (1935); Benjamin M. Palmer, Rights of the South Defended in the Pulpits (1860).

19. Zephaniah Kingsley, A Treatise on the Patriarchal, or Co-operative System of Society . . . under the Name of Slavery 6, 8 (2d ed. 1829); Nehemiah Adams, A South-Side View of Slavery; or, Three Months at the South in 1854, at 119, 121–22 (1854); John H. Hopkins, A Scriptural, Ecclesiastical, and Historical View of Slavery 32–33 (1864).

20. Thomas R. Dew, Review of the Debate in the Virginia Legislature, of 1831 and 1832, at 288, 359, 387 (1832), *quoted in* William M. Wiecek, The Sources of Antislavery Constitutionalism in America, 1760–1848, at 147–48 (1977).

21. *See, e.g.*, Cobb, *supra*, at 39–41.

22. Personal Slavery Established 18–19 (1773); 2 Edward Long, History of Jamaica 353–54, 360, 365, 370 (1774).

23. Samuel Cartwright, *Prognathous Species of Mankind, in* Slavery Defended: The Views of the Old South 139 (1963); George S. Sawyer, Southern Institutes 195 (1858); Letter from Josiah C. Nott to J. D. B. De Bow, *in* Two Lectures on the Connection

between the Biblical and Physical History of Man 5, 5 (1849); Josiah C. Nott and George R. Gliddon, Types of Mankind: Or Ethnological Researches 50 (1854); John H. Van Evrie, White Supremacy and Negro Subordination 90–91, 117, 188 (1868).

24. W. Gilmore Simms, *The Morals of Slavery, in* The Pro-Slavery Argument 175, 258 (1852) (orig. pub. in Southern Literary Messenger 1837).

25. Albert G. Brown, Cong. Globe, 33d Cong., 1st Sess., appendix 230 (Feb. 24, 1854); W. Gilmore Simms, *supra*, at 259.

26. 5 The Works of John C. Calhoun 333, 339 (Richard K. Crallé ed., 1851–56); A Debate on Slavery: Held in the City of Cincinnati on . . . 1845 . . . 33–34 (1846); James K. Paulding, Slavery in the United States 82–83 (1836).

27. American Anti-Slavery Society, *Declaration of the Anti-Slavery Convention,* Dec. 4, 1833; Proceedings of the Anti-Slavery Convention, Assembled at Philadelphia 12, 12–13 (1833).

28. Letter from Weld to Elizur Wright, Jr. (Jan. 10, 1833), *in* 1 Letters of Theodore Dwight Weld, Angelina Grimké Weld, and Sarah M. Grimké 99, 99 (Gilbert H. Barnes and Dwight L. Dumond eds., 1965).

29. Brougham, *The Liberator,* Jan. 22, 1831, Liberator, at 13, cl. 1; W. E. Channing, Slavery 47–48, 51 (3d ed. 1835; 1969); The National Anti-Slavery Standard, February 21, 1857, quoted in William E. Nelson, *The Impact of the Antislavery Movement upon Styles of Judicial Reasoning in Nineteenth Century America,* 87 Harv. L. Rev. 513, 536 (1974); Cong. Globe, 33rd Cong., 1st Sess., appendix 268 (Feb. 24, 1854); Weld, Slavery, *supra* at 5.

30. George W. F. Mellen, An Argument on the Unconstitutionality of Slavery 55–56, 62–63 (1841); Charles Olcott, Two Lectures on Slavery and Abolition 88 (1838); Theodore Parker, The Dangers from Slavery (July 2, 1854), *in* 4 Old South Leaflets 1–3 (1897).

31. William Lloyd Garrison, An Address Delivered before the Old Colony Anti-Slavery Society . . ., July 4, 1839, at 17 (1839); James McPherson, The Struggle for Equality: Abolitionists and the Negro in the Civil War and Reconstruction 3 (1964).

32. Bourne, The Book and Slavery Irreconcilable 139–40 (1816); Elizabeth Heyrick, Immediate, Not Gradual Abolitionism 13, 16 (1824); Garrison, Address, *supra,* at 17 (1839).

33. Amos A. Phelps, Lectures on Slavery and Its Remedy 177–79 (1834); *Constitution of the New-England Anti-Slavery Society, in* 1 The Abolitionist: Or Record of the New England Anti-Slavery Society 2 (January 1833); Elizur Wright, Jr., The Sin of Slavery, and Its Remedy 40 (1833).

34. Angelina E. Grimké, letter XII, Oct. 2, 1837, *in* Letters to Catherine E. Beecher . . . 114, 114–15 (rev. ed. 1838).

35. *Quoted in* Bruce Laurie, Beyond Garrison: Antislavery and Social Reform 36–37 (2005).

36. Peter Smith, Letters of Theodore Dwight Weld . . ., *supra,* at 133; Wright, *supra,* at 40; A Statement of the Reasons which Induced the Students of Lane Seminary to Dissolve Their Connection with That Institution (1834); Sydney Strong, *The Exodus of Students from Lane Seminary to Oberlin in 1834, in* 4 Papers of the Ohio Church History Society 1, 4–9 (Delavan L. Leonard ed., 1893); Letter from Birney to Joseph Healy, Oct. 2, 1835, *in* 1 Letters of James Gillespie Birney, 1831–1857, at 249, 250 (Dwight L. Dumond ed., 1938).

37. Weld to Ray Potter (June 11, 1836), *in* 1 Letters of Theodore Dwight Weld, *supra,* at 309–10.

38. 3 Wendell P. and Francis J. Garrison, William Lloyd Garrison, 1805–1879, at 412

(1889); Wendell Phillips, Review of Lysander Spooner's Essay on the Unconstitutionality of Slavery 3–4 (1847).

39. Joel Tiffany, A Treatise on the Unconstitutionality of American Slavery 9, 19, 120 (1849); Proceedings of the Convention of Radical Political Abolitionists . . . Slavery an Outlaw 7, 15–19, 42–44 (1855); Mellen, *supra*, at 427; Alvan Stewart, A Legal Argument Before the Supreme Court of the State of New Jersey at the May Term, 1845, at 35 (1845); Lewis Tappan, Address to the Non-slaveholders of the South 4 (1843); William Goodell, Slavery and Anti-Slavery 588 (1852).

40. Mellen, *supra*, at 55–56, 61, 63 (1841); Tiffany, *supra*, at 36–37; Spooner, *Has Slavery in the United States a Legal Basis?*, 1 Mass. Q. Rev. 273, 285–89 (1848); Letter from Gerrit Smith to Salmon P. Chase, On the Unconstitutionality of Every Part of American Slavery 3 (1847); Charles Olcott, *supra*, 87–88 (1838).

41. Tiffany, *supra*, at 84-89, 91; Address of the Free Constitutionalists to the People of the United States 10-11 (2d ed. 1860); Lysander Spooner, The Unconstitutionality of Slavery 99–100 (1845); Mellen, *supra*, at 87–88; William Goodell, Address of the Macedon Convention 3 (1847); Alvan Stewart, *Argument, on the Question Whether the New Constitution of 1844 Abolished Slavery in New Jersey, in* Writings and Speeches of Alvan Stewart, on Slavery 272, 336–37 (Luther R. Marsh ed., 1860).

42. Letter of Smith to Chase, *supra*, at 5–10.

CHAPTER FOUR. Sectional Compromise and National Conflict

1. Annals of Cong. 15th Cong., 2d Sess. 1166, 1169–70 (1819); *id.* at 1203–4; Letter from Jefferson to John Holmes (Apr. 22, 1820), *in* 10 The Writings of Thomas Jefferson 157 (Paul L. Ford ed., 1899).

2. Annals of Cong. 15th Cong., 2d Sess. 1180 (February 1819); *id.* 16th Cong., 1st Sess. 279 (January 1820).

3. *Id.* 15th Cong., 2d Sess. 1191–93 (February 1819).

4. *Id.* 16th Cong., 1st Sess. 149 (January 1820); *id.* 15th Cong., 2d Sess. 1170, 1174–75 (February 1819).

5. *Id.* at 1185, 1188; on the Senate side see *id.* 16th Cong., 1st Sess. 195–99 (January 1820); *id.* at 390–92 (February 1820).

6. The Life and Writings of Thomas Jefferson 287 (1798; S. E. Forman ed., 2d ed. 1900); Frederic Bancroft, Calhoun and the South Carolina Nullification Movement 28–29, 47–48 (1928).

7. Samuel F. Bemis, John Quincy Adams and the Union 260–68 (1956; 1984).

8. John C. Calhoun *quoted in* William W. Freehling, Prelude to Civil War: The Nullification Controversy in South Carolina, 1816–1836, at 257 (1966); Bancroft, *supra*, at 28–29; John C. Calhoun *quoted in* Henry Wilson, *This Conspiracy against the Unity of the Republic, in* Slavery as a Cause of the Civil War 40–41 (Edwin C. Rozwenc ed., 1963); James Madison *quoted in id.* at 40.

9. David Wilmot *quoted in* A. Cash Koeniger, *Ken Burns's "The Civil War": Triumph or Travesty?*, 55 J. Military Hist. 225, 232 (1991) (review).

10. 4 A Compilation of the Messages and Papers of the Presidents 456 (James D. Richardson ed., 1904) (Polk's message); Cong. Globe, 29th Cong., 1st Sess. 1213 (Aug. 8, 1846) (proposed bill); *id.* at 1213–14 (White); *id.* at 1214, 1217–18 (Wilmot); Charles B. Going, David Wilmot, Free Soiler 51, 61 (1924); Harold M. Hyman and William M. Wiecek, Equal Justice under Law 129 (1982).

11. *See, e.g.,* Cong. Globe 31st Cong., 1st Sess. 86 (Dec. 27, 1849) (offering constitutional language for Utah); *id.* at 99–100 (Jan. 4, 1850) (proposing admitting California, New Mexico, and Utah with no restriction on slavery); *id.* at 103 (Jan. 4, 1850) (proposing a fugitive slave clause); *id.* at 165–71 (Jan. 16, 1850) (proposing Texas boundaries that excluded slavery from the North and Northwest but establishing an additional slave state, Jacinto).

12. 2 Carl Schurz, Life of Henry Clay 166 (1887); *Reminiscences of Washington,* 47 Atlantic Monthly 234, 241 (February 1881); William E. Dodd, Jefferson Davis 118–19 (1907); 2 Thurlow W. Barnes, Memoir of Thurlow Weed 176–77 (1884); 2 George T. Curtis, Life of Daniel Webster 397–98 (1870).

13. Robert R. Russel, *What Was the Compromise of 1850?,* 22 J. S. Hist. 292 (1956); F. H. Hodder, *The Authorship of the Compromise of 1850,* 22 Miss. Valley Hist. Rev. 525 (1936); 1 James F. Rhodes, History of the United States from the Compromise of 1850, at 99–198 (1893); 1 Allan Nevins, Ordeal of the Union 229–345 (1947).

14. 1 Stat. 302 (1793).

15. 41 U.S. (16 Pet.) 539 (1842).

16. Joseph Nogee, *The Prigg Case and Fugitive Slavery, 1842–1850,* 39 J. Negro Hist. 185, 198–201 (1954); R. L. Morrow, *The Liberty Party in Vermont,* 2 New Eng. Q. 234, 234 (1929).

17. Marion G. McDougall, Fugitive Slaves 112–15 (1969), provides the text of the Fugitive Slave Act of 1850.

18. Nogee, *supra,* at 198–99.

19. David M. Potter, The Impending Crisis, 1848–1861, at 130–32 (1976).

20. Arthur C. Cole, The Era of the Civil War 228–29 (1919); Emmett D. Preston, *The Fugitive Slave Acts in Ohio,* 28 J. Negro Hist 422, 433–34, 457 (1943); Louis Filler, The Crusade Against Slavery, 1830–1860, at 202–3 (1960); Ella Forbes, *"By My Own Right Arm": Redemptive Violence and the 1951 Christiana, Pennsylvania, Resistance,* 83 J. Negro Hist. 159, 164–65 (1998); Michael Fellman, *Theodore Parker and the Abolitionist Role in the 1850s,* 61 J. Am. Hist. 666, 672–73 (1974); Harold Schwartz, *Fugitive Slave Days in Boston,* 27 N. Eng. Q. 191, 193, 195–96 (1954).

21. 62 U.S. (21 How.) 506, 524, 526 (1858).

22. Abraham Lincoln, *Speech at Peoria, Illinois, in Reply to Senator Douglas, in* 2 The Writings of Abraham Lincoln 190, 234–35 (Arthur B. Lapsley ed., 1905) (Oct. 16, 1854).

23. James F. Rhodes, *Antecedents of the American Civil War, in* The Causes of the American Civil War 56 (Edwin C. Rozwenc ed., 2d ed. 1972); Joseph H. Parks, *The Tennessee Whigs and the Kansas-Nebraska Bill,* 10 J. S. Hist. 308, 315 (1944); Robert R. Russel, Critical Studies in Antebellum Sectionalism 25 (1972); 2 Nevins, *supra,* at 86–88, 92, 98, 103–8, 121; Cong. Globe 33rd Cong., 1st Sess. 175 (Jan 16, 1854).

24. Cong. Globe 33rd Cong., 1st Sess. 281–82 (first published *in* National Era (Jan. 24, 1854)); Cong. Globe 33rd Cong., 1st Sess., appendix 268 (Feb. 24, 1854); Cong. Globe, 33rd Cong., 1st. Sess., appendix, 155 (Feb. 17, 1854).

25. 60 U.S. (19 How.) 393 (1857).

26. Potter, *supra,* at 268–69, 276–77; Don E. Fehrenbacher, The Dred Scott Case: Its Significance in American Law and Politics 239–83 (1978); Walter Ehrlich, They Have No Rights: Dred Scott's Struggle for Freedom 9–81 (1979); Walter Ehrlich, *Was the Dred Scott Case Valid?,* 55 J. Am. Hist. 256, 264 (1968). A court reporter misspelled Sanford's name, calling the case "Dred Scott v. Sandford." G. Edward White, *The Constitutional Journey of Marbury v. Madison,* 89 Va. L. Rev. 1463, 1507 n. 175 (2003); Christopher L. Eisgruber, Dred *Again: Originalism's Forgotten Past,* 10 Const. Comment. 37, 37 n. 3 (1993).

27. Carl B. Swisher, Roger B. Taney 93–95, 154 (1935); Henry G. Connor, John Archibald Campbell: Associate Justice of the United States Supreme Court, 1853–1861, at 71 (1920); Alexander A. Lawrence, James Moore Wayne: Southern Unionist 144–45 (1943); John P. Frank, Justice Daniel Dissenting 58 (1964); J. Merton England, *The Free Negro in Ante-Bellum Tennessee,* 9 J. S. Hist. 37, 46–47 (1943); Donald M. Roper, *In Quest of Judicial Objectivity: The Marshall Court and the Legitimation of Slavery,* 21 Stan. L. Rev. 532, 535 n. 17 (1969); In re Charge to Grand Jury, 30 F. Cas. 1013, 1014 (C.C.N.D. N.Y. 1851) (Nelson put the Onus of Unity on the North helping in the capture of fugitives: "They must determine it, and the responsibility rests upon them. If they abide by the constitution—the whole and every part of it—all will be well. If they expect the Union to be saved, and to enjoy the blessings flowing from it, short of this, they will find themselves mistaken when it is too late."); Charge to Grand Jury, 30 F. Cas. 1007 (C.C.S.D. N.Y. 1851) (Nelson); Ex parte Jenkins, 13 F. Cas. 445 (C.C.E.D. Pa. 1853) (Grier); Van Metre v. Mitchell, 28 F. Cas. 1036 (C.C.W.D. Pa. 1853) (Grier).

28. Mark A. Graber, Dred Scott and the Problem of Constitutional Evil (2006).

29. Abraham Lincoln at Springfield, June 16, 1858, *in* Created Equal? The Complete Lincoln-Douglas Debates of 1858 1, 7 (Paul M. Angle ed., 1958).

30. *A Declaration of the Immediate Causes Which Induce and Justify the Secession of South Carolina, in* Slavery as a Cause of the Civil War, *supra,* at 29–30; *also available at* http://history.furman.edu/benson/docs/scdebate2.htm.

CHAPTER FIVE. Reconstructing the American Dream

1. 1 William H. Herndon and Jesse W. Weik, Abraham Lincoln: The True Story of a Great Life 66–67 (1888; 1923); 2 Emanuel Hertz, Abraham Lincoln: A New Portrait 531 (1931) (there is some question on the attribution of the Cincinnati speech; see 4 The Collected Works of Abraham Lincoln 156 (Roy P. Basler *et al.* eds., 1953); http://memory.loc.gov/ammem/today/apr16.html (1849 bill).

2. Abraham Lincoln, *Speech at Peoria, Illinois, in Reply to Senator Douglas, in* 2 The Writings of Abraham Lincoln 190–92, 208–10, 216–17 (Arthur B. Lapsley ed., 1905) (Oct. 16, 1854); Abraham Lincoln, *Fragment on Slavery, in* 2 The Collected Works of Abraham Lincoln, *supra,* at 222–23 (July 1, 1854?); Letter of Lincoln to Horace Greeley, *quoted in* Lorraine A. Williams, *Northern Intellectual Reaction to the Policy of Emancipation,* 46 J. Negro Hist. 174, 182 (1961) ("What I do about slavery and the colored race, I do because I believe it will help to save the Union; and what I forbear, I forbear because I do not believe it will help save the Union.").

3. Douglas, The Lincoln-Douglas Debates: The First Complete, Unexpurgated Text 54–55 (Harold Holzer ed., 1993) (Aug. 21, 1858).

4. 3 The Collected Works of Abraham Lincoln, *supra,* at 16; Gabor Boritt, *Did He Dream of a Lily-White America? The Voyage of Linconia, in* The Lincoln Enigma 2–5 (Gabor Boritt ed., 2001); Don E. Fehrenbacher, *Only His Stepchildren: Lincoln and the Negro, in* A Nation Divided: Problems and Issues of the Civil War and Reconstruction 47–48 (George M. Fredrickson ed., 1975).

5. 3 The Collected Works of Abraham Lincoln, *supra,* at 92–93 (Sept. 11, 1858); *id.* at 327 (Oct. 18, 1858); James M. McPherson, Battle Cry of Freedom: The Civil War Era 129 (1988; 1989); Waldo W. Braden, Abraham Lincoln: Public Speaker 35–36 (1988).

6. Cong. Globe, 36th Cong., 2d Sess. 1285 (House vote) (Feb. 28, 1861), 1364 (text)

(Mar. 2, 1861), 1402–3 (Senate vote) (Mar. 2, 1861); R. Alton Lee, *The Corwin Amendment in the Secession Crisis*, 70 Ohio Hist. Q. 1 (1961).

7. 3 Official Records of the Union and Confederate Armies 466–67 (Robert N. Scott ed., ser. 1, 1882) (proclamation); 12 Stat. 319 (1861) (First Confiscation Act).

8. Joint Resolution . . ., ch. 26, 12 Stat. 617 (1862).

9. Harry S. Blackiston, *Lincoln's Emancipation Plan*, 7 J. Negro Hist. 257, 269–70 (1922) (on Hunter).

10. W. M. Brewer, *Lincoln and the Border States*, 34 J. Negro Hist. 46, 59–60 (1949); Abraham Lincoln, *Appeal to Border State Representatives to Favor Compensated Emancipation*, in 5 The Collected Works of Abraham Lincoln, *supra*, at 317–19 (July 12, 1862).

11. 12 Stat. 589, 591 (Second Confiscation Act) (July 17, 1862); *id.* at 597, 599 (Militia Act) (July 17, 1862); *id.* at 432 (Act to Secure Freedom in the Territories) (June 19, 1862); *id.* at 376 (Act for Release in the District of Columbia) (Apr. 16, 1862).

12. Letter from Lincoln to Orville H. Browning (Sept. 22, 1861), *in* 4 The Collected Works of Abraham Lincoln, *supra*, at 532; Letter from Lincoln to Horace Greeley (Aug. 22, 1862), *in* Abraham Lincoln: Speeches and Writings, 1859–1865, at 358 (Don E. Fehrenbacher ed., 1989).

13. Gideon Welles, *The History of Emancipation*, 14 The Galaxy 842–44 (Dec. 1872); Francis B. Carpenter, Six Months at the White House with Abraham Lincoln 21–23 (1867).

14. http://www.loc.gov/exhibits/treasures/trt025.html (original draft of Proclamation); Salmon P. Chase, Inside Lincoln's Cabinet: The Civil War Diaries of Salmon P. Chase 149–52 (David Donald ed., 1954); Abraham Lincoln, *Address on Colonization to a Deputation of Negroes*, in 5 The Collected Works of Abraham Lincoln, *supra*, at 370 (first published in New York Tribune, Aug. 15, 1862); James D. Lockett, *Abraham Lincoln and Colonization: An Episode That Ends in Tragedy at L'Ile à Vache, Haiti, 1863–1864*, 21 J. Black Stud. 428, 435 (1991).

15. Mark M. Krug, *The Republican Party and the Emancipation Proclamation*, 48 J. Negro Hist. 98, 114 (1963); Frederick Douglass, Speech at Cooper Institute, February 1863, *quoted in* Lincoln on Black and White 133, 135 (Arthur Zilversmit ed., 1971); James M. McPherson, The Struggle for Equality 119 (2d ed. 1995); Louis Ruchames, *William Lloyd Garrison and the Negro Franchise*, 50 J. Negro Hist. 37, 39 (1965); Elsie M. Lewis, *Liberty and Reaction*, 32 J. Negro Educ. 251, 252 (1963); Clarence E. Walker, *Book Review*, 65 J. Am. Hist. 1130, 1131 (1979) (reviewing Daniel A. Novak, The Wheel of Servitude: Black Forced Labor after Slavery) (quoting Phillips).

16. Leonard P. Stavisky, *Book Review* 35 J. Negro Hist. 323, 325 (1950) (reviewing Ralph Korngold, Two Friends of Man) (quoting Illinois legislature).

17. Alexander Tsesis, The Thirteenth Amendment and American Freedom: A Legal History (2004); Michael Vorenberg, Final Freedom: The Civil War, the Abolition of Slavery, and the Thirteenth Amendment (2001); Abraham Lincoln, *Annual Message to Congress*, in 8 The Collected Works of Abraham Lincoln, *supra*, at 149 (Dec. 6, 1864); Noah Brooks, Washington in Lincoln's Time 141–42 (1895; Herbert Mitgang ed., 1958); *Reply to the Committee Notifying Lincoln of His Renomination*, 7 The Collected Works of Abraham Lincoln, *supra*, at 380 (June 9, 1864); LaWanda Cox and John H. Cox, Politics, Principle, and Prejudice, 1865–1866, at 30 (1969).

18. 13 Stat. 326, 329 (July 1, 1864) (Act regulating the D.C. Railroad Company); 13 Stat. 536, 537 (Mar. 3, 1865) (Act regulating the D.C. Railroad Company); U.S. Const. art. I, 8, cl. 17; Railroad Co. v. Brown, 84 U.S. 445 (1873).

19. Cong. Globe, 38th Cong., 1st Sess. 19 (Dec. 14, 1863) (Ashley); *id.* at 21 (Wilson); *id.* at 521 (Feb. 8, 1864) (Sumner's equality language); *id.* at 1488 (Apr. 8, 1864) (exchange between Sumner and Howard).

20. *Id.* 1439–40 (Apr. 6, 1864) (Harlan); *id.* at 1324 (Mar. 28, 1864) (Wilson).

21. *Id.* at 2990 (June 15, 1864) (Ingersoll); see also *id.* at 1324 (Mar. 28, 1864) (Wilson); *id.* at 1199 (Mar. 19, 1864) (Wilson). Even a Democratic supporter of the proposal, Representative James S. Rollins, who held slaves in Missouri, used the Declaration to argue that race was an accidental circumstance, and all men are created equal. Cong. Globe, 38th Cong. 2d Sess. 260 (Jan. 13, 1865).

22. *Id.* at 244 (Jan. 12, 1865) (Vermont Representative Frederick E. Woodbridge); Cong. Globe, 39th Cong., 1st Sess. 1151 (Mar. 2, 1866) (Pennsylvania Representative M. Russell Thayer); Cong. Globe, 38th Cong., 1st Sess. 1439 (Apr. 6, 1864) (Harlan); Cong. Globe, 38th Cong., 2d Sess. 154 (Jan. 10, 1865) (Kasson).

23. Cong. Globe, 38th Cong., 1st Sess. 2982 (June 15, 1864) (Mallory).

24. McPherson, *supra,* at 126.

25. Isaac N. Arnold, The History of Abraham Lincoln, and the Overthrow of Slavery 587–88 (1866); 2 Documentary History of the Constitution of the United States of America, 1786–1870, at 636–37 (1894); http://www.nps.gov/archive/malu/documents/amend13 .htm.

26. Weevils in the Wheat: Interviews with Virginia Ex-Slaves 58–59 (Perdue *et al.* eds., 1976); Leon F. Litwack, Been in the Storm So Long: The Aftermath of Slavery 374 (1979); Peter Kolchin, American Slavery, 1619–1877, at 216–18 (1993).

27. Peter Kolchin, American Slavery, 1619–1877, at 217–21 (1993); Whitelaw Reid, After the War: A Tour of the Southern States, May 1, 1865–May 1, 1866, at 387, 389 (1866); 5 American Slave: A Composite Autobiography 153 (George Rawick ed., 1972).

28. William Preston Vaughn, Schools for All: The Blacks and Public Education in the South, 1865–1877, at 1 (1974); Eric Foner, Reconstruction: America's Unfinished Revolution, 1863–1877, at 96 (1988; 1989); Ivan E. McDougle, *The Social Status of the Slave,* 3 J. Negro Hist. 281, 289 (1918); *Danger: An Educated Black Man,* 22 J. Blacks in Higher Educ. 19 (Winter 1998–99); Janet Cornelius, *"We Slipped and Learned to Read": Slave Accounts of the Literacy Process, 1830–1865,* 44 Phylon 171, 176, 183 (1983); James A. Padgett, *From Slavery to Prominence in North Carolina: Preparation,* 22 J. Negro Hist. 433, 435 (1937); John B. Myers, *The Education of the Alabama Freedmen during Presidential Reconstruction, 1865– 1867,* 40 J. Negro Educ. 163, 167 (1971); Sandra E. Small, *The Yankee Schoolmarm in Freedmen's Schools: An Analysis of Attitudes,* 45 J. S. Hist. 381, 381 (1979); Letter from Edmonia G. Highgate to M. E. Strieby, Dec. 17, 1866, *in* We Are Your Sisters: Black Women in the Nineteenth Century 298–99 (Dorothy Sterling ed., 1984); Kenneth M. Stampp, The Era of Reconstruction, 1865–1877, at 139 (1969).

29. Kolchin, *supra,* at 63–67, 220–21 (1993); Litwack, *supra,* at 191, 237–38; James Hammond, *Letter to an English Abolitionist, in* The Ideology of Slavery 191–92 (1981); Avery Craven, Reconstruction: The Ending of the Civil War 119–20 (1969); Gilbert T. Stephenson, *Racial Distinctions in Southern Law,* 1 Am. Pol. Sci. Rev. 44, 47–48 (1906); Herbert G. Gutman, Black Family in Slavery and Freedom, 1750–1925, at 207–9 (1976).

30. Andrew E. Taslitz, *Slaves no More! The Implications of the Informed Citizen Ideal for Discovery Before Fourth Amendment Suppression Hearings,* 15 Ga. St. U. L. Rev. 709, 747 (1999); Donald G. Nieman, To Set the Law in Motion: The Freedmen's Bureau and the Legal Rights of Blacks, 1865–68, at 98 (1979); Cong. Globe, 39th Cong., 1st Sess. III (Dec. 21, 1865).

31. *Id.* at 39 (Dec. 13, 1865); W. E. B. Du Bois, Black Reconstruction 167 (1935; 1973); David Oshinsky, Worse Than Slavery (1996); Benjamin B. Kendrick, Journal of the Joint Committee of Fifteen on Reconstruction 274–75 (1914).

32. Barton Shaw, *Book Review,* 57 J. S. Hist. 782, 782–83 (1991) (reviewing Race, Class, and Politics in Southern History (Jeffrey J. Crow *et al.* eds.)).

33. Ch. 31, 14 Stat. 27 (1866) (Civil Rights Act of 1866); ch. 86, 14 Stat. 50 (1866) (Slave Kidnaping Act); ch. 187, 14 Stat. 546 (1867) (Peonage Act of 1867); ch. 27, 14 Stat. 385 (Act of Feb. 5, 1867, expanding the scope of habeas corpus statutes).

34. Cong. Globe, 39th Cong., 1st Sess. 211–12 (Jan. 12, 1866); Civil Rights Act, 14 Stat. 27 (1866).

35. The congressional vote overriding President Johnson's veto of the Civil Rights Act of 1866 is found at Cong. Globe, 39th Cong., 1st Sess. 1809 (Senate) (Apr. 6, 1866), 1861 (House) (Apr. 9, 1866). For some insights that the Civil Rights Act of 1866 provides for understanding the Fourteenth Amendment, see Robert J. Kaczorowski, *Congress's Power to Enforce Fourteenth Amendment Rights: Lessons from Federal Remedies the Framers Enacted,* 42 Harv. J. on Legis. 187 (2005).

36. United States v. Virginia, 518 U.S. 515 (1996); Brown v. Board of Ed., 347 U.S. 483 (1954); Tennessee v. Lane, 541 U.S. 509 (2004); Lawrence v. Texas, 539 U.S. 558 (2003).

37. Cong. Globe, 39th Cong., 1st Sess. 2459 (May 8, 1866) (Thaddeus Stevens, explaining the Fourteenth Amendment); *id.* at 2764 (May 23, 1866) (introducing the joint resolution on the Fourteenth Amendment in the Senate); *id.* at 3042 (June 8, 1866) (Senate vote passing the joint resolution); *id.* at 3149 (June 13, 1866) (House vote passing the joint resolution).

38. Kendrick, *supra,* at 46 (Congressman Thaddeus Stevens's proposal); *id.* at 51 (Congressman John A. Bingham's proposal); Cong. Globe, 39th Cong., 1st Sess. 1033–34 (Feb. 26, 1866) (proposed joint resolution); *id.* at 157–58 (Jan. 9, 1866) (Bingham's initial outline of the Fourteenth Amendment).

39. *Id.* at 2079–81 (Apr. 21, 1866) (Nicholson of Delaware); *id.* at App. at 133 (Feb. 26, 1866) (Rogers of New Jersey).

40. For the House votes on the Civil Rights Act of 1866 and the veto override see Cong. Globe, 39th Cong., 1st Sess. 1367, 1861 (1866).

41. Cong. Globe, 39th Cong., 1st Sess. 1063–64 (Feb. 27, 1866) (Hale of New York); *id.* at 1086 (Feb. 28, 1866) (Davis of New York); *id.* at 1088 (Woodbridge) (Feb. 28, 1866); *id.* at 1095 (Feb. 28, 1866) (postponement).

42. *Id.* at 2530 (May 10, 1866).

43. Laurent B. Frantz, *Congressional Power to Enforce the Fourteenth Amendment against Private Acts,* 73 Yale L.J. 1353, 1355 (1964) (quoting Freedmen's Bureau agent).

44. Cong. Globe, 39th Cong., 1st Sess. 2765–66 (May 23, 1866); Corfield v. Coryell, 6 F. Cas. 546, 551–52 (C.C.E.D. Pa. 1823) (dicta of Washington, as designated Circuit Court justice); Cong. Globe, 39th Cong., 1st Sess. 1088 (Feb. 28, 1866).

45. 59 Mass. 198.

46. Cong. Globe, 39th Cong., 2d Sess. 124 (Dec. 14, 1866); *id.* at 128; *id.* at 252.

47. 14 Stat. 428, 429 (Mar. 2, 1867); 15 Stat. 72 (June 22, 1868); 15 Stat. 73 (June 25, 1868).

48. *Petition from South Carolina Black Citizens,* June 29, 1865, *in* 8 The Papers of Andrew Johnson 317 (1989); Letter from Joseph Noxon to Johnson (May 27, 1865), *in* 8 *id.* at 119.

49. Letter from William Johnson to Johnson (June 6, 1865), *in* 8 *id.* at 190; Letter from

J. Rhodes Mayo to Johnson (June 17, 1865), *in* 8 *id.* at 252; Letter from J. G. Dodge to Johnson (June 20, 1865), *in* 8 *id.* at 263.

50. Leon F. Litwack, North of Slavery: The Negro in the Free States, 1790–1860, at 74–75 (1961); Lawrence Grossman, The Democratic Party and the Negro: Northern and National Politics, 1868–1892, at 16 (1976).

51. James Blaine, James Garfield, *et al., Ought the Negro to be Disfranchised? Ought He to Have Been Enfranchised?*, 128 North Am. Rev. 225, 225–26, 244–47 (1879).

52. William Gillette, Retreat from Reconstruction, 1869–1879, at 18–19 (1979); William Gillette, The Right to Vote: Politics and the Passage of the Fifteenth Amendment (1969); LaWanda Cox and John H. Cox, *Negro Suffrage and Republican Politics: The Problem of Motivation in Reconstruction Historiography,* 33 J. S. Hist. 303, 318–20, 327–30 (1967).

53. Michael Les Benedict, A Compromise of Principle: Congressional Republicans and Reconstruction, 1863–1869, at 325–27 (1974); Cong. Globe 40th Cong., 3d Sess. 560 (Jan. 23, 1869); *id.* at 639 (Jan. 27, 1869); H.R. Res. 1531, 40th Cong. 3d Sess. (Dec. 14, 1868); Cong. Globe, 40th Cong. 3d Sess. 708 (Jan. 29, 1869).

54. *Id.* at 861–62 (Feb. 4, 1869) (Warner); *id.* at 863 (Morton); *id.* at 1626–27 (Feb. 26, 1869) (Wilson).

55. *See* John M. Mathews, Legislative and Judicial History of the Fifteenth Amendment 35–36, 44–45, 48 (1909).

56. H.R. Rep. No. 22, 41st Cong., 3d Sess. (Jan. 30 1871); S. Rep. No. 21, 42d Cong., 2d Sess. (Jan. 25, 1872).

57. H.R. Rep. No. 37, 41st Cong., 3d Sess. at 2–3 (1871).

58. John A. Carpenter, *Atrocities in the Reconstruction Period,* 47 J. Negro Hist. 234, 242–44 (1962); Herbert Shapiro, *The Ku Klux Klan During Reconstruction: The South Carolina Episode,* 49 J. Negro Hist. 34, 36–38, 40–41 (1964).

59. 16 Stat. 140 (Mar. 31, 1870).

60. 16 Stat. 433 (Feb. 28, 1871); 17 Stat. 13 (Apr. 20, 1871).

61. Cong. Globe, 42d Cong., 1st Sess. App. 85–86 (Mar. 31, 1871) (Bingham); *id.* at 501 (1871).

62. Cong. Globe, 42d Cong., 1st Sess. 693–94 (Apr. 14, 1871) (Edmunds); Cong. Globe, 42d Cong., 1st Sess. App. 150 (Apr. 4, 1871).

63. Stephen Cresswell, *Enforcing the Enforcement Acts: The Department of Justice in Northern Mississippi, 1870–1890,* 53 J. S. Hist. 421, 425 (1987); Everette Swinney, *Enforcing the Fifteenth Amendment, 1870–1877,* 28 J. S. Hist. 202, 217–18 (1962); Eric Foner, Reconstruction: America's Unfinished Revolution, 1863–1877, at 457 (1988); Louis F. Williams, The Great South Carolina Ku Klux Klan Trials, 1871–1872 (1996); Shapiro, *supra;* Michael E. Deutsch, *The Improper Use of the Federal Grand Jury: An Instrument for the Internment of Political Activists,* 75 J. Crim. L. and Criminology 1159, 1170 n. 56 (1984).

64. Cong. Globe, 42d Cong., 2d Sess. 382–83 (Jan. 15, 1872) (Sumner).

65. Cong. Globe, 41st Cong., 2d Sess. 3434 (May 13, 1870) (proposed bill); Cong. Globe, 42d Cong., 2d Sess. 244 (Dec. 20, 1871) (proposed bill); *id.* 429 (Jan. 17, 1872) (Quarles); *id.* at 431 (Griffing); *id.* (Sykes).

66. Sumner, New Nat'l Era, May 5, 1870, *quoted in* Bertram Wyatt-Brown, *The Civil Rights Act of 1875,* 18 W. Pol. Q. 763, 763–64 (1965); Cong. Record, 43 Cong., 1st Sess. 4173 (May 22, 1874) (Edmunds); *id.* at 4114–15 (May 21, 1874) (Johnston).

67. David Donald, Charles Sumner and the Rights of Man 586–87 (1970).

68. Alfred H. Kelly, *The Congressional Controversy over School Segregation, 1867–1875,*

64 Am. Historical Rev. 537, 552–56, 563 n. 143 (1959) (on North Carolina and Georgia segregation).

69. Civil Rights Act of 1875, ch. 114, 1–4, 18 Stat. 335; Civil Rights Cases, 109 U.S. 3 (1883).

70. Cong. Globe 40th Cong., 1st Sess. 203 (Mar. 19, 1867) (Stevens' Confiscation and Apportionment Bill); William L. Richter, American Reconstruction, 1862–1877, at 240–41 (1996) (concerning Julian's land reapportionment plan); *What the Black Man Wants: An Address Delivered in Boston, Massachusetts, on 26 January 1865, in* 4 The Frederick Douglass Papers 59, 68 (J. Blassingame and J. McKivigan eds., 1991).

CHAPTER SIX. Unraveling Constitutional Reconstruction

1. Buford Satcher, Blacks in Mississippi Politics, 1865–1900, at 38–39 (1978); Lerone Bennett, Jr., Black Power U.S.A.: The Human Side of Reconstruction, 1867–1877, at 226–29 (1967); 9 The American Slave: A Composite Autobiography 4:42 (George P. Rawick ed., 1972); J. Mason Brewer, Negro Legislators of Texas 51–52 (1970); Richard Bardolph, *The Distinguished Negro in America, 1770–1936,* 60 Am. Hist. Rev. 527, 538 n. 20 (1955).

2. Rutherford B. Hayes *quoted in* Vincent P. De Santis, Republicans Face the Southern Question: The New Departure Years, 1877–1897, at 100–101 (1959); Stanley P. Hirshson, Farewell to the Bloody Shirt: Northern Republicans and the Southern Negro, 1877–1893, at 47–48 (1962).

3. Live-Stock Dealers' and Butchers' Ass'n v. Crescent City Live-Stock Landing and Slaughter-House Co., 15 F. Cas. 649, 652, 653 (1870).

4. Bradwell v. Illinois, 83 U.S. (16 Wall.) 130, 139 (1873).

5. The Slaughter-House Cases, 83 U.S. (16 Wall.) 36, 66–83 (1873).

6. *Id.* at 125, 128–29 (Swayne, J., dissenting).

7. *Id.* at 112, 114–16 (Bradley, J., dissenting).

8. *Id.* at 90, 100–101 (Field, J., dissenting).

9. United States v. Cruikshank, 92 U.S. 542, 560 (1875) (Clifford, J., dissenting); Robert Kaczorowski, The Politics of Judicial Interpretation: The Federal Courts, Department of Justice and Civil Rights, 1866–1876, at 176 (1985); Eric Foner, Reconstruction: America's Unfinished Revolution, 1863–1877, at 530–31 (1988; 1989); Everette Swinney, *Enforcing the Fifteenth Amendment, 1870–1877,* 28 J. S. Hist. 202, 207 (1962).

10. Cruikshank, 92 U.S. at 552–53, 554, 557–59.

11. Hall v. DeCuir, 95 U.S. 485 (1877).

12. Civil Rights Cases, 109 U.S. 3 (1883).

13. *Id.* at 13–15.

14. Malvina S. Harlan, Some Memories of a Long Life, 1854–1911, at 112–13 (2002).

15. Alan F. Westin, *John Marshall Harlan and the Constitutional Rights of Negroes: The Transformation of a Southerner,* 66 Yale L.J. 637, 681–82 (1957).

16. *Divided Feeling in Atlanta on the Vexed Question,* N.Y. Times, Oct. 18, 1883, at 1 (concerning Atlanta opera house and Bullock reactions); *If Eloquence and Pen Fail the Negro Must Use Pistol and Bludgeon,* Chi. Daily Trib., Oct. 16, 1883, at 1 (Greener); *A Word to the Colored Men,* Chi. Daily Trib., Oct. 18, 1883, at 4 (Springfield, Ill.); *Colored Citizens Enter a Loud Protest against the Supreme Court Decision,* Chi. Daily Trib., Oct. 25, 1883 (Chicago); *Large Meeting Held at Indianapolis, Ind., to Consider the Recent Supreme Court Decision,* Chi. Daily Trib., Oct. 23, 1883, at 3; *The Action of the Supreme Court Condemned,*

Chi. Daily Trib., Oct. 18, 1883, at 1 (Pittsburgh); *Division of Opinion among Colored Leaders Regarding the Recent Decision,* Chi. Daily Trib., Oct. 18, 1883, at 1 (Douglass).

17. *See An Important Decision by the United States Supreme Court,* Chi. Daily, Oct. 16, 1883, at 1 (contemporary reactions); *Effects of Civil Rights Decision on District of Columbia Suits: Probability of a New Issue Growing Out of the Court's Action,* Chi. Daily, Oct. 17, 1883, at 1 (Republican response).

18. C. Vann Woodward, *The Case of the Louisiana Traveler, in* Quarrels That Have Shaped the Constitution 145, 145–46 (John A. Garraty ed., 1966); Howard N. Rabinowitz, *From Exclusion to Segregation: Southern Race Relations, 1865–1890,* 63 J. Am. Hist. 325, 336–37 (1976).

19. Owen Fiss, *Troubled Beginnings of the Modern State, 1888–1910,* in 8 History of the Supreme Court of the United States 352–85 (1993) (discussing Supreme Court case law about the time of *Plessy*); Plessy v. Ferguson, 163 U.S. 537 (1896).

20. *See, e.g.,* A Fool's Errand. By One of the Fools, *available at* http://docsouth.unc .edu/church/tourgee/tourgee.html 163, 172–74.

21. Abbott v. Hicks, 11 So. 74, 76 (La. 1892).

22. Woodward, *supra,* at 164; Charles A. Lofgren, The Plessy Case: A Legal-Historical Interpretation 34 (1987); John M. Wisdom, *Plessy v. Ferguson—100 Years Later,* 53 Wash. and Lee L. Rev. 9, 14 (1996).

23. Brook Thomas, *Plessy v. Ferguson and the Literary Imagination,* 9 Cardozo Stud. L. and Literature 45, 46 (1997); Peter Irons, A People's History of the Supreme Court 225–26 (1999); Ex Parte Plessy, 11 So. 948 (1892).

24. James W. Ely, Jr., The Chief Justiceship of Melville W. Fuller, 1888–1910, at 8 (1995); Robert L. McCaul, The Black Struggle for Public Schooling in Nineteenth-Century Illinois 61 (1987).

25. Barton J. Bernstein, *Plessy V. Ferguson: Conservative Sociological Jurisprudence,* 48 J. Negro Hist. 196, 200 (1963) (S.C. and Va.); Hall v. DeCuir, 95 U.S. 485, 485–86 (1877) (La.).

26. Chesapeake, 179 U.S. 388; Ray S. Baker, Following the Color Line: American Negro Citizenship in the Progressive Era 44 (1908; 1964).

27. *Id.* at 34; August Meier and Elliott Rudwick, *The Boycott Movement against Jim Crow Streetcars in the South, 1900–1906,* 55 J. Am. Hist. 756, 756–57 (1969) (streetcar ordinances and statutes); T. B. Benson, *Segregation Ordinances,* 1 Va. L. Reg. 330 (1915) (Baltimore); Milton R. Konvitz, *Segregation and the Civil Rights of Negroes: The Extent and Character of Legally-Enforced Segregation,* 20 J. Negro Educ. 425, 431 (1951) (listing various statutes and ordinances).

28. Gilbert T. Stephenson, Race Distinctions in American Law 190–92 (1910; 1969).

29. Lawrence J. Friedman, *The Search for Docility: Racial Thought in the White South, 1861–1917,* 31 Phylon 313, 320 (1970).

CHAPTER SEVEN. Political Restrictions and Developments

1. John Hosmer and Joseph Fineman, *Black Congressmen in Reconstruction Historiography,* 39 Phylon 97, 97 (1978); Monroe N. Work *et al., Some Negro Members of Reconstruction Conventions and Legislatures and of Congress,* 5 J. Negro Hist. 63, 105 (1920); Samuel DuBois Cook, *Democracy and Tyranny in America: The Radical Paradox of the Bicentennial and Blacks in the American Political System,* 38 J. of Pol. 276, 287 (1976).

2. Byron D'Andra Orey, *Black Legislative Politics in Mississippi,* 30 J. Black Stud. 791,

793 (2000); Vernon Lane Wharton, The Negro in Mississippi, 1865–1890, at 202 (1947); William Cohen, At Freedom's Edge: Black Mobility and the Southern White Quest for Racial Control, 1861–1915, at 205–6 (1991) (Louisiana and vote reduction percentages); Joseph H. Cartwright, Triumph of Jim Crow: Tennessee Race Relations in the 1880s, at 65–66, 95–96 (1976); Mark T. Carleton, *What Has Happened since 1921, in* Gateway to Tomorrow: A New Constitution for Louisiana's People 27 (1973).

3. Richard H. Pildes, *Democracy, Anti-Democracy, and the Canon,* 17 Const. Comment. 295, 308–16 (2000); J. Morgan Kousser, The Shaping of Southern Politics: Suffrage, Restriction, and the Establishment of the One-Party South, 1880–1910, at 263 (1974).

4. In an influential study, Key claimed that "formal disfranchisement measures did not lie at the bottom of the decimation of the southern electorate. They, rather, recorded a *fait accompli* brought about, or destined to be brought about, by more fundamental political processes." Southern Politics in State and Nation 533 (1949). Klarman follows Key, writing that "it is not much of an exaggeration to say that blacks already had been effectively disfranchised," primarily through violence and fraud, even "before state constitutional suffrage restrictions were implemented." *The Plessy Era,* 1998 Sup. Ct. Rev. 303, 406 (1998). Klarman does acknowledge that "while fraud and violence were critical to black disfranchisement, one must not unduly minimize the significance of legal restrictions." *Id.* at 405. The effectiveness of the new provisions in virtually eliminating blacks and illiterate and poor whites from political power has been documented by C. Vann Woodward, Origins of the New South, 1877–1913, at 342–47 (1951); Kousser, *supra,* at 50, 238–46 (1974); Charles D. Farris, *The Re-Enfranchisement of Negroes in Florida,* 39 J. Negro Hist. 259, 261 (1954); George B. Tindall, *The Campaign for the Disfranchisement of Negroes in South Carolina,* 15 J. S. Hist. 212, 214–17 (1949); A. A. Taylor, *The Aftermath of Reconstruction,* 9 J. Negro Hist. 546, 549, 562–63 (1924).

5. Pildes, *supra,* at 301–3; Farris, *supra,* at 262.

6. William Cohen, At Freedom's Edge: Black Mobility and the Southern White Quest for Racial Control, 1861–1915, at 207 (1991) ("afford to die . . . ").

7. Stephen Cresswell, Multiparty Politics in Mississippi, 1877–1902, at 220–21 (1955); Earl M. Lewis, *The Negro Voter in Mississippi,* 26 J. Negro Ed. 329, 336–38 (1957).

8. Williams v. Mississippi, 170 U.S. 213, 215 (1898) (pre-1890 figures); James H. Stone, *A Note on Voter Registration under the Mississippi Understanding Clause, 1892,* 38 J. S. Hist. 293, 293, 295 (1972); B. E. H. and J. J. K., Jr., Note, *Federal Protection of Negro Voting Rights,* 51 Va. L. Rev. 1051, 1080 n. 93 (1965) (1899 figures); Albert B. Hart, *The Realities of Negro Suffrage,* 2 Proc. Am. Pol. Sci. Ass'n 149, 160 (1905) (Miss., S.C., La., Ala., and Va. did not put their constitutions to popular vote).

9. Williams, 170 U.S. 213.

10. Quoted in *Ben Tillman: Memories of an Agrarian Racist,* 32 J. Black Higher Educ. 48, 49 (2001) ("You dirty . . . "); Cong. Record, 56 Cong., 1st Sess. 2245 (Feb. 26, 1900) ("We had a hundred . . . ").

11. Francis B. Simkins, The Tillman Movement in South Carolina 212–17 (1926); Cong. Record, 56 Cong., 1st Sess. 3223–24 (Mar. 23, 1900); Francis B. Simkins and Robert H. Woody, South Carolina during Reconstruction 550 (1932).

12. Quiet Revolution in the South 194 (Chandler Davidson and Bernard Grofman eds., 1994); William Simpson, *Note, The Primary Runoff: Racism Reprieve,* 65 N.C. L. Rev. 359, 361 n. 13 (1987); Woodward, *supra,* at 372 n. 11 (1951); Thomas D. Clark and Albert D. Kirwan, The South since Appomattox: A Century of Regional Change 109 (1967).

13. State ex rel. Labauve v. Michel, 46 So. 430, 432 (La. 1908); Leo Alilunas, *A Study of Judicial Cases Which Have Developed as the Result of "White Prymary" Laws,* 25 J. Negro Hist. 172, 173–74 (1940); Paul A. Kunkel, *Modifications in Louisiana Negro Legal Status under Louisiana Constitutions, 1812–1957,* 44 J. Negro Hist. 1, 17–18 (1959) ("this convention has been called . . . "); John C. Rose, *Negro Suffrage: The Constitutional Point of View,* 1 Am. Pol. Sci. Rev. 17, 26–30 (1906) (constitutional provisions); Daniel Brantley, *Blacks and Louisiana Constitutional Development, 1890–Present: A Study in Southern Political Thought and Race Relations,* 48 Phylon 51, 53–56 (1987) (constitutional provisions and 1904 figure); U.S. v. Louisiana, 225 F.Supp. 353, 374 (E.D. La. 1963) (providing voting figures); Kunkel, *supra,* at 19 (1912 grandfather clause amendment).

14. James Knox, Speech (May 22, 1901), *in* 1 Official Proceedings of the Constitutional Convention of the State of Alabama, May 21, 1901 to September 3, 1901, at 9, 12, 18 (1901) ("we must . . . ") and ("descended from a race . . . "); Giles v. Teasley, 193 U.S. 146, 148 (1904) (Alabama population).

15. Francis G. Caffey, *Suffrage Limitations at the South,* 20 Pol. Sci. Q. 53, 56–57 (1905).

16. Joseph H. Taylor, *Populism and Disfranchisement in Alabama,* 34 J. Negro Hist. 410, 425 (1949); Wayne Flynt, *Alabama's Shame: The Historical Origins of the 1901 Constitution,* 53 Ala. L. Rev. 67, 74–75 (2001).

17. Caffey, *supra,* at 54–55 (constitutional provisions); Kirk H. Porter, A History of Suffrage in the United States 213 (1918) (same); Malcolm C. McMillan, Constitutional Development in Alabama, 1798–1901: A Study in Politics, the Negro, and Sectionalism 352–53 (1955) (number of registered voters by race).

18. Louis R. Harlan, *The Secret Life of Booker T. Washington,* 37 J. S. Hist. 393, 397–98 (1971); Giles v. Harris, 189 U.S. 475; Giles v. Teasley, 193 U.S. 146.

19. J. Morgan Kousser, Colorblind Injustice: Minority Voting Rights and the Undoing of the Second Reconstruction 318–22 (1999).

20. Giles v. Teasley, 33 So. 819 (1903).

21. Gray v. Sanders, 372 U.S. 368, 381 (1963) ("the conception of political equality from the Declaration of Independence, to Lincoln's Gettysburg Address, to the Fifteenth, Seventeenth, and Nineteenth Amendments can mean only one thing—one person, one vote"); Wesberry v. Sanders, 376 U.S. 1, 18 (1964) (deciding one-person, one-vote issues to be justiciable); Reynolds v. Sims, 377 U.S. 533, 560–61 (1964) (using one-person, one-vote standards to find a state apportionment plan to be in violation of the Equal Protection Clause); Pub. L. No. 89-110, 79 Stat. 437 (codified as amended in scattered sections of 42 U.S.C.) (VRA).

22. Kousser, The Shaping of Southern Politics, *supra,* at 172, 241 (reduction in black vote); Charles E. Wynes, Race Relations in Virginia, 1870–1902, at 40–41, 64, 66 (1961) (providing details on the Virginia constitution's specific provisions and on the general voter turnout); Wythe W. Holt, Jr., *Constitutional Revision in Virginia, 1902 and 1928: Some Lessons on Roadblocks to Institutional Reform,* 54 Va. L. Rev. 903, 913 (1968).

23. Lawrence D. Rice, The Negro in Texas, 1874–1900, at 132 (1971); Henry A. Bullock, *The Expansion of Negro Suffrage in Texas,* 26 J. Negro Educ. 369, 370 (1957) (Terrell law); Robert W. Hainsworth, *The Negro and the Texas Primaries,* 18 J. Negro Hist. 426, 426 (1933); Edward L. Ayers, The Promise of the New South: Life after Reconstruction 309 (1992) (Georgia); Dewey W. Grantham, Jr., *Hoke Smith: Progressive Governor of Georgia, 1907–1909,* 15 J. S. Hist. 423, 433 (1949).

24. Guinn v. United States, 238 U.S. 347 (1915); Benno C. Schmidt, Jr., *Black Dis-*

franchisement from the KKK to the Grandfather Clause, 82 Colum. L. Rev. 835, 852 (1982); Nixon v. Herndon, 273 U.S. 536 (1927); Nixon v. Condon, 286 U.S. 73 (1932); Smith v. Allwright, 321 U.S. 649 (1944); Terry v. Adams, 345 U.S. 461 (1953).

25. 1 Adams Family Correspondence 370, 381–82 (L. H. Butterfield *et al.* eds., 1963) (Mar. 31, 1776, and Apr. 14, 1776).

26. Angelina Grimké *quoted in* Catherine H. Birney, Grimké Sisters: . . . The First American Women Advocates of Abolition and Woman's Rights 194 (1885); Sarah Grimké, Letters on the Equality of the Sexes and the Condition of Woman 79–83 (1837).

27. Douglas H. Maynard, *The World's Anti-Slavery Convention of 1840,* 47 Miss. Valley Hist. Rev. 452, 459–60, 465 (1960); Jane H. Pease and William H. Pease, *Black Power—The Debate in 1840,* 29 Phylon 19, 25 (1968).

28. 1 A History of Woman Suffrage, 1848–1861, at 70–71 (Elizabeth Cady Stanton ed., 1881); Benjamin Quarles, *Frederick Douglass and the Woman's Rights Movement,* 25 J. Negro Hist. 35 (1940); Proceedings of the Woman's Rights Conventions Held at Seneca Falls and Rochester N.Y., July and August, 1848 (1848).

29. *American Anti-Slavery Society,* National Anti-Slavery Standard, May 13, 1865, at 2 (Phillips quotation); Barbara Allen Babcock, *A Place in the Palladium: Women's Rights and Jury Service,* 61 U. Cin. L. Rev. 1139, 1164–65 (1993) (Stanton); Letter from Stanton to Phillips, May 25, 1865, *in* 2 Elizabeth Cady Stanton as Revealed in Her Letters, Diary and Reminiscences 104–5 (Theodore Stanton and Harriot Stanton Blatch eds., 1922).

30. Babcock, *supra,* at 1164–65 (Truth); National Woman Suffrage Association, *Declaration of Rights for Women, in* A Concise History of Woman Suffrage 302 (1978) (Mary Jo Buhle and Paul Buhle eds., 1978) ("aristocracy"); Woman's Journal, Dec. 6, 1879, at 388 (California petition and supporting argument).

31. 2 A History of Woman Suffrage, 1861–1876, at 91–92 (Elizabeth Cady Stanton, Susan B. Anthony, and Matilda Joslyn Gage eds., 1881; facsimile 1985); Letter from Stanton to Smith (Jan. 1, 1866), *in* Ellen Carol DuBois, Feminism and Suffrage: The Emergence of an Independent Women's Movement in America, 1848–1869, at 61 (1978); Carrie Chapman Catt and Nettie Rogers Shuler, Woman Suffrage and Politics: The Inner Story of the Suffrage Movement 37–41 (1923); William L. O'Neill, Everyone Was Brave: A History of Feminism in America 17 (1971) (Anthony).

32. Gretchen Ritter, *Jury Service and Women's Citizenship before and after the Nineteenth Amendment,* 20 L. and Hist. Rev. 479, 495 (2002) (quoting Stanton, "The noble . . . "); 2 History of Woman Suffrage, 1861–1876, *supra,* at 349–50. Julian's proposal may be found at Cong. Globe 41st Cong., 1st Sess. 72 (Mar. 15, 1869), and H.R.J. Res. 15, 41st Cong. 41 (Mar. 15, 1869). Stanton's endorsement of the proposed sixteenth amendment appears at *The Sixteenth Amendment,* Revolution, Apr. 29, 1869, at 266.

33. 2 History of Woman Suffrage, 1861–1876, *supra,* at 407–10 (1881).

34. Ellen Carol DuBois, *Outgrowing the Compact of the Fathers: Equal Rights, Woman Suffrage, and the United States Constitution, 1820–1878,* 74 J. Am. Hist. 836, 854 (1987).

35. United States v. Anthony, 24 F. Cas. 829 (N.D.N.Y. 1873). Anthony's speech is reproduced in A Concise History of Woman Suffrage, *supra,* at 293–96.

36. *Id.* at 288–90 (Minor's complaint).

37. Minor v. Happersett, 88 U.S. (21 Wall.) 162.

38. Louis Filler, *Parker Pillsbury: An Anti-Slavery Apostle,* 19 New Eng. Q. 315, 333 (1946); Jean V. Matthews, Women's Struggle for Equality: The First Phase, 1828–1876, at 129 (1997).

39. Geoffrey C. Ward, Not for Ourselves Alone: The Story of Elizabeth Cady Stanton and Susan B. Anthony 108, 110 (1999) (quoting Train and Anthony); David Donald, Charles Sumner and the Rights of Man 83-84 (1970) (quoting Train); Garrison to Stanton (Jan. 4, 1868), *quoted in* Garth E. Pauley, *W. E. B. Du Bois on Woman Suffrage: A Critical Analysis of His Crisis Writings,* 30 J. Black Stud. 383, 408 n. 3 (1981).

40. Robert E. Riegel, *The Split of Feminist Movement in 1869,* 49 Miss. Valley Hist. Rev. 485, 491 (1962); William Lloyd Garrison and the Fight against Slavery: Selections from *The Liberator* (William E. Cain ed., 1995); Wendy Hamand Venet, A Strong-Minded Woman: The Life of Mary Livermore (2005); Julia Ward Howe and the Woman Suffrage Movement: A Selection from Her Speeches and Essays (1913); Thomas Wentworth Higginson, Army Life in a Black Regiment (1870).

41. *Debates at the American Equal Rights Association Meeting, New York City, May 12–14, 1869, in* A Concise History of Woman Suffrage, *supra,* at 257–74.

42. *Id.* 259, 259–60, 262–63; *The Sixteenth Amendment,* Revolution, Apr. 29, 1869, at 266; Ellen Carol DuBois, Feminism and Suffrage: The Emergence of an Independent Women's Movement in America, 1848–1869, at 178 (1978).

43. *Debates at the American Equal Rights Association Meeting, supra,* at 258–59.

44. *Id.* at 258–59, 267.

45. *Id.* at 260–63, 267.

46. Lawrence M. Friedman, Joanna L. Grossman, and Chris Guthrie, *Guardians: A Research Note,* 40 Am. J. Leg. Hist. 146, 152–53 (1996); Michael Grossberg, Governing the Hearth: Law and the Family in Nineteenth-Century America 234–37, 244–47 (1985).

47. Elizabeth B. Clark, *Matrimonial Bonds: Slavery and Divorce in Nineteenth-Century America,* 8 L. and Hist. Rev. 25, 46–48 (1990); Elizabeth Pleck, *Feminist Responses to "Crimes against Women," 1868–1896,* 8 Signs 451, 455–56 (1983); Mary Lyndon Shanley, *Marital Slavery and Friendship: John Stuart Mill's The Subjection of Women,* 9 Pol. Theory 229, 230–35 (1981); Eric Foner, The Story of American Freedom 83–84 (1998).

48. Ida B. Wells, Crusade for Justice: The Autobiography of Ida B. Wells 229–30 (Alfreda M. Duster ed., 1970).

49. Mary Cady Stanton, *quoted in* James M. McPherson, The Abolitionist Legacy: From Reconstruction to the NAACP 319 (1975).

50. Paula Giddings, When and Where I Enter: The Impact of Black Women on Race and Sex in America 126–27 (1984) (quoting Anthony from the 1899 meeting); McPherson, *supra,* at 321–22; Belle Kearney, *The South and Woman Suffrage,* Woman's J., Apr. 4, 1903, at 106–7.

51. *Henry B. Blackwell, Address to the NAWSA Convention, Atlanta, Georgia, . . . 1895, in* A Concise History of Woman Suffrage, *supra,* at 337.

52. Wyo. Laws 1869, ch. 31, 1–2; Wyo. Const. art. 6, 1 (1890); M. Ostrogoski, *Woman Suffrage in Local Self-Government,* 6 Pol. Sci. Q. 677, 707—8 (1891).

53. Suzanne M. Marilley, Woman Suffrage and the Origins of Liberal Feminism in the United States, 1820–1920, at 124–58 (1996) (Colorado); Jennifer Frost et al., *Why Did Colorado Suffragists Fail to Win the Right to Vote in 1877, but Succeed in 1893?, available at* http://www.binghamton.edu/womhist/colosuff/intro.htm; http://www.binghamton.edu/womhist/teacher/colosuff.htm.

54. Utah Const., art. 4, 1; *Utah: Women in Church, Marriage, and Politics, available at* http://www.museumoftheamericanwest.org/explore/exhibits/suffrage/suffrage—ut.html; Taylor v. Louisiana, 419 U.S. 522, 533 n. 13 (1975) (Utah juries); ID. Const. art. 6, 2;

Beverly Beeton, Women Vote in the West: The Woman Suffrage Movement, 1869–1986, at 116–33 (1986) (Idaho).

55. G. Thomas Edwards, Sowing Good Seeds, The Northwest Suffrage Campaigns of Susan B. Anthony 19–153 (1990); *Abigail Scott Duniway and Idaho Suffrage, available at* http://farrit.lili.org/node/104; Washington Territory, Act of Nov. 23, 1883; F. M. Butlin, *International Congress of Women,* 9 Econ. J. 450, 450 (1899) (1888 convention).

56. Mildred Andrews, *Women in Washington State Win the Vote on Nov. 8, 1910,* http:// www.historylink.org/essays/output.cfm?file_id=5213; T. A. Larson, *The Woman Suffrage Movement in Washington,* 67 Pac. Northwest Q. 49 (1976).

57. Barbara Allen Babcock, *Clara Shortridge Foltz: "First Woman,"* 30 Ariz. L. Rev. 673, 673–74, 695–715 (1988); John Calvin Sherer, History of Glendale and Vicinity 321 (1922) (Braly); *Charming Women in Suffragette Lobby,* L.A. Times, Nov. 10, 1910, at II1; Eileen L. McDonagh and H. Douglas Price, *Woman Suffrage in the Progressive Era: Patterns of Opposition and Support in Referenda Voting, 1910–1918,* 79 Am. Pol. Sci. Rev. 415, 416 (1985).

58. *Suffrage Gains Jewish Women,* L.A. Times, May 9, 1911, at II6; *Talks Suffrage to Footlights, id.,* Sept. 19, 1911, at I6 (rabbi); *Law Student Heads Aliens,* L.A. Times, Apr. 2, 1911, at II13; *Suffragists' New Machine,* L.A. Times, July 15, 1911, at II3.

59. *Antis Voice Their Protest,* L.A. Times, Dec. 17, 1910, at II6; *Suffrage Fad of Minority: Antis Want Men to Understand Women's Position, id.,* Feb. 6, 1911, at I11. *See also* Dora Oliphant Coe, *California Opposes Woman Suffrage, id.,* Aug. 30, 1911, at II7.

60. *Suffrage Wins by 2,500,* N.Y. Times, Oct. 14, 1911, at 13.

61. *Virginia Rejects Suffrage,* N.Y. Times, Feb. 9, 1912, at 1; *Suffragists Beaten, But Still Hopeful, id.,* Mar. 20, 1912, at 8; *Suffrage Wins, Then Is Shelved, id.,* Mar. 30, 1912, at 2; *Weep at Suffrage Defeat: Connecticut Women Grieve in House Gallery as Amended Bill Is Rejected, id.,* Apr. 3, 1913, at 11; *Woman Suffrage in Defeat,* Chi. Daily Trib., Apr. 10, 1912, at 1.

62. Scown v. Czarnecki, 106 N.E. 276, 277 (Ill. 1914) (constitutional and statutory text); John A. Fairlie, *The Illinois Legislature,* 7 Am. Pol. Sci. Rev. 435, 436–37 (1913); Steven M. Buechler, The Transformation of the Woman Suffrage Movement: The Case of Illinois, 1850–1920 (1986); Jane Addams, *Society and Women's Clubs,* Chi. Daily Trib., Feb. 4, 1912, at I1; *One Woman's Kiss Gives Illinois Suffrage,* L.A. Times, June 14, 1913, at I1.

63. Christine A. Lunardini and Thomas J. Knock, *Woodrow Wilson and Woman Suffrage: A New Look,* 95 Pol. Sci. Q. 655, 661 (1980–81); *Defeat of Woman Suffrage,* N.Y. Times, Nov. 3. 1915, at 14; Arthur Connors, *Constitutional Amendments and Referenda Measures, 1917,* 12 Am. Pol. Sci. Rev. 268, 269 (1918); *Woman Suffrage,* N.Y. Times, Nov. 7, 1917, at 12 ("The *Times* will . . ."); *Urges Suffragists Not to Stand Alone,* N.Y. Times, Dec. 7, 1917, at 12 (quoting Blatch).

64. *Breaks Silence: President Wilson Congratulates Mrs. Carrie Chapman Catt on Suffragists' Success in North Dakota,* Chi. Daily Trib., Jan. 27, 1917, at 5; A Surprising Victory for Suffrage, http://www.nebraskastudies.org/0700/frameset_reset.html?http://www.ne braskastudies.org/0700/stories/0701_0111.html (Nebraska); 1917 R.I. Pub. Laws 1507; In re Opinion to the Governor, 109 A. 84, 85 (R.I. 1920); Eileen L. McDonagh and H. Douglas Price, *Woman Suffrage in the Progressive Era: Patterns of Opposition and Support in Referenda Voting, 1910–1918,* 79 Am. Pol. Sci. Rev. 415, 417 (1985) (Ohio, Indiana, Michigan, and laws of 1919 and 1920); *Women's Suffrage in Arkansas,* http://asms.k12.ar.us/ar mem/wallace/History.htm; Deborah P. Clifford, *Recalling the Women's Suffrage Struggle in Vt.,* http://www.vermonttoday.com/century/otherviews/dclifford.html; *Chronology of Michigan Women's History,* http://www.h-net.org/michigan/timeline/miwchron.html.

65. Eleanor Flexner, Century of Struggle: The Women's Rights Movement in the United States 289–93 (1975); Paula Baker, *The Domestication of Politics: Women and American Political Society, 1780–1920,* 89 Am. Hist. Rev. 620, 642–43 (1984).

66. *Favor Woman Suffrage,* N.Y. Times, Nov. 7, 1910, at 10 (poll of congressional candidates).

67. Sandra Day O'Connor, *The History of the Women's Suffrage Movement,* 49 Vand. L. Rev. 657, 667–68 (1996).

68. John A. Moon, Cong. Record, 65th Cong., 2d Sess. 765–66 (Jan. 10, 1918); Rankin, *id.* at 771; Raker, *id.* at 772–73; Philip N. Cohen, *Nationalism and Suffrage: Gender Struggle in Nation-Building America,* 21 Signs 707, 719–25 (1996).

69. Campbell, Cong. Record, 65th Cong., 2d Sess. 767; Cantrill, *id.* at 765; Kelly, *id.* at 769–70.

70. Wilson, Cong. Record, 65th Cong., 2d Sess. 10, 928–29 (Sept. 30, 1918); Lisa A. Marovich, *Fueling the Fires of Genius: Women's Inventive Activities in American War Eras,* 59 J. Econ. Hist. 462, 464–65 (1999); Ellen S. More, *"A Certain Restless Ambition": Women Physicians and World War I,* 41 Am. Q. 636, 652–53 (1989).

71. E. O. Phillips, *Women's Vote Is Ratified by Three States: Illinois First, Then Wisconsin and Michigan,* Chi. Daily Trib., Jun. 11, 1919, at 1; *Colby Proclaims Woman Suffrage,* N.Y. Times, Aug. 27, 1920, at 1.

72. Kenneth R. Johnson, *White Racial Attitudes as a Factor in the Arguments against the Nineteenth Amendment,* 31 Phylon 31, 31–32 (1970); U.S. Department of Interior, *19th. Amendment to the U.S. Constitution,* available at http://www.nps.gov/malu/documents/amend19.htm.

73. *Thousands Carry Lunches to Polls,* N.Y. Times, Nov. 3, 1920, at 11; *Sees Women's Influence: Miss Paul Says They Will Be Better Organized Next Time,* N.Y. Times, Nov. 3, 1920, at 22.

74. *Negro Women Are Refused Ballots,* L.A. Times, Nov. 3, 1920, at 19; on Paul's unwillingness to help black women voters see Nancy F. Cott, *Feminist Politics in the 1920s: The National Woman's Party,* 71 J. Am. Hist. 43, 50–54 (1984); Anne Firor Scott, *After Suffrage: Southern Women in the Twenties,* 30 J. S. Hist. 298, 309–10 (1964).

CHAPTER EIGHT. Progressive Transitions

1. Nicholas Lemann, The Promised Land: The Great Black Migration and How It Changed America (1991); Douglas Massey and Nancy Denton, American Apartheid: Segregation and the Making of the Underclass (1993).

2. Michael Jones-Correa, *The Origins and Diffusion of Racial Restrictive Covenants,* 115 Pol. Sci. Q. 541, 547–48 (2000–2001); Buchanan v. Warley, 245 U.S. 60 (1917); David E. Bernstein and Ilya Somin, *Judicial Power and Civil Rights Reconsidered,* 114 Yale L.J. 591, 627 (2004) (on NAACP successes).

3. La. Stat. R.S. 33:5066 (1924), repealed by Acts 1972, no. 257, 1; Tyler v. Harmon, 104 So. 200 (La. 1925); Tylor v. Harmon, 107 So. 704 (La. 1926); Harmon v. Tyler, 273 U.S. 668 (1927); Corrigan, 271 U.S. 323 (1926).

4. Joel Williamson, The Crucible of Race: Black-White Relations in the American South Since Emancipation 388–92 (1984); *Vardaman Opposes Negro,* N.Y. Times, Jan. 22, 1914, at 8.

5. Kevin K. Gaines, Uplifting the Race: Black Leadership, Politics, and Culture in

the Twentieth Century 215 (1996); August Meier and Elliott Rudwick, *The Rise of Segregation in the Federal Bureaucracy, 1900–1930,* 28 Phylon 178, 178–81 (1967); Stephen R. Fox, The Guardian of Boston: William Monroe Trotter 179–80, 182 (1971); Letter from William M. Trotter to President Woodrow Wilson, Nov. 6, 1913, *in* 8 The Papers of Woodrow Wilson 491, 491–93 (1978); Williamson, *supra,* at 386–87 (on enforcement); *President Resents Negro's Criticism,* N.Y. Times, at 1; Letter from Wilson to Oswald Garrison Villard, Aug. 28, 1913, *in* 8 The Papers of Woodrow Wilson, *supra,* at 245 (defending segregation); Letter from Wilson to Howard A. Bridgman, Sept. 8, 1913, *in* 8 *id.* at 491, 491–93 (same).

6. Meier and Rudwick, *supra,* at 181–83.

7. 163 U.S. 537, 561 (Harlan, J., dissenting).

8. Gandolfo v. Hartman, 49 F. 181 (C.C.S.D. Cal. 1892); Dale Baum, *Woman Suffrage and the "Chinese Question": The Limits of Radical Republicanism in Massachusetts, 1865–1876,* 56 New Eng. Q. 60, 74 (1983) (on Sumner and other Radicals); Act of May 6, 1882, ch. 126 , 22 Stat. 58 1; Act of May 5, 1892, ch. 60, 27 Stat. 25 1; Act of Apr. 29, 1902, ch. 641, 32 Stat. 176 1; Act of Apr. 27, 1904, ch. 1630, 33 Stat. 394, 428; Act of Mar. 3, 1911, ch. 1015, 36 Stat. 1087, 1094 25 (granting district courts jurisdiction over Chinese Exclusion Cases); Act of Sept. 13, 1888, ch. 1015, 25 Stat. 476 5–6; Chae Chan Ping, 130 U.S. 581, 603–7 (1889); Act of Dec. 17, 1943, ch. 344, 57 Stat. 600. *See also* Nishimura Ekiu v. United States, 142 U.S. 651, 659 (1892); Fong Yue Ting v. United States, 159 U.S. 698, 705–7 (1893).

9. Yick Wo v. Hopkins, 118 U.S. 356 (1886); Wong Wing v. United States, 163 U.S. 228 (1896).

10. Dorothee Schneider, *"I Know All about Emma Lazarus": Nationalism and Its Contradictions in Congressional Rhetoric of Immigration Restriction,* 13 Cultural Anthropology 82, 89 (1998); Bernard Axelrod, *Historical Studies of Emigration from the United States,* 6 Int'l Migration Rev. 32, 38 (1972); Act of Feb. 5, 1917, ch. 29, 39 Stat. 874, 876, 877; Roger Daniels, Guarding the Golden Door: American Immigration Policy and Immigrants Since 1882, at 46 (2004).

11. *Id.* at 47–48 (quoting Johnson); 66 Cong. Rec. 3 Sess., 178–79 (Dec. 10, 1920) (Huddleston).

12. Carey McWilliams, Prejudice: Japanese-Americans, Symbol of Racial Intolerance 58–59, 60–61 (1944); *Once-Over for Anti-Jap Bills,* L.A. Times, Feb. 2, 1920, at I4; Peter B. Kyne, The Pride of Palomar 124–25 (1922 ed.).

13. Act of May 19, 1921, ch. 8, 42 Stat. 5; John Higham, Strangers in the Land: Patterns of American Nativism, 1860–1925, at 310–11 (1955).

14. Act of May 26, 1924, ch. 190, 43 Stat.153, 159; Bill O. Hing, Defining America through Immigration Policy 68–69 (2004); David M. Reimers, Unwelcome Strangers: American Identity and the Turn against Immigration 22 (1998) (Italian and Greek immigration).

15. Gabriel J. Chin, *Segregation's Last Stronghold: Race Discrimination and the Constitutional Law of Immigration,* 46 UCLA L. Rev. 1, 14 (1998); Kevin R. Johnson and Bill Ong Hing, *National Identity in a Multicultural Nation,* 103 Mich. L. Rev. 1347, 1372 (2005) (Japanese-U.S. gentlemen's agreement (1907, 1908)); Act of Mar. 24, 1934, ch. 84, 8(a)(1), 48 Stat. 456, 462 (1934) (Filipinos); Leti Volpp, *Divesting Citizenship,* 53 UCLA L. Rev. 405, 415 (2005).

16. Junzo Hishi, *The Root of War,* N.Y. Times, May 3, 1915, at 10; William E. Leuchtenburg, The Perils of Prosperity, 1914–32, at 10, 206–7 (1958); Higham, *supra,* at 273, 283,

285; *Ford Apology Kills Off Two $1,000,000 Suits,* Chi. Daily Trib., July 9, 1927, at 1; Marc Dollinger, *The Other War,* 89 Am. Jewish Hist. 437, 457 (2002); Marcia G. Synnott, *The Admission and Assimilation of Minority Students at Harvard, Yale, and Princeton, 1900–1970,* 19 Hist. Educ. Q. 285, 289–90 (1979).

17. Leonard Dinnerstein, The Leo Frank Case 53, 60 (1966); *Troops on Alert for Mob,* N.Y. Times, May 2, 1913, at 5; *Burns Attacked by Mob,* N.Y. Times, May 2, 1913, at 1; Frank v. Georgia, 80 S.E. 1016 (Ga. 1914).

18. Frank v. Mangum, 237 U.S. 309 (1915).

19. Walter White, A Man Called White 25–26 (1948); http://en.wikipedia.org/wiki/Image:FrankLynchedLarge.jpg (photo).

20. Anne S. Emanuel, *Lynching and the Law of Georgia,* 5 Wm. and Mary Bill Rts. J. 215, 219 (1996) (Knights of Mary Phagan); Monroe H. Freedman, *Atticus Finch—Right and Wrong,* 45 Ala. L. Rev. 473, 473–74 (1994); Shawn Lay, *Ku Klux Klan in the Twentieth Century,* New Ga. Encyclopedia *at* http://www.georgiaencyclopedia.org/nge/Article.jsp?path=/HistoryArchaeology/TheProgressiveEraandWorldWarI/GroupsOrganizations-6&id=h-2730; David M. Chalmers, Hooded Americanism: The First Century of the Ku Klux Klan, 1865–1965, at 29–31 (1965) (Simmons and Klan); Arnold S. Rice, The Ku Klux Klan in American Politics 13 (1962).

21. *Induct 2,000 in the Klan,* N.Y. Times, Jun. 19, 1921, at 4.

22. *Pacifist Whipped in Kuklux Style,* N.Y. Times, Oct. 30, 1917, at 3; *Night Rider Raids Spread in South,* N.Y. Times, Oct. 11, 1920, at 1; *Governor's Exposé Arouses Georgians,* N.Y. Times, May 1, 1921, at 25; *Negro Churches Burned,* N.Y. Times, May 29, 1919, at 13; Charles P. Sweeney, *The Great Bigotry Merger,* 115 Nation 8 (1922); *Abductors Injure Editor,* N.Y. Times, July 2, 1922, at 8; *Masked Floggers,* N.Y. Times, Mar. 22, 1922, at 2; *Klansmen Admit Attacking Doctor,* N.Y. Times, June 16, 1922, at 13.

23. *Ask Texas Governor to Curb,* N.Y. Times, July 22, 1921, at 4; *Mayors Warn Ku Klux,* N.Y. Times, Oct. 7, 1922, at 11; *The Klan Defies a State,* 77 Literary Dig. 12 (June 9, 1923) (N.Y. and Smith); *Oklahoma Klan Bars Masked Parades,* N.Y. Times, Sept. 11, 1923, at 19; *Illinois Anti-Klan Bill Is Law,* N.Y. Times, June 28, 1923, at 2; *Michigan Mask Law Aimed at Klan,* N.Y. Times, Aug. 31, 1923, at 10; *Two States Forbid Masks,* N.Y. Times, Apr. 10, 1923, at 26 (Minn. and Ia.).

24. Leonard J. Moore. Citizen Klansmen: The Ku Klux Klan in Indiana, 1921–1928, at xii, 1–2 (1991); Nancy MacLean, Behind the Mask of Chivalry: The Making of the Second Ku Klux Klan xi–xii (1994); Robert A. Goldberg, Hooded Empire: The Ku Klux Klan in Colorado 178–80 (1981); Leuchtenburg, *supra,* at 208–13.

CHAPTER NINE. Rights in the Regulatory State

1. Richard Hofstadter, Social Darwinism in American Thought 34, 41 (1944; 1955).

2. Eric Foner, The Story of American Freedom 123 (1998); Harry A. Millis and Royal E. Montgomery, Organized Labor 630-31 (1945).

3. Cass R. Sunstein, The Partial Constitution 48-49 (1993).

4. Holden v. Hardy, 169 U.S. 366 (1898) (Utah statute). Utah also forbade women and children from working in mines for health-related reasons.

5. Lochner v. New York, 198 U.S. 45 (1905); Paul Kens, Lochner v. New York: Economic Regulation on Trial (1998).

6. William E. Forbath, *The Shaping of the American Labor Movement,* 102 Harv. L.

Rev. 1111, 1155 (1989); Wayne McCormack, *Economic Substantive Due Process and the Right of Livelihood*, 82 KY. L.J. 397, 399–400 (1994); Muller v. Oregon, 208 U.S. 412 (1908); Adkins v. Children's Hosp., 261 U.S. 525 (1923).

7. Herbert K. Abrams, *A Short History of Occupational Health*, 22 J. Public Health Policy 34, 64 (2001); Robert E. Prasch, *Retrospectives: American Economists in the Progressive Era on the Minimum Wage*, 13 J. Econ. Perspectives 221 (1999); George G. Groat, *Economic Wage and Legal Wage*, 33 Yale L.J. 489, 492 (1924).

8. Clayton Act, 15 U.S.C. 17 (1914).

9. Duplex Printing Press Co. v. Deering, 254 U.S. 443 (1921).

10. Norris-LaGuardia Act, 29 U.S.C. 101–15; see also United States v. Hutchinson, 312 U.S. 219, 231 (1941).

11. Hammer v. Dagenhart, 247 U.S. 251 (1918), overruled by United States v. Darby, 312 U.S. 100 (1941); Bailey v. Drexel Furniture Co., (Child Labor Tax Case), 259 U.S. 20 (1922); Adkins v. Children's Hospital, 261 U.S. 525 (1923), overruled in part by West Coast Hotel Co. v. Parrish, 300 U.S. 379, 388–400 (1937).

12. Daniel J. Hulsebosch, *The New Deal Court: Emergence of a New Reason*, 90 Colum. L. Rev. 1973, 1974–75 (1990); Risa L. Goluboff, *Deaths Greatly Exaggerated*, 24 Law and Hist. Rev. 201, 203–4 (2006) (quoting "the crucial . . . ").

13. Dorothy Dunbar Bromley, *Vanishing Wages*, New Outlook 52 (1933) (wage comparisons); Howard B. Myers, *The Earnings of Labor*, 37 Am. J. Soc. 896, 902 (1932) (same).

14. Christina D. Romer, *The Nation in Depression*, 7 J. Econ. Persp. 19, 32 (1993) (1932 statistics); Christopher G. Wye, *The New Deal and the Negro Community*, 59 J. Am. Hist. 621, 631 (1972); Charles H. Martin, *Negro Leaders, The Republican Party, and the Election of 1932*, 32 Phylon 85, 85 (1971).

15. *The Next Labor Offensive*, Fortune 58, 58 (January 1933).

16. 5 Public Papers and Addresses of Franklin D. Roosevelt 233 (Samuel I. Rosenman ed., 1938); 2 *id.* 5.

17. Lewis L. Gould, The Modern American Presidency 91–92 (2003); John B. Kirby, Black Americans in the Roosevelt Era: Liberalism and Race 32 (1980); Jayne R. Beilke, *The Changing Emphasis of the Rosenwald Fellowship Program, 1928–1948*, 66 J. Negro Educ. 3, 7 (1997).

18. *Getting to Know the Racial Views of Our Past Presidents: What about FDR?*, 38 J. Blacks in Higher Educ. 44, 44–45 (Winter 2002–3); Harvard Sitkoff, A New Deal for Blacks: The Emergency of Civil Rights as a National Issue 40 (1978); Richard M. Dalfiume, *Military Segregation and the 1940 Presidential Election*, 30 Phylon 42, 49–50 (1969).

19. Arthur F. Raper, Tragedy of Lynching 25–26, 36–37, 46–47 (1933); Gunnar Myrdal, An American Dilemma: The Negro Problem and Modern Democracy 560–61 (1944).

20. W. Fitzhugh Brundage, Lynching in the New South: Georgia and Virginia, 1880–1930, at 238 (1993); Myrdal, *supra*, at 565; Henry E. Barber, *The Association of Southern Women for the Prevention of Lynching, 1930–1942*, 34 Phylon 378, 382 (1973); *Women of the South Ask Roosevelt to End Lynching*, N.Y. Times, Jan. 10, 1934, at 1; *Roosevelt Action on Lynching Asked*, N.Y. Times, Oct. 28, 1934, at 1.

21. Charles S. Mangum, Jr., The Legal Status of the Negro 291, 292 (1940); Moore v. Dempsey, 261 U.S. 86 (1923).

22. Brown v. State, 36 So. 73 (Miss. 1904); Uzzle v. Com., 60 S.E. 52 (Va. 1908).

23. Browder v. Commonwealth, 123 S.W. 328 (Ct. App. Ky. 1909); Fountain v. State, 107 A. 554, 554 (Ct. of App. Md. 1919); Mickle v. State 213 S.W. 665 (Ct. Crim. App. Tx. 1919).

24. 2 The Public Papers and Addresses of Franklin D. Roosevelt 517, 519 (Samuel I. Rosenman ed., 1938) ("vile . . . "); 3 *id.* 8, 12–13 (Samuel I. Rosenman ed., 1938) ("banditry . . . "); 3 Complete Presidential Press Conferences of Franklin D. Roosevelt, Press Conference no. 125, at 375, 376 (May 25, 1934).

25. *The Best of the Anti-Lynching Fights,* Editorial, Crisis, June 1935, at 177; Roger Biles, A New Deal for the American People 180–81 (1991); Donald W. Jackson and James W. Riddlesperger, Jr., *Federalism, the Roosevelt Coalition, and Civil Rights, in* Franklin D. Roosevelt and the Transformation of the Supreme Court 170–71 (Stephen K. Shaw *et al.* eds., 2004); Mary White Ovington, The Walls Came Tumbling Down 257–63 (1947); Walter White, A Man Called White 169–70 (1948).

26. George B. Tindall, The Emergence of the New South, 1913–1945, at 553–55 (1967); Frank Freidel, Franklin D. Roosevelt: A Rendezvous with Destiny 246 (1990).

27. Kenneth O'Reilly, Nixon's Piano: Presidents and Racial Politics from Washington to Clinton 122 (1995); *"Civil Rights" Unit Set Up by Murphy,* N.Y. Times, Feb. 4, 1939, at 2.

28. 18 U.S.C. 241; 18 U.S.C. 242.

29. United States v. Classic, 313 U.S. 299 (1941); 18 U.S.C. 51; 18 U.S.C. 52.

30. Screws v. United States, 325 U.S. 91 (1945); Daniel C. Richman, *Federal Criminal Law, Congressional Delegation, and Enforcement Discretion,* 46 UCLA L. Rev. 757, 797 (1999); Tom C. Clark, *A Federal Prosecutor Looks at the Civil Rights Statute,* 47 Colum. L. Rev. 175 (1947); Kevin J. McMahon, Reconsidering Roosevelt on Race: How the Presidency Paved the Road to Brown 168–69 (2004). Justices Roberts, Frankfurter, and Jackson dissented because they thought charging law to be unconstitutional.

31. Exec. Order No. 8802, 6 Fed. Reg. 3109 (June 25, 1941); Merl E. Reed, Seedtime for the Modern Civil Rights Movement: The President's Committee on Fair Employment Practice, 1941–1946, at 14–15 (1991).

32. *See* Jane P. Clark, The Rise of a New Federalism: Federal-State Cooperation in the United States 103–4 (1938); Henry J. Bitterman, State and Federal Grants-in-Aid 364 (1938).

33. Francis Hoague *et al., Wartime Conscription and Control of Labor,* 54 Harv. L. Rev. 50, 64 (1940); John A. Pandiani, *The Crime Control Corps: An Invisible New Deal Program,* 33 Brit. J. Soc. 348, 350 (1982); 2 Arthur M. Schlesinger, Jr., The Age of Roosevelt: The Coming of the New Deal 336–39, 341 (1959); David C. Coyle, Conservation: An American Story of Conflict and Accomplishment 103–4 (1957); Aubrey Williams, *The Work of the National Youth Administration,* 1 Living 65, 65 (1939).

34. Act of Mar. 31, 1933, ch. 17, 48 Stat. 22, 22–23; Raymond A. Mohl and Neil Betten, *Ethnic Adjustment in the Industrial City: The International Institute of Gary, 1919–1940,* 6 Int'l Migration Rev. 361, 375 (1972); Robert Ritzenthaler, *The Impact of War on an Indian Community,* 45 Am. Anthropologist 325, 325 (1943).

35. Sharon Hartman Storm, *Challenging "Woman's Place": Feminism, the Left, and Industrial Unionism in the 1930s,* 9 Feminist Stud. 359 (1983).

36. Luther C. Wandall, *A Negro in the CCC,* 42 Crisis 244, 244–53 (1935).

37. Kenneth Holland and Frank E. Hill, Youth in the CCC 111–12 (1942); Calvin W. Gower, *The Struggle of Blacks for Leadership Positions in the Civilian Conservation Corps, 1933–1942,* 61 J. Negro Hist. 123, 128–29 (1976); Kenneth S. Davis, FDR: The New Deal Years, 1933–1937, at 630 (1986); John A. Salmond, *The Civilian Conservation Corps and the Negro,* 52 J. Am. Hist. 75, 77–79 (1965).

38. Arthur E. Morgan, *Social Methods of the Tennessee Valley Authority,* 8 J. Educ. Soc.

261, 262 (1935); Earle S. Draper and Tracy B. Augur, *The Regional Approach to the Housing Problem,* 1 Law and Contemp. Probs. 168, 172–74 (1934); Alonzo L. Hamby, Liberalism and Its Challengers: From FDR to Reagan 26 (2d ed. 1992); Salmond, *supra* at 82.

39. John P. Davis, *A Survey of the Problems of the Negro Under the New Deal,* 5 J. Negro Educ. 3, 11 (1936); John P. Davis, *A Black Inventory of the New Deal,* 42 Crisis 141, 142 (1935); John P. Davis, *The Plight of the Negro in the Tennessee Valley,* 42 Crisis 294, 294–95 (1935).

40. Morton Keller, *The New Deal: A New Look,* 31 Polity 657, 661 (1999); John P. Davis, *Black Inventory, supra,* at 142.

41. Act of May 12, 1933, ch. 25, 48 Stat. 31; D. W. Brogan, Roosevelt and the New Deal 99–100 (1952).

42. Warren C. Whatley, *Labor for the Picking: The New Deal in the South,* 43 J. Econ. Hist. 905, 913 (1983).

43. Arthur F. Raper, Preface to Peasantry: A Tale of Two Black Belt Counties 6–7 (1936; 1968); M. S. Venkataramani, *Norman Thomas, Arkansas Sharecroppers, and the Roosevelt Agricultural Policies, 1933–1937,* 47 Miss. Valley Hist. Soc'y 225, 234–37; Will W. Alexander. The Collapse of Cotton Tenancy 57–61 (1935); Thomas J. Woofter *et al.,* Landlord and Tenant on the Cotton Plantation 66–67 (1936).

44. Ward H. Rodgers, *Sharecroppers Drop Color Line,* 42 Crisis 168, 168–69 (1935); Harold Hoffsommer, *The AAA and the Cropper,* 13 Soc. Forces 494, 497, 499 (1935); Jean Collier Brown, *The Negro Woman Worker,* Bulletin of the Women's Bureau, no. 165 Dept. of Labor 7 (1938).

45. Louis Cantor, *A Prologue to the Protest Movement: The Missouri Sharecropper Roadside Demonstration of 1939,* 55 J. Am. Hist. 804, 809 (1969); Arthur Raper, *The Role of Agricultural Technology in Southern Social Change,* 25 Soc. Forces 21, 23 (1946); Allen F. Kifer, The Negro under the New Deal, 1933–1941, at 152 (1961) (Ph.D. diss., University of Wisconsin (Madison)); Myrdal, *supra,* at 257–58.

46. Raymond Wolters, Negroes and the Great Depression: The Problem of Economic Recovery 78–79 (1970); Biles, *supra,* at 176–77.

47. Elias Huzar, *Federal Unemployment Relief Policies,* 2 J. Pol. 321, 325 (1940); J. Kerwin Williams, *The Status of Cities under Recent Federal Legislation,* 30 J. Am. Pol. Sci. Rev. 1107, 1111 (1936); Procedural Issuance from Harry L. Hopkins to the State Emergency Relief Administrations (Nov. 29, 1933), quoted in Deborah C. Malamud, *"Who They Are—or Were": Middle-Class Welfare in the Early New Deal,* 151 U. Pa. L. Rev. 2019, 2042–43 n. 62 (2003).

48. John P. Murchison, *Some Major Aspects of the Economic Status of the Negro,* 14 Soc. Forces 114, 115–16 (1935); Ralph J. Bunche, *A Critique of New Deal Social Planning as It Affects Negroes,* 5 J. Negro Educ. 59, 63 (1936); Walter G. Daniel, *F.E.R.A. Help for Negro Education,* 4 J. Negro Educ. 278, 280 (1935); James M. Sears, *Black Americans and the New Deal,* 10 Hist. Teacher 89, 94 (1976).

49. Edward Lewis, *The Negro on Relief,* 5 J. Negro Educ. 73, 74–75 (1936); Leslie H. Fisher, Jr., *The Negro in the New Deal Era, in* The Negro in Depression and War: Prelude to Revolution 1930–1945, at 10 (Bernard Sternsher ed., 1969); Roger Biles, *The Urban South in the Great Depression,* 56 J. S. Hist. 71, 98 (1990).

50. Arthur R. Jarvis, *Opportunity, Experience, and Recognition: Black Participation in Philadelphia's New Deal Arts Projects, 1936–1942,* 85 J. Negro Hist. 241, 241 (2000); Elias Huzar, *Federal Unemployment Relief Policies: The First Decade,* 2 J. Pol. 321, 330 (1940); Arthur E. Burns and Peyton Kerr, *Recent Changes in Work-Relief Wage Policy,* 31 Am. Econ.

Rev. 56, 58 (1941); Edwin Amenta and Drew Halfmann, *Wage Wars: Institutional Politics, WPA Wages, and the Struggle for U.S. Social Policy,* 65 Am. Soc. Rev. 506, 511–13 (2000); W. J. Trent, Jr., *Federal Sanctions Directed against Racial Discrimination,* 3 Phylon 171, 176 (1942) (statutory language); Helen Carlson, *Nevada,* 14 Western Folklore 44, 45 (1955); David La Vere, Life among the Texas Indians: The WPA Narratives (1998); W. E. B. Du Bois, *A Chronicle of Race Relations,* 2 Phylon 388, 400 (1941); Kenya C. Dworkin y Méndez, *The Tradition of Hispanic Theater and the WPA Federal Theater Project in Tampa-Ybor City, Florida, in* 2 Recovering the U.S. Hispanic Literary Heritage Project 282 (1996); Ruth Lopez, *The Role of Hispanic Artists in the WPA,* Santa Fe New Mexican, Oct. 23, 1998, at 8.

51. Rita Werner Gordon, *The Change in the Political Alignment of Chicago's Negroes during the New Deal,* 56 J. Am. Hist 584, 594–95 (1969); Carl N. Degler, Out of Our Past 398 (1959) ("Negroes don't . . . "); Christopher G. Wye, *The New Deal and the Negro Community: Toward a Broader Conceptualization,* 59 J. Am. Hist. 621, 634–35 (1972).

52. Richard Kluger, Simple Justice: The History of Brown v. Board of Education and Black America's Struggle for Equality 217 (1976); Pub. Res. no. 1, 76th Cong. 1st Sess. (Feb. 4, 1939); Leo M. Alpert, *The Alien and the Public Charge Clauses,* 49 Yale L.J. 18, 23 (1939); Mimi Abramovitz, Regulating the Lives of Women 283–84 (1996); A. Mohl and Neil Betten, *Gary, Indiana: The Urban Laboratory as a Teaching Tool,* 4 Hist. Teacher 5, 15 (1971).

53. B. Joyce Ross, *Mary McLeod Bethune and the National Youth Administration: A Case Study of Power Relationships in the Black Cabinet of Franklin D. Roosevelt,* 60 J. Negro Hist. 1 (1975); Walter G. Daniel and Carroll L. Miller, *The Participation of the Negro in the National Youth Administration Program,* 7 J. Negro Educ. 357–60 (1938); Sitkoff, *supra,* at 73 (insult about Williams); Monroe Billington, *Lyndon B. Johnson and Blacks: The Early Years,* 62 J. Negro Hist. 26, 28–31 (1977).

54. Marian Thompson Wright, *Negro Youth and the Federal Emergency Programs: CCC and NYA,* 9 J. Negro Educ. 397, 402 (1940).

55. Stanley High, Roosevelt—and Then? 201–2 (1937); Daniel and Miller, *supra,* at 360–61; Chas H. Thompson, *The Status of Education of and for the Negro in the American Social Order,* 8 J. Negro Educ. 489, 490 (1939); Fred McCuistion, *The Present Status of Higher Education of Negroes,* 2 J. Negro Educ. 379, 381 (1933).

56. Ira De A. Reid, *The Development of Adult Education for Negroes in the United States,* 14 J. Negro Educ. 299, 305 (1945); Walter G. Daniel, *Federal Activities and Negro Education, and General Progress,* 6 J. Negro Educ. 101, 104 (1937).

57. Mickey Kaus, The End of Equality 259 (1992).

58. Trent, *supra,* at 177.

59. John B. Parrish, *Women in the Nation's Labor Market,* 54 Q. J. of Econ. 527, 527–29 (1940).

60. Arthur E. Burns and Peyton Kerr, *Recent Changes in Work-Relief Wage Policy,* 31 Am. Econ. Rev. 56, 63 (1941) (WPA and women); Chase Going Woodhouse, *Some Trends in Women's Work,* 16 Soc. Forces 543, 548 (1938); Susan Ware, Holding Their Own: American Women in the 1930s 40, 42 (1982); Women Workers through the Depression 104–5 (Lorine Pruette, ed., 1934); Suzanne Mettler, Dividing Citizens: Gender and Federalism in New Deal Public Policy 41–43 (1998).

61. Throughout the discussion on women's wages and hours that follows I have relied on a Department of Labor publication. Brown, *supra,* at 2—8, 11–13.

62. *Id.;* Schechter Poultry Corp. v. United States, 295 U.S. 495 (1935) (finding that the NIRA delegated government authority to private business); United States v. Butler, 297

U.S. 1 (1936) (holding that Congress had overstepped its authority in trying to regulate agriculture pursuant to the AAA); Carter v. Carter Coal Co., 298 U.S. 238 (1936) (striking Bituminous Coal Act); Morehead v. New York, 298 U.S. 587 (1936). For a more complete list of Supreme Court decisions finding New Deal laws unconstitutional see Benjamin F. Wright, The Growth of American Constitutional Law ch. 9 (1942; 1967).

63. Arthur Krocks, *Roosevelt Asks Power to Reform Courts, Increasing the Supreme Bench to 15 Justices; Congress Startled, but Expected to Approve,* N.Y. Times, Feb. 6, 1937 at 1; *Aim To Pack Court, Declares Hoover,* N.Y. Times, Feb. 6, 1937, at 1; 6 The Public Papers and Addresses of Franklin D. Roosevelt 51–66 (Samuel I. Rosenman ed., 1941). For more detail on the court-packing plan see Robert H. Jackson, The Struggle for Judicial Supremacy (1941); William E. Leuchtenburg, Franklin D. Roosevelt and the New Deal, 1932–1940, at 231–35 (1963); Michael E. Parrish, *The Great Depression, the New Deal, and the American Legal Order,* 59 Wash. L. Rev. 723, 737–38 (1984).

64. West Coast Hotel Co. v. Parrish, 300 U.S. 379 (1937); William E. Leuchtenburg, The Supreme Court Reborn: The Constitutional Revolution in the Age of Roosevelt 163–65 (1995). Some scholars have recently debated the extent to which Roosevelt threatened the Court's decisionmaking. *See, e.g.,* Barry Cushman, Rethinking the New Deal Court: The Structure of a Constitutional Revolution (2002).

65. Muller v. Oregon, 208 U.S. 412 (1908).

66. Arthur F. Lucas, The Legal Minimum Wage in Massachusetts iv (1927); Adkins v. Children's Hospital of the District of Columbia, 261 U.S. 525 (1923); Planned Parenthood v. Casey, 505 U.S. 833, 861 (1992).

67. U. S. Dept of Labor, Women's Bureau, Women at Work: A Century of Industrial Change 8–9 (1933) (bulletin no. 115); Josephine Goldmark, *The New Menace in Industry,* 43 Scribner's 141, 141, 143 (March 1933).

68. According to Justice Roberts, the fifth and deciding vote upholding the Washington minimum wage statute was taken on February 1, 1937, and Roosevelt announced his plan on February 5, 1937. According to Roberts's recollection, he cast his vote on December 19, 1936. *See* Felix Frankfurter, *Mr. Justice Roberts,* 104 U. Pa. L. Rev. 311, 315 (1955). *Few of Justices Read Message Immediately,* N.Y. Times, Feb. 6, 1937, at 8. Morehead, 298 U.S. at 604–5. Nebbia v. New York, 291 U.S. 502 (1934) (Roberts's majority opinion upholding New York's order fixing the price of milk); Ashwander v. Tennessee Valley Authority, 297 U.S. 288 (1936) (Hughes's opinion upholding the TVA's right to contract with private party).

69. Parrish, 300 U.S. at 391, 398–99.

70. An academic debate rages about the extent to which the post-1937 cases were novel. *See* Bruce Ackerman, We the People: Foundations 105–30 (1991); Cass R. Sunstein, *Lochner's Legacy, in* Law and Liberalism in the 1980s 157–90 (Vincent Blasi ed., 1991); James A. Henretta, *Charles Evans Hughes and the Strange Death of Liberal America,* 24 Law and Hist. Rev. 115 (2006). *But see* Cushman, *supra;* Richard Friedman, *Switching Time and Other Thought Experiments: The Hughes Court and Constitutional Transformation,* 142 U. Pa. L. Rev. 1891 (1994); G. Edward White, The Constitution and the New Deal 235, 204–5 (2000).

71. On some of the constitutional implications of *West Coast Hotel see* Laurence H. Tribe, *Unraveling* National League of Cities: *The New Federalism and Affirmative Rights to Essential Government Services,* 90 Harv. L. Rev. 1065, 1086–89 (1977); Edward S. Corwin, Constitutional Revolution, Ltd. 78–79 (1941). Decisions following *Parrish:* NLRB v. Jones

and Laughlin Steel Corp., 301 U.S. 1 (1937); Helvering, 301 U.S. 619 (1937); *see also* Steward Mach. Co. v. Davis, 301 U.S. 548 (1937) (upholding the unemployment compensation plan through the Social Security Act).

72. *Campaign Address at the Commonwealth Club, San Francisco, Cal.* (Sept. 23, 1932), in 1 Franklin D. Roosevelt, The Public Papers and Addresses of Franklin D. Roosevelt 742, 752, 754, 756 (Samuel I. Rosenman ed., 1938); J. Joseph Huthmacher, Senator Robert F. Wagner and the Rise of Urban Liberalism 131 (1968); William E. Forbath, *The New Deal Constitution in Exile,* 51 Duke L.J. 165, 174–77 (2001).

73. *Fate of Court Bill Decided by President, but He Waits Till Today to Reveal Stand,* Aug. 25, 1937, N.Y. Times, at 1; *Court Plan Fight Will Be Renewed by the President,* Aug. 26, 1937, at 1; *Calls Court Plan Dead,* N.Y. Times, Oct. 1, 1937, at 10; *Inquiry into Black on Klan Urged,* N.Y. Times, Aug. 17, 1937, at 9; *Black Confirmed by Senate, 63–16,* N.Y. Times, Aug. 18, 1937, at 1.

74. Strauder v. West Virginia, 100 U.S. 303 (1880); Virginia v. Rives, 100 U.S. 313 (1880); Neal v. Delaware, 103 U.S. 370 (1881); Bush v. Kentucky, 107 U.S. 110 (1883); Andrews v. Swartz, 156 U.S. 272 (1895); Gibson v. Mississippi, 162 U.S. 565 (1896); Smith v. Mississippi, 162 U.S. 592 (1896); Murray v. Louisiana, 163 U.S. 101 (1896); Williams v. Mississippi, 170 U.S. 213 (1898); Carter v. Texas, 177 U.S. 442 (1900); Rogers v. Alabama, 192 U.S. 226 (1904); Martin v. Texas, 200 U.S. 316 (1906); Thomas v. Texas, 212 U.S. 278 (1909); Moore v. Dempsey, 261 U.S. 86 (1923).

75. Powell v. Alabama, 287 U.S. 45. *See generally* Dan T. Carter, Scottsboro: A Tragedy of the American South (1969); James Goodman, Stories of Scottsboro (1994).

76. Emmanuel O. Iheukwumere, *Judicial Independence and the Minority Jurist,* 78 Temp. L. Rev. 379, 394–96 (2005); N. Jeremi Duru, *The Central Park Five, the Scottsboro Boys, and the Myth of the Bestial Black Man,* 25 Cardozo L. Rev. 1315, 1336 (2004); Katharine K. Baker, *The Wigmorian Defense of Feminist Method,* 49 Hastings L.J. 861, 866 n. 22 (1998); Andrew E. Taslitz, *Patriarchal Stories I: Cultural Rape Narratives in the Courtroom,* 5 S. Cal. Rev. L. and Women's Stud. 387, 455 (1996); Note, 32 Colum. L. Rev. 1430 (1932).

77. Weems v. State, 141 So. 215 (1932); Patterson v. State, 141 So. 195 (1932); Powell v. State, 141 So. 201 (1932).

78. The names of the released were Willie Robertson, Roy Wright, Eugene Williams, and Olen Montgommery. After the Supreme Court decision, Ozie Powell was kept in jail for five years without retrial. He tried to escape by slitting a jail guard's throat. Powell was shot in the face during the escape attempt but survived. Then Powell was tried and convicted for assault. He received twenty years without receiving credit for the time he had spent in jail awaiting retrial. He was paroled in 1946. For a fascinating portrait of all the Scottsboro boys *see* http://www.pbs.org/wgbh/amex/scottsboro/peopleevents/index.html.

79. Robert A. Burt, Brown's *Reflection,* 103 Yale L.J. 1483, 1492 (1994); Stephen B. Bright and Patrick J. Keenan, *Judges and the Politics of Death: Deciding between the Bill of Rights and the Next Election in Capital Cases,* 75 B.U. L. Rev. 759, 765 n. 32 (1995); Patterson v. State, 156 So. 567 (1934); Norris v. Alabama, 156 So. 556 (1934); Benno C. Schmidt, Jr., *Juries, Jurisdiction, and Race Discrimination: The Lost Promise of Strauder v. West Virginia,* 61 Tex. L. Rev. 1401, 1477–79 (1983).

80. Norris v. Alabama, 294 U.S. 587 (1935); Patterson v. Alabama, 294 U.S. 600 (1935); Schmidt, Jr., *supra,* at 1477–79.

81. Street v. National Broadcasting Co., 645 F.2d 1227, 1230 (6th Cir. 1981); Hugo A.

Bedau and Michael L. Radelet, *Miscarriages of Justice in Potentially Capital Cases*, 40 Stan. L. Rev. 21, 148 (1987); Hale v. Kentucky, 303 U.S. 613 (1938); Pierre v. Louisiana, 306 U.S. 354 (1939); Smith v. Texas, 311 U.S. 128 (1940).

82. Cumming v. Board of Ed., 175 U.S. 528 (1899) (equal protection, public high school); Berea College v. Kentucky, 211 U.S. 45 (1908) (private college that was incorporated under Ky. law); Gong Lum v. Rice, 275 U.S. 78, 85 (1927) (equal protection, public high school).

83. Missouri ex rel. Gaines v. Canada, 305 U.S. 337.

84. Mark V. Tushnet, Making Civil Rights Law: Thurgood Marshall and the Supreme Court, 1936–1961, at 122 (1994); Charles J. Ogletree, Jr., *From Brown to Tulsa: Defining Our Own Future*, 47 How. L.J. 499, 521 (2004); Robert C. Downs *et al.*, *A Partial History of UMKC Law School: The "Minority Report,"* 68 UMKC L. Rev. 511, 521–22 (2000).

85. Sipuel v. Board of Regents of University of Oklahoma, 332 U.S. 631.

86. Sweatt v. Painter, 339 U.S. 629.

87. McLaurin v. Oklahoma State Regents, 339 U.S. 637 (1950).

88. Shelley v. Kraemer, 334 U.S. 1; Hurd v. Hodge, 334 U.S. 24 (1948) (finding that judicial enforcement of racial covenants in the District of Columbia violates the Civil Rights Act of 1866); Barrows v. Jackson, 346 U.S. 249 (1953) (holding that state court enforcement of damages for a restrictive covenant failed to provide equal protection).

89. Mitchell v. U.S., 313 U.S. 80 (1941) (failure of an interstate carrier to provide first-class accommodation for a black person violated the "unjust discrimination" provision of the Interstate Commerce Act); Morgan v. Virginia, 328 U.S. 373 (1946) (Virginia statute and criminal conviction punishing a black passenger of a segregated vehicle on an interstate trip, who refused to change seats to comply with the discriminatory policy, was an undue burden on interstate commerce); Henderson v. U.S., 339 U.S. 816 (1950) (segregation in dining car of an interstate train was an undue and unreasonable prejudice or violation).

90. United States v. Carolene Prods. Co., 304 U.S. 144, 152 n. 4 (1938).

91. Louis Lusky, *Footnote Redux: A Carolene Products Reminiscence*, 82 Colum. L. Rev. 1093, 1098 (1982).

92. Lewis F. Powell, Jr., *Carolene Products Revisited*, 82 Colum. L. Rev. 1087 (1982); Bruce A. Ackerman, *Beyond Carolene Products*, 98 Harv. L. Rev. 713, 745–46 (1985); Laurence H. Tribe, *The Puzzling Persistence of Process-Based Constitutional Theories*, 89 Yale L.J. 1063, 1073, 1075–77 (1979–80); Ronald Dworkin, A Matter of Principle 66 (1985); G. Edward White, *Historicizing Judicial Scrutiny*, 57 S.C. L. Rev. 1, 68–72 (2005).

93. Schneider v. New Jersey, 308 U.S. 147, 160–61 (1939); West Virginia State Board of Education v. Barnette, 319 U.S. 624, 638–39 (1943).

94. Skinner v. Oklahoma, 316 U.S. 535, 536–37, 541.

95. Missouri ex rel. Gaines v. Canada, 305 U.S. 337 (1938); Norris v. Alabama, 294 U.S. 587 (1935); Powell v. Alabama, 287 U.S. 45 (1932); Shelley v. Kraemer, 334 U.S. 1 (1948); Pollock v. Williams, 322 U.S. 4, 17 (1944); Nixon v. Condon, 286 U.S. 73 (1932); Smith v. Allwright, 321 U.S. 649 (1944); Sitkoff, *supra*, at 243.

96. In Harold Ickes's words: "Rugged individualism does not mean freedom for the mass of the people, but oppression. It implies exploitation of the many by the few. It means regimentation in mill, mine and factory so that a few may grow rich and powerful at the expense of the many. It is the doctrine of ruthlessness, the imposition by the strong of their

will upon the weak. It stands for the denial of social responsibility, the negation of the theory that the individual owes any duty to the mass." Harold L. Ickes, The New Democracy 32 (1934).

CHAPTER TEN. The War against Tyranny

1. *In* 13 Public Papers of Franklin Delano Roosevelt 34 (Samuel I. Rosenman ed., 1950); Hughes, *My America, in* What the Negro Wants 299, 307 (Rayford W. Logan ed., 1944).

2. Cumming v. Board of Ed., 175 U.S. 528 (1899); Gong Lum v. Rice, 275 U.S. 78 (1927); Guey Heung Lee v. Johnson, 404 U.S. 1215, 1215 ftn. (1974) (citing a California segregation statute); Lueras v. Town of Lafayette, 65 P.2d 1431 (Colo. 1937); Terrell Wells Swimming Pool v. Rodriguez, 182 S.W.2d 824 (Tex. Ct. App. 1944); Ronald Takaki, A Different Mirror: A History of Multicultural American 374 (1993).

3. Lou Potter with William Miles and Nina Rosenblum, Liberators: Fighting on Two Fronts in World War II 242 (1992) ("Emotionally and . . . "); W. E. B. Du Bois, *Chronicle of Race Relations,* 4 Phylon 270, 287 (1943) (quoting "we fight Hitler . . . " and quoting "be fought more vigorously . . . "); Harvard Sitkoff, A New Deal for Blacks: The Emergence of Civil Rights as a National Issue, vol. 1, The Depression Decade 299–300 (1978) (Wagner and Murphy).

4. *Nazi Principles and the Ku Klux Klan,* Editorial, Birmingham News, Oct. 13, 1933, at 8; Eric Keyser, *Protection of Jews in Germany Assured by Hitler Lieutenant,* Commercial Appeal (Memphis, Tenn.), Mar. 26, 1933, at 1; *Hitler Running Amuck,* Editorial, *id.* at 6; *Lynching Is Here,* Editorial, News and Observer (Raleigh, N.C.), Nov. 24, 1938, at 4.

5. Johnpeter Horst Grill and Robert L. Jenkins, *The Nazis and the American South in the 1930s: A Mirror Image?,* 58, J. S. Hist. 667, 669 (1992).

6. Franklin Delano Roosevelt: The Four Freedoms, *available at* http://americanrh etoric.com/speeches/fdrthefourfreedoms.htm; Frank Freidel, Franklin D. Roosevelt: A Rendezvous with Destiny 360–61 (1990); Paul G. Lauren, Power and Prejudice: The Politics and Diplomacy of Racial Discrimination 151 (2d ed. 1996) (quoting Gandhi and Buck); Buck, American Unity and Asia 29 (1942).

7. Gregory M. Hooks, Forging the Military-Industrial Complex: World War II's Battle of the Potomac 90–91 (1991); Michael R. Darby, *Three-and-a-Half Million U.S. Employees Have Been Mislaid: Or, an Explanation of Unemployment, 1934–1941,* 84 J. Pol. Econ. 1, 4 (1976).

8. Landon G. Rockwell, *The Planning Function of the National Resources Planning Board,* 7 J. of Pol. 169 (1945); Caroline F. Ware, *Implication for Negro Americans of the Post-War Planning Activities of the U.S. Government,* 12 J. Negro Educ. 543, 544, 550–52 (1943); National Resources Planning Board, National Resources Development: Report for 1942, at 1, 8; 12 The Public Papers and Addresses of Franklin D. Roosevelt 21, 30–31 (Samuel I. Rosenman ed., 1950); John D. Skrentny, The Minority Rights Revolution 78 (2002).

9. 13 Public Papers of Franklin Delano Roosevelt 32, 40–42 (Samuel I. Rosenman ed., 1950).

10. James Baldwin, The Fire Next Time 68 (1963).

11. Note, *Disenfranchisement by Means of the Poll Tax,* 53 Harv. L. Rev. 645, 645 (1940); William M. Brewer, *The Poll Tax and Poll Taxers,* 29 J. Negro Hist. 260, 287–88 (1944); Fred G. Folsom, Jr., *Federal Elections and the White Primary,* 43 Colum. L. Rev. 1026, 1026–

27 (1943); Ralph J. Bunche, *The Negro in the Political Life of the United States*, 10 J. Negro Educ. 567, 573 (1941); Rayford W. Logan, *The Negro Wants First-Class Citizenship*, in What the Negro Wants 10–11 (Rayford W. Logan ed., 1944).

12. Smith v. Allwright, 321 U.S. 649; Grovey v. Townsend, 295 U.S. 45 (1935).

13. C. H. Parrish, Jr., *Negro Higher and Professional Education in Kentucky*, 17 J. Negro Educ. 289, 294 (1948); Helen Harris Bracey, *The Education of Negroes in Florida*, 16 J. Negro Educ. 340, 345 (1947); Frank A. DeCosta, *The Education of Negroes in South Carolina*, 16 J. Negro Educ. 405, 407 (1947); S. O. Roberts, *Negro Higher and Professional Education in Tennessee*, 17 J. Negro Educ. 361, 362–63 (1948).

14. Martha Menchaca and Richard R. Valencia, *Anglo-Saxon Ideologies in the 1920s–1930s: Their Impact on the Segregation of Mexican Students in California*, 21 Anthropology and Educ. Q. 222, 223–32 (1990); Westminster v. Mendez, 161 F.2d 774, 780–81 (1947).

15. Donald W. Jackson and James W. Riddlesperger, Jr., *Federalism, the Roosevelt Coalition, and Civil Rights*, in Franklin D. Roosevelt and the Transformation of the Supreme Court 179 (Stephen K. Shaw *et al.* eds., 2004) (quoting Roosevelt); Kenneth O'Reilly, Nixon's Piano: Presidents and Racial Politics from Washington to Clinton 127–28, 135 (1995).

16. Godfrey Hodgson, The Colonel: The Life and Wars of Henry Stimson, 1867–1952, at 249 (1990); Ulysses Lee, The United States Army in World War II, Special Studies: The Employment of Negro Troops 44–45 (1966); Doris Kearns Goodwin, No Ordinary Time: Franklin and Eleanor Roosevelt: The Home Front in World War II 169–70 (1994).

17. Doris Kearns Goodwin, No Ordinary Time: Franklin and Eleanor Roosevelt: The Home Front in World War II 169 (1994) (quoting Army War College Report); E. Franklin Frazier, The Negro in the United States 682 (rev. ed. 1957) (quoted sociological statement); Bernard C. Nalty, Strength for the Fight: A History of Black Americans In the Military 134 (1986); Pete Daniel, *Going among Strangers: Southern Reactions to World War II*, 77 J. Am. Hist. 886, 893 (1990) (Coahoma County quotations).

18. P. L. Prattis, *The Morale of the Negro in the Armed Services of the United States*, 12 J. Negro Educ. 355, 359 (1943); Harvard Sitkoff, *Racial Militancy and Interracial Violence in the Second World War*, 58 J. Am. Hist. 661, 668–69 (1971); 5 Blacks in the United States Armed Forces: Basic Documents 270 (Morris J. MacGregor and Bernard C. Nalty eds., 1977).

19. Phillip McGuire, Taps for a Jim Crow Army: Letters From Black Soldiers in World War II 183–88 (1983); Richard M. Dalfiume, Desegregation of the U.S. Armed Forces: Fighting on Two Fronts, 1939–1953, at 72–73 (1969); Roscoe E. Lewis, The *Role of Pressure Groups in Maintaining Morale among Negroes*, 12 J. Negro Educ. 464, 469–70 (1943); *Racial Integration: What America's Universities Might Learn from the Success of the United States Army*, 31 J. Negro Higher Educ. 34 (2001).

20. Sitkoff, New Deal, *supra*, at 300; Charles H. Houston, *Critical Summary: The Negro in the U.S. Armed Forces in World Wars I and II*, 12 J. Negro Educ. 364, 365 (1943).

21. William Brink and Louis Harris, The Negro Revolution in America 50 (1964) ("headed overseas . . . "); Francis Biddle, In Brief Authority 155–56 (1962) ("a welding school . . . "); 1 Samuel A. Stouffer *et al.*, The American Soldier: Adjustment During Army Life 502–6 (1949) (survey); Robert J. Norrell, Reaping the Whirlwind: The Civil Rights Movement in Tuskegee 61 (1985) (Pinkard); Jennifer E. Brooks, *Winning the Peace: Georgia Veterans and the Struggle to Define the Political Legacy of World War II*, 66 J. S. Hist. 563, 572, 576 (2000).

22. Donald R. McCoy and Richard T. Ruetten, Quest and Response: Minority Rights and the Truman Administration 9–10 (1973); Neil A. Wynn, *The Impact of the Second World War on the American Negro,* 6 J. Contemp. Hist. 42, 45 (1971); Phillip McGuire, *Desegregation of the Armed Forces: Black Leadership, Protest, and World War II,* 68 J. Negro Hist. 147, 155 (1983); L. D. Reddick, *The Negro Policy of the United States Army, 1775–1945,* 34 J. Negro Hist. 9, 26–27 (1949); Howard H. Long, *The Negro Soldier in the Army of the United States,* 12 J. Negro Educ. 307, 314–15 (1943); Prattis, *supra,* at 361–62; Charles C. Moskos, Jr., *Racial Integration in the Armed Forces,* 72 Am. J. Soc. 132, 134 (1966).

23. Dalfiume, *supra,* at 88.

24. Charles C. Moskos, Jr., *Racial Integration in the Armed Forces,* 72 Am. J. Soc. 132, 134 (1966); Dalfiume, *supra,* at 93; Wynn, *supra,* at 46; Philip A. Klinkner with Rogers M. Smith, The Unsteady March 187–89 (1997).

25. President's Civil Rights Commission, To Secure These Rights 47.

26. Dalfiume, *supra,* at 88; Richard Stillman II, *Negroes in the Armed Forces,* 30 Phylon 139, 141 (1969).

27. Louis C. Kesselman, The Social Politics of FEPC: A Study in Reform Pressure Movements 9–10 (1948); Neil A. Wynn, The Afro-American and the Second World War 40–41 (1976); Raymond W. Goldsmith, *The Power of Victory: Munitions Output in World War II,* 10 Military Aff. 69, 73 (1946); Richard M. Dalfiume, *The "Forgotten Years" of the Negro Revolution, in* The Negro in Depression and War: Prelude to Revolution in 1930–1945, at 298–99 (Bernard Sternsher ed., 1969).

28. Robert C. Weaver, *Racial Employment Trends in National Defense, Part II,* 3 Phylon 22, 24, 27 (1942); Louis C. Kesselman, *The Fair Employment Practice Commission Movement in Perspective,* 31 J. Negro Hist. 30, 36–37 (1946); Leon A. Ransom, *Combating Discrimination in the Employment of Negroes in War Industries and Government Agencies,* 12 J. Negro Educ. 405, 411 (1943); Robert C. Weaver, *Recent Events in Negro Union Relationships,* 52 J. Pol. Econ. 234, 236 (1944).

29. Sitkoff, New Deal, *supra,* at 301.

30. Harold G. Vatter, The U.S. Economy in World War II 132 (1985); O'Reilly, *supra,* at 127; McGuire, *Desegregation, supra,* at 147.

31. Sitkoff, New Deal, *supra,* at 307 (quoting "at a time . . . "); Paula F. Pfeffer, A. Philip Randolph, Pioneer of the Civil Rights Movement 46–49 (1990); Executive Order 8802, June 25, 1941; Executive Order 8823, July 18, 1941; Executive Order 9111, May 25, 1942; Executive Order 9346, May 27, 1943; First Report of F.E.P.C. 43 (1945) (providing information on discrimination in industries like railroads, shipbuilding, and oil).

32. Roy Wilkins, *The Negro Wants Full Equality, in* What the Negro Wants 126 (Rayford W. Logan, ed., 1944) ("the sure justification . . . ") Louis Ruchames, Race, Jobs, and Politics: The Story of FEPC 22–23 (1952) (all other quotations).

33. Louis Starks, *FEPC Defied by Railroads in South on Hiring Negroes,* N.Y. Times, Dec. 14, 1943, at 1; *Rail Job Bias Case Certified to President by the FEPC,* N.Y. Times, Dec. 28 1943, at 1; *The New York State Commission against Discrimination: A New Technique for an Old Problem,* 56 Yale L.J. 837, 842–44 (1947); Chas. H. Thompson, Editorial Comment, *FEPC Hearings Reduce Race Problem to Lowest Terms—Equal Economic Opportunity,* 12 J. Negro Hist. 585, 585–86 (1943); William J. Collins, *Race, Roosevelt, and Wartime Production: Fair Employment in World War II Labor Markets,* 91 Am. Econ. Rev. 272, 274 (2001).

34. Alexa B. Henderson, *FEPC and the Southern Railway Case: An Investigation into the Discriminatory Practices of Railroads during World War II,* 61 J. Negro Hist. 173, 187

(1976); Collins, *supra*, at 284–85; Goodwin, *supra*, at 539; Alan Clive, State of War: Michigan in World War II 141 (1979); Robert C. Weaver, Negro Labor: A National Problem 223 (1946).

35. There are slight statistical discrepancies, which I account for by differing authors' breadth of understanding of "manufacturing jobs." I have used Weaver's prewar figures: Robert C. Weaver, *The Employment of the Negro in War Industries*, 12 J. Negro Educ. 386, 387–89 (1943); Eric Foner, *Expert Report on Behalf of the University of Michigan: The Compelling Need for Diversity in Higher Education*, 5 Mich. J. Race and L. 311, 330 (1999); Harold G. Vatter, The U.S. Economy in World War II 126, 130–31(1985); Robert H. Zieger, American Workers, American Unions, 1920–1985, at 81–82 (1986); Robert C. Weaver, *The Economic Status of the Negro in the United States*, 19 J. Negro Educ. 232, 237–39 (1950).

36. John Hope II and Edward E. Shelton, *The Negro in the Federal Government*, 32 J. Negro Educ. 367, 371–72 (1963); John A. Davis and Cornelius L. Golightly, *Negro Employment in the Federal Government*, 6 Phylon 337, 343 (1945).

37. Steele v. Louisville and Nashville R.R. Co., 323 U.S. 192, 202 (1944); Tunstall v. Brotherhood of Locomotive Firemen and Enginemen, 323 U.S. 210 (1944).

38. Susan B. Anthony II, Out of the Kitchen—Into the War: Woman's Winning Role in the Nation's Drama 114–15 (1943).

39. Paul V. McNutt, *Our Production Line Amazons*, N.Y. Times Rev. Books, July 4, 1943, at 1, 12.

40. *See, e.g.,* Helen Hull Jacobs, "By Your Leave, Sir": The Story of a WAVE (1943); Josephine von Miklos, I Took a War Job (1943); Ann Pendleton, Hit the Rivet, Sister (1943); Susan B. Anthony, Out of the Kitchen—Into the War: Woman's Winning Role in the Nation's Drama (1943).

41. Maureen Honey, *The "Womanpower" Campaign: Advertising and Recruitment Propaganda during World War II*, 6 Frontiers 50, 50 (1981); Advertisement for Acme Steel Company, Business Week, Oct. 2, 1943, at 52 ("keeping the production . . . "); Sherrie A. Kossoudji and Laura J. Dresser, *Working Class Rosies: Women Industrial Workers during World War II*, 52 J. Econ. Hist. 431, 432 (1992) ("large numbers of women . . . "); Carolyn C. Jones, *Split Income and Separate Spheres: Tax Law and Gender Roles in the 1940s*, 6 L. and Hist. Rev. 259, 286 (1988); Maureen Honey, *The Working-Class Woman and Recruitment Propaganda during World War II: Class Differences in the Portrayal of War Work*, 8 Signs 672, 677–78 (1983); U.S. Department of Labor, Women's Bureau, Women on the Industrial Front (June 4, 1942) (W042–78).

42. Phyllis T. Bookspan, *A Delicate Imbalance: Family and Work*, 5 Tex. J. Women and L. 37, 45 (1995); Abby J. Cohen, *A Brief History of Federal Financing for Child Care in the United States*, 6 Future of Children 26, 29–30 (1996); Lanham Act, Pub. L. No. 76-849, 54 Stat. 1125 (1940); Deborah Phillips and Edward Zigler, *The Checkered History of Federal Child Care Regulation*, 14 Rev. Research and Educ. 3, 11–12 (1987).

43. Mary M. Schweitzer, *World War II and Female Labor Force Participation Rates*, 40 J. Econ. Hist. 89, 89–90 (1980); Marguerite J. Fisher, *Equal Pay for Equal Work Legislation*, 2 Industrial and Labor Relations Rev. 50, 51 (1948); Hazel Davis, *Teachers' Salaries*, 16 Rev. Educ. Res. 262, 263 (1946); Kossoudji and Dresser, *supra*, at 441, 443; George Q. Flynn, The Mess in Washington: Manpower Mobilization in World War II 181 (1979); Nancy Gabin, *"They Have Placed a Penalty on Womanhood": The Protest Actions of Women Auto Workers in Detroit-Area UAW Locals, 1945–1947*, 8 Feminist Stud. 373, 376 (1982).

44. Valerie Kincade Oppenheimer, The Female Labor Force in the United States: Demographic and Economic Factors Governing Its Growth and Changing Composition 44–45 (1970) (citing AIPO poll numbers); Hazel Erskine, *The Polls: Women's Role,* 35 Pub. Opinion Q. 275, 286 (1971) (citing *Fortune* poll); William H. Chafe, The American Woman: Her Changing Social, Economic, and Political Roles, 1920–1970, at 193–95 (1972). *But see* Leila J. Rupp, Mobilizing Women for War: German and American Propaganda, 1939–1945, at 177, 180 (1978).

45. Nancy Gabin, *Women and the United Automobile Workers' Union in the 1950s, in* Women Work and Protest: A Century of U.S. Women's Labor History 259, 264 (Ruth Milkman ed., 1985); Vilma R. Hunt, *Reproduction and Work,* 1 Signs 543, 548 (1975); Marc Miller, *Working Women and World War II,* 53 New Eng. Q. 42, 58 (1980); Mary Dublin Keyserling, *The Economic Status of Women in the United States,* 66 Am. Econ. Rev. 205, 205 (1976); Mary E. Guy, *Workplace Productivity and Gender Issues,* 53 Pub. Admin. Rev. 279, 279 (1993); Emmy E. Werner, *Women in Congress: 1917–1964,* 19 W. Pol. Q. 16, 28 (1966); Carol Nechemias, *Changes in the Election of Women to U.S. State Legislative Seats,* 12 Legis. Stud. Q. 125, 129–30 (1987); Malcolm Jewell and Marcia Lynn Whicker, *The Feminization of Leadership in State Legislatures,* 26 Pol. Sci. and Pol. 705, 705 (1993).

46. Tsutomu Obana, *The Changing Japanese Situation in California,* 5 Pac. Aff. 954, 956 (1932); Robert Higgs, *Landless by Law: Japanese Immigrants in California Agriculture to 1941,* 38 J. Econ. Hist. 205, 206–7 (1978); Harold G. Vatter, The U.S. Economy in World War II 135 (1985); Oliver C. Cox, *The Nature of the Anti-Asiatic Movement on the Pacific Coast,* 15 J. Negro Educ. 603 (1946); Raymond L. Buell, *Some Legal Aspects of the Japanese Question,* 17 Am. J. Int'l L. 29, 36 (1923); Miriam J. Wells, *Social Conflict, Commodity Constraints, and Labor Market Structure in Agriculture,* 23 Comp. Stud. Soc'y and Hist. 679, 686 (1981).

47. Paul L. Murphy, The Constitution in Crisis Times, 1918–1969, at 234 (1972); 7 Fed. Reg. 1407 (1942); Biddle, *supra,* ch. 13; Hodgson, *supra,* at 258.

48. Warren's testimony in America at War: The Home Front, 1941–1945, at 98, 98, 101, 103 (1968); Carey McWilliams, Prejudice: Japanese-Americans: Symbol of Racial Intolerance 119–21 (1945).

49. Robert R. Wilson, Editorial, *Some Legal Questions Concerning War Relocation,* 39 Am. J. Int'l L. 314, 315 (1945); Hohri v. United States, 782 F.2d 227, 231 (D.C. Cir. 1986) (quoting "The Japanese race . . . "); Morris E. Opler, *The Bio-Social Basis of Thought in the Third Reich,* 10 Am. Soc. Rev. 776, 785 (1945) (quoting "A Jap's a Jap"); 50 U.S.C. app. 1989a(a) (1988).

50. *Comm'n on Wartime Relocation and Internment of Civilians, Personal Justice Denied* (1982), *reprinted in* Justice Delayed: The Record of the Japanese American Internment Cases 103, 113 (Peter Irons ed., 1989).

51. Jacobus tenBroek *et al.,* Prejudice, War, and the Constitution 135 (1954); *Comm'n on Wartime Relocation and Internment of Civilians, Personal Justice Denied* (1982), *supra,* at 115.

52. Eugene V. Rostow, *The Japanese American Cases: A Disaster,* 54 Yale L.J. 489, 494 (1945); Peter Irons, Justice at War 198–201 (1983); Bill Hosokawa, Nisei: The Quiet Americans 409 (1969).

53. Ex parte Kanai, 46 F.Supp. 286, 288 (E.D. Wis.).

54. Hirabayashi v. United States, 320 U.S. 81. *See also* Yasui v. United States, 320 U.S. 115 (1943).

55. In Ex parte Endo, 323 U.S. 283 (1944).

56. Korematsu v. United States, 323 U.S. 214.

57. tenBroek, *supra*, at 262 ,265, 302 (1954); Rostow, *supra*, at 496; Rostow, *Our Worst Wartime Mistake*, 191 Harper's 193, 193–94 (Sept. 1945).

58. Hirabayashi v. United States, 627 F.Supp. 1445 (W.D. Wash. 1986); Korematsu v. United States, 584 F.Supp. 1406 (N.D. Cal. 1984); Presidential Proclamation no. 4417 (Feb. 20, 1976); Pub. L. No. 100-383, 102 Stat. 903 (1988).

CHAPTER ELEVEN. Expanding Civil Rights

1. Sipuel v. Board of Regents of the University of Oklahoma, 332 U.S. 631 (1948); Shelley v. Kraemer, 334 U.S. 1 (1948); Oyama v. California, 332 U.S. 633 (1948); Takahashi v. Fish and Game Commission, 334 U.S. 410 (1948).

2. K. J. McMahon, Reconsidering Roosevelt on Race 186 (2004) (quoting Truman's executive order.)

3. To Secure These Rights: The Report of the President's Committee on Civil Rights 79, 99–101 (1947); *id.* at 146–47 (quoting Acheson).

4. M. M. Hoffman, *The Illegitimate President*, 105 Yale L.J. 935, 950 (1996); J. M. Balkin, *What "Brown" Teaches Us about Constitutional Theory*, 90 Va. L. Rev. 1537, 1547 (2004); M. Billington, *Civil Rights, President Truman, and the South*, 58 J. Negro Hist. 127, 132–33, 137 (1973); H. Sitkoff, *Harry Truman and the Election of 1948*, 37 J. S. Hist. 597, 600–602 (1971) (Thurmond's resolution).

5. M. J. Klarman, *The Puzzling Resistance to Political Process Theory*, 77 Va. L. Rev. 747, 799–801 (1991); M. R. Gardner, Harry Truman and Civil Rights: Moral Courage and Political Risks 219 (2002).

6. Billington, *supra*, at 137; E. B. Ader, *Why the Dixiecrats Failed*, 15 J. Pol. 356 (1953); M. R. Frankel and L. R. Frankel, *Fifty Years of Survey Sampling in the United States*, 51 Pub. Opinion Q. S127, S129 (1987); D. J. Hutchinson, *A Social of Social Reform: The Judicial Role*, 4 Green Bag 2d 157, 165 (2001); Thomas M. Holbrook, *Did the Whistle-Stop Campaign Matter?*, 35 Pol. Sci. and Politics 59 (2002).

7. H. O. Reid, *Efforts to Eliminate Legally-Enforced Segregation through Federal, State, and Local Legislation*, 20 J. Negro Educ. 436, 440, 442 (1951).

8. M. R. Gardner, Harry Truman and Civil Rights 152–57 (2002); Leslie H. Fisher, Jr., *The Negro in the New Deal Era, in* The Negro in Depression and War: Prelude to Revolution, 1930–1945, at 21–23 (B. Sternsher ed., 1969); Jordan D. Luttrell, *The Public Housing Administration and Discrimination in Federally Assisted Low-Rent Housing*, 64 Mich. L. Rev. 871, 875–76 (1966); Oscar Cohen, *The Case for Benign Quotas for Housing*, 21 Phylon 20, 20–21 (1960).

9. W. Maslow and J. B. Robison, *Civil Rights Legislation and the Fight for Equality, 1862–1952*, 20 U. Chi. L. Rev. 363, 387 nn. 133, 134 (1953); C. S. Johnson, *American Minorities and Civil Rights in 1950*, 20 J. Negro Educ. 485, 485–88 (1951); P. Murphy Malin, *The Status of Civil Rights in the United States in 1950*, 20 J. Negro Educ. 279, 280 (1951); Max Meenes, *American Jews and Anti-Semitism*, 10 J. Negro Educ. 557, 557–58 (1941).

10. Maslow and Robison, *supra*, at 387, 391; Malin, *supra*, at 280.

11. H. Putzel, Jr., *Federal Civil Rights Enforcement: A Current Appraisal*, 99 U. Pa. L. Rev. 439, 441–45 (1951); Act of May 31, 1870, ch. 114, 6, 16 Stat. 141 (codified as amended at 18 U.S.C. 241); Act of May 31, 1870, ch. 114, 17, 16 Stat. 144 (codified as amended at 18 U.S.C. 242).

12. Pub. L. No. 85-315 (Sept. 9, 1957); 71 Stat. 634 *et seq.* (1957); Warren M. Christopher, *The Constitutionality of the Voting Rights Act of 1965*, 18 Stan. L. Rev. 1 (1965); Thomas R. Winquist, *Civil Rights: Legislation: The Civil Rights Act of 1957*, 56 Mich. L. Rev. 619 (1958).

13. Pub. L. No. 86-449; 74 Stat. 86 *et seq.* (1960); Christopher, *supra*, at 6; Daniel M. Berman, A Bill Becomes a Law: The Civil Rights Act of 1960 (1962).

14. Taylor Branch, Parting the Waters: America in the King Years, 1954–63, at 304 (1989) ("unsolved problems . . . ").

15. Julius A. Amin, *The Peace Corps and the Struggle for African American Equality*, 29 J. Black Stud. 809, 810 (1999); D. A. Horowitz, *White Southerners' Alienation and Civil Rights*, 54 J. S. Hist. 173, 179 (1988); C. Sitton, *Wallace Ends Resistance as Guard Is Federalized*, N.Y. Times, Sept. 11, 1963, at 1; C. M. Brauer, *Kennedy, Johnson, and the War on Poverty*, 69 J. Am. Hist. 98, 105 (1982); C. M. Brauer, John F. Kennedy and the Second Reconstruction 29, 316 (1977); S. F. Lawson, *"I Got It from the New York Times'": Lyndon Johnson and the Kennedy Civil Rights Program*, 67 J. Negro Hist. 159, 161–62 (1982) (quoting Johnson).

16. *Radio and Television Report to the American People on Civil Rights*, *in* Public Papers of the Presidents of the United States: John F. Kennedy, 1963, at 468–70 (1964).

17. 109 Cong. Rec. 22,838–39 (Nov. 27, 1963) (Johnson's statement).

18. Quoted in Hugh D. Graham, The Civil Rights Era: Origins and Development of National Policy, 1960–1972, at 6 (1990).

19. Civil Rights Act of 1964, Pub. L. No.88-352, 78 Stat. 241-68.

20. Lucas A. Powe, Jr., The Warren Court and American Politics 232–33 (2000); M. Webster, Note, *The Warren Court's Struggle with the Sit-in Cases . . .*, 17 J.L. and Pol. 373, 383–88 (2001); F. M. Riddick and M. Zweben, *The Eighty-Eighth Congress*, 18 W. Pol. Q. 334, 336 (1965); R. Weisbrot, Freedom Bound 91 (1991).

21. Melville B. Nimmer, *A Proposal for Judicial Validation of a Previously Unconstitutional Law: The Civil Rights Act of 1875*, 65 Colum. L. Rev. 1394 (1965).

22. John R. Lewis, Walking with the Wind: A Memoir of the Movement 50 (1988).

23. Franks v. Bowman Transportation Company, 424 U.S. 747, 764–66 (1976); McDonnell Douglas Corp. v. Green, 411 U.S. 792, 802–4 (1973) (disparate treatment); Griggs v. Duke Power Co., 401 U.S. 424, 430-33 (1971) (disparate impact); Albemarle Paper Co. v. Moody, 422 U.S. 405, 425 (1975) (about business necessity defense and reply).

24. Pub. L. No. 89-110, 79 Stat. 437; *The Voting Rights Act of 1965*, Duke L.J. 463, 467–69 (1966); Christopher, *supra*, at 8; South Carolina v. Katzenbach, 383 U.S. 301, 328 (1966).

25. Milton R. Konvitz, *The Flower and the Thorn*, *in* The Pulse of Freedom: American Liberties: 1920–1970s, at 237–39 (Alan Reitman ed., 1975); Ronald J. Terchek, *Political Participation and Political Structures: The Voting Rights Act of 1965*, 41 Phylon 25, 28 (1980); Arthur Eisenberg, *The Millian Thought of Lani Guinier*, 21 N.Y.U. Rev. L. and Soc. Change 617, 619 n. 9 (1994–95); Tracey L. Meares and Dan M. Kahan, *The Wages of Antiquated Procedural Thinking*, 1998 U. Chi. Legal F. 197, 207 (1998).

26. Pub. L. No. 89-87, 79 Stat. 286, 290; Pub. L. No. 89-239, 79 Stat. 926; Pub. L. No. 89-329, 79 Stat. 1219; Pub. L. No. 89-10, 79 Stat. 27; Pub. L. No. 89-333, 79 Stat. 1282.

27. Pub. L. No. 90-201, 81 Stat. 607; Pub. L. No. 95-256; Pub. L. No. 99-592, 100 Stat. 3342; Pub. L. No. 90-284, 82 Stat. 81; Pub. L. No. 93-383, 88 Stat. 633, 729; Pub. L. No. 100-430, 102 Stat. 1619.

28. Pub. L. No. 88-38, 77 Stat. 56.

29. Mary L. Dudziak, Cold War Civil Rights: Race and the Image of American Democracy (2000).

CHAPTER TWELVE. The Warren Court's Achievements

1. United States v. Carolene Prods. Co., 304 U.S. 144, 152 n. 4 (1938); John H. Ely, Democracy and Distrust 73, 75–77 (1980).

2. Missouri ex rel. Gaines v. Canada, 305 U.S. 337 (1938); Sipuel v. Board of Regents of University of Oklahoma, 332 U.S. 631 (1948); Sweatt v. Painter, 339 U.S. 629 (1950); McLaurin v. Oklahoma State Regents, 339 U.S. 637 (1950); Plessy v. Ferguson, 163 U.S. 537 (1896).

3. Brown v. Board of Education, 347 U.S. 483 (1954); Bolling v. Sharpe, 347 U.S. 497 (1954); A. Reynaldo Contreras and Leonard A. Valverde, *The Impact of Brown on the Education of Latinos*, 63 J. Negro Educ. 470 (1994); Keyes v. School District No. 1, 413 U.S. 189 (1973); J. Milton Yinger and George E. Simpson, *The Integration of Americans of Mexican, Puerto Rican, and Oriental Descent*, 304 Annals Am. Acad. Pol. and Soc. Sci. 124, 131 (1956).

4. Alexander M. Bickel, *The Original Understanding and the Segregation Decision*, 69 Harv. L. Rev. 1, 63–65 (1955); Michael W. McConnell, *Originalism and the Desegregation Decisions*, 81 Va. L. Rev. 947, 1078–79, 1092–1100 (1995).

5. *See, e.g.,* Florida Dept. of Health v. Florida, 450 U.S. 147, 152 n. 6 (1981) (Stevens, J., concurring); Milliken v. Bradley, 418 U.S. 717, 767 (1974) (White, J., dissenting). *But see* J. M. Balkin, *What "Brown" Teaches Us about Constitutional Theory*, 90 Va. L. Rev. 1537, 1548 (2004); Neal Katyal, *Sunsetting Judicial Opinions*, 79 Notre Dame L. Rev. 1237, 1245 n. 31 (2004).

6. Herbert Wechsler, *Toward Neutral Principles of Constitutional Law*, 73 Harv. L. Rev. 1, 33 (1959).

7. Bell, Silent Covenants: Brown v. Board of Education and the Unfulfilled Hopes for Racial Reform 20–27 (2004).

8. W. E. B. Du Bois, *Does the Negro Need Separate Schools?*, 4 J. Negro Educ. 328, 335 (1935); Horace Mann Bond, *The Extent and Character of Separate Schools in the United States*, 4 J. Negro Educ. 321, 324 (1935); Howard Hale Long, *Some Psychogenic Hazards of Segregated Education of Negroes*, 4 J. Negro Educ. 336, 343, 349 (1935).

9. Richard Kluger, Simple Justice 706 (1975) (pointing out that Warren stressed "that the sociology was merely supportive and not the substance of the holding"); E. Barrett Prettyman, Jr., Brown v. Board of Education: *An Exercise in Advocacy*, 52 Mercer L. Rev. 581, 602 (2001) (former clerk for Justice Jackson recalling the surprise about the fuss made about footnote 11).

10. Muller v. Oregon, 208 U.S. 412 (1908); Kluger, *supra*, at 254; *Brennan Backs Use of Non-Legal Data*, N.Y. Times, Nov. 26, 1957, at 17.

11. Brown v. Bd. of Educ., 349 U.S. 294, 299, 301 (1955); Harrell R. Rodgers, Jr., *The Supreme Court and School Desegregation: Twenty Years Later*, 89 Pol. Sci. Q., 751, 755 (Winter 1974–75).

12. Quoted in Paul Gewirtz, *Remedies and Resistance*, 92 Yale L.J. 585, 612 (1983).

13. Cooper v. Aaron, 358 U.S. 1, 18–20 (1958).

14. Aaron v. McKinley, 173 F.Supp. 944 (E.D. Ark. 1959), aff'd per curiam, 361 U.S. 197

(1959); Aaron v. Cooper, 261 F.2d 97 (8th Cir. 1958); Clark v. Board of Ed. of Little Rock School Dist., 369 F.2d 661, 663–64 (8th Cir. 1966).

15. Lia B. Epperson, *Resisting Retreat: The Struggle for Equality in Educational Opportunity in the Post-Brown Era*, 66 U. Pitt. L. Rev. 131, 133 n. 8 (2004); Dennis J. Hutchinson, *Perspectives on Brown*, 8 Green Bag 2d 43, 45–46 (2004) ("Without the support . . . ").

16. *See, e.g.*, Bush v. Orleans Parish Sch. Bd., 138 F. Supp. 337 (E.D. La. 1956), aff'd, 242 F.2d 156 (5th Cir. 1957).

17. Daniel J. Meador, *The Constitution and the Assignment of Pupils to Public Schools*, 45 Va. L. Rev. 517, 527 (1959).

18. See, *e.g.*, Carson v. Warlick, 238 F.2d 724 (4th Cir. 1956); Orleans Parish School Bd. v. Bush, 268 F.2d 78 (5th Cir. 1959); Romero v. Weakley, 226 F.2d 399 (9th Cir. 1955); Brewer v. Hoxie School Dist., Ark., 238 F.2d 91 (8th Cir. 1956).

19. *See, e.g.*, Miss. Code Ann. 6334-02–03 (Supp. 1960); S.C. Code 21-247.2 (Supp. 1960); Tenn. Code Ann. 49-1749–1761 (Supp. 1962). *See, e.g.*, Woods v. Wright, 334 F.2d 369, 374 (5th Cir. 1964); Clemons v. Board of Ed. of Hillsboro, Ohio, 228 F.2d 853, 858 (6th Cir. 1956); Orleans Parish School Bd. v. Bush, 242 F.2d 156, 165 (5th Cir. 1957).

20. Borders v. Rippey, 184 F.Supp. 402, 420 (N.D. Tex. 1960); Comm. on Civil Rights, Survey of School Desegregation in the Southern and Border States, 1965–66, at 51, quoted in U.S. v. Jefferson County Bd. of Educ. 372 F.2d 836, 888 n. 110 (5th Cir. 1966).

21. Quoted in United States v. Jefferson County Bd. of Educ., 372 F.2d 836, 854 n. 40 (1966).

22. Griffin v. County School Bd., 377 U.S. 218, 234 (1964); Green v. County Sch. Bd., 391 U.S. 430, 439 (1968); *Justices Tell South to Spur Integration of All Its Schools*, N.Y. Times, May 28, 1968, at 1.

23. Alexander v. Holmes County Bd. of Educ., 396 U.S. 19, 20 (1969) (per curiam); Swann v. Charlotte-Mecklenburg Bd. of Educ., 402 U.S. 1 (1971).

24. Gerald N. Rosenberg, The Hollow Hope: Can Courts Bring About Social Change? 50, 99–100 (1991); John C. Boger, *Education's "Perfect Storm"? Racial Resegregation, High-Stakes Testing, and School Resource Inequities: The Case of North Carolina*, 81 N.C. L. Rev. 1375, 1387 (2003). Latino student enrollment in largely minority schools increased after 1968. Michael A. Boozer *et al.*, *Race and School Quality since Brown v. Board of Education*, 1992, Brookings Papers on Econ. Activity. Microecon., 269, 277–81 (1992).

25. Michael J. Klarman, From Jim Crow to Civil Rights ch. 7 (2004); Paul Finkelman, *Civil Rights in Historical Context: In Defense of Brown*, 118 Harv. L. Rev. 973, 1017–18, 1029 (2005) (book review of Klarman, From Jim Crow . . .); David E. Bernstein and Ilya Somin, *Judicial Power and Civil Rights Reconsidered*, 114 Yale L.J. 591, 645–47, 650–56 (2004) (book review of same).

26. Muir v. Louisville Park Theatrical Association, 347 U.S. 971 (1954); 347 U.S. 971 (1954); Gayle v. Browder, 352 U.S. 903 (1956); Turner v. City of Memphis, 369 U.S. 350, 353 (1962).

27. Runyon v. McCrary, 427 U.S. 160 (1976).

28. Mitchell v. United States, 313 U.S. 80 (1941).

29. Morgan v. Virginia, 328 U.S. 373, 377 (1946) (holding); Morgan v. Virginia 184 Va. 24, 27–31 (1945) (facts); Henderson v. United States, 339 U.S. 816 (1950).

30. Gayle v. Browder, 352 U.S. 903 (1956).

31. Daniel H. Pollitt, *Dime Store Demonstrations: Events and Legal Problems of First*

Sixty Days, 1960 Duke L.J. 315, 317–18 (1960); Milton R. Konvitz, *The Flower and the Thorn, in* The Pulse of Freedom: American Liberties, 1920–1970s, at 227–28 (Alan Reitman ed., 1975); Anna Leon-Guerrero, Social Problems: Community, Policy, and Social Action 436–37 (2005); Martin Oppenheimer, *The Southern Student Movement: Year 1,* 33 J. Negro Hist. 396, 401 (1964); Melvin I. Urofsky, *The Supreme Court and Civil Rights since 1940,* 4 Barry L. Rev. 39, 51 n. 78 (2003); Tilman C. Cothran, *The Negro Protest against Segregation in the South,* 357 Annals Am. Acad Pol. Soc. Sci. 65, 69 (1965).

32. Garner v. Louisiana, 368 U.S. 157 (1961).

33. Taylor v. Louisiana, 370 U.S. 154 (1962).

34. Peterson v. City of Greenville, 373 U.S. 244 (1963).

35. Bell v. Maryland, 378 U.S. 226 (1964).

36. 78 Stat. 243 *et seq.*

37. Heart of Atlanta Motel, Inc., v. United States, 379 U.S. 241 (1964).

38. Katzenbach v. McClung, 379 U.S. 294 (1964); Brief for the Appellant at 3, 5–6, Katzenbach v. McClung, 379 U.S. 294 (1964) (found at 1964 WL 72715).

39. Daniel v. Paul, 395 U.S. 298 (1969).

40. Jones v. Alfred H. Mayer, 392 U.S. 409 (1968).

41. Williams v. Mississippi, 170 U.S. 213 (1898); Giles v. Harris, 189 U.S. 475 (1903); Giles v. Teasley, 193 U.S. 146 (1904).

42. H. C. Nixon, *The Southern Legislature and Legislation,* 10 J. Pol. 410, 412 (1948); Anthony Lewis, *Legislative Apportionment and the Federal Courts,* 71 Harv. L. Rev. 1057, 1064 (1957); Baker v. Carr, 369 U.S. 186 (1962); Morton J. Horwitz, The Warren Court and the Pursuit of Justice 82–84 (1998); Malcolm E. Jewell, State Legislatures in Southern Politics, 26 J. Pol. 177, 177–78 (1964); Gary W. Copeland and Jean G. McDonald, *Reapportionment and Partisan Competition: When Does Reapportionment Matter?,* 9 Pol. Behav. 160, 163 (1987).

43. Wesberry v. Sanders, 376 U.S. 1, 49 (1964) (Harlan, J., dissenting).

44. Colegrove v. Green, 328 U.S. 549 (1946).

45. Baker v. Carr, 369 U.S. at 210, 237–38, 262–64.

46. Wesberry v. Sanders, 376 U.S. 1, 7–9 (1964).

47. Reynolds v. Sims, 377 U.S. 533, 565 (1964).

48. Gray v. Sanders, 372 U.S. 368, 379–80 (1963).

49. Reynolds v. Sims, 377 U.S. at 566, 579.

50. Kirkpatrick v. Preisler, 394 U.S. 526, 530–31 (1969).

51. *Compare* Karcher v. Daggett, 462 U.S. 725 (1983) (congressional deviations); Mahan v. Howell, 410 U.S. 315, 319, 333 (1973) (state district deviations); Connor v. Finch, 431 U.S. 407, 418 (1977) (state district deviations).

52. Lassiter v. Northampton Bd. of Elections, 360 U.S. 45 (1959); Katzenbach v. Morgan, 384 U.S. 641 (1966); South Carolina v. Katzenbach, 383 U.S. 301 (1966).

53. Robert B. McKay, *Reapportionment: Success Story of the Warren Court,* 67 Mich. L. Rev. 223, 229 (1968).

54. H. George Frederickson and Yong Hyo Cho, *Legislative Apportionment and Fiscal Policy in the American States,* 27 W. Pol. Q. 5, 30, 35 (1974); A. Spencer Hill, *The Reapportionment Decisions: A Return to Dogma?,* 31 J. Pol. 186, 209–10 (1969).

55. Griswold v. Connecticut, 381 U.S. 479 (1965).

56. William O. Douglas, We the Judges 429 (1955).

57. Mapp v. Ohio, 367 U.S. 643, 656 (1961) (search and seizure); Griswold v. Connecti-

cut, 381 U.S. at 484 (self-incrimination); Boyd v. United States, 116 U.S. 616, 630 (1886); NAACP v. Alabama, 357 U.S. 449, 462 (1957) (association); NAACP v. Button, 371 U.S. 415, 430–31 (1963) (association); Skinner v. Oklahoma, 316 U.S. 535, 541 (1942); Public Utilities Commission v. Pollak, 343 U.S. 451, 467 (1952) (Douglas, J., dissenting); William O. Douglas, The Right of the People 89–90 (1958).

58. Wechsler, *supra;* John Hart Ely, Democracy and Distrust: A Theory of Judicial Review (1980).

59. Pace v. Alabama, 106 U.S. 583 (1882); Myrdal, An American Dilemma 590–91 (1944); George E. Simpson and J. Milton Yinger, Racial and Cultural Minorities: An Analysis of Prejudice and Discrimination 504–5 (4th ed. 1972).

60. Naim v. Naim, 87 S.E.2d 749, 750–51, 756 (Va. 1955); Naim v. Naim, 350 U.S. 891 (1955); Naim v. Naim, 90 S.E.2d 849 (Va. 1956); Naim v. Naim, 350 U.S. 985 (1956); Gregory M. Dorr, *Principled Expediency: Eugenics, Naim v. Naim, and the Supreme Court,* 42 Am. J. Legal Hist. 119, 130–31 (1998).

61. Naim v. Naim, 350 U.S. 985 (1956); Lucas A. Powe, Jr., The Warren Court and American Politics 285–87 (2000) ("total bullshit"); Loving v. Virginia, 388 U.S. 1, 6 n. 5 (1967).

62. David Margolick, *A Mixed Marriage's 25th Anniversary of Legality,* N.Y. Times, June 12, 1992, at B20; Robert A. Pratt, *Crossing the Color Line: A Historical Assessment and Personal Narrative of Loving v. Virginia,* 41 How. L.J. 229 (1998); Loving, 388 U.S. at 3.

63. Richard Delgado, *The Current Landscape on Race,* 104 Mich. L. Rev. 1269, 1280 n. 49 (2006); Loving v. Virginia, 388 U.S. at 11 n. 11.

64. Pratt, *supra,* at 240–41.

65. Mapp v. Ohio, 367 U.S. at 654–55; Robinson v. California, 370 U.S. 660 (1962); Malloy v. Hogan, 378 U.S. 1, 6 (1964) (self-incrimination); Benton v. Maryland, 395 U.S. 784 (1969) (double jeopardy); Pointer v. Texas, 380 U.S. 400, 403–5 (1965) (cross-examination); Klopfer v. North Carolina, 386 U.S. 213, 223 (1967) (speedy trial); Washington v. Texas, 388 U.S. 14 (1967) (compulsory process); Duncan v. Louisiana, 391 U.S. 145, 149–50 (1968) (jury trial).

66. Gideon v. Wainwright, 372 U.S. 335, 344–45 (1963); Douglas v. California, 372 U.S. 353, 354–58 (1963); Griffin v. Illinois, 351 U.S. 12, 17–19 (1956) (Black, J., plurality opinion); Miranda v. Arizona, 384 U.S. 436 (1966); Bernard Schwartz, Superchief: Earl Warren and His Supreme Court 591 (1983).

67. Harper v. Va. Bd. Of Elections, 383 U.S. 663, 668 1966).

68. Washington v. Davis, 426 U.S. 229, 242 (1976); Pers. Adm'r of Mass. v. Feeney, 442 U.S. 256, 274 (1979); Regents of the Univ. of Cal. v. Bakke, 438 U.S. 265, 290–91 (1978); Ross v. Moffit, 417 U.S. 600, 610 (1974).

69. Milliken v. Bradley, 418 U.S. 717, 748–49 (1974); Dayton Bd. of Educ. v. Brinkman, 433 U.S. 406, 416, 420 (1977); Dayton Bd. of Educ. v. Brinkman, 443 U.S. 526, 541 (1979); School Dist. of Omaha v. United States, 433 U.S. 667 (1977); Brennan v. Armstrong, 433 U.S. 672 (1977); San Antonio Independent School District v. Rodriguez, 411 U.S. 1 (1973).

70. Bd. of Educ. of Okla. City Pub. Schs. v. Dowell, 498 U.S. 237, 247 (1991).

71. *See, e.g.,* United States v. Ash, 413 U.S. 300, 315–16, 321 (1973); Strickland v. Washington, 466 U.S. 668, 700 (1984); Gustafson v. Florida, 414 U.S. 260, 265 (1973).

72. Whren v. United States, 517 U.S. 806 (1996) (pretextual searches); Atwater v. City of Lago Vista, 532 U.S. 318 (2001) (minor traffic violation); Chavez v. Martinez, 538 U.S. 760 (2003) (self-incriminating statement).

73. Note, *The Equal Protection Clause as a Limitation on the States' Power to Disenfranchise Those Convicted of a Crime,* 21 Rutgers L. Rev. 297, 299 n. 17 (1967); Douglas R. Tims, *The Disenfranchisement of Ex-Felons: A Cruelly Excessive Punishment,* 7 Sw. U. L. Rev. 124, 125 nn. 8, 9 (1975); Note, *Civil Disabilities,* 23 Vand. L. Rev. 931, 975–77 (1970); Note, *Disenfranchisement of Ex-Felons,* 25 Stan. L. Rev. 845, 845–46 (1973).

74. Davis v. Beason, 133 U.S. 333 (1890), *abrogated on other grounds;* Romer v. Evans, 517 U.S. 620 (1996); Richardson, 418 U.S. 24, 54–56 (1974).

75. Hunter v. Underwood, 471 U.S. 222, 233 (1985); Alexander Keyssar, The Right to Vote: The Contested History of Democracy in the United States 306 (2000).

76. Daniel P. Tokaji, *The New Vote Denial: Where Election Reform Meets the Voting Rights Act,* 57 S.C. L. Rev. 689, 700 (2006); Christopher Uggen and Jeff Manza, *Democratic Contraction? Political Consequences of Felon Disenfranchisement in the United States,* 67 Am. Sociological Rev. 777, 793 tbl.4a (2002); Katherine Shaw, Note, *Invoking the Penalty,* 100 Nw. U. L. Rev. 1439, 1441 (2006).

CHAPTER THIRTEEN. Sketches of the Continuing Legal Effort

1. Bradwell v. Illinois, 83 U.S. 130 (1872) (attorney); Goesaert v. Cleary, 335 U.S. 464 (1948) (bartender); Reed v. Reed, 404 U.S. 71, 74, 76–77 (1971).

2. Frontiero v. Richardson, 411 U.S. 677, 687–88 (1973) (plurality); *id.* at 691–92 (Powell, J., concurring joined by Burger and Blackmun).

3. Craig v. Boren, 429 U.S. 190, 197-210 (1976).

4. Mississippi Univ. for Women v. Hogan, 458 U.S. 718, 726 (1982).

5. United States v. Virginia (1996), 518 U.S. 515, 524, 531, 533, 540, 555-56 (1996); *Other Judicial Decisions,* 18 NO. 7 Jud./Legis. Watch Rep. 1, 2 (1997) (quoting Ginsburg).

6. Nguyen v. INS, 533 U.S. 53, 54, 64, 70 (2001).

7. *Id.* at 92 (O'Connor, J., dissenting).

8. Nevada Department of Human Resources v. Hibbs, 538 U.S. 721, 730, 731 n. 5.

9. Roe, 410 U.S. 113, 129, 153 (1973).

10. *Id.* at 164–65.

11. Planned Parenthood v. Casey, 505 U.S. 833, 860, 872–75 (O'Connor, Kennedy, Souter, JJ.); *id.* at 99 (Stevens, J., concurring in part and dissenting in part); *id.* at 926 (Blackmun, J., concurring in part and dissenting in part); Stenberg v. Carhart, 530 U.S. 914, 921 (2000).

12. Ayotte v. Planned Parenthood, 126 S.Ct. 961 (2006); Bellotti v. Baird, 443 U.S. 622, 640 (1979).

13. Casey, 505 U.S. at 897-98.

14. Harris v. McRae, 448 U.S. 297, 315–16 (1980).

15. Cynthia Harrison, On Account of Sex: The Politics of Women's Issues, 1945–1968, at 179 (1988); Hugh D. Graham, The Civil Rights Era: Origins and Development of National Policy, 1960–1970, at 136 (1990).

16. John D. Skrentny, The Minority Rights Revolution 96, 98–99 (2002) (quoting Green); Harris, *supra,* at 177; Abigail C. Saguy, *Employment Discrimination or Sexual Violence? Defining Sexual Harassment in American and French Law,* 34 Law and Soc'y Rev. 1091, 1102 (2000).

17. 20 U.S.C. 1681(a) (2005); 20 U.S.C. 1681(c) (2005); Gebser v. Lago Vista Independent School Dist., 524 U.S. 274, 287 (1998); *A Policy Interpretation: Title IX and Intercollegi-*

ate Athletics, 44 Federal Register (no. 239) (1979), *available at* http://www.ed.gov/about/offices/list/ocr/docs/t9interp.html; Cannon v. Univ. of Chicago, 441 U.S. 677 (1979); Horner v. Ky. High Sch. Athletic Ass'n, 206 F.3d 685, 689 (6th Cir. 2000) (disparate impact approach *unavailable* for Title IX cases); Weser v. Glen, 190 F.Supp.2d 384, 395 (E.D.N.Y. 2002) (disp. impact unavailable); Cohen v. Brown Univ., 991 F.2d 888, 895 (1st Cir. 1993) (disp. impact available); Mabry v. State Bd. of Cmty. Colls. and Occupational Educ., 813 F.2d 311, 316 n. 6 (10th Cir. 1987) (disp. impact available); Cannon v. University of Chicago, 648 F.2d 1104, 1109 (7th Cir.) (disp. impact unavailable for Title IX cases); Mehus v. Emporia State Univ., 295 F.Supp. 2d 1258, 1271 (D. Kan. 2004) (disp. impact available).

18. Lisa Yonka Stevens, Note, *The Sport of Numbers: Manipulating Title IX to Rationalize Discrimination against Women,* 2004 B.Y.U. Educ. and L.J. 155, 186 (2004); Ted Leland and Karen Peters, *Title IX: Unresolved Public Policy Issues,* 14 Marq. Sports L. Rev. 1, 9 (2003) (list of scholarships at top 18 awarding universities).

19. Federal Water Pollution Control Act Amendments of 1972, Pub. L. No. 92-500, 13, 86 Stat. 816, 903; Comprehensive Health Manpower Training Act of 1971, Pub. L. No. 92-157, 101, 85 Stat. 431, 461; Aug. 5, 1971, Pub. L. No. 92-65, 112, 214, 85 Stat. 166, 168, 173; Nurses Training Act of 1971, Pub. L. No. 92-158, 11, 85 Stat. 465, 479–80.

20. 42 U.S.C.A. 1398l, found unconstitutional by United States v. Morrison, 529 U.S. 598 (2000).

21. U.S. Department of Justice, Bureau of Justice Statistics, *Crime Characteristics, available at* http://www.ojp.usdoj.gov/bjs/cvict_c.htm; Kay L. Levine, *No Penis, No Problem,* 33 Fordham Urb. L.J. 357. 381 (2006); Eliza Hirst, *The Housing Crisis for Victims of Domestic Violence,* 10 Geo. J. on Poverty L. and Pol'y 131, 131 n. 5 (2003); Victoria F. Nourse, *Where Violence, Relationship, and Equality Meet: The Violence against Women Act's Civil Rights Remedy,* 11 Wis. Women's L.J. 1, 5 (1996); S. Rep. No. 103-138, at 54 (1993) ("in certain areas . . . "); S. Rep. No. 101-545, at 37 (1990).

22. 42 U.S.C.A. 1398l; United States v. Morrison, 529 U.S. 598, 628–31 (2000) (Souter, J., dissenting); S. Rep. No. 103-138, at 54 (1993); Julie Goldscheid, *The Civil Rights Remedy of the 1994 Violence against Women Act,* 39 Fam. L.Q. 157, 160–61 (2005); Rebecca E. Zietlow, *Juriscentrism and the Original Meaning of Section Five,* 13 Temp. Pol. and Civ. Rts. L. Rev. 485, 512 (2004); Sally F. Goldfarb, *Violence against Women and the Persistence of Privacy,* 61 Ohio St. L.J. 1, 16–18 (2000); Linda C. McClain, *Toward a Formative Project of Securing Freedom and Equality,* 85 Cornell L. Rev. 1221, 1246 (2000); 18 U.S.C.A. 2264 (listing civil penalties).

23. H.R. Conf. Rep. No. 103-711, at 385 (1994) ("bias and discrimination . . . "); S. Rep. No. 103-138, at 44–47 (1993); Andrew E. Taslitz, Rape and the Culture of the Courtroom (1999); Cass R. Sunstein, The Partial Constitution 340 (1993).

24. United States v. Morrison, 529 U.S. 598, 617, 621 (2000); Civil Rights Cases, 109 U.S. 3 (1883); Heart of Atlanta Motel, Inc. v. United States, 379 U.S. 241 (1964); Katzenbach v. McClung, 379 U.S. 294 (1964); Hodel v. Virginia Surface Mining and Reclamation Assn., 452 U.S. 264, 312 (1981) (Rehnquist, J., concurring).

25. URA, 48 Stat. 22, 23 (1993); CCC, 50 Stat. 319, 320 (1937); CPT, 53 Stat. 855, 856 (1939); NTA, 57 Stat. 153, 153 (1943); Exec. Order No. 8802 (June 25, 1941).

26. Exec. Order No. 10,925 (Mar. 6, 1961); Graham, *supra,* at 35; James E. Jones, Jr., *The Origins of Affirmative Action,* 21 U.C. Davis L. Rev. 383, 396–97 (1988).

27. Exec. Order No. 11,246 (Sept. 24, 1965); Exec. Order No. 11,375 (Oct. 13, 1967); Graham, *supra,* at 187; Elliot G. Hicks, *What Is This Thing You Call "Affirmative Action"?,*

12 OCT W.Va. Law. 4, 4 (1998); Bernard F. Ashe, *Racial Progress in the New Millennium—A Different Shade,* 11 Experience 13 (2001); Legal Aid Soc. of Alameda County v. Brennan, 381 F.Supp. 125, 136 (N.D. Cal. 1974); 41 C.F.R. 60-2.11 (1973); 29 C.F.R. 1607 *et seq.* (1978).

28. *It Can't Happen Here—Can It?,* Newsweek, May 5, 1969, at 26, 28; Robert M. O'Neil, Discriminating against Discrimination 67 (1975); John S. Wellington and Pilar Montero, *Equal Educational Opportunity Programs in American Medical Schools,* 53 J. Med. Educ. 633, 637–39 (1978).

29. John A. Douglass, *Anatomy of Conflict: The Making and Unmaking of Affirmative Action at the University of California, in* Color Lines 118, 125 (John D. Skrentny ed., 2001); Bernard Schwartz, Behind *Bakke* 4 (1988); Regents of the University of California v. Bakke, 438 U.S. 265, 273–75 (1978).

30. *Id.* at 276-77.

31. *Id.* at 290, 299, 316–20, 323.

32. *Id.* at 353, 356–58 (Brennan, J., concurring in the judgment and dissenting in part).

33. *Id.* at 396 (Marshall, J., dissenting).

34. City of Richmond v. J. A. Croson Co., 488 U.S. 469, 505 (1989); Adarand Constructors, Inc. v. Pena, 515 U.S. 200, 205 (1995).

35. Gratz v. Bollinger, 539 U.S. 244, 249–51 (2003).

36. *Id.* at 246, 270; *id.* at 295 (Souter, J., dissenting); *id.* at 301, 303–4 (Ginsburg, J., dissenting).

37. Bakke, 438 U.S., at 289–90; Grutter v. Bollinger, 539 U.S. 306, 323–24 (2003).

38. Robert C. Post, *Fashioning the Legal Constitution: Culture, Courts, and Law,* 117 Harv. L. Rev. 4, 71–75 (2003); Reva B. Siegel, *Equality Talk: Antisubordination and Anticlassification Values in Constitutional Struggles over Brown,* 117 Harv. L. Rev. 1470, 1538–39 (2004).

39. Grutter v. Bollinger, 539 U.S. 306, 346 (Ginsburg, J., concurring); James E. Ryan, *Schools, Race, and Money,* 109 Yale L.J. 249, 273–75 (1999); Gary Orfield, *Metropolitan School Desegregation: Impacts on Metropolitan Society,* 80 Minn. L. Rev. 825, 842 (1996); Roslyn Arlin Mickelson, *Achieving Equality of Educational Opportunity in the Wake of Judicial Retreat from Race Sensitive Remedies,* 52 Am. U. L. Rev. 1477, 1485 (2003).

40. *See, e.g.,* San Antonio Indep. Sch. Dist. v. Rodriguez, 411 U.S. 1, 35 (1973).

41. U.S. Department of Health and Human Services, A Nation's Shame: Fatal Child Abuse and Neglect . . . viii–xiii, 39–40 (1995); DeShaney v. Winnebago County Dep't of Soc. Servs., 489 U.S. 189, 201 (1989); Castle Rock v. Gonzales, 545 U.S. 748 (2005).

42. Adoption and Safe Families Act of 1997, Pub. L. 105-89, 111 Stat. 2115; Deborah Paruch, *The Orphaning of Underprivileged Children,* 8 J. L. and Fam. Stud. 119, 137–38 (2006); MaryLee Allen and Mary Bissell, *Safety and Stability for Foster Children,* 14 Future of Children 49, 54–55 (2004).

43. Tanya Krupat, *Visiting Improvement Efforts: The Importance of Maintaining Family,* 191 PLI/Crim 167, 202 (2002); Susan H. Badeau *et al., Looking to the Future,* 14 Future of Children 175, 179 (2004); Ruth Massinga and Peter J. Pecora, *Providing Better Opportunities for Older Children in the Child Welfare System,* 14 Future of Children 151, 153 (2004).

44. *Cf.* Annette Ruth Appell, *Uneasy Tensions between Children's Rights and Civil Rights,* 5 Nev. L.J. 141, 154–61 (2004) (distinguishing between children's and dependency rights).

45. In re Gault, 387 U.S. 1; Richard Kay and Daniel Segal, *The Role of the Attorney in Juvenile Court Proceedings,* 61 Geo. L.J. 1401, 1403 (1973); Richard J. Bonnie and Thomas Grisso, *Adjudicative Competence and Youthful Offenders, in* Youth on Trial: A Developmen-

tal Perspective on Juvenile Justice 73, 80, 82–83 (Thomas Grisso and Robert G. Schwartz eds., 2000); C. Antoinette Clarke, *The Baby and the Bathwater: Adolescent Offending and Punitive Juvenile Justice Reform,* 53 U. Kan. L. Rev. 659, 667 (2005); Julian W. Mack, *The Juvenile Court,* 23 Harv. L. Rev. 104, 109–11 (1909); Note, *Juvenile Delinquents: The Police, State Courts, and Individualized Justice,* 79 Harv. L. Rev. 775 (1966); President's Commission on Law Enforcement and Administration of Justice, Task Force Report: Juvenile Delinquency and Youth Crime 7 (1967).

46. *See* Conn. Gen. Stat. Ann. 51-299 (West 1985); Fla. Stat. Ann. 938.29 (2003); Tex. Fam. Code Ann. 51.10(k) and 51.10(l) (Vernon 2002); In re Ricky H., 468 P.2d 204, 205–6, 211 (Cal. 1970).

47. In re Winship, 397 U.S. 358 (1970).

48. McKeiver v. Pennsylvania, 403 U.S. 528, 541, 543 (1971). While this is a plurality case, six justices, counting Justices White's and Brennan's concurrences, agreed that delinquency hearings need not include a jury.

49. McKeiver, 403 U.S. at 553 (White, J., concurring); Neal Miller, *State Laws on Prosecutors' and Judges' Use of Juvenile Records,* Nat'l Inst. of Just Res. in Brief, *available at* http://www.ncjrs.gov/txtfiles/juvrecs.txt (1995); Sara E. Kropf, Note, *Overturning McKeiver v. Pennsylvania,* 87 Geo. L.J. 2149, 2175 (1999); Julian V. Roberts, *The Role of Criminal Record in the Sentencing Process,* 22 Crime and Just. 303, 329–31 (1997); United States v. Gardner, 860 F.2d 1391, 1399–1400 (7th Cir. 1988); Commonwealth v. Phillips, 492 A.2d 55, 57–58 (Pa. 1985); U.S. Sentencing Guidelines Manual 4A1.2 (1998).

50. Blakely v. Washington, 542 U.S. 296, 303 (2004); Apprendi v. New Jersey, 530 U.S. 466, 490 (2000); Jones v. United States, 526 U.S. 227, 248–49 (1999).

51. United States v. Tighe, 266 F.3d 1187, 1193–95 (9th Cir. 2001); United States v. Smalley, 294 F.3d 1030, 1033 (8th Cir. 2002).

52. Parham v. J.R., 442 U.S. 584, 609 (1979); Alexander V. Tsesis, *Protecting Children against Unnecessary Institutionalizations,* 39 S. Tex. L. Rev. 995 (1998).

53. Holly Metz, *Branding Juveniles against Their Will,* Student Law., Feb. 1992, at 21, 28; Lois A. Weithorn, Note, *Mental Hospitalization of Troublesome Youth: An Analysis of Skyrocketing Admission Rates,* 40 Stan. L. Rev. 773, 813 (1988); Katherine Barrett and Richard Greene, *"Mom, Please Get Me Out!,"* 107 Ladies Home J. 98, 103 (May 1990); Arnold Binder and Virginia L. Binder, *The Incarceration of Juveniles, from the Era of Crouse to That of Freud and Skinner,* 18 Legal Stud. F. 349, 357 (1994).

54. Richard E. Redding, *Children's Competence to Provide Informed Consent for Mental Health Treatment,* 50 Wash. and Lee L. Rev. 695, 702 (1993); Binder and Binder, *supra,* at 357 ("severe disabilities . . . ").

55. Jan C. Costello, *Why Have Hearings for Kids If You're Not Going to Listen? A Therapeutic Jurisprudence Approach to Mental Disability Proceedings for Minors,* 71 U. Cin. L. Rev. 19, 25 (2002).

56. Utah Code Ann. 62A-15-620, 625(2)(b) 628(2), 631(6), 62A-15-701 *et seq.*; Mich. Comp. Laws 330.1498e(3)(a)-(b); Cal. Welf. and Inst. Code 5150, 5250, 5275, 5350–71, 5585.50, 5585.52.

57. Griswold v. Connecticut, 381 U.S. 479 (1965); Eisenstadt v. Baird, 405 U.S. 438 (1972); Roe v. Wade, 410 U.S. 113 (1973); Planned Parenthood v. Casey, 505 U.S. 833 (1992); Carey v. Population Services, 431 U.S. 678 (1977).

58. Bowers v. Hardwick, 478 U.S. 186, 190–93 (1986).

59. Romer v. Evans, 517 U.S. 620, 623–34 (1996).

60. Lawrence v. Texas, 539 U.S. 558 (2003).

Index